an IISS *strategic dossier*

IRAN'S NETWORKS OF INFLUENCE IN THE MIDDLE EAST

published by

The International Inst

ARUNDEL HOUSE | 6 TEMPLE PLACE | LONDON | WC2R 2PG | UK

IRAN'S NETWORKS OF INFLUENCE IN THE MIDDLE EAST

The International Institute for Strategic Studies
ARUNDEL HOUSE | 6 TEMPLE PLACE | LONDON | WC2R 2PG | UK

DIRECTOR-GENERAL AND CHIEF EXECUTIVE **Dr John Chipman**

This publication has been prepared by the Director-General and Chief Executive of the Institute and his staff. It incorporates commissioned contributions from recognised subject experts, which were reviewed by a range of experts in the field. The IISS would like to thank the various individuals who contributed their expertise to the compilation of this dossier. The responsibility for the contents is ours alone. The views expressed herein do not, and indeed cannot, represent a consensus of views among the worldwide membership of the Institute as a whole.

First published November 2019 by the International Institute for Strategic Studies.

© 2019 The International Institute for Strategic Studies

COVER IMAGES: Top: Background: A Lebanese Hizbullah fighter near Arsal, Lebanon, 26 July 2017 (Anwar Amro/AFP/Getty Images); main images, top–bottom: Popular Mobilisation Units fighters launch missiles targeting the village of Salmani, south of Mosul, in Iraq's Nineva province, 30 October 2016 (Ahmad Al-Rubaye/AFP/Getty Images); Major-General Qasem Soleimani, commander of Iran's Islamic Revolutionary Guard Corps (IRGC) attends a meeting between Supreme Leader Ayatollah Ali Khamenei (not pictured) and the IRGC in Tehran, 18 September 2016 (by Pool/Press Office of Iranian Supreme Leader/Anadolu Agency/Getty Images); Pro-government forces at a funeral ceremony at the Sayyida Zainab mosque in Damascus, Syria, 26 April 2017 (Louai Beshara/AFP/Getty Images)

Printed and bound in the UK by Hobbs the Printers Ltd.

All rights reserved. No part of this book may be reprinted or reproduced or utilised in any form or by any electronic, mechanical, or other means, now known or hereafter invented, including photocopying and recording, or in any information storage or retrieval system, without permission in writing from the publishers.

British Library Cataloguing in Publication Data
A catalogue record for this book is available from the British Library

Library of Congress Cataloging in Publication Data
A catalog record for this book has been requested

ISBN 978-0-86079-218-5

About The International Institute for Strategic Studies

The International Institute for Strategic Studies is an independent centre for research, information and debate on the problems of conflict, however caused, that have, or potentially have, an important military content. The Staff of the Institute is international in composition and IISS work is international in its perspective and reach. The Institute is independent and it alone decides what activities to conduct. It owes no allegiance to any government, any group of governments or any political or other organisation. The IISS stresses rigorous fact-based research with a forward-looking policy orientation that can improve wider public understanding of international security problems and influence the development of sounder public policy, and more effective business decisions in the international arena.

CONTENTS

INTRODUCTION	**7**
CHAPTER ONE **Tehran's strategic intent**	**11**
CHAPTER TWO **Lebanese Hizbullah**	**39**
CHAPTER THREE **Syria**	**85**
CHAPTER FOUR **Iraq**	**121**
CHAPTER FIVE **Yemen**	**159**
CHAPTER SIX **Bahrain, Saudi Arabia and Kuwait**	**179**
CONCLUSION	**195**
APPENDICES **Key individuals** **Iran-backed militias** **Order organising the Syrian Local Defence Forces**	**207** **213** **216**
INDEX	**219**

COMMON ABBREVIATIONS

AAB	Al-Ashtar Brigades
AAH	Asaib Ahl al-Haq
AQAP	Al-Qaeda in the Arabian Peninsula
EFP	explosively formed penetrator
ESO	External Service Organisation
GCC	Gulf Cooperation Council
HHN	Harakat Hizbullah al-Nujaba
IDF	Israeli Defense Forces
IED	improvised explosive device
IFLB	Islamic Front for the Liberation of Bahrain
INA	Islamic National Alliance
IRGC	Islamic Revolutionary Guard Corps
ISCI	Islamic Supreme Council of Iraq
ISF	Iraqi Security Forces
ISIS	Islamic State in Iraq and Syria
JAM	Jaish al-Mahdi
KH	Kataib Hizbullah
KSS	Kataib Sayyid al-Shuhada
KDP	Kurdistan Democratic Party
LAF	Lebanese Armed Forces
LAFA	Liwa Abu al-Fadl al-Abbas
LB	Liwa al-Baqir
LDF	Local Defence Forces
NDF	National Defence Forces
OIRAP	Organisation for the Islamic Revolution in the Arabian Peninsula
PIJ	Palestinian Islamic Jihad
PMU	Popular Mobilisation Units
PUK	Patriotic Union of Kurdistan
SCIRI	Supreme Council for the Islamic Revolution in Iraq
SSRC	Syrian Scientific Studies and Research Center
UAV	uninhabited aerial vehicle
UNIFIL	United Nations Interim Force in Lebanon

GLOSSARY OF TERMS

Artesh Abbreviation of 'Artesh-e Jomhouri-ye Eslami-ye Iran', or 'Islamic Republic of Iran Army'. The common name by which the regular army in Iran is known, as opposed to the Islamic Revolutionary Guard Corps

Ayatollah 'Sign of God', a Twelver Shia honorific title predominantly used for high-ranking jurists who can command informal authority over fellow clerics and lay people

Fatwa A ruling issued by an Islamic jurist with recognised authority on a point of Islamic law

Hojjat ol-Eslam 'Proof of Islam', a Twelver Shia honorific title used for those jurists who are considered advanced in Islamic learning but below the level of an Ayatollah

Khomeinism See 'Velayat-e Faqih'

Labayke ya Zainab 'At your service, Zainab', Arabic phrase used on flags and branding of many Shia militias with links to Iran. Zainab refers to the granddaughter of the Prophet Muhammad, Sayyida Zainab, whose tomb in Damascus is a highly revered Shia pilgrimage site

Mahvar-e/Jeb-heh-ye Mogha-vamat 'Axis/Front of Resistance', term used to group those states/actors who oppose a US military and Israeli presence in the Middle East

Mahwar/Jabhat al-Muqawamah Arabic equivalent of Mahvar-e/Jebheh-ye Moghavamat

Marja al-taqlid 'Source of emulation', a Twelver Shia religious term for a jurist with the highest-ranking religious authority. The individual derives their authority from their adherents choosing to follow their religious explanations and interpretations rather than those of another marja

Modafean-e Haram 'Holy Shrine Defenders', the title by which the Iranian state refers to those (mainly) Shia soldiers who have fought in Iraq and Syria against Sunni takfiri extremists and Syrian rebels in defence of important Shia religious sites such as the Shrine of Sayyida Zainab in Damascus

Sayyid Islamic title used by those who claim direct descendance from the Prophet Muhammad

Takfiri A Muslim who accuses another Muslim of being an unbeliever (kafir), e.g., ISIS members accusing Shia Muslims of not being Muslim

Velayat-e Faqih 'Guardianship of the Jurist', a Shia Islam political concept formulated by Ayatollah Ruhollah Khomeini whereby an Islamic scholar/jurist is the source of the state's supreme political authority. In the Islamic Republic of Iran, this individual holds the constitutionally recognised position of 'Supreme Leader'

Wilayat al-Faqih Arabic equivalent of Velayat-e Faqih

INTRODUCTION

> 'We also have important capabilities outside of the country. We have supporters, we have strategic depth, both across the region and in this country. Some support us because of Islam, others because of the language, and others because of Shia Islam. They all constitute the country's strategic depth.'[1]
>
> **Iranian Supreme Leader Ayatollah Ali Khamenei, 2014**

Since the Islamic Revolution in 1979, an understanding of the capabilities and strategic intent of Iran has been essential for the security and defence strategies of regional actors and global powers alike. This has in the past decade translated into a requirement for an understanding of Iran's military capabilities.

The International Institute for Strategic Studies (IISS) has contributed to this understanding through Strategic Dossiers on Iran's two most salient sovereign capabilities: its ballistic-missile and nuclear programmes (published in 2008 and 2011, respectively). Both these subjects continue to be relevant, as tension between Iran and the United States and regional states continues to rise. Iran's missile capability, both within its sovereign territory and through the missile systems operated by the partners it supports, continues to be a major consideration in any strategic calculation in Tehran, or Washington, of escalation.

However, in the contemporary Middle East a third Iranian strategic capability is proving the determinant of strategic advantage: the ability to fight by, with and through third parties. This subject forms the basis of the third Iran dossier by the IISS: *Iran's Networks of Influence*. Iran has possessed a form of this capability since 1979, but its potency and significance has risen sharply in the past decade, to the point where it has brought Iran more regional influence and status than either its nuclear or ballistic-missile programme.

Terminology

The relationships between Iran and a number of non-state actors vary widely. Each has ideological, strategic, political and logistical dimensions. Some are organic and structured; others opportunistic.

According to traditional definitions, a 'proxy' is the relatively weaker non-state actor that depends on a state sponsor for its power and relevance, and receives and carries out the preferences of its 'patron'. The term 'proxy' does not accurately describe the variety of relationships Iran has with its partners. For example, the media regularly describes Lebanese Hizbullah and the Houthis as Iran's 'proxies'. The former was set up by Iranian agents and abides by *Velayat-e Faqih* (religious jurisprudence); the latter is an emanation of a tribal group that belongs to a Shia branch, Zaydism, that does not recognise *Velayat-e Faqih*. As well as being different entities in kind, each has a different utility and standing for Iran.

The term 'proxy' also implies a directive relationship, which allows Iran to direct while the proxy obeys. If applied across the influence network, it would imply in turn a uniform level of control and orchestration of the groups by Iran, which

IISS research has not found to be the case. There is undoubtedly sufficient use made by Tehran of all the relationships it has with regional non-state actors for it to constitute a network of influence, but not to suggest a more consolidated structure.

Significantly, Tehran has made no attempt to formalise the status of any of these relationships or the network as a whole. There are no charters and treaties and no formal agreements on the status of the various groups. Tehran most commonly refers to non-state parties in emotive or religious language, which does not precisely reflect the nature of the relationship. Unusually, the network itself has been given more of a coherent and cohesive identity by commentators and adversaries than by the regime, which prefers a broad and all-inclusive reference to 'Resistance', the ideological, military and cultural opposition to perceived Western domination and Israel's existence, and to Arab governments accused of subordination to Western powers and Israel.

The term 'proxy' has therefore been used sparingly and selectively in this dossier. The most generally useful term is 'partner', which covers the full range of operational relationships or, where Iran

This regional influence comes from enduring partnerships between Iran and active civilian or military entities in foreign jurisdictions. Iran has developed and maintained an ability to use these relationships with extraterritorial entities to achieve its strategic ends. They have become a highly valuable and effective sovereign capability.

Of all the players in the wars in Iraq and Syria, Iran has arguably come out of these campaigns better placed than any other, with the possible exception of Russia. It has achieved maximum expansion (if not consolidation) of its influence in return for minimal Iranian casualties. In each of the key theatres for Iran (Iraq, Lebanon and Syria), it has achieved its aims through other parties. It is doing the same in Yemen (a non-essential but strategically valuable theatre for Tehran).

Understanding how Iran builds, operates and uses this capability is the subject of the central chapters of this dossier. The conclusion analyses the strategic significance of the capability and how it could be deployed in the future. It also examines the wider significance of this type of sovereign capability, given the evolving nature of conflict and the advan-

tages that Iran possesses through its recent experience of conflict and its ability to mobilise and deploy the global Shia community across theatres.

The dossier does not make policy recommendations but is intended through objective, fact-based analysis to inform both policymakers and practitioners. More broadly, it also aims to stimulate debate on what capabilities are required to prevail in contemporary and possible future conflicts. In the case of Iran's third-party capability, the significance of this in remote, asymmetric and complex warfare will rise and could determine strategic advantage.

How Iran has developed and maintained influence over a group of mainly non-state actors across the Middle East and what in practice this influence amounts to requires careful examination and nuance. Descriptors and analyses have tended to reflect states' policy positions towards the Iranian regime. However, this politicised analysis can obscure rather than illuminate. It can, for example, exaggerate the degree to which Iran exercises control over its partners (inherent in the use of the word 'proxy') or mislead as to how far Iran has copied techniques and objectives from one theatre to another.

	Partner	Strategic ally	Ideological ally	Proxy	State organ
Key criterion	The client pursues its relationship with the patron due only to political or transactional expediency, and may or may not continue to pursue objectives in common with the patron absent its support	Without the patron's support, the client would continue to pursue objectives in common with the patron based on strategic convergence, albeit with more limited resources	Without the patron's support, the client would continue to pursue objectives in common with the patron owing to their ideological affinity, albeit with more limited resources	Without the patron's support, the client would continue to hold objectives in common with the patron (owing to either common ideology or expedient interests) but be unable to pursue them	Without the patron's support, the client would cease to exist
Example(s)	Hamas	Houthi movement (Ansarullah)	Hizbullah	Syrian National Defence Force	Liwa Fatemiyoun; Liwa Zainabiyoun

is engaged in a conflict, 'third parties'. Relationships with Iran are differentiated by assessing each group against four criteria:

- Ideological affinity: the level of ideological alignment and the corresponding loyalty it generates;
- Strategic convergence: the level of strategic alignment (i.e., of visions and interests regarding the shape of the regional order, the nature of the threats and enemies and the strategies deployed to that effect);
- Political expediency: the level and nature of the political benefits generated by the relationship; and

- Transactional value: the level of the mutual security, military, political and economic returns created by the relationship.

These criteria are then used to assess the actor's classification: partner, strategic ally, ideological ally, proxy or state organ (see table above).

These criteria allow for a more nuanced understanding of each partner's relationship with Iran, and to make weighted comparisons between the groups and judgements about the likely durability and future course of their relationships with Iran.

It can also result in too categorical a designation of an influence structure, which in reality is neither static nor typical. This has become particularly problematic with the designation of the Islamic Revolutionary Guard Corps (IRGC) by the US as a terrorist organisation. By association, those whom the IRGC supports or vice versa share that designation. This has lent a technical justification to the hitherto rhetorical depictions of the IRGC Quds Force's partnerships overseas as a 'network of terrorism'.[2] Similarly, descriptions of the network as expansionist and substantial can be simplistic. The network is expansionist in that it has steadily extended Iran's reach into other jurisdictions, but it has not imposed, for example, Iranian administrators or garrisons. Nor does Tehran expect an economic return from its partners. On the contrary: Iran finances them.

While the evidence considered by *Iran's Networks of Influence* in some cases supports value-based descriptions (in particular, 'proxy'), it is important to capture the texture and variety of Iran's relationships and to avoid generalisations.

'Capability' is a neutral concept intended to facilitate a dispassionate study of the mechanics of Iran's

relationships and partnerships. This dossier conducts an audit of Tehran's capability in relevant theatres, including an examination of elements such as recruitment, weapons supply and command-and-control systems, based on original field research, open-source information, and interviews with a range of Western and regional government sources. The result of this audit forms the basis of a strategic analysis in each of the chapters on individual theatres and, in the conclusion, on the capability as a whole. The first chapter explores the wider context in which this capability has evolved.

As Iran's capability is a strongly military one, this dossier has made extensive use of IISS defence data and analysis, including details of the military equipment of Iranian partners. It focuses on the theatres of Lebanon, Syria, Iraq and Yemen. In each of these, a military conflict has been or is in progress that Iran has entered by supporting one of the protagonists: the state but also allied non-state armed groups in Iraq and Syria, a separate entity (Hizbullah) in Lebanon and the opposition (the Houthis) in Yemen. However, there is another theatre in which Iran has extended or attempted to extend its influence through a variant of this capability, but in which there has been no relevant armed conflict: the Gulf states. This dossier therefore includes a chapter on Bahrain, Saudi Arabia and Kuwait, covering aspects of Iranian power projection, primarily Iranian support for the Bahraini militant groups. In the Syria chapter, the dossier also covers Iran's recruitment of Shia militia fighters from Afghanistan and Pakistan, and their deployment.

Iran's means of extending its influence are not restricted to partnerships with other entities. It also makes extensive use of soft power, cultural diplomacy and terrorist operations overseas against hostile states and domestic opponents. A detailed study of these forms of influence lies outside the scope of this dossier. Similarly, the details of Iran's financing of its partners are in many cases opaque and this dossier has confined itself to using figures already published. While the role of cyber power as a capability for Iran to deploy offensively is well documented, IISS research has not found any evidence of its use in direct support of overseas partners. There is, however, evidence of a transfer of some cyber capabilities to Hizbullah.

Notes

[1] 'Basij-e zharfa-ye rahbordi va eghtedar-e melli-ye Iran-e islami' [The mobilisation of Islamic Iran's strategic depth and national capability], Rasa News, 21 November 2015, http://rasanews.ir/fa/news/303858/بسیج-ژرفای-راهبردی-و-اقتدار-ملی-ایران-اسلامی.

[2] Yeganeh Torbati and Jonathan Landay, 'U.S. calls on Iran to halt support for "destabilising forces"', Reuters, 20 May 2017, https://uk.reuters.com/article/uk-iran-election-usa/u-s-calls-on-iran-to-halt-support-for-destabilising-forces-idUKKCN18G0PV; White House, 'Remarks by National Security Advisor Ambassador John Bolton to the Zionist Organization of America', 5 November 2018, https://www.whitehouse.gov/briefings-statements/remarks-ambassador-john-bolton-zionist-organization-america/.

CHAPTER ONE

TEHRAN'S STRATEGIC INTENT

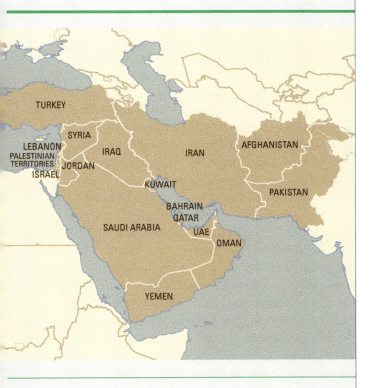

On 19 March 2003, American cruise missiles hit Baghdad, beginning a series of high-intensity, precision salvos. Within three weeks, the US-led international coalition had occupied the Iraqi capital and effectively ended a regime that Iran had failed to defeat during the eight-year Iran–Iraq War, a conflict that had consumed a generation of Iranians and crippled Iran's economy.

Within months, Iran had executed the initial stages of an aggressive hybrid-warfare strategy[1] aimed at frustrating US objectives in Iraq, while simultaneously attempting to reshape Iraq's political dynamic to favour Iran. The campaign drew upon a military doctrine that acknowledged Iran's conventional military weakness and avoided direct confrontation with powerful adversaries. The doctrine eschewed operations that might invite heavy casualties and instead focused on the use of unconventional forces and proxies.

Relying on unconstrained logistics lines, Tehran exported a relatively seasoned group of Iran-based Iraqi surrogates and developed its first foreign militia since the creation of Lebanese Hizbullah. Iran enabled these militias by providing military technology that was tailored for its lethality to Western military forces. The rapid collapse of political stability in Iraq, combined with an absence of a Western strategy either to prevent or levy a price for Iran's intervention in Iraq, allowed Tehran to manipulate the political evolution of a collapsed Arab state for the first time since Lebanon in the 1980s. By 2011, Iran's forces and political allies were entrenched in Iraq, and Tehran's influence there acknowledged by the international community.

The collapse of Syria in 2011 threatened Iran with the loss of its only state ally and the logistical architecture it relied upon to sustain Lebanese Hizbullah.

Table 1.1: **Regional strategic assessment: the Shia element**

State	Political–military situation	Social fabric	Shia community's attitude toward Iran	Level of cohesion within the Shia community	Nature and level of political power
Bahrain	Stable	Shia majority	Ambivalent	● Low	● Low
Iraq	Post-conflict	Shia majority	Leaning towards	●● Medium	●●● High Fragmented / Institutionalised / Non-state
Lebanon	Stable	Largest community (non-majority)	Leaning towards	●●● High	●●● High Unified / Institutionalised / Non-state
Syria	Conflict	Shia minority*	Leaning towards	●●● High	●● Medium Unified / Low institutionalisation / Non-state
Yemen	Conflict	Shia (Zaydi) minority	Leaning towards	●● Medium	●●● High Institutionalised / Non-state

*Excludes Alawites

Source: IISS

●●● High   ●● Medium   ● Low

Furthermore, the intensity of the Syrian civil war challenged a military doctrine best suited for low-intensity conflict. However, an unconstrained logistics channel in the form of an air bridge, the availability of nearby surrogates, and the absence of any Western effort to block Iran's involvement during a time of diplomatic engagement on nuclear issues allowed Tehran time to shape a strategy that achieved objectives without challenging its fundamental doctrinal principles.

However, Iran's regional adventurism required a domestic narrative to blunt opposition. Tehran's state-controlled media and religious institutions initially masked or minimised its involvement in Syria, framing its actions as the protection of Syria's Shia community and important shrines from Sunni militants. Potential domestic criticism was stifled by aggressive state-security elements or muted in the wake of Sunni militant terrorism in Ahvaz and Chabahar in 2018, which validated the need for extraterritorial counter-terrorist operations. Although the extent of personnel losses and resource costs would eventually be revealed, domestic opposition never reached the point where Iran's leaders needed to consider compromise on critical objectives, let alone withdrawal from the conflict.

The unexpected fall of the Yemeni city of Sanaa to the Houthi rebels in September 2014 provided Iran with an opportunity to inflict damage on Saudi Arabia and the United Arab Emirates for the first time since the Islamic Revolution in 1979. By then accustomed to an absence of Western reaction to its interventions, Tehran might also have considered the Yemen conflict as a chance to extend Iran's influence into the southern Red Sea.[2] However, intervention in this conflict would not be easy. Tehran's focus at the time could not be shifted from Syria, and its logistics channel to Yemen would be constrained. Iran's relations with the Houthi leadership extended to the first days of the 1979 revolution, but the political and operational connections were shallow compared to those with the Syrian regime. The Houthis brought years of experience as insurgents, but their battlefield sophistication was more akin to that of the Taliban than Lebanese Hizbullah. Once again, an unconstrained, if less efficient, logistics channel and the absence of international opposition eventually enabled Iran to introduce advisers, funds, advanced ballistic-missile technology, armed uninhabited aerial vehicles (UAVs) and explosive remote-controlled boats, which significantly altered the course of the conflict.

By 2019, Iran's influence in Iraq, Lebanon, Syria and Yemen had become a new normal in a region where such a concept would have once been unthinkable by the region's leaders, including those in Tehran. Iran had achieved much of this change using a transnational Shia militancy, capable of fighting with varying degrees of skill and discipline, which

Map 1.1: **Iran: overview of influence in the Middle East**

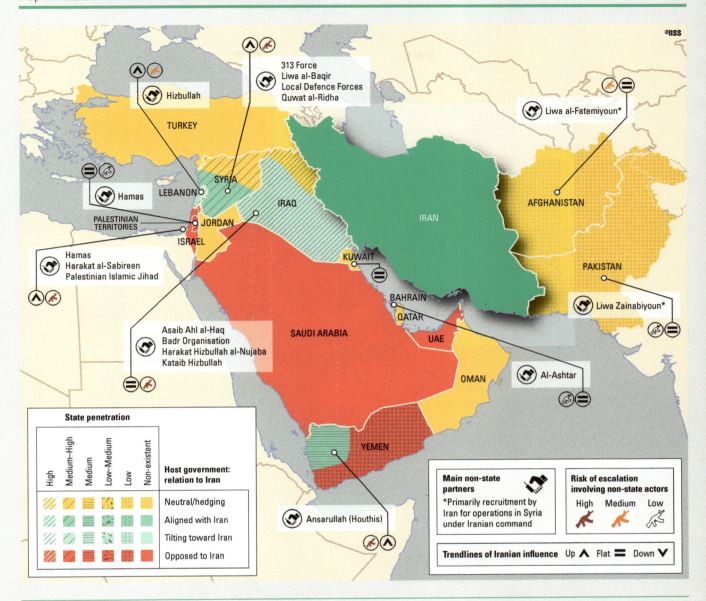

Source: IISS

confronted different Iranian adversaries on disconnected battlefields simultaneously.

No state has been so active, and perhaps as effective, as Iran in regional conflicts in modern times. The list of Iran's actions against regional targets is long: Iranian personnel and equipment have conducted offensive cyber attacks, enabled naval attacks in the Red Sea, and missile and UAV attacks on Saudi Arabia and its population. The Islamic Revolutionary Guard Corps' (IRGC's) Quds Force operations have sparked hundreds of Israeli airstrikes against Iranian and Iranian-backed-group sites in Syria. Iran has also maintained small ground forces in Syria, Yemen and sometimes Iraq.

To the chagrin of those Arab states under attack by Iranian-backed groups and which had only recently survived the threats of the Arab Spring, there has been insufficient international response to deter Iran from developing and deploying this capability. Moscow blocked action at the United Nations Security Council (UNSC), and some Western leaders advocated a role for Iran in the economic development of the region's Arab states.[3] This perception, and a sense that the US was turning away from the region, has played an influential role in how Israel and the Sunni Arab states have responded to perceived Iranian threats.

Tehran has, to some extent, anticipated and carefully managed this strategic expansion – its

Figure 1.1: **Iran's Supreme National Security Council: structure and participants**

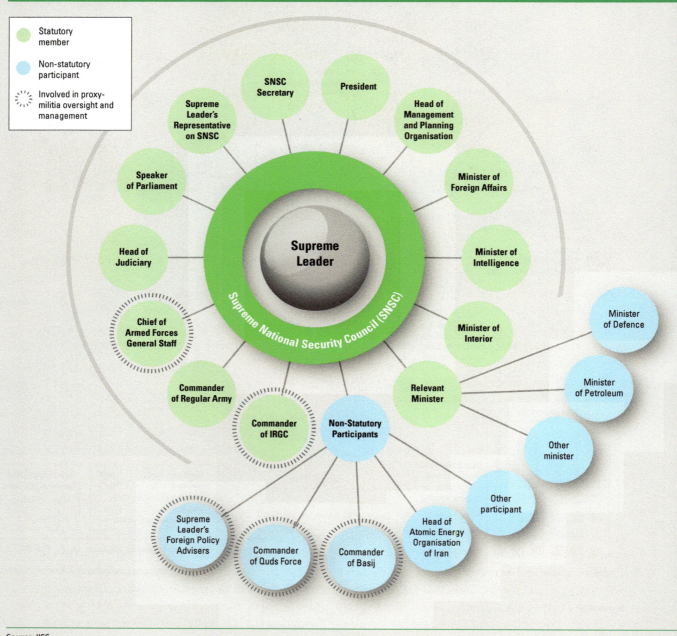

Source: IISS

extraterritorial ambitions are laid out in its constitution and the rhetoric of its leadership – though it could not predict the regional seismic shifts and international apathy that have enabled its success. However, there were also several points in each of these conflicts when it appeared as if the balance might shift against Tehran.

Iran's expeditionary security and military capacity evolved to meet new demands, including increased intra-service military collaboration beyond that anticipated by the Islamic Republic's founders. Regional interventions have also cost Iran hundreds of lives and billions of dollars at a time when it is also facing unprecedented international sanctions pressure and mounting domestic discontent.

The drivers and history behind Iran's transformation since the 2003 Iraq conflict can be observed by analysis of Tehran's involvement in Iraq, Syria and Yemen. These theatres illustrate how Iran's military strategy has shaped its actions, even as it evolved to meet unexpected challenges. Examination of the growth and use of Lebanese Hizbullah, and of Iran's reach into Bahrain, Saudi Arabia and Kuwait, completes the picture.

(l) Supreme Leader Ayatollah Ali Khamenei, September 2016

(r) Members of the Islamic Revolutionary Guard Corps in parliament, Tehran, October 2018

Iran's doctrinal framework and the tools behind its execution

Iran's response to regional challenges and opportunities in the aftermath of its war with Iraq involved an offensive and defensive strategy shaped by increasingly ambitious goals, resource limitations and unanticipated situational demands. Through rigorous self-control over the extent of its direct involvement in conflicts, Tehran has avoided the high costs of undertaking conventional warfare. It has also refrained from overt attacks on more powerful actors that could have threatened the regime.

Iran's lack of state allies, a plethora of well-resourced regional and international adversaries, and antiquated and sanctions-constrained armed forces compelled Tehran to develop a military doctrine that avoided direct or extended conflict with superior conventional powers. The doctrine drew from both the Soviet and US systems, Iran's revolutionary goals and experiences from the 1981–88 Iran–Iraq War, and observations of US performance against Iraq in 1991's *Operation Desert Storm*. It is also possible that those who developed the strategy also studied the US covert campaign in Afghanistan against the Soviet Union.

An important factor in Iran's consistency of doctrine is the longevity of its revolutionary leadership. Since 1989, Supreme Leader Ayatollah Ali Khamenei has been the ultimate guardian of Iran's strategic posture and has staffed security elements with senior officers he trusts to share his hardline views. Similarly, Iran's military leaders often remain in their positions for a considerable number of years. Few of Iran's adversaries can match such consistency of leadership.

Tehran's experience in the Iran–Iraq War formed the foundation of its military paradigm. Iran endured more than a million casualties, including 300,000 fatalities. The war cost Tehran as much as US$645 billion and left its economy and infrastructure in ruins.[4] Its survivors had witnessed Iran's survival in a war it fought without allies, with a military using (by the end of the conflict) outdated technology. Its perseverance required the determination of its people, thousands of whom died. The war taught Iran that its domestic defence and external operations needed to rely upon layered defences and asymmetric responses if Tehran were to prevail against stronger powers.

In addition, the Islamic Republic's constitution includes several sections that could be interpreted as a mandate to export Iran's revolution.[5] Iran's involvement in Lebanon and the Gulf in the 1980s demonstrated its willingness to do so. Since the 1979 revolution, Iran's Supreme Leaders have led a foreign policy in which Iran acts as the self-appointed leader of the world's Shia Muslims, with an emphasis on those in Iran's near abroad. Regional intervention in defence of Shia Islam provides evidence of its commitment to devote resources to do so. Tehran's role in the Sunni-dominated Middle East also aims to achieve greater empowerment for the region's Shi'ites.[6]

The military doctrine Iran adopted in 1992 in its 'Complete Regulations of the Islamic Republic of Iran Armed Forces' reflected an intention to draw upon an atypical combination of conventional forces (with an emphasis on ballistic-missile programmes), the exploitation of geography and Islamic Revolutionary energy.[7] Tehran's doctrine required collaboration from an unusual military architecture consisting of a then politically suspect Western-style Islamic Republic of Iran Army (*Artesh-e Jomhouri-ye Eslami-ye Iran*, or 'Artesh' for short) and a more ideologically reliable, if inexperienced, revolutionary military force called the IRGC (*Sepah-e Pasdaran-e Enghelab-e Eslami*).

(l) Supreme Leader Ayatollah Ruhollah Khomeini, February 1979

(r) Islamic Revolutionary Guard Corps personnel in Imam Hussein Square, Tehran, during the Iran–Iraq War, May 1985

Establishment of the Islamic Revolutionary Guard Corps

Eventually, the IRGC would become Iran's foremost offensive and defensive actor. Established on 22 April 1979 by Ayatollah Ruhollah Khomeini, the IRGC was born at a time when the *Artesh* was deeply distrusted by Iran's revolutionary leaders and its personnel were being systematically purged. Formation of the IRGC not only provided a counterweight to the *Artesh* but also allowed Iran's new leaders to gather the hundreds of armed groups associated with the hundreds, if not thousands, of revolutionary committees that dominated Iran in 1979. Article 150 of Iran's constitution mandated vaguely that the IRGC protect the nascent revolution and its future achievements.[8] As a force orientated to the socio-political values of the revolution's leadership, the IRGC was also tasked to support liberation movements and oppressed Muslims abroad.[9]

The IRGC focused on destroying the myriad armed leftist, monarchist, communist and ethnic elements who opposed the new Islamic Republic's ideology. Gradually, the group developed bureaucratic cohesion and professionalism, aided by the lessons taught in the Iran–Iraq War, and a systematic removal of members deemed lacking in ideological adherence to Islamic values and the concept of political rule by a supreme religious jurisprudent (*Velayat-e Faqih*), an important component of Khomeinism. Following the end of the Iran–Iraq War, the IRGC gradually became an important domestic economic player through its role in reconstruction, and its veterans could be increasingly found in parliament and government positions.

The relationship between the IRGC and the *Artesh* during the Iran–Iraq War was strained. The IRGC suspected the latter's loyalty while the *Artesh* focused on the IRGC's lack of professionalism and use of ambiguous demarcations of its responsibility to encroach on what it saw as *Artesh* roles. However, the two forces are meant to collaborate in times of war on missile activity and control of the shipping channels of the Persian Gulf. In terms of defence, they share a responsibility to execute a 'mosaic' defence response, which would draw on unconventional operations, guerrilla actions and the exploitation of Iran's terrain.[10] Domestically, Iran's deterrence-based doctrine 'stresses raising an adversary's risks and costs rather than reducing its own'.[11] Externally, the doctrine aims to raise the risk to adversaries without increasing the risks and costs to Iranian forces. Proxy partners abroad are also of use to Tehran in terms of perception management. Adversaries would need to consider the possibility that a strike on Iran could produce a counter-attack by multinational surrogate militias at a location and time of Iran's choosing.[12]

Although the *Artesh* remained the model of a traditional military force, charged with the defence of Iran's territorial integrity, the IRGC became Iran's dominant military organisation. The IRGC's aggressive loyalty to the regime won it a superior budget, greater prestige, access to Iran's senior leadership, the ability to operate large parastatal commercial enterprises and greater autonomy from civilian control.[13] Its ownership of companies involved in rebuilding war-damaged Iran provided it with vast resources, as well as a web of commercial and political interests. As its power grew, and despite Ayatollah Khomeini's call for the IRGC to refrain from involvement in politics, the Corps increasingly criticised Iran's civilian leaders when it perceived the latter's actions as threatening the revolution's (or its own) values or interests.[14]

Establishment of the Quds Force

The IRGC's extraterritorial mission to support revolutionary movements relies upon its subordinate element, the Quds Force (Jerusalem Force, or

Figure 1.2: **Structure of the Islamic Revolutionary Guard Corps**

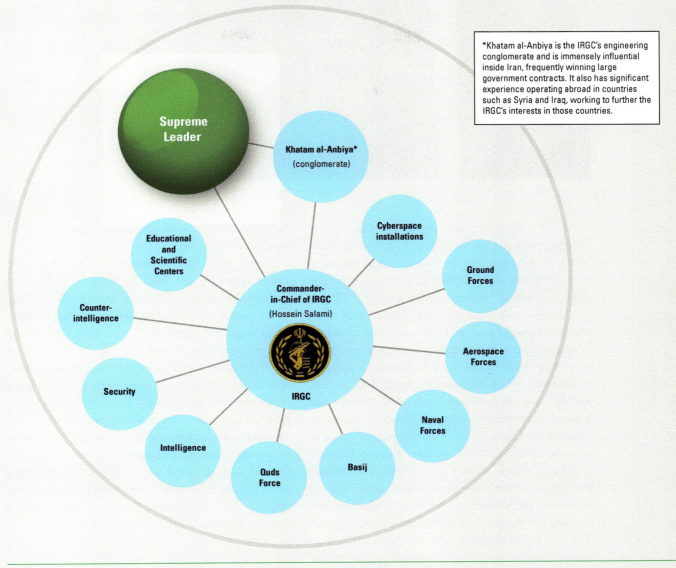

*Khatam al-Anbiya is the IRGC's engineering conglomerate and is immensely influential inside Iran, frequently winning large government contracts. It also has significant experience operating abroad in countries such as Syria and Iraq, working to further the IRGC's interests in those countries.

Source: IISS

Niru-ye Quds), an unconventional force established in the first years of the Iran–Iraq War from intelligence and special-forces units with a mandate to engage in extraterritorial low-intensity conflicts in support of 'oppressed' Muslims.

Ayatollah Khamenei said in 1990 that the Quds Force's mission was to 'establish popular Hezbollah cells all over the world'.[15] The IRGC Commander-in-Chief Mohammad Ali Jafari illustrated the consistency of this assignment in his 2016 claim that 'the mission of the Quds Force is extraterritorial, to help Islamic movements, expand the Islamic Revolution and to bolster the resistance and endurance of suffering people throughout the world and to people who need help in such countries as Lebanon, Syria, and Iraq'.[16]

The early years of the Quds Force were occupied by the conflict with Iraq and cooperation with Lebanese Hizbullah. During the tenure of its first chief, IRGC Brigadier-General Ahmad Vahidi,[17] the Quds Force adopted a structure to enable operations in Afghanistan, Africa, Asia, Central Asia, Iraq, Lebanon, Latin America and the Arabian Peninsula. It established approximately 20 militant training camps in Iran,[18] as well as camps in Lebanon and eventually Sudan.[19] Its creation of a specialised logistics element allowed it to manage covert weapons shipments internationally.

AN IISS STRATEGIC DOSSIER   TEHRAN'S STRATEGIC INTENT   17

(l) Islamic Revolutionary Guard Corps commander Mohammad Ali Jafari, September 2012

(r) US and Saudi military personnel survey the damage to Khobar Towers, Saudi Arabia, June 1996

As the group's reach expanded, Quds Force officers provided a safe haven, funds, terrorist training, weapons and ideological nourishment to a broad group of international militants, including Afghan Hazaras, Balkan Muslims, Gulf militants, Palestinians and even al-Qaeda.[20] As this list illustrates, the Quds Force can be ideologically flexible. It provides support to any group that it might consider part of the international 'Axis of Resistance', willing to confront Iran's adversaries, particularly the US, and increase Iran's regional influence. Western and regional governments during this period repeatedly accused the Quds Force of having played a role in terrorist operations in Argentina, Kuwait, Lebanon and Saudi Arabia, as well as attempts to destabilise Bahrain and other Gulf governments. Some of these operations (for example, in Beirut in 1983 and Khobar in 1996) left hundreds of Americans dead or injured. The 1994 AMIA bombing in Buenos Aires left 85 dead and hundreds wounded.[21] However, international reaction was limited to relatively modest economic sanctions and diplomatic démarches, which did little to constrain Quds Force activity.

In circa 1998, then IRGC Brigadier-General Qasem Soleimani replaced Vahidi, who moved to Iran's Ministry of Defence. Born in March 1957 into a farming family in southeastern Iran and forced by poverty to leave home at age 13 in search of work, Soleimani found employment in the municipal water department in Kerman. He played no part in the 1979 revolution, and his first role in the war with Iraq was to ensure the delivery of water to front-line soldiers. As the conflict attrited Iran's cadre of officers, Soleimani was moved to a battlefield position and here – despite an absence of military or indeed much formal education – he thrived and enjoyed a reputation for bravery. His early military career included the suppression of Kurdish uprisings along Iran's northwest border with Iraq and participation in the Iran–Iraq War's major battles.[22]

After the war, Soleimani was appointed commander of an IRGC division tasked with suppressing unrest and narcotics trafficking along Iran's eastern border. Tehran's tensions with Taliban-ruled Afghanistan increased soon after he assumed this assignment. In August 1998, the Taliban captured and later killed Iranian diplomats and a press correspondent, and a war was only narrowly averted. Soleimani would likely have been active during this time working with sources within the Taliban community on the status of the captured Iranians, negotiating their return, and participating in any Iranian military planning for an attack on Afghanistan. During this same period, Soleimani maintained the Quds Force relationship with Lebanese Hizbullah and expanded training facilities in Lebanon and Sudan.[23]

Iraq

The US-led invasion of Iraq provided Iran with the first real opportunity to exercise the offensive aspects of its 1992 military doctrine. The Iran–Iraq War had ended only 15 years before, and Iran would have felt compelled to do everything possible to defang Baghdad permanently and to establish a relatively compliant and benign government in its place. In addition, the spectre of a long-term American presence in Iraq would have been seen as unacceptable.

Iraq's Shia majority offered the prospect of a large Arab state sympathetic to Tehran. Influence over Iraq would provide Tehran with strategic depth and some purchase over Iraq's Kurds, as well as new opportunities to pressure Iraq's neighbours – Jordan, Kuwait and Saudi Arabia. Although most Iraqi Shi'ites were not adherents of Khomeinism,[24] a sufficient number were committed to (and had been trained by) Iran to allow

Conditions for Iranian intervention

The Iraqi conflict offered four characteristics that became essential to the success of Iran's intervention there, as well as in its future adventurism:

| A failed state of geostrategic significance with a disorganised opposition and local partners willing to employ lethal force to achieve Iran's goals.

| A Shia community that believed itself to be under existential threat. (However, the fractious Shia community in Iraq was such that no single umbrella organisation like Lebanese Hizbullah could ever be created and some Shia elements – such as that led by Muqtada al-Sadr – would challenge Tehran as much as Washington.)

| A logistics pipeline, which allowed Iran to transfer personnel, materiel and weapons in support of its allies, as well as enabling it to bring surrogates to Iran for training.

| The absence of an external actor with the will and capacity to threaten Iran's core interests sufficiently to end its intervention.

Tehran some confidence that it would have powerful Shia allies in the social and political chaos that followed the 2003 invasion. Iran could gain additional partners through financial inducements or political pressure.

In 2001–03, Tehran watched as Washington's relationship with Baghdad worsened, and the likelihood of war grew. Iran undertook preparations that reflected its strategic drivers and many of the extraterritorial elements of its military doctrine.

Tehran positioned the Badr Corps (later the Badr Organisation), an Iran-based Iraqi exile force, at the Iraqi border with Iran with orders to return to Iran as soon as conditions permitted.[25] Established in 1982 as the military wing of the Supreme Council for the Islamic Revolution in Iraq (SCIRI), the Badr Corps was formed first from Iraqi Shia prisoners of war and later those Iraqi Shia who fled to Iran to escape persecution in Saddam Hussein's Iraq.[26] By 2003, the group – entirely dependent on Iran – could be considered to be a somewhat well-trained, ideologically sound and disciplined unit that could be deployed into Iraq's Shia population to establish nodes of Shia authority sympathetic to Iran.[27] The Iranian plan also called for the Badr Corps to disrupt the post-invasion American occupation using political, military and social means to supplant US influence.[28]

By 2005, US commanders accepted that the Quds Force had initiated a large-scale unconventional military campaign aimed at Iranian domination of Iraq's emerging government and deeper influence over Kurdish groups in the north. As part of this campaign, Iran enabled, and sometimes directed, attacks on US personnel using Iranian-manufactured explosively formed penetrators (EFPs) and improvised rocket-assisted munitions.[29] Tehran's introduction of these highly effective weapons resulted in a significant increase in coalition dead and wounded. Their use also marked the first of many examples of the Quds Force empowering third-party groups with more advanced weapons technology tailored to a specific battlefield.[30] But their introduction also underscored a second lesson: Iran's provision of lethal weapons to surrogates allowed it to damage adversaries without concern that its targets would retaliate against Tehran.

During 2007 and 2008, Iraqi officials served as intermediaries between the US commander General David Petraeus and Qasem Soleimani. Soleimani sent the following message:

> General Petraeus, you should know that I, Qassem Suleimani, control the policy for Iran with respect to Iraq, Lebanon, Gaza, and Afghanistan. And indeed, the ambassador in Baghdad is a Quds Force member. The individual who's going to replace him is a Qods Force member.[31]

Although such dialogue would periodically continue, Soleimani avoided Iraq during Petraeus's time, likely believing that the American commander would not hesitate to order his detention.

The inability of Quds Force leaders to travel freely in Iraq did little to impact Iran's growing influence. By 2011, Iran's influence over Baghdad's political, security and media architecture was significant. The Quds Force ensured that it had sufficient funds, weapons and political guidance to be successful and those who opposed Iran's interests were either sidelined or threatened into compliance. Soleimani played an increasingly open role in Iraq's political process, resolving factional disputes among the Iranian militias and Muqtada al-Sadr, as well as seeking the election of Nouri al-Maliki as prime minister, who was considered sufficiently compliant that he would neither challenge Shia militia influence nor aggressively oppose Iran's activities in Iraq.[32]

Map 1.2: **IRGC Quds Force Major-General Qasem Soleimani: reported presence in Iraq, Lebanon, Syria and Russia, 2012–18**

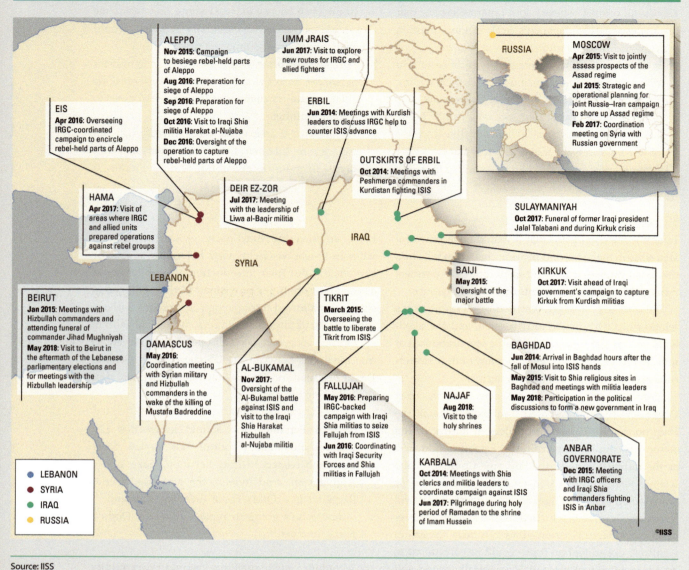

Source: IISS

Iran's experience in Iraq provided important lessons. Just as Iran had escaped international retaliation for its years of support for terrorism, its overt challenge to Western powers in Iraq demonstrated that there were few actual red lines regarding Tehran's use of unconventional forces and surrogates in its near abroad. Iran paid no price for its repeated lethal attacks on coalition forces or its interference in Iraqi affairs.

By 2011, Tehran had achieved its strategic goal of a relatively stable Iraq that no longer posed a military threat to Iran. By relying on a small footprint of forces and using third-party militias to confront British and US forces, Iran had minimised its own losses. While US domestic support for its involvement in Iraq had plummeted, there was little visible dissent from Iranians for their government's role, even during election unrest in 2009.

The Iraqi conflict also helped to transform the role and stature of the Quds Force. Soleimani's relationship with the Supreme Leader considerably deepened during this period. As a result, the Quds Force's domination of Iran's policy in Iraq stood in stark contrast to the limited role played by Iran's foreign ministry, especially as the Quds Force assigned its senior officers as Iran's ambassadors to Baghdad.[33] A new generation of the Quds Force cadre acquired valuable experiences in working with Arab militias against Western forces in Iraq and saw that they could undertake indirect threats against them without incurring any direct response against Iran.

Iran had also created a new generation of militia allies who offered political and military support for its interests.[34] Tehran gained loyal partners in such Iraqi Shi'ite figures as Hadi al-Ameri, head of the Badr Organisation; Qais al-Khazali, head of Asaib Ahl al-Haq; Jamal Jaafar Mohammad al-Ibrahimi (otherwise known as Abu Mahdi al-Muhandis), deputy chairman of the Popular Mobilisation Units (al-Hashd al-Shaabi, or PMU); and Abu Mustafa al-Shaibani, one of the founders of Kataib Sayyid al-Shuhada.[35]

A significant challenge to Iran's success came with the rise of the Islamic State, also known as ISIS or ISIL. The dramatic initial success of ISIS forces in Iraq in June 2014 compelled Soleimani to play a more significant role in the direction of Iraqi militias in combat to sustain Iraqi allies, and to prevent the collapse of Iraq and establishment of an ISIS state on Iran's western border. Iran transferred hundreds of advisers to the Iraqi government, shipped tonnes of weapons to the Kurds and recalled Shia militias from Syria to confront ISIS forces, which seemed at one point close to threatening Baghdad.[36] In an unprecedented example of its new regional assertiveness and willingness to operate militarily near Western forces, Iran provided close air support to Kurdish Peshmerga forces, Badr Organisation militia forces and Iraqi special-operations units. The operations also enabled Iran to test indigenous guided ordinance.[37]

As part of its effort to enhance the effectiveness of Iraqi militias against ISIS during this period, Iran aggressively supported the creation of the PMU in June 2014. The PMU was initially composed largely of Shia militias, as well as Christian, Sunni and Turkmen forces. Although some of the Shia were loyal to Iraq's Grand Ayatollah Ali al-Sistani and Muqtada al-Sadr, the majority of these militias fell under Iran's influence. In an attempt to place these forces under greater central-government control, the Iraqi government adopted a December 2016 law that incorporated them into Iraq's armed forces. The effort had mixed results and little genuine Iranian support.[38] A March 2018 decree provided PMU fighters with the same benefits as their defence-ministry counterparts, seemingly strengthening the militia's separate identity. Iran's significant influence over the Shia elements within this force and Iraq itself remained unchallenged.[39]

The Arab Spring and Syria

The 2011 Arab Spring unleashed a region-wide wave of political and economic turmoil. Having survived domestic unrest in 2009, Iran looked well positioned to exploit such events. The Sunni Gulf states no doubt appeared attractive targets, given their large Shia populations. However, Tehran's failure to instigate any pro-Iranian unrest revealed both that its long-feared influence over Gulf-based Shia was overblown and that the Quds Force could not overmatch the Gulf states' security services. Public and private rhetoric between the Gulf states and Iran became increasingly hostile.

Any disappointment Tehran might have felt at this failure was no doubt forgotten at the alarm that accompanied the political collapse of Syria, despite thousands of arrests by Damascus's increasingly outmatched security services. More and more, it looked as if President Bashar al-Assad's regime would unravel as had those of Hosni Mubarak of

"THE SYRIAN CONFLICT WOULD SERVE AS A POWERFUL TEST OF IRAN'S EXTERNAL MILITARY DOCTRINE"

Egypt and Zine al-Abidine Ben Ali in Tunisia. The amount of territory under the control of its fatigued military and security services, which were designed to fight a conventional war against Israel or to serve as a check against other Syrian institutions that might move against the regime, seemed to shrink daily.

For Tehran, the loss of Syria would cost it its only state ally and dramatically reduce its ability to support Lebanese Hizbullah, as well as impede its ability to work with Palestinian militants. Assad's Syria also provided Iran with access to the borders of Israel and Jordan, along with some protection to Iraq. For these reasons, Tehran considered the survival of Assad as a high priority.[40]

The Syrian conflict would serve as a powerful test of Iran's external military doctrine. The conflict demands were a mirror opposite to those in Iraq between 2003 and 2008. In Iraq, the Iranians used insurgents to attack the regular US Army; in Syria, Soleimani would need to bolster a regular army fighting against multinational insurgents supported by the US.

Quds Force in the lead

As in Iraq, the Quds Force took the lead, shaping Iran's operations to protect Shia shrines from Sunni militants and to sustain the Assad regime itself.[41] Within months, the Quds Force would also see the war as an indirect conflict against the Gulf states and the US. In early 2011, Tehran dispatched a small group of senior Quds Force officials to Syria to assess the situation. The group included Soleimani and Hossein Hamadani, the commander of the IRGC's Mohammad Rasulullah Corps of Greater Tehran. A close associate of Soleimani, Hamadani had helped put down the 2009 Green Movement and some in Tehran likely believed Damascus would benefit from this experience.[42] The state of Syria's military capability and its eroding fighting capacity were immediately apparent.[43]

More than any other element, the air-transport links between Iran and Syria would prove critical to Tehran's success in that theatre. This link enabled the Quds Force to import advisers and technical support to allow Assad to monitor opposition communications, crowd-control equipment, UAVs

"GRADUALLY, IRAN ADMITTED THAT A NUMBER OF IRANIAN VOLUNTEERS WERE FIGHTING IN THE CONFLICT"

and ammunition. Tehran reportedly used a variety of military, civilian and charter aircraft, as well as Syrian military aircraft, to sustain this supply line.[44] Its use of Iraqi airspace was enabled by allies in Baghdad who accepted the fiction that the flights carried humanitarian supplies.[45] Despite widespread reporting of Iran's growing military involvement in Syria, the international community did not attempt to cut Iran's air link with Damascus.

Tehran was concerned as to how its people would respond to this campaign. While they would support an Iranian effort to protect important Shia shrines and the Shia community, there would likely be little support for an expenditure of blood and treasure to sustain an Arab dictator. Iranian statements either downplayed or outright denied involvement, such as that of Jafari, in which he insisted that the IRGC provided 'assistance in planning, as well as financial help', but did not have a military presence in Syria.[46] The involvement of hundreds of Quds Force and Lebanese Hizbullah personnel, who provided intelligence, training and battlefield support in Syria, made this narrative increasingly difficult to sustain.[47]

The presence of Iranian military officials in Syria was exposed in August 2012, when Syrian opposition forces captured 48 Iranian 'military pilgrims' allegedly visiting the Shrine of Sayyida Zainab in Damascus. The detainees included IRGC Ground Force commanders with experience in counter-insurgent operations,

providing the first evidence that non-Quds Force personnel were also operating in Syria. The Quds Force and Syrian government worked to gain their release, eventually doing so on 9 January 2013 in exchange for 2,130 opposition prisoners.[48]

Gradually, Iran admitted that a number of Iranian volunteers were fighting in the conflict, but insisted they did so only to protect Shia shrines.[49] Hizbullah similarly denied its involvement until a growing number of combat-related obituaries and the October 2012 death of a senior Hizbullah official made it impossible to continue denials.[50]

By early 2013, the growing number of military funerals of war casualties demanded a more compelling narrative. The February 2013 ceremony that commemorated the death of IRGC Major-General Hassan Shateri (otherwise known as Hesam Khushnevis) came with the claim that he had died not in combat, but at the hands of Israeli agents.[51] Iran's domestic narrative shifted to highlight the importance to Iran itself of victory against the opposition forces. In February 2013, hardline Iranian cleric Mehdi Taeb stressed the significance of Iran's role in Syria to a group of Basij paramilitary militia students, describing Syria as 'the 35th province' of Iran and exclaiming that if 'we lose Syria, we cannot keep Tehran'.[52]

By early 2013, Iran's involvement appeared to be only slowing what then seemed to be the inevitable collapse of the Assad regime. Iran responded with four initiatives. Firstly, Soleimani discouraged Assad from confronting opposition forces throughout Syria and instead urged him to stabilise the southern and western fronts, which were most important to the regime's survival.[53] Secondly, the Quds Force undertook a reorganisation of Syria's various paramilitary forces into a new 50,000-strong unit called the National Defence Forces (NDF).[54] Thirdly, Iran increased the number of Lebanese Hizbullah and Iraqi militia forces in the country. Members of Iraq's Asaib Ahl al-Haq, Badr Organisation and Kataib Hizbullah (named collectively the *Haidariyoun*) soon highlighted their Syrian operations on social media.[55] Finally, Iranian Foreign Minister Mohammad Javad Zarif undertook an aggressive diplomatic campaign that criticised US and Sunni involvement in the conflict, while simultaneously urging a political settlement with the opposition that would keep Assad in power and Iran's interests intact. Iran was excluded from peace talks in Geneva, but its diplomatic voice on Syria was growing.[56]

Gradually, the situation stabilised.[57] On 19 May 2013, Iran joined Syrian forces in a major battle to capture the city of Qusayr, which had been under opposition control since early in the conflict. Restoration of government control was an essential element in the Quds Force's strategy: the city enjoyed a strategic location, sitting along the supply route for opposition forces in Homs, as well as splitting Damascus from Assad's traditional Alawite stronghold on the Syrian coast. The city also sits near the entrance to the Bekaa Valley, the traditional channel for Iran's movement of personnel and weapons to Lebanese Hizbullah. Soleimani reportedly took personal charge of a large body of Lebanese Hizbullah, NDF, Quds Force and Syrian military personnel in the battle.[58] After severe fighting, the city fell to Assad's government on 5 June.[59] By the end of 2013, Iran's increasingly dominant role in directing Syrian battlefield operations was widely known, and opposition elements began to claim that Soleimani had more power in Syria than Assad.[60]

An increasing Iranian and Iranian-backed group presence

Despite these successes, the intensity of the conflict and weak morale were attriting Assad's overstretched forces. In addition, the rise of ISIS in Iraq and the fall of Mosul in June 2014 required the return of Iraqi militia personnel from Syria. Lacking any other local resources and constrained by a doctrine that limited substantial deployment of Iranian forces but had no such prohibition against third-country nationals, the Quds Force introduced Afghan Shia fighters to the conflict.

Drawing first upon a small number of Afghans who had fought with the Quds Force during the Iran–Iraq War and later against the Taliban, Iran recruited a new force from the large pool of Afghan refugees resident in Iran, as well as Hazara Shi'ites from Afghanistan itself.[61] Named the *Fatemiyoun*, the Afghans were soon joined (albeit in smaller numbers) by Pakistanis (called *Zainabiyoun*). These fighters generally received only basic combat training and consequently suffered high casualties.[62] Iran would have no choice but to increase its presence in Syria if the Assad regime was to survive.

By late 2014, Iran was sending hundreds of military personnel, as well as increasingly advanced missiles and UAVs, into the conflict with diminishing impact. Syrian forces were also increasingly operating under Iranian direction.[63] Tehran was now immersed in a conflict that it could not unilaterally win militarily, but from which withdrawal or defeat was unac-

Quds Force commander Qasem Soleimani, Tehran, September 2016

ceptable politically and strategically. Furthermore, Iran's growing presence in Syria suggested a new relationship with Damascus that offered long-term advantages in terms of power projection that Iran could not afford to lose.

The year 2015 began badly for Iran and its Syrian allies. Attempts to recapture Aleppo, Syria's largest city, had stalled. The Syrian opposition was increasingly well armed, battle hardened and showing signs of improved inter-factional coordination. Idlib fell to the opposition and ancient Palmyra to ISIS.[64] By August 2015, Assad's forces controlled only about one-sixth of pre-conflict Syria.[65]

Iranian losses were also spiking. Iranian media reported that 18 high-ranking IRGC officers and at least 400 Afghan and Iranian 'volunteers' had died in Syria since 2012.[66] Funerals for high-ranking officers killed in fighting came at a pace not seen since the Iran–Iraq War. Some, such as Hamadani, were close friends of Soleimani and received state funerals.[67] The reported locations where these generals died show how widespread senior Iranian personnel were operating in Syria. Hamadani died near Aleppo. Brigadier-General Mohammad Allahdadi was killed along with Hizbullah fighters in an airstrike in southern Syria. Major-General Hadi Kajbaf and three other Iranians were killed south of Damascus. Brigadier-General Reza Khavari died near Hama in central Syria. Surrogates were killed as well, although their losses were seldom reported.[68] For example, the commander of the Fatemiyoun Division, Ali Reza Tavassoli, died at Deraa. The Quds Force responded to these reports with an aggressive media campaign (in which Soleimani prominently appeared) highlighting Syrian successes and reminding audiences of the need to protect Shia shrines. However, this trend could not be sustained.[69]

IRGC Major-General Mohammad Bagheri in Russia, November 2017

Enter Russia

Soleimani's battlefield weaknesses included a lack of combat air support, advanced artillery, missile coordination and sophisticated special-operations partners. Given Moscow's long history in Syria, President Vladimir Putin's animosity towards US President Barack Obama, concerns that the Arab Spring would diminish Russian regional influence and Russia's traditional lack of objection to Iran's activities in Syria with Hizbullah, Russia was an obvious choice.

Such an expansion of Russo-Iranian military cooperation would be a dramatic shift in what had been a complicated historical relationship. The years following the collapse of the Soviet Union witnessed deepening relations. Moscow's willingness to sell Iran weapons and nuclear technology, and Russian support for Iran at the UNSC, as well as its attempts to build a relationship with Iranian President Mahmoud Ahmadinejad, gradually made Russia seem less hostile.[70] In July 2015, Soleimani flew to Moscow and met President Putin to negotiate joint military involvement in the conflict.[71] On 30 September, Russia's parliament approved Putin's request to launch airstrikes in Syria. Russia's presence and the intensity of its operations quickly escalated.[72]

In mid-April 2016, Russia launched bombers from Hamadan air base in Iran, which enabled it to strike multiple targets in Syria, the first time a foreign state had operated in Iran since the Second World War.[73] Russian use of Iranian bases was significant given Iran's constitutional prohibition forbidding the establishment of 'any kind of foreign military base in the country, even for peaceful purposes'.[74] A significant victory came with the fall of Aleppo to Syrian government control on 26 December 2016.[75] Although the ferocity of the war would continue unabated, the Assad regime's survival appeared increasingly assured.

IRGC–Artesh collaboration

In June 2016, Iran's Supreme Leader replaced Major-General Hassan Firouzabadi, who had been the Chief of Iran's Armed Forces General Staff since 1989, with IRGC Major-General Mohammad Bagheri, a close friend of Qasem Soleimani.[76] Bagheri promptly selected a prominent *Artesh* commander, Major-General Abdolrahim Mousavi, as his deputy. In July the same year, IRGC Major-General Gholam Ali Rashid was assigned command of the Khatam al-Anbiya Central Headquarters, the element responsible for actual command and control of Iran's combat forces.[77] These changes augured increased emphasis on IRGC–*Artesh* extraterritorial collaboration.

Increasing cooperation between the IRGC and the *Artesh* had been apparent since at least 2011 and 2012, when they conducted large joint exercises, the first such manoeuvres since the 1979 revolution.[78] Joint domestic mosaic defence exercises have also taken place.[79] As Iran's involvement in the Syria conflict entered its fifth year, reform appeared to be spurred by battlefield demands, as well as shifts in Iran's perception of its strategic threats. Such joint exercises continued through 2018.[80]

The involvement of *Artesh* ground forces in Syria marked a profound shift from its traditional and constitutionally mandated defence-focused paradigm and the first time the *Artesh* had fought abroad since the end of the Iran–Iraq War.[81] Iran's public learned of this growing involvement much as the IRGC first disclosed its role: funeral announcements. In April 2016, Iran announced the deaths of three junior *Artesh* personnel, likely from the 65th Airborne Special Forces Brigade. *Artesh* forces also suffered casualties in fighting near Aleppo.[82]

Iran's use of ballistic missiles

It was likely that with the involvement of so many other Iranian military elements in Syria, Iranian missiles would also play a role.[83] On 18 June 2017, the IRGC fired six medium-range surface-to-surface missiles at ISIS forces in Syria in response to an ISIS attack in Tehran earlier in the month.[84] On 30 September 2018 and in response to a terrorist attack by Sunni militants against IRGC personnel that month, Iran again fired six medium-range ballistic missiles across Iraqi airspace against ISIS strongholds in Syria.[85] The attacks also demonstrated Iran's capability to Israel and the Sunni Gulf states.

Map 1.3: **Iranian regional missile reach: selected ballistic and cruise missiles**

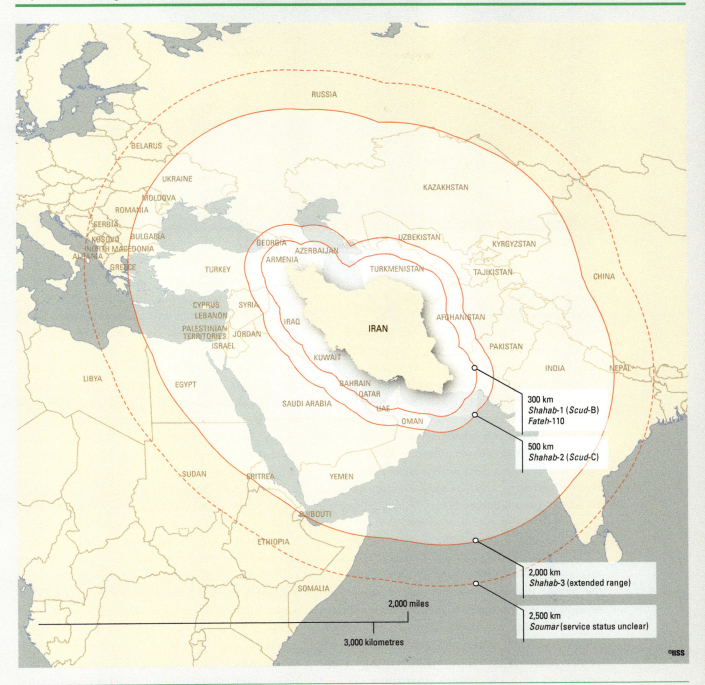

Maximum missile ranges assuming standard payload and most forward deployment. Distances shown are approximate.
Source: IISS

By 2017, Iran's operations in Syria represented a blend of conventional and unconventional forces and surrogate and allied actors. Personnel costs in the conflict had been significant. The number of Iranians killed in Syria had reached hundreds, perhaps more than 2,100, and with many more wounded.[86] Casualties among Iran's multinational militias were undoubtedly several times higher.[87]

However, Iran's sacrifices had salvaged an ally, extended regional power projection and provided valuable battlefield experience to its forces. The death of at least one student from the IRGC's officer-training Imam Hossein University may be evidence that Iran incorporated the conflict into its force training.[88] Tehran's forces also acquired significant military experience (especially concerning air support

The Islamic Revolutionary Guard Corps fires ballistic missiles from Kermanshah, Iran, reportedly hitting Al-Bukamal in Syria's Deir ez-Zor governorate, October 2018

of combat operations and the combat integration of surface-to-surface missile capabilities) through joint operations with Russia.

Much as it did in Lebanon and Iraq, Iran has sought to sustain the paramilitary structures it created in Syria. In 2017, Iran's IRGC Commander-in-Chief Jafari called upon the Syrian government to formalise the existence of Syria's National Defence Forces and allow it to remain in existence following the end of the conflict, much as Iraq had formalised the existence of the PMU.[89] It is likely that Iran's political allies in Syria will be encouraged by Tehran to pursue positions of authority, much as their counterparts have been in Iraq and Lebanon.

Yemen

Yemen's Houthis had maintained a relationship with the Islamic Republic since the earliest days of the revolution, and some of its leadership had spent years in Iran.[90] During the 2000s, Sanaa would routinely complain of Iran's relationship with the Houthis, but outside observers discounted much of this as propaganda. In 2007, the Yemeni government expelled Tehran's ambassador reportedly over Iranian efforts to destabilise the fragile country.[91] In 2009, Yemeni authorities intercepted two Iranian arms shipments bound for the Houthis.[92] Nonetheless, the relationship did not appear to be a priority for either side until after the Yemeni government began to unravel in 2011. Even then, Iran's security services had more urgent demands in Iraq and Syria.[93]

The situation changed dramatically when the Houthis captured Sanaa on 21 September 2014 and expelled the Yemeni government. Shortly thereafter, the Houthis moved to seize the port of Aden and Saudi Arabia and the UAE formed an Arab coalition to restore the Yemeni government to power.[94] Iran realised that the conflict offered an opportunity to injure Riyadh and perhaps gain a partner with the capability to threaten commerce in the southern Red Sea and the strategic Bab al-Mandeb choke point. Iran's influence over that geography, along with its existing control of the Strait of Hormuz, would allow Tehran to respond to any US action with an asymmetric threat to global energy and trade shipments. Tehran also likely recognised that the international community – which did little to challenge its actions in Iraq and Syria – would have no appetite to obstruct it.

As in the case of Syria, Iran's first response involved the transfer of advisers and weapons via an air bridge managed by its civilian airlines, and later maritime smuggling from civilian ports and small boats.[95] A small contingent of Lebanese Hizbullah military specialists were active on the ground. The Arab coalition quickly ended Iran's ability to conduct flights and open naval shipments, but smuggling via Oman and the Arabian Sea coast enabled Iran to introduce increasingly sophisticated missile and UAV technology, advanced anti-tank guided missiles, sniper rifles, rocket-propelled grenades, small arms and ammunition at a sufficient pace to allow the Houthis to maintain the initiative.[96] The Houthi capture of Yemen's main port of Hudaydah in 2014 further enabled Iran to ship ballistic missiles and advisers to its new partner.[97]

Despite this success, Tehran's engagement with the Houthis was challenging. Iran's arrival in Iraq, Syria and even Lebanon in the 1980s relied heavily on the support of Iran-based allies or local contacts Tehran had dealt with for years, if not decades. No such architecture existed in Yemen. The Houthis had

Cyber

Iran's approach to the new threats and opportunities presented by cyberspace and cyber operations is inherently bound to its strategic outlook. This applies particularly to its doctrine of strategic depth, both as it opposes its traditional regional adversaries (the Sunnis led by Saudi Arabia; and Israel) and as it sees a new and unique opportunity to reach into the homeland networks of the global superpower ally of those adversaries, the United States. As with other levers of power, Iran's cyber capabilities are born of internal organisational rivalry and are sometimes 'outsourced' to non-state actors. As with Iranian strategy in general, its use of cyberspace has an innate duality, with pragmatic regional defence partnering uncomfortably with a more dogmatic attempt to protect and export Iran's Islamic Revolution.

The context for Iran's approach to cyber is provided by its comparatively well-educated and computer-literate young population, and two strategic shocks. The first shock was the role the internet played in the flow of ideas that fuelled the Green Movement in 2009. This led to the IRGC being given a mandate and large investment to improve Iran's domestic-information security; essentially, to protect the Iranian Revolution in cyberspace. This included the use of non-state cyber 'proxies' – the Gerdab.ir hacker group was reportedly tasked with hacking internal opponents of the regime, while the IRGC-affiliated Iranian Cyber Army hacker group markedly increased its activity from 2009 onwards. The second shock was Iran's realisation that in 2010 its adversaries had successfully used a cyber capability (Stuxnet) to impede its development of a nuclear-weapons capability. Iran seemed to draw two main conclusions: the need to continue to strengthen its own cyber defences and an appreciation of the 'offensive' reach Iran itself might be able to achieve across cyberspace.

In 2011–12, and in addition to the similarly tasked IRGC Cyber Defence Command already in place, Iran established its Joint Chiefs of Staff Cyber Command, tasked with thwarting attacks against Iranian nuclear facilities and coordinating national cyber warfare and information security. In 2015, Ayatollah Ali Khamenei appointed a Supreme Council for Cyber Space, reportedly a policymaking and supervisory body. Between 2009–10 and 2019, and often via non-state proxies such as the Iranian Cyber Army, Iran has invested heavily in developing and using cyber capabilities, for propaganda, intelligence exploitation and disruption. This appears to be an attempt to offset its conventional military weakness when compared with Saudi Arabia and the US, with an IRGC general claiming in 2013 that Iran was the 'fourth biggest cyber power among the world's cyber armies'. Of particular note has been Iran's development of the Shamoon 'wiper' virus in imitation of Stuxnet, and its use against (among others) the Saudi oil industry and Western (including US) financial services. But reportedly Iran's main cyber priority remains the need to identify the 'vital points of vulnerability' in its own infrastructure, to boost its own cyber defence. A report by the British Technology firm Small Media indicated that in 2015 Tehran had increased its spending on cyber security by 1,200% over a two-year period.

There is ample evidence from the last decade that Iran has provided cyber tools and training to its favoured proxy militia, Lebanese Hizbullah, helping to improve the latter's capability as a cyber actor. The degree to which Iran may have shared some of its more advanced cyber capabilities is an open question, as is the degree to which Iran's own cyber capabilities may have benefited from greater cooperation on intelligence matters with Russia in the wake of the war in Syria.

As of 2018, reporting from cyber-security companies (e.g., the 2018 Cloudstrike report) revealed ongoing Iranian cyber operations across the Middle East, but also against Western companies that do business or maintain infrastructure in the region, in some cases reaching into infrastructure provided by those companies in Western countries. The 2011 DigiNotar attack, the 2013 attack against the US Navy, the 2014 attack against the Las Vegas Sands Casino, the 176 days of distributed denial of service (DDoS) attacks against US banks (which took place as US sanctions were being ratcheted up on Iran), and the attacks on the British and Canadian parliaments illustrate the range of Iranian cyber attacks. New tactics have also been reported, with a greater prevalence of information operations conducted on Western social-media platforms. Overall, Iran's current cyber activity seems designed to conduct espionage against regional rivals, to control dissident activity and to further hybrid-war campaigns internationally. Cyberspace has given Iran a new international reach. The Shamoon wiper has re-emerged as a destructive threat, as part of the Iranian response to the collapse of the Joint Comprehensive Plan of Action (JCPOA, also known as the Iran nuclear deal) and the renewal of sanctions.

few advanced technical skills and rejected domination by any outside party, including Iran. The ideological grooming and technical training of the Houthis required working with them in Iran as well as Yemen. Nonetheless, the Houthis were tenacious and possessed a deep antipathy towards Saudi Arabia and the West. It soon became clear that Iran could sustain a conflict with Riyadh at a low cost: a limited number of advisers and weapons, training in Yemen and Iran, and sufficient funds to help the Houthis buy influence among other tribes.

The gradual improvement of Houthi missile and UAV skills, as well as their ideological harmony with Hizbullah, likely indicates that Iran has achieved some degree of success in both areas. Houthi rhetoric (and the group's flag) share Hizbullah's tone and

> **"WESTERN OBSERVERS ACKNOWLEDGE IRAN'S ROLE IN YEMEN, BUT TEHRAN HAS FACED NO CONSEQUENCES FOR ITS ACTIONS"**

language, and Houthi leaders met Hizbullah leader Secretary-General Hassan Nasrallah in August 2018.[98]

By 2016, Iranian weaponry in Yemen was visible on every front. The Houthi's use of Iranian explosive remote-controlled boats enabled attacks on Emirati, Saudi and US military vessels, oil tankers and oil terminals in the Red Sea.[99] With Iranian technical assistance, the Houthis were able to increase the range of pre-conflict missiles to target first Jeddah and by 2017 Riyadh itself. On 6 November 2017, an extended-range Houthi missile struck close to Riyadh International Airport. The Saudi foreign minister issued a statement that his government saw Iran's role in the attacks as 'an act of war … Iran cannot lob missiles at Saudi cities and towns and expect us not to take steps.'[100] The comments were ignored, and a month later, the Houthis launched a missile at King Salman's Riyadh palace.[101]

Western observers routinely acknowledge Iran's role in exacerbating the conflict and the extent of the civilian disaster, but Tehran has faced no specific consequences for its actions in Yemen. Emirati and Saudi leaders reportedly remain convinced that Iran intends to establish the same missile and UAV programme in Yemen targeting them as it achieved in Lebanon against Israel after 2006.[102] This argument failed to sway the international community, although Iran-enabled missile attacks also threaten expatriates in Saudi Arabia. As in Iraq, Iran has not only injured an adversary but has been able to use the conflict itself to do additional damage to that adversary's international reputation.

Iran's regional success: the enabling framework

The success of Iran's military doctrine relied on a series of components:

Consistent application of hybrid-war techniques

Iran's regional success was not guaranteed, but its refusal to involve large numbers of its forces did protect it from the risks of overextension. Tehran's operations displayed similar activity profiles, with deployment pace and intensity dependent upon battlefield requirements and the level of sophistication of its surrogate militias. All of these tools were used in Iraq and Syria, and most apply to Yemen as well:

- The deployment of senior Quds Force officers as advisers.
- Financial, materiel, communications and cyber support.
- The training of third-party militias – locally and in Iran – aimed at enhancing their sophistication, effectiveness and ideological reliability.
- The deployment of small numbers of IRGC or Lebanese Hizbullah specialists.
- The provision of advanced weaponry tailored to battlefield requirements (e.g., EFPs, advanced surveillance and armed UAVs, advanced ballistic-missile technology, explosive remote-controlled boats) to increase the power of surrogate and partner militias.
- The gradual involvement of non-IRGC Iranian elements, including the *Artesh*, the foreign ministry and other civilian ministries.
- Initial denial of involvement in the conflict, followed by gradual admission of activities as losses become undeniable.
- The development of militias into Hizbullah-like organisations, with local security and political roles, under Iran's influence.
- The exploitation of soft-power potential.

The main advantage of this profile is that it has allowed Tehran to test (and successively breach) perceived international red lines. The absence of red lines risked Iran and the West stumbling into conflict as a result of increasingly aggressive Iranian and Iranian-proxy actions. Instead, regional states have seemingly grown accustomed to conventional military operations instigated by Iran, but limited to front-line states.

Table 1.2: **Iranian assistance to Shia groups**

Nationality	Location of recruitment	Location of training	Critical enablers	IRGC commanders deployed on battlefield	Level of direct battlefield involvement	Level of funding	Known location of operations
Afghan	Mostly in Iran	Iran Syria	Direct recruitment Training Organisation Funding Command	Yes	●	●	Syria
Bahraini	Bahrain Iran Iraq	Iran Iraq	Explosively formed penetrators	No	○	●	Bahrain
Iraqi	Iraq	Mostly Iraq Iran	Explosively formed penetrators Training Mentoring Organisation	Yes	●●	●●	Iraq Syria
Lebanese	Lebanon	Mostly Lebanon Iran	Training Organisation Funding Rockets Missiles Uninhabited aerial vehicles Anti-tank guided missiles	Yes	●	●●●	Lebanon Syria Iraq Yemen
Pakistani	Pakistan	Iran Syria	Direct recruitment Training Organisation Funding Command	Yes	○	●	Syria
Syrian	Syria	Mostly Syria Iran	Direct recruitment Training Organisation Funding Command Rockets Uninhabited aerial vehicles Anti-tank guided missiles	Yes	●●●	●●●	Syria
Yemeni	N/A	Yemen	Funding Missiles Missile training Uninhabited aerial vehicles	Yes	●	●	Yemen

Source: IISS ●●● High ●● Medium ● Limited ○ None

Significant expenditure of financial resources

Despite the demands of the regional conflicts in which it has been involved, Tehran has limited the numbers of Iranian personnel deployed in theatre, instead deploying only senior personnel and specialists. In contrast, its expenditure of financial resources faced few constraints. However, it is difficult to estimate the costs of Iran's regional interventions. Its expenditures include not only billions of dollars in direct cash payments and oil deliveries, but also weapons and equipment from national stockpiles. Funding for its allies and surrogates in the region includes payments and training expenses for thousands of militia fighters, as well as the costs of operating Iranian military and civilian airlines.

Expenditures in the Iraq, Syria and Yemen conflicts are estimated to have cost the Iranian economy as much as US\$16bn.[103] These costs are in addition to as much as US\$700 million reportedly paid annually to Lebanese Hizbullah, as well as millions of dollars to various Palestinian militants.[104] The strain of such expenditures on Iran's flagging economy has been considerable, although the impact has been eased by the fact that the cost has been spread over more than eight years. In terms of specific conflict costs, Iran's support to Syria since 2011 has been the most significant expenditure of

Figure 1.3: **Ideological affiliation with key allies/proxies**

Qais al-Khazali | JAN 2018
We are part of the Axis of Resistance, but the political situation of Iraq is not so clear … The events which happened in Iraq after the invasion of ISIS in June 2014 confirmed that the majority of Iraqis are a people of resistance and they believe in it.

Abu Mahdi al-Muhandis
The support of the Islamic Republic [of Iran] has been essential, and the youth of Hezbollah had an essential role in training, planning, and supporting [the PMU].

Hassan Nasrallah
It's the Axis of Resistance's responsibility, at a state, movement, and individual level to prepare itself and not lose sight of the fact that if we prepare ourselves for the day that war comes, we can change this war from an historic threat to an historic opportunity.

Abu Mahdi al-Muhandis | AUG 2017
(in letter to Hassan Nasrallah)
Sayyid of the Resistance, in the past, present and future your name is associated with splendour and greatness, a form of conscious opposition. In the past, present and future we stand with you on the same path that is stretched from the sky to the Earth.

Bashar al-Assad
The fighters of Hizbullah … played no less a role in defending Syrian soil than their brothers in courage, the fighters of the Syrian armed forces. When we talk about them, we speak with a pride that equals our pride in any Syrian fighter who defends his homeland. The same goes for their martyrs, their wounded, and their heroic families. As for Iran, it did not hesitate to stand alongside us from day one. It gave us unlimited weapons and equipment, it sent us military advisors and officers to help us with planning, and it gave us economic support during the very difficult circumstances we underwent.

Qais al-Khazali | SEP 2018
As for the support from Iran, I previously mentioned that it has been openly supporting the resistance in Iraq and around the world. It is no big secret … Iran would benefit from weakening the US, and we share this interest.

Ali Akbar Velayati | MAY 2018
Today we have won in Syria, we have won in Lebanon and Iraq, and we are in the process of winning in Yemen.

Hossein Salami | APR 2018
You [Israelis] don't have an escape route and you live in the dragon's mouth. So be aware that the Resistance Front is much stronger than before … You've seen how the Resistance Front has fought on the ground against the *takfiris*, how it has thoroughly cleared them away. And you're not ever going to be as strong as they were.

Mohammad Ali Falaki | AUG 2016
In Iran, we sometimes used to look at [Afghans] like they were drug-dealers, criminals or construction labourers … but because of their support for those who are Shia they have fought in Syria … This [younger] generation came and in Syria under the command of Iranian forces they shone with their courage, bravery, self-sacrifice and honour.

We go from here [Iran] to south Lebanon and support the Shia there, we go to Bahrain and Yemen, too. We provide money to all of them and support the Shia there.

Zainabiyoun commander | JUL 2016
God willing, the Zainabiyoun fighters will return [to Pakistan] after the end of the Syrian civil war and will act in the Supreme Leader's interest throughout the world.

Qasem Soleimani | JUN 2016
The Al Khalifa (rulers of Bahrain) surely know their aggression against Sheikh Isa Qassim is a red line that crossing it would set Bahrain and the whole region on fire, and it would leave no choice for people but to resort to armed resistance.

Hossein Amir Abdollahian | FEB 2015
(Deputy Foreign Minister for Arab and African Affairs)
Yemeni Ansarullah movement has taken major steps to restore domestic peace and stability to the country through completing political procedure.

Hossein Salami | NOV 2018
Yemen will never die and now it's regaining its historic identity. Yemen, Syria, Lebanon and Palestine are still alive and it's the Zionists who've become trapped.

Nouri al-Maliki
The Axis of Resistance, represented by Lebanese Hizbullah, the Houthis, the Popular Mobilisation Units and the IRGC, will soon liberate Palestine.

Foreign Ministry spokeswoman | MAR 2015
Claims about the dispatch of weapons from the Islamic Republic of Iran to Yemen are completely fabricated and sheer lies.

Ali Shirazi | JAN 2015
(Supreme Leader's representative to the IRGC)
The popular mobilisation of Iraq and Syria is also like what happened for Hizbullah and Ansarullah. In each country that our enemies have entered to try to destroy Islam, the exact opposite has occurred. Their coming has acted as a catalyst for mobilisation and has provoked a feeling of national defence.

LEBANON

Source: IISS

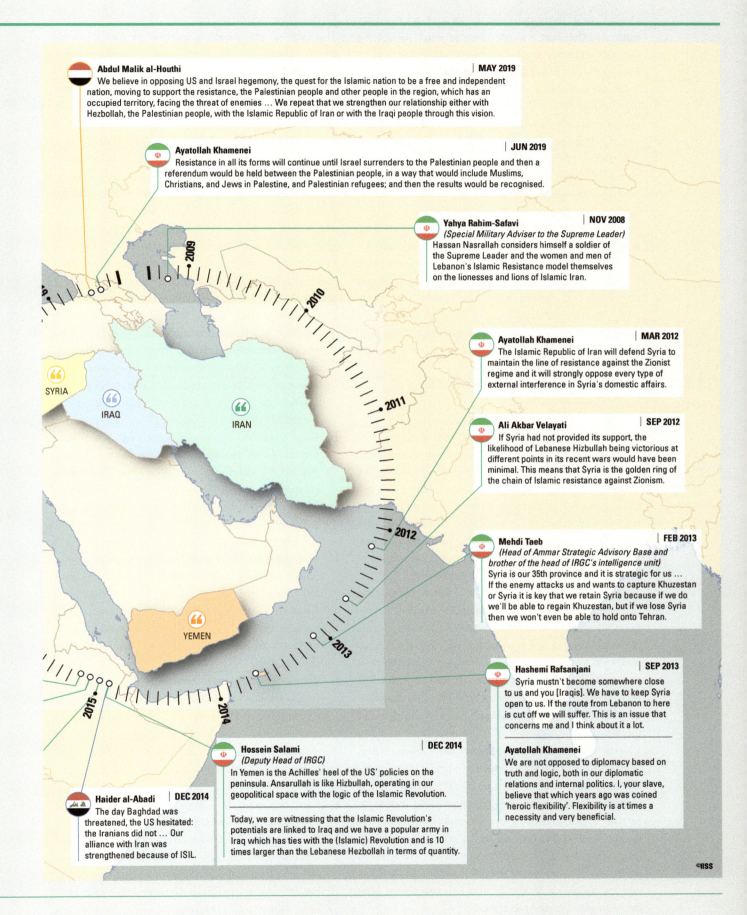

foreign aid in its modern history. In 2015, a UN envoy estimated that Iran was spending as much as US$6bn per year on its Syrian operations, although it is unclear how much of this aid came in cash and oil as compared to excess materiel Iran had already produced for its own armed forces.[105] According to IMF figures, Iran also provided Syria with credit lines totalling US$1.9bn in 2013, US$3bn in 2014 and US$0.97bn in 2015.[106] In addition, Iran reportedly transferred about 60,000 barrels of oil per day to Syria.[107]

Reliance on third parties to fight conflicts

Since 2003, the Quds Force has created or nurtured, armed, funded, trained and transported an increasingly seasoned transnational Shia (and sometimes Sunni) militancy capable of fighting against different opponents on disconnected battlefields simultaneously. Iran's militia partners – some of whom only came into existence after 2011 – may number as high as 200,000.[108] However, Iran's control over surrogate

"IRAN'S CONTROL OVER SURROGATE OPERATIONS VARIES"

operations varies. In some cases, Iran seeks only to influence their actions (e.g., elements of the Taliban). In others, its goal is to enable partners with parallel interests (e.g., the Houthis, and to an extent Lebanese Hizbullah). But in many cases, Iran's control has been routine and direct (e.g., the Shia militias in Iraq and Syria). The Sunni components of this militancy (Hamas, Palestinian Islamic Jihad and Taliban elements) underscore that Iran's interests are also geopolitical.[109]

The loyalty of these militias – when considered collectively – has been enough to achieve Iran's regional goals, whereas cohesion among Iran's regional adversaries is weaker. The fact that thousands of Arabs have fought for years under Iranian command has also shown that Tehran had eroded at least some of the traditional Arab–Persian hostility that had long confounded its ability to build pools of influence in the region.

Iran's surrogates and partners are also evolving. Iraqi and Lebanese surrogates have undertaken expeditionary operations that would have been deemed improbable only a decade ago, providing Iran with further opportunities to evade responsibility for its regional interventions. As Iran's proxy partners in Iraq, Lebanon, Syria and Yemen assert themselves politically, it is likely that they will allow Iran to maintain its influence in the political development and decision-making of Arab states.[110]

An assertive foreign policy

The lack of international reaction to Iran's adventurism resulted from a mixture of crisis fatigue, competing priority issues, a decline in direct US involvement in the region and Russian obstructionism in the UNSC. But Iran's willingness to undertake an assertive foreign policy to exploit fissures in the international community did deflect pressure from Tehran, allowing the Quds Force to create facts on the ground. This foreign policy has been directed by the Supreme Leader but dominated by two actors: Major-General Soleimani, who engaged directly with Iraqi, Russian and Syrian leaders, and Iran's Foreign Minister Zarif, who focused on communicating with the broader international community. In their engagement with foreign officials, and despite differences in style and personality, they displayed common qualities:

- Both represent Iran's incoming generation of leaders: assertive, pragmatic and committed to the revolution's principles. They are unwilling to compromise on Iran's claimed role as a regional hegemon, and are committed to the sustenance of the Axis of Resistance against Israel and the need for the US to leave the region.

- Each has relied on powerful patrons, whom they are likely to influence. Soleimani's ties to the Supreme Leader are as well known as Zarif's relationship with President Hassan Rouhani. Soleimani is likely to survive under future hardline supreme leaders, but Zarif's position may not survive the end of Rouhani's term in 2021.

- Their stature is in part due to their longevity. Soleimani has led the Quds Force since 1998 and had considerable experience with Afghan and Kurdish issues before taking command. Zarif became foreign minister in 2013, before which he had periodic interaction with US officials and long service at the UN.

- Their status has been elevated by significant US foreign-policy decisions: Soleimani's operational world burgeoned after the US-led invasion of Iraq; for Zarif, the Joint Comprehensive Plan of Action nuclear deal provided unprecedented engagement with China, Russia, the US and major European leaders.

- Each has been the target of Western outreach. Zarif used the discussions to build a working relationship with the US secretary of state and other leaders. Soleimani rejects direct contact, but periodically, if only briefly and through intermediaries, has engaged with the US. These engagements may have allowed each an understanding of Western negotiating style to a degree not shared by their Western intermediaries regarding Iran.

- Each exploited the West's willingness to negotiate at times of weakness or geopolitical necessity. Examples include Soleimani's indirect outreach before the US invasions of Afghanistan and Iraq, and his willingness to authorise discussions following the US crackdown on Iranian forces in Iraq. Zarif's engagement during pre-invasion discussions, support for nuclear talks as sanctions pressure reached its height, and engagement of the Geneva process on Syria when Assad was at his weakest, were similar.
- Each is adept at using the media and social media. Zarif routinely engages Western press and social media, while Soleimani appears on social media and makes widely reported anti-Western speeches.

Strategic assessment

Iran's interventions have validated an external military doctrine emphasising hybrid-war techniques and cooperation with state and sub-state actors. Iran has been able to threaten international energy and shipping arteries in the Persian Gulf and the Strait of Hormuz, and to some extent the Red Sea and Bab al-Mandeb. A large number of Iranian military personnel have fought difficult and multi-year conflicts in which they may believe they not only achieved strategic objectives but did so at the expense of Arab regional powers, Israel and the US. This confidence will likely guide Tehran's view as to how it will manage future conflicts.

The conflicts in Syria and Yemen are far from over, but as they do wind down, Iran will be faced with a series of challenges. Iran's clients are well positioned to protect its interests, and the international community has yet to develop a strategy capable of dismantling Tehran's militias. However, Iran will also be challenged to produce the resources required to sustain post-conflict reconstruction. Failure to do so could easily erode Iran's influence at the expense of external powers. Tehran's execution of its military doctrine has won it unprecedented regional influence during periods of equally unprecedented conflict. Whether this doctrine can deliver substantive returns in times of peace, as it did in Lebanon, will be tested in Syria and elsewhere.

Notes

[1] Hybrid war (also known as grey-zone conflict) is a blend of conventional and unconventional forces engaged in asymmetric actions, which avoid conventional conflict but are designed to achieve strategic goals. Such tools are often employed by weaker powers against powerful adversaries. Actions involved in this conflict exploit uncertain policy, legal frameworks and the openness of free societies. Likewise, they are gradually undertaken along an escalatory ladder in which specific steps are deniable, yet still attributable to the aggressor. See US Special Operations Command, 'The Gray Zone', 9 September 2015, https://info.publicintelligence. net/USSOCOM-GrayZones.pdf; US Department of State, 'International Security Advisory Board: Report on Gray Zone Conflict', 3 January 2017, https://www.state.gov/t/avc/isab/266650.htm#gzconflict.

[2] James Howard-Johnston, *East Rome, Sasanian Persia and the End of Antiquity* (Abingdon: Routledge, 2006), p. 21.

[3] Jeffrey Goldberg, 'The Obama Doctrine', *Atlantic*, April 2016, https://www.theatlantic.com/magazine/archive/2016/04/the-obama-doctrine/471525.

[4] Pierre Razoux, *The Iran–Iraq War* (Cambridge, MA: Belknap Press, 2015), p. 574.

[5] 'Constitution of the Islamic Republic of Iran', https://www.wipo.int/edocs/lexdocs/laws/en/ir/ir001en.pdf; Richard Horowitz, 'A Detailed Analysis of Iran's Constitution', World Policy, 12 October 2010, https://worldpolicy.org/2010/10/12/a-detailed-analysis-of-irans-constitution. In terms of external adventurism, Article 3(5) declares 'unsparing support to the mustad'afun [oppressed of the world]'. Article 154 adds that Iran 'supports the just struggles of the mustad'afun against the mustakbirun [tyrants] in every corner of the globe'.

[6] Moshe Ma'oz, 'The "Shi'i Crescent": Myth and Reality', Brookings Analysis Paper, no. 15, November 2017, https://www.brookings.edu/wp-content/uploads/2016/06/11_middle_east_maoz.pdf.

[7] Firas Elias, 'Iranian Military Doctrine', Fikra Forum, Washington Institute, 15 November 2017, https://www.washingtoninstitute.org/fikraforum/view/iranian-military-doctrine; Robert Czulda, 'The Defensive Dimension of Iran's Military Doctrine: How Would They Fight?', *Middle East Policy*, vol. 23, no. 1, Spring 2017, https://www.mepc.org/journal/defensive-dimension-irans-military-doctrine-how-would-they-fight; Michael Connell, 'Iran's Military Doctrine', United States Institute of Peace, https://iranprimer.usip.org/resource/irans-military-doctrine; Steven R. Ward, *Immortal: A Military History of Iran and Its Armed Forces* (Washington, DC: Georgetown University Press, 2009), p. 302; Steven R. Ward, 'The Continuing Evolution of Iran's Military Doctrine', *Middle East Journal*, vol. 59, no. 4, Autumn 2005, p. 560, http://www.jstor.org/stable/4330184.

8 Constitution of the Islamic Republic of Iran, p. 5; Horowitz, 'A Detailed Analysis of Iran's Constitution'.

9 Bayram Sinkaya, *Revolutionary Guards in Iranian Politics: Elites and Shifting Relations* (Abingdon: Routledge, 2016), pp. 20–21, 42–46; Frederic Wehrey et al., *The Rise of the Pasdaran* (Santa Monica, CA: RAND Corporation, 2009), p. 22, https://www.rand.org/content/dam/rand/pubs/monographs/2008/RAND_MG821.pdf.

10 Czulda, 'The Defensive Dimension of Iran's Military Doctrine'.

11 Ward, 'The Continuing Evolution of Iran's Military Doctrine', p. 567.

12 'Doktrin-e defa'i-ye Iran az "defa'e sarf" beh "afzayesh-e tahdid bara-ye doshman" taghyir yafteh' [Iran's Defence Doctrine has changed from 'cost-inducing defence' to 'increasing the threat to the enemy'], speech by IRGC media adviser to IRGC command Hamid Reza Moqaddamfar, 1 October 2016, https://www.tasnimnews.com/fa/news/1395/07/10/1198210.

13 Ali Alfoneh, 'Eternal Rivals? The Artesh and the IRGC', Middle East Institute, 28 November 2011, https://www.aei.org/publication/eternal-rivals-the-artesh-and-the-irgc; Julian Borger and Robert Tait, 'The financial power of the revolutionary guards', *Guardian*, 15 February 2010, https://www.theguardian.com/world/2010/feb/15/financial-power-revolutionary-guard.

14 Sinkaya, *Revolutionary Guards in Iranian Politics: Elites and Shifting Relations*, p. 47; Houchang Hassan-Yari, 'Iran: Defending the Islamic Revolution – The Corps of the Matter', Radio Free Europe, 5 August 2005, https://www.rferl.org/a/1060431.html.

15 Dexter Filkins, 'The Shadow Commander', *New Yorker*, 23 September 2013, https://www.newyorker.com/magazine/2013/09/30/the-shadow-commander.

16 'Ma'muriyat-e niru-ye qods towse'eh-ye enghelab-e eslami dar jahan ast' [The Quds Force's Mission is to Expand the Islamic Revolution Throughout the World], *Kayhan*, 2 October 2014, http://kayhan.ir/fa/news/24370.

17 Mehran Riazaty, *Khomeini's Warriors: Foundation of Iran's Regime, Its Guardians, Allies Around the World* (Bloomington, IN: Xlibris, 2016), pp. 226–27.

18 *Ibid.*, pp. 230–31.

19 Anthony H. Cordesman and Bryan Gold, *The Gulf Military Balance: The Conventional and Asymmetric Dimensions* (Washington, DC: Center for Strategic and International Studies, 2014), pp. 148–49.

20 National Commission on Terrorist Attacks upon the United States, 'The 9/11 Commission Report', 22 July 2004, p. 61, https://www.9-11commission.gov/report/911Report.pdf; Anthony H. Cordesman, 'Iran's Revolutionary Guards, the Al Quds Force, and Other Intelligence and Paramilitary Forces', Center for Strategic and International Studies, 16 August 2007, p. 8, https://csis-prod.s3.amazonaws.com/s3fs-public/legacy_files/files/media/csis/pubs/070816_cordesman_report.

pdf; US Department of the Treasury, 'Fact Sheet: Designation of Iranian Entities and Individuals for Proliferation Activities and Support for Terrorism', 25 October 2007, https://www.treasury.gov/press-center/press-releases/pages/hp644.aspx.

21 'Iran Charged Over Argentina Bomb', BBC News, 25 October 2006, http://news.bbc.co.uk/2/hi/americas/6085768.stm.

22 Riazaty, *Khomeini's Warriors: Foundation of Iran's Regime, Its Guardians, Allies Around the World*, pp. 230–31; Ali Alfoneh, 'Brigadier General Qassem Suleimani: a biography', Middle Eastern Outlook, 24 January 2011, https://www.aei.org/publication/brigadier-general-qassem-suleimani-a-biography; Filkins, 'The Shadow Commander'; Shirin Samara, '*Shakhsiyyat Iraniyyah: Qasim Sulaymani … min al-thul ila wajihat hurub al-iqlim*' [Iranian characters: Qasem Soleimani … From the shadows to the front line of the region's wars], Iran Lens, 22 December 2018, https://jadehiran.com/archives/4073.

23 Riazaty, *Khomeini's Warriors: Foundation of Iran's Regime, Its Guardians, Allies Around the World*, pp. 230–31; Alfoneh, 'Brigadier General Qassem Suleimani: a biography'; Filkins, 'The Shadow Commander'; Samara, 'Iranian Characters: Qasem Soleimani'.

24 'Khomenism', Counter Extremism Project, https://www.counterextremism.com/khomeinism.

25 Borzou Daragahi, 'Badr Brigade: Among Most Consequential Outcomes of the Iran–Iraq War', Atlantic Council, 16 August 2018, https://www.atlanticcouncil.org/blogs/iransource/badr-brigade-among-most-consequential-outcomes-of-the-iran-iraq-war-2.

26 *Ibid.*

27 Nader Uskowi, *Temperature Rising: Iran's Revolutionary Guards and Wars in the Middle East* (Lanham, MD: Rowman and Littlefield, 2018), pp. 35–37.

28 Joel D. Rayburn and Frank K. Sobchak (eds), *The U.S. Army in the Iraq War – Volume 2: Surge and Withdrawal, 2007–2011* (Carlisle, PA: U.S. Army War College Press, 2019), pp. 74–75, https://ssi.armywarcollege.edu/pubs/display.cfm?pubID=1376; Michael Ware, 'Inside Iran's Secret War for Iraq', *Time*, 22 August 2005, http://www.mickware.info/Past/2005/files/1ed99b0a67b6c013794d8844a97615ab-11.php.

29 Rayburn and Sobchak (eds), *The U.S. Army in the Iraq War – Volume 2: Surge and Withdrawal, 2007–2011*, pp. 275–76, 620.

30 Andrew deGrandpre and Andrew Tilghman, 'Iran linked to deaths of 500 U.S. troops in Iraq, Afghanistan', *Military Times*, 14 July 2015, https://www.militarytimes.com/news/pentagon-congress/2015/07/14/iran-linked-to-deaths-of-500-u-s-troops-in-iraq-afghanistan.

31 Martin Chulov, 'Qassem Suleimani: the Iranian general "secretly running" Iraq', *Guardian*, 28 July 2011, https://www.theguardian.com/world/2011/jul/28/qassem-suleimani-iran-iraq-influence.

32 Hesam Forozan, *The Military in Post-Revolutionary Iran: The Evolution and Roles of the Revolutionary Guards* (New York:

Routledge, 2016), p. 198.

33 Chulov, 'Qassem Suleimani: the Iranian general "secretly running" Iraq'.

34 Garrett Nada and Mattisan Rowan, 'Pro-Iran Militias in Iraq', The Wilson Center, 27 April 2018, https://www.wilson-center.org/article/part-2-pro-iran-militias-iraq.

35 Declassified Tactical Interrogation Report of Qayis Hadi Sa'id Al-Khazali, no. 200243-062.

36 Missy Ryan and Loveday Morris, 'The U.S. and Iran are Aligned Against the Islamic State – For Now', *Washington Post*, 27 December 2014, https://www.washingtonpost.com/world/national-security/the-us-and-iran-are-aligned-in-iraq-against-the-islamic-state--for-now/2014/12/27/353a748c-8d0d-11e4-a085-34e9b9f09a58_story.html?utm_term=.c20399991d5f; Jim Sciutto and Greg Botelho, 'Iraqis "up against the wall" as ISIS threatens province near Baghdad', CNN, 11 October 2014, https://www.cnn.com/2014/10/10/world/meast/isis-threat/index.html.

37 David Cenciotti, 'Previously unknown details about Iranian F-4, F-5, Su-24 and UAVs involvement in air strikes on ISIS targets in Iraq', *Aviationist*, 4 December 2014, https://theaviationist.com/2014/12/04/iriaf-strikes-isis-in-iraq.

38 Tamer El-Ghobashy and Mustafa Salim, 'As Iraq's Shiite militias expand their reach, concerns about an ISIS revival grow', *Washington Post*, 9 January 2019, https://www.washingtonpost.com/world/as-iraqs-shiite-militias-expand-their-reach-concerns-about-an-isis-revival-grow/2019/01/09/52da575e-eda9-11e8-8b47-bd0975fd6199_story.html?utm_term=.6c34d7c6d250.

39 Nada and Rowan, 'Pro-Iran Militias in Iraq'.

40 Ali Hashem, 'In Syria, Iran sees necessary war', *Al-Monitor*, 16 March 2017, https://www.al-monitor.com/pulse/originals/2017/03/iran-syria-intervention-hamedani-Qods-force-memoir.html.

41 Garrett Nada, 'Shiite Holy Sites in Syria', United States Institute of Peace, 3 June 2013, https://iranprimer.usip.org/blog/2013/jun/03/part-ii-shiite-holy-sites-syria.

42 Farnaz Fassihi and Jay Solomon, 'Top Iranian Official Acknowledges Syria Role', *Wall Street Journal*, 16 September 2012, https://www.wsj.com/articles/SB10000872396390443720204578000482831419570.

43 Filkins, 'The Shadow Commander'.

44 Farzin Nadimi, 'Iran Is Still Using Pseudo-Civilian Airlines to Resupply Assad', Washington Institute for Near East Policy, Policywatch no. 2785, 13 April 2017, https://www.washingtoninstitute.org/policy-analysis/view/iran-is-still-using-pseudo-civilian-airlines-to-resupply-assad.

45 'Kerry scolds Iraq about Iran', *Politico*, 24 March 2013, https://www.politico.com/story/2013/03/john-kerry-iraq-iran-089257.

46 Christopher Phillips, *The Battle for Syria: International Rivalry in the New Middle East* (New Haven, CT: Yale University Press), p. 161.

47 Con Coughlin, 'Iran sends elite troops to aid Bashar al-Assad regime in Syria', *Telegraph*, 6 September 2012, https://www.telegraph.co.uk/news/worldnews/middleeast/iran/9526858/Iran-sends-elite-troops-to-aid-Bashar-al-Assad-regime-in-Syria.html; Farnaz Fassihi, 'Iran Said to Send Troops to Bolster Syria', *Wall Street Journal*, 27 August 2012, https://www.wsj.com/articles/SB10000872396390444230504577615393756632230.

48 Anne Barnard and Sebnem Arsu, 'Iranian Captives Freed in Prisoner Exchange in Syria', *New York Times*, 9 January 2013, https://www.nytimes.com/2013/01/10/world/middleeast/syria-iranians-prisoner-exchange.html.

49 Robin Wright, 'Iran's Generals Are Dying in Syria', *New Yorker*, 26 October 2015, https://www.newyorker.com/news/news-desk/irans-generals-are-dying-in-syria.

50 'Hezbollah Military Commander '"Killed in Syria"', BBC News, 2 October 2012, https://www.bbc.com/news/world-middle-east-19801884.

51 Dominic Evans and Mariam Karouny, 'Iranian Guards Commander Killed in Syria', Reuters, 15 February 2013, https://www.reuters.com/article/us-syria-crisis-iran-idUS-BRE91D0EY20130215.

52 'Iranian Cleric: Losing Syria is Like Losing Tehran', YaLibnan, 16 February 2013, http://yalibnan.com/2013/02/16/iranian-cleric-losing-syria-is-like-losing-tehran.

53 Phillips, *The Battle for Syria: International Rivalry in the New Middle East*, pp. 150–51.

54 *Ibid.*, p. 161.

55 *Ibid.*, pp. 157, 163.

56 Thomas Erdbrink, Sewell Chan and David E. Sanger, 'After a U.S. Shift, Iran Has a Seat at Talks on War in Syria', *New York Times*, 28 October 2015, https://www.nytimes.com/2015/10/29/world/middleeast/syria-talks-vienna-iran.html.

57 William J. Burns, *The Back Channel: A Memoir of American Diplomacy and the Case for Its Renewal* (London: Hurst & Co., 2019), p. 326.

58 Phillips, *The Battle for Syria: International Rivalry in the New Middle East*, pp. 160–62.

59 Uskowi, *Temperature Rising: Iran's Revolutionary Guards and Wars in the Middle East*, p. 82.

60 Phillips, *The Battle for Syria: International Rivalry in the New Middle East*, pp. 150, 160.

61 Uskowi, *Temperature Rising: Iran's Revolutionary Guards and Wars in the Middle East*, pp. 133–34; 'Bazgasht-e jangjuyan-e Afghan az Surieh; negarani-ye tazeh-ye Afghanestan' [The return of Afghan fighters from Syria; Afghanistan's recent worry], *Deutsche Welle*, 29 November 2017, https://www.dw.com/fa-ir/a-41568824.

62 Tobias Schneider, 'The Fatemiyoun Division: Afghan fighters in the Syrian civil war', Middle East Institute Policy Paper 2018–9, 15 October 2018, pp. 9–10, https://www.mei.edu/sites/default/files/2018-11/PP11_Schneider.pdf.

63 Jonathan Saul and Parisa Hafezi, 'Iran boosts military support in Syria to bolster Assad', Reuters, 21 February 2014,

https://www.reuters.com/article/us-syria-crisis-iran-insight/
iran-boosts-military-support-in-syria-to-bolster-assad-idUS
BREA1K0TV20140221?feedType=RSS&feedName=world
News; Paul Bucala, 'The Artesh in Syria: A fundamental
shift in Iranian hard power', Critical Threats, 4 May 2016,
https://www.criticalthreats.org/analysis/the-artesh-in-syria-
a-fundamental-shift-in-iranian-hard-power.

64 Phillips, *The Battle for Syria: International Rivalry in the New
Middle East*, p. 215.

65 Columb Strack, 'Country Risk: Syrian Government No
Longer Controls 83% of the Country', Jane's 360, 24 August
2015, https://www.janes.com/article/53771/syrian-govern-
ment-no-longer-controls-83-of-the-country.

66 Hossein Bastani, 'Iran Quietly Deepens Involvement in
Syria's War', BBC Persian, 20 October 2015, https://www.
bbc.com/news/world-middle-east-34572756.

67 Wright, 'Iran's Generals Are Dying in Syria'.

68 Sam Wilkin, 'Iran brings home body of top general killed
in Syria', *Lebanon Daily Star*, 13 June 2015, https://www.
dailystar.com.lb/News/Middle-East/2015/Jun-13/301944-
iran-brings-home-body-of-top-general-killed-in-syria.ashx.

69 Bastani, 'Iran Quietly Deepens Involvement in Syria's War';
Nada, 'Shiite Holy Sites in Syria'.

70 Mark Katz, 'Russia and Iran', *Middle East Policy*, vol. 19,
no. 3, 2012, https://www.mepc.org/russia-and-iran.

71 Uskowi, *Temperature Rising: Iran's Revolutionary Guards and
Wars in the Middle East*, pp. 65–66.

72 'Russia Joins War in Syria: Five Key Points', BBC News, 1
October 2015, https://www.bbc.com/news/world-middle-
east-34416519; Phillips, *The Battle for Syria: International
Rivalry in the New Middle East*, pp. 213–14.

73 Neil MacFarquhar and David E. Sanger, 'Russia Sends
Bombers to Syria Using Base in Iran', *New York Times*, 16
August 2016, https://www.nytimes.com/2016/08/17/world/
middleeast/russia-iran-base-syria.html.

74 Constitution of the Islamic Republic of Iran, Article 146;
Horowitz, 'A Detailed Analysis of Iran's Constitution'.

75 Uskowi, *Temperature Rising: Iran's Revolutionary Guards and
Wars in the Middle East*, pp. 65–66.

76 Amir Toumaj, 'Death of a General: What Shaban Nasiri
Reveals About Iran's Secretive Qods Force', *War on the
Rocks*, 23 March 2018, https://warontherocks.com/2018/03/
death-of-a-general-what-shaban-nasiri-reveals-about-irans-
secretive-qods-force.

77 Sam Tamiz, 'Why Is Iran Shaking Up Its Military Leadership?',
National Interest, 27 July 2016, https://nationalinterest.org/
feature/why-iran-shaking-its-military-leadership-17133; Will
Fulton, 'IRGC Command Network: Formal Structures and
Informal Influence', Critical Threats, 10 July 2013, https://www.
criticalthreats.org/wp-content/uploads/2016/07/pdf_uploadan-
alysisThe_IRGC_Command_Network-1.pdf.

78 'Iran's Army chief reaffirms unity with IRGC', Iran Project,

17 January 2019, https://theiranproject.com/blog/2019/01/17/
irans-army-chief-reaffirms-unity-with-irgc; 'Iran announces
plans for military drills', United Press International, 12
April 2012, https://www.upi.com/Iran-announces-plans-for-
military-drills/66271334240186.

79 'IRGC begins military drills near Iran's northwest border',
Press TV, 24 September 2017, https://www.presstv.com/
DetailFr/2017/09/24/536292/Iran-IRGC-Ground-Forces-
Moharram-Army.

80 Yusef Jalali, 'Iran's army, IRGC hold massive joint air
defense drills', PressTV, 6 November 2018, https://www.
presstv.com/Detail/2018/11/06/579203/Irans-army-IRGC-
hold-massive-joint-air-defense-drills.

81 Paul Bucala and Marie Donovan, 'A New Era for Iran's
Military Leadership', Critical Threats, 1 December 2016,
https://www.criticalthreats.org/analysis/a-new-era-for-
irans-military-leadership; Constitution of the Islamic
Republic of Iran, Article 143; Horowitz, 'A Detailed
Analysis of Iran's Constitution'.

82 Farzin Nadimi, 'Iran's Army Suffers Its First Casualties in
Syria', Washington Institute, 12 April 2016, https://www.
washingtoninstitute.org/policy-analysis/view/irans-army-
suffers-its-first-casualties-in-syria.

83 Robert Einhorn and Vann H. Van Diepen, 'Constraining
Iran's missile capabilities', Brookings Institution, March
2019, https://www.brookings.edu/research/constraining-
irans-missile-capabilities.

84 Babak Dehghanpisheh, 'Iran Fires Missiles at Militant Groups
in Eastern Syria', Reuters, 18 June 2017, https://www.reuters.
com/article/us-mideast-crisis-syria-iran-idUSKBN1990WI.

85 Hwaida Saad and Rod Nordland, 'Iran Fires a Ballistic Missile
at ISIS in Syria, Avenging an Earlier Attack', *New York Times*,
1 October 2018, https://www.nytimes.com/2018/10/01/world/
middleeast/iran-isis-missile-syria.html.

86 '2,100 Iran fighters killed in Iraq, Syria: official', *Al-Monitor*,
7 March 2017, https://al-monitor.com/pulse/afp/2017/03/iraq-
syria-conflict-iran-toll.html.

87 Ali Alfoneh and Michael Eisenstadt, 'Iranian Casualties in
Syria and the Strategic Logic of Intervention', Washington
Institute for Near East Policy, Policywatch no. 2585,
11 March 2016, http://www.washingtoninstitute.org/
policy-analysis/view/iranian-casualties-in-syria-and-the-
strategic-logic-of-intervention.

88 'Ashk-e daneshjuyan-e daneshgah-e afsari-ye Emam
Hossein dar feragh-e Shahid "Abbas Daneshgar"' [The
tears of the students of the officer-training Imam Hussein
University after the passing away of the martyr, student
Abbas], Tasnim News, https://www.tasnimnews.com/fa/
news/1395/03/24/1103749.

89 Anton Mardasov, 'Russia Eyes Role in Formation of Syria's
National Defence Forces', *Al-Monitor*, 27 August 2018,
https://www.al-monitor.com/pulse/originals/2018/08/

russia-syria-idlib-ndf.html; Phillips, *The Battle for Syria: International Rivalry in the New Middle East*, pp. 160–62.

90 Marieke Brandt, *Tribes and Politics in Yemen: A History of the Houthi Conflict* (London: Hurst & Company, 2017), p. 115.

91 Barak A. Salmoni, Bryce Loidolt and Madeleine Wells, *Regime and Periphery in Northern Yemen: The Huthi Phenomenon* (Santa Monica, CA: Rand National Defense Research Institute, 2010), p. 170; Brandt, *Tribes and Politics in Yemen: A History of the Houthi Conflict*, p. 205.

92 Michael Knights, 'The Houthi War Machine: From Guerrilla War to State Capture', *CTC Sentinel*, September 2018, p. 17, https://www.washingtoninstitute.org/uploads/Documents/opeds/Knights20180910-CTCSentinel.pdf.

93 Uskowi, *Temperature Rising: Iran's Revolutionary Guards and Wars in the Middle East*, pp. 28, 115–28.

94 David B. Ottaway, 'Saudi Arabia Forms a Pan-Arab Sunni Alliance Against the Houthis', Wilson Center, Middle East Program Viewpoints, no. 74, March 2015, https://www.wilsoncenter.org/sites/default/files/saudi_arabia_forms_pan-arab_sunni_alliance_against_houthis_0.pdf.

95 'Iranian Flight Lands in Yemen After Aviation Deal', Radio Free Europe, 1 March 2015, https://www.rferl.org/a/iran-mahan-flight-lands-yemen/26875916.html.

96 Yara Bayoumy and Phil Stewart, 'Exclusive: Iran steps up weapons supply to Yemen's Houthis via Oman – Officials', Reuters, 20 October 2016, https://www.reuters.com/article/us-yemen-security-iran/exclusive-iran-steps-up-weapons-supply-to-yemens-houthis-via-oman-officials-idUSKCN12K0CX; Ashraf al-Falahi, 'Just How Neutral Is Oman in Yemen War?', *Al-Monitor*, 12 October 2016, https://www.al-monitor.com/pulse/originals/2016/10/oman-neutral-saudi-war-iran-houthis.html.

97 'Yemen rebels take port city Hodeida', *Al-Masdar News*, 14 October 2014, https://www.almasdarnews.com/article/yemen-rebels-take-port-city-hodeida; Samer al-Atrush, 'Fears for Yemen civilians as battle to retake Hodeidah reaches residential areas around port', *Telegraph*, 20 June 2018, https://www.telegraph.co.uk/news/2018/06/20/saudi-military-coalition-seizes-yemen-airport-rebels.

98 'Hezbollah's Nasrallah Met With Iran-backed Yemeni Rebels', Haaretz, 19 August 2018, https://www.haaretz.com/middle-east-news/hezbollah-s-nasrallah-met-with-iran-backed-yemeni-rebels-1.6389613.

99 Phil Stewart, 'U.S. sees mounting evidence of Houthi role in strike on U.S. warship', Reuters, 12 October 2016, https://www.reuters.com/article/us-yemen-security-usa-idUSKCN12C0DV; Sarah Dadouch, 'Saudi-led coalition says it thwarts Houthi attack on oil tanker', Reuters, 10 January 2018, https://uk.reuters.com/article/uk-shipping-redsea-attack/saudi-led-coalition-says-it-thwarts-houthi-attack-on-oil-tanker-idUKKBN1EZ2GC; 'Iranian Technology Transfers to Yemen', Conflict Armament Research, March 2017, http://www.conflictarm.com/perspectives/iranian-technology-transfers-to-yemen; Cameron Glenn, 'Who Are Yemen's Houthis', Wilson Center, 29 April 2015, https://www.wilsoncenter.org/article/who-are-yemens-houthis.

100 David J. Kirkpatrick, 'Saudi Arabia Charges Iran With "Act of War," Raising Threat of Military Clash', *New York Times*, 6 November 2017, https://www.nytimes.com/2017/11/06/world/middleeast/yemen-saudi-iran-missile.html.

101 Katie Paul and Rania El Gamal, 'Saudi Arabia intercepts Houthi missile fired toward Riyadh; no reported casualties', Reuters, 19 December 2017, https://www.reuters.com/article/us-saudi-blast/saudi-arabia-intercepts-houthi-missile-fired-toward-riyadh-no-reported-casualties-idUSKBN1ED17Y.

102 Author discussion with senior Saudi and Emirati policy and security officials.

103 US Secretary of State Mike Pompeo, 'Remarks to Congress on Yemen', 28 November 2018, https://content.govdelivery.com/attachments/USSTATEBPA/2018/11/28/file_attachments/1114183/S%20Yemen%20Briefing%2011%20 2018%20.pdf.

104 Joyce Karam, 'Iran pays Hezbollah $700 million a year, US official says', *National*, 5 June 2018, https://www.thenational.ae/world/the-americas/iran-pays-hezbollah-700-million-a-year-us-official-says-1.737347; Lisa Barrington, 'U.S. pressure on Hezbollah, Iran is working, Pompeo says in Beirut', Reuters, 22 March 2019, https://www.reuters.com/article/us-usa-pompeo-lebanon/u-s-pressure-on-hezbollah-iran-is-working-pompeo-says-in-beirut-idUSKCN1R31IV.

105 Eli Lake, 'Iran Spends Billions to Prop Up Assad', Bloomberg Opinion, 9 June 2015, https://www.bloomberg.com/opinion/articles/2015-06-09/iran-spends-billions-to-prop-up-assad.

106 Jeanne Gobat and Kristina Kostial, 'Syria's Conflict Economy', International Monetary Fund Working Paper 16/123, 29 June 2016, https://www.imf.org/en/Publications/WP/Issues/2016/12/31/Syrias-Conflict-Economy-44033.

107 'The Toll of War: The Economic and Social Consequences of the Conflict in Syria', World Bank, p. 56.

108 Sune Engel Rasmussen and Isabel Coles, 'Iran's Allies Target Its Rivals, Risking Conflict', *Wall Street Journal*, 24 May 2019, https://www.wsj.com/articles/irans-allies-target-its-rivals-risking-conflict-11558690326.

109 'Tripartite Military Meeting to Secure Tehran–Damascus Road', *Asharq Al-Awsat*, 18 March 2019, https://aawsat.com/english/home/article/1639126/tripartite-military-meeting-secure-tehran-damascus-road; Uskowi, *Temperature Rising: Iran's Revolutionary Guards and Wars in the Middle East*, p. xiv.

110 Brian Katz, 'Axis Rising: Iran's Evolving Regional Strategy and Non-State Partnerships in the Middle East', Center for Strategic and International Studies, 11 October 2018, https://www.csis.org/analysis/axis-rising-irans-evolving-regional-strategy-and-non-state-partnerships-middle-east.

CHAPTER TWO

LEBANESE HIZBULLAH

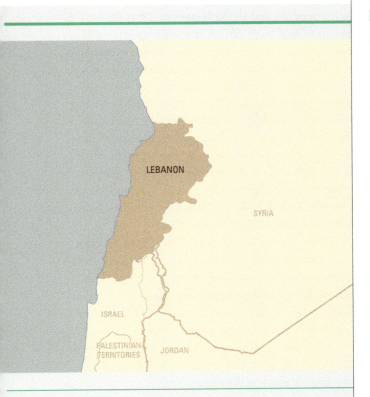

- The intimate relationship between Iran and Hizbullah is of immense and lasting strategic value to both
- Iran has been central to the development and use of Hizbullah's three strategic capabilities: its rocket and missile arsenal, its foreign operations and its regional power projection (including its expeditionary war-fighting role)
- Hizbullah has become the mentor of choice for Iran's other regional partners and the key facilitator of their relationships

Of the many non-state actors Iran supports, none is as identified with, and as instrumental to its regional goals and activities, as Hizbullah (*Hizb Allah*, or Party of God). Its rise from a guerrilla group in Lebanon to the most powerful and versatile transnational Middle Eastern non-state actor ranks among the Islamic Republic of Iran's greatest accomplishments.

In less than four decades, Tehran has nurtured and developed a deployable asymmetric capability that no other regional, or indeed global, power possesses, and that has delivered significant security and strategic returns for the ambitious but isolated power. For Iran, Hizbullah's strategic relevance and operational utility stems from three sets of capabilities that can be directly credited to Tehran's guidance, as well as its material and organisational contributions: its missile (and more recently, uninhabited aerial vehicle) arsenal, its foreign-operations activities and its regional power-projection capacity. The group's reach is also unprecedented for a non-state actor, with its fundraising, propaganda and operations reaching well beyond the Middle East and as far as Europe, the Americas, Africa and Asia.

Indeed, Iranian doctrine, statecraft and resources have been essential to Hizbullah's growth. In comparison to more recent efforts to support surrogates and partners, Tehran focused on nurturing a single,

Syrian President Bashar al-Assad with Iranian President Mahmoud Ahmadinejad alongside Hizbullah Secretary-General Hassan Nasrallah in Damascus, Syria, February 2010

consolidated organisation, reflecting the early ambitions and strategic aims of the Islamic Republic.

The many facets of Hizbullah and the myriad roles it plays in the Lebanese, Middle Eastern and international arenas are, for officials and observers alike, cause for debate about the identity, purpose and inner workings of the group, and about its relationship with Tehran.

Simultaneously a political party, social provider, sectarian actor, armed militia and foreign operator, Hizbullah confounds, shocks, inspires and repels. Having survived and emerged victorious, though at considerable cost to itself and to its environment, from several wars and political challenges, it has morphed from an organisation struggling to survive Lebanese politics into a regional actor with undeniable reach and potency. In the process, it has become the dominant force in Lebanon, able to check a weak state, overpower its rivals and ultimately set the country's trajectory and security policy.

Hizbullah serves as the ideological and operational cornerstone of the *Mumanaa* (described by an intellectual close to the party as a middle ground between 'steadfastness' and 'forbiddance') and the Axis of Resistance that have propelled Iran into the politics of the Arab world and which structure Iran's various regional activities.[1] For Hizbullah, *Muqawamah* (resistance to foreign oppression and to assaults on sovereignty, exemplified by the Western hegemony and Israel, as well as their alleged Middle Eastern clients) is an all-encompassing culture and lifestyle, not just a military pursuit. It fuses personal *jihad* (struggle) and *ijtihad* (independent reasoning), communal cohesion and the quest for political power. Strategically, *Muqawamah* has served as a rallying cry for the players in the Middle East who have sought to oppose the dominance of the United States and the existence of Israel.

Hizbullah's leaders and core members acknowledge the centrality of Iran to its identity, development and current operations. However much its rivals and enemies see it as a stigma, this affiliation is a matter of pride for the *Hizbullahi* (members of Hizbullah) and of an existential nature for the group's leadership.

For those in power in Iran, Hizbullah carries a special meaning: it is the main product of decades of ideological and material investment that has paid off substantially. For hardline Iranian conservatives, *Hizbullahis* are exemplars who advance Iran's interests and validate its ideology. At a gathering in Isfahan in 2008, then-commander of the Islamic Revolutionary Guard Corps (IRGC) Major-General Yahya Rahim-Safavi (now adviser to the Supreme Leader) celebrated Hizbullah's current secretary-general, Hassan Nasrallah, and his followers: 'Nasrallah considers himself a soldier of the Supreme Leader, and the men and women of Lebanon's Islamic resistance have followed the pattern of Iran's lionesses and honourable men.'[2]

Support is evident across the Iranian political spectrum: Hizbullah is considered, at the very least, as a privileged and laudable partner. Perspectives on the costs and trade-offs over the group may differ, but Iran's core leadership is fully invested in the relationship as a central element in its security strategy. Hizbullah is a deployable force that allows Iran to pursue policy objectives at reach, at limited cost and with plausible deniability. Importantly, Hizbullah's Arab and anti-Israeli character have enabled Iran to mollify Arab distrust of Tehran's intentions, be at the forefront of the resistance against perceived Western imperialism and Zionism, and drive a wedge between Arab populations and their elites who tend to be more antagonistic toward Iran.

While Iran is clearly Hizbullah's spiritual reference and the more powerful of the two actors, their interactions are fluid and complex enough that a traditional proxy–client analysis based on material dependency and command-and-control considerations obscures their true nature. Indeed, Hizbullah has achieved unique status among Iran's partners, akin to a brother in arms in Tehran's pursuit of security and influence in the region.

The organic and ideological nature of Iranian–*Hizbullahi* relations

Separating the intrinsic and domestic factors that explain Hizbullah's rise and success from the external contribution made by Iran is necessary in order to appreciate the political and military resilience and overall success of the militant organisation.

Lebanon's ties to Iran predate the emergence of Hizbullah, explaining in part the success and resilience of the Hizbullah project. They go back to the sixteenth century, when the Safavid dynasty converted Persia to Twelver Shi'ism with the aid of Lebanese Shi'ite clerics. Centuries of religious and societal relations left an imprint on both communities.[3]

However, Hizbullah was born out of the convergence of powerful forces that shook Iran and Lebanon throughout the 1970s and 1980s and which, later on, defined them. The social and political turmoil of the Lebanese Civil War (1975–90) fuelled the awakening and empowerment of a Shia Muslim community long relegated to a secondary political and economic role by the dominant Christian and Sunni sects. The community was ruled by quasi-feudal leaders and traditional families, affected by state abandonment and politicised through ambivalent relations with Palestinian *Fedayin* (fighters belonging to various Palestinian groups waging war against Israel from Lebanon). Compounding this were the Israeli invasions of 1978 and 1982 and Israel's subsequent occupation of Lebanon. This imposed significant human and political costs on the Shia community, which, over time, mobilised around resistance fighters using asymmetric methods against a militarily superior opponent. Furthermore, the regional geopolitical power play of Syria, whose forces entered the Lebanese conflict in 1976 and which served as Lebanon's suzerain until 2005, favoured the development of Hizbullah.

A key figure in the process of Shia awakening in the twentieth century was Imam Musa al-Sadr, an Iranian cleric with Iraqi and Lebanese origins. Trained in the holy cities of Qom in Iran and Najaf in Iraq, Sadr played a major role in mobilising the Lebanese Shia community in the 1960s and 1970s and co-founding the Amal Movement and its militia, from which many early Hizbullah leaders would emerge. However, Sadr had a complex and ultimately competitive relationship with Grand Ayatollah Ruhollah Khomeini, notably over the leadership of the Shia community. His mysterious disappearance in 1978 in Libya, before Khomeini's ascendance to power, removed a considerable obstacle to the latter's *Velayat-e Faqih* concept of theocratic governance.

Essential to Hizbullah's genesis was the Iranian revolutionary movement that culminated in the 1979 Islamic Revolution, which thereafter sought to export its model of political–religious governance, but faced extensive regional and international pushback. Indeed, the special relationship between Hizbullah and Iran owes much to the presence in Lebanon from the early 1970s of an Iranian revolutionary cadre that would join the inner circle of Ayatollah Khomeini in his successful attempt to dethrone the Shah of Iran and establish a theocracy.[4] As Khomeini was articulating and propagating both *Velayat-e Faqih* and his world view, he was reaching out to and recruiting followers motivated ideologically and by socio-political dynamics in Iran and beyond. Lebanon was particularly attractive, thanks to its growing and vibrant Twelver Shia community and long ties with the Iranian clerical establishment. Khomeini himself had taken an interest in Lebanese and Palestinian affairs from the 1960s, cultivating a

"HIZBULLAH HAS ACHIEVED UNIQUE STATUS AMONG IRAN'S PARTNERS"

cadre of Iranian and Lebanese interlocutors, with the goal of recruiting them into the 'resistance' against Israel (then secretly aligned to the regime of the Shah). From an early stage, Khomeini's ideological outlook extended to all Shi'ites and other disenfranchised Arabs.

While the groups that coalesced into Hizbullah started forming during Israel's invasion of Lebanon in 1982, and the official announcement of its establishment came with the 1985 'Open Letter' – its ambitious ideological and political manifesto – the ingredients and personalities had coalesced earlier.[5] During the 1970s, as Lebanon disintegrated into civil war, the existence of militant networks there attracted Iranians opposed to the Pahlavi regime, who joined the numerous left-wing, Palestinian and Shia armed groups that would play a central role in the conflict. However, anti-Shah politics, ideologies and personalities in Lebanon were often in conflict, reflecting political battles within the Iranian opposition, as well as the chaotic politics of the Shia community in Lebanon.[6]

Most prominent among these Iranians was Mostafa Chamran, a student activist who fled Iran and studied in the US before moving to Lebanon to become a guerrilla commander, fighting at one time as part of the Amal militia. Chamran and his allies, who prioritised the rights and interests of the underprivileged Shia community, were at odds with a more hardline faction led by Ayatollah Hossein Montazeri, which had a more revolutionary outlook

Iranian Minister of Interior Ali Akbar Mohtashami-Pur, Tehran, July 1988

The rise of Hizbullah

In December 1979, the radical faction of Montazeri mounted the first effort to send revolutionary Iranian volunteers to Lebanon to fight alongside their Shia brethren; this failed due to Syrian unease with Islamist radicalism and factional disputes in Beirut and Tehran.[7] However, by 1980, Iran had established small, client-like proto-organisations in Lebanon that vied for power in a crowded arena with larger and more established militias.

1980s

The trigger for Hizbullah's rise was Israel's invasion of Lebanon in 1982. The destruction, human suffering and humiliation of the following 18-year occupation left a deep mark on the Shia community, but also galvanised it to reassert a sense of pride and ownership over its politics and future. Conveniently, Khomeini's revolution, with its claim to represent the rights of the downtrodden, its aim of exporting its ideals and its defensive-turned-offensive war against Saddam Hussein's Iraq, served as an inspiration and as an enabler.

These external dynamics – the Iranian revolution and the Israeli invasion – added to an already favourable social and political context for the formation of a movement such as Hizbullah. Although Iran sought to court Shia communities elsewhere in the Arab world, notably in Bahrain and Iraq, Lebanon's civil war and its already politicised Shia community provided a unique opportunity. As Iranian ambassador to Lebanon Musa Fakhr Rouhani tellingly remarked in January 1984:

> If we concentrate on the point that Lebanon is considered the heart of the Arab countries in the Middle East, a platform from which different ideas have been directed to the rest of the Arab world, we can conclude that the existence of an Islamic movement in that country will result in Islamic movements throughout the Arab world.[8]

Iran was quick to mobilise in favour of its Lebanese Shia brethren: as Israeli forces pushed towards Beirut in June 1982, Ragheb Harb, Ibrahim al-Amine and Subhi Tufayli were actively lobbying Iran for help, while Shia militants, including Imad Mughniyah, fought the advancing force. Tehran deployed hundreds of military advisers from the newly established IRGC to the Bekaa Valley in eastern Lebanon, then under Syrian occupation. Uneasy about religious fundamentalism, given its own struggles at home,

and embraced the Palestinian liberation struggle alongside the Palestinian Liberation Organisation and other groups as part of an anti-imperialist agenda. Montazeri's faction, more tightly aligned with ayatollahs Khomeini and Beheshti, included Iranians who later would play prominent roles in Iran's security policy, notably Ali Akbar Mohtashami-Pur, who was Iranian ambassador to Syria from 1981 to 1986, and in the 1970s was active as a member of revolutionary armed groups in Lebanon and an early adviser of Khomeini. When the Islamic Revolution succeeded, Chamran left for Iran with a delegation of Amal leaders and members of Lebanon's Supreme Islamic Shia Council; he became defence minister and an early architect of Tehran's security strategy, including the establishment of the IRGC, before dying in 1981 in the Iran–Iraq War.

Dozens of Iranian and Lebanese commanders and militia members involved in the struggles of the 1970s and the Iranian Revolution would later create militant cells and structures that formed the basis of Hizbullah. These figures included some of Hizbullah's most important leaders – notably, its first leaders, Ragheb Harb and Abbas al-Musawi; its current secretary-general, Hassan Nasrallah; leading ideologues, such as Ibrahim al-Amine and Muhammad Yazbek; and its best-known security commanders, Imad Mughniyah and Mustafa Badreddine, many of whom remained active for decades. This created a sense of comradeship among the early recruits, based on trust, reciprocity and mutual dependency. This legacy and the personal ties that developed explain in large part the endurance and strength of the Iran–Hizbullah relationship.

(l) IRGC commander Mohsen Rafighdoust, September 1996

(r) Syrian armed forces in Beirut, Lebanon, May 1988

and eager to maintain unchallenged dominance over Lebanon, although militarily defeated by Israel there, the Syrian regime of Hafez al-Assad assented to Iranian insistence to help establish a new Shia movement in Lebanon.[9] The architect of this strategy was Mohtashami-Pur.[10] Its implementer was Ahmad Motevasselian, an IRGC commander with experience in the Iran–Iraq War, who apparently arrived in Beirut within a week of the Israeli invasion but who disappeared in July 1982. An early commander of the first IRGC contingent was Mohsen Rafighdoust, who had trained in refugee camps in Lebanon in the 1970s, was Ayatollah Ruhollah Khomeini's bodyguard in 1979 and would later serve as the first Minister of the Revolutionary Guards from 1982 to 1988. This ministry was dissolved in 1989.[11] Another IRGC officer in Lebanon at the time was Hossein Dehghan, who would serve as Iran's defence minister from 2013 to 2017 and become a senior military adviser to Supreme Leader Ayatollah Ali Khamenei.

The contribution of these Iranian military advisers boosted the already battle-hardened guerrillas and helped grow the ranks of the disparate Shia groups. But more than the training itself, it was the ideological direction, organisational framework and material support extended by Iran that proved instrumental to the merging of the fragmented Shia militant groups into the Islamic Resistance, which later announced itself as Hizbullah. Backed by committed IRGC personnel, the early members of Hizbullah were highly ideological, and often puritanical, presenting themselves as a vanguard rather than a mass movement. Parts of the Bekaa Valley, if only for a few years, became an experiment in Islamist governance. These early members included both established and new associates from the Amal Movement, which was seen as too moderate and accommodating of Israel and the Lebanese power structure, and from left-wing and Palestinian groups; young and ambitious clerics; members of the Da'wa Party; and Shia villagers from the valley. Hizbullah's appeal quickly spread to Beirut's southern suburbs, where large numbers of Shia citizens lived in parlous conditions, but was slower to reach southern Lebanon, where the Amal Movement's historic presence and the legacy of Imam Musa al-Sadr constrained its growth.

Hizbullah's ideological affiliation to Iran was absolute, as evidenced in the 1985 Open Letter:

> We, the sons of Hizbullah's *umma* [Muslim community], whose vanguard God has given victory in Iran and which has established the nucleus of the world's central Islamic state, abide by the orders of a single, wise and just command represented by the guardianship of the jurisprudent (*waliyy al-faqih*), currently embodied in the supreme Ayatullah Ruhallah al-Musawi al-Khumayni.[12]

Early on, Iran served as Hizbullah's protector and enabler. Throughout its first decade, Hizbullah operated in a hostile environment, where it had no clear comparative advantage. It faced a militarily superior occupier, Israel; it vied for control over the anti-Israel resistance with left-wing and other groups; and it challenged the preeminence of the better-established, mainstream Shia Amal Movement. Most importantly, it operated in a setting where an often sceptical, at times antagonistic, Syria was the dominant security and political power. Between 1985 and 1990, Hizbullah clashed repeatedly with Amal and Syrian forces. Tehran provided political guidance, financial support and military assistance, even deploying IRGC fighters alongside Hizbullah in its armed competition with the Amal Movement, and mediating Syrian–*Hizbullahi* tensions.[13]

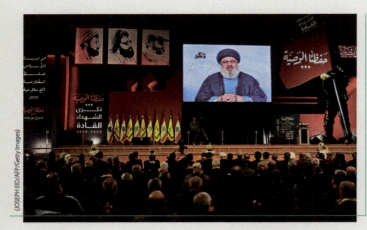

Hizbullah Secretary-General Hassan Nasrallah delivers a televised speech, February 2018

Syria's tolerance of Hizbullah and its sponsorship by Iran was enabled by Damascus and Tehran's alliance against Saddam Hussein and Iran's provision of discounted oil to the Assad regime during the 1980s. Over time, Syria developed its own appreciation of the strategic and operational value in the militant group. Indeed, it was Syrian geopolitical calculations that allowed Hizbullah to emerge unscathed from the Lebanese civil war and that paved the way for its political and military growth.

1990s

Lebanese militias were disarmed and disbanded after the 1989 adoption of the Taif Agreement (a political settlement that rearranged power-sharing among Lebanese sects) and the end of the civil war in 1990. However, seeking leverage in its negotiations with Israel over the Golan Heights and possible peace, and at Iran's behest, Damascus insisted that Hizbullah maintain its armed status as a resistance force against Israel. In exchange, Damascus demanded that Hizbullah recognise its dominance in Lebanese politics and abide by its parameters in fighting Israel. The Shia organisation pragmatically acquiesced and focused primarily on fighting Israel's occupying forces in southern Lebanon.

Acknowledging that pursuing and imposing Khomeinist ideals in Lebanon was at the time impossible, Hizbullah toned down its Islamist revolutionary outlook, at least momentarily and after a divisive internal debate over the Taif Agreement, and entered the political arena. Hizbullah began to soften the requirements for membership and tone down the centrality of *Velayat-e Faqih*,[14] allowing more Shi'ites to embrace the movement politically, while following the religious leaders of their choosing. Hizbullah abandoned its original aspiration to establish Islamist governance in Lebanon in favour of a more gradual strategy, but without relinquishing its overall objectives.

At the same time, Hizbullah continued to regard the relationship with Iran as essential. However, the end of the Iran–Iraq War, the death of Ayatollah Khomeini and the focus on containing Saddam Hussein's Iraq translated into a detente in the 1990s between Iran and its Gulf neighbours. As a result, Iran froze its export of revolutionary ideals and had a reduced need to use Hizbullah to injure the Gulf states, as it had done during the 1980s to punish them for siding with Saddam Hussein or to challenge their ruling families. Even then, the fragile Saudi–Iranian rapprochement under Crown Prince Abdullah and then Iranian president Akbar Hashemi Rafsanjani, and later president Mohammad Khatami, did not preclude Iranian-supported coercion: in 1996, Iran directed and Hizbullah supported the bombing of a US military installation in the Saudi city of Khobar. For Hizbullah, however, Tehran's shifting foreign policy had no effect: Iran's unwavering hostility to Israel and commitment to drive its forces out of Lebanon secured reliable support for Hizbullah's activities.

These evolutions coincided with the elevation of Hassan Nasrallah as Hizbullah secretary-general in 1992. Nasrallah's charisma and political shrewdness helped Hizbullah to highlight its Lebanese identity while remaining firmly in Iran's orbit. Under Nasrallah, the group also began its transformation into a mass movement, political party and social-services provider, as well as evolving into a more effective military actor.

In parallel, and with Syrian facilitation, the movement was able to develop better and more secure links to Iran, while Damascus and Tehran also oversaw Hizbullah's growth in military strength. Syria supervised an increasingly sophisticated supply chain for the organisation, comprising civilian and military airports and seaports, storage facilities and ground routes. This role allowed Damascus to regulate Hizbullah's activities, maintaining a degree of control over the group, as well as deniability in terms of Syria's complex relationship with Israel and the US.

What followed was a steady political rise, along with several strategic successes, that put Hizbullah at the centre of regional politics. Throughout the 1990s – and in contrast to the mismanagement and corruption of other parties – discipline, organisational competence and Iranian funding became the essential ingredients of Hizbullah's success. While it ran in national and municipal elections, at the time, the group chose not to seek direct institutional power through the control of ministries or bureaucracies, as the preservation of its armed status – its main priority – was guaranteed by Syria. Deliberately staying on the margins of politics also allowed it to avoid taking responsibility for running the disordered affairs of the Lebanese state, thereby maintaining an image of political purity while cultivating its own constituency.

To cater to, mobilise and eventually enlarge this constituency, Hizbullah invested in the provision of social services, such as healthcare and poverty relief, to the Shia community.[15] Uniquely among Lebanese political parties, Hizbullah had no need to control ministries or divert state resources to provide services to its base. Indeed, Iranian financial backing, later supplemented with funding from legal and illegal sources, guaranteed that Hizbullah could maintain its autonomy, and fulfil its goal of remaining unimpeded by the state and political constraints.

A central element of this strategy was Hizbullah's network of charities, social organisations and construction firms. This ensured strong community ties and cohesion, and aided recruitment in peacetime. In times of conflict, the network could be deployed to support Hizbullah's military operations, as well as to provide community relief, and later engage in reconstruction activities. Such activities amounted to a form of Iranian-backed parallel state-building.[16] Of paramount importance was the provision of salaries and benefits to fighters and their families, who received no direct assistance from the Lebanese state, while Hizbullah's construction arm, Jihad al-Binaa, which was intimately tied to the Iranian Ministry of Construction Jihad, ensured that Hizbullah could engage in immediate post-conflict relief and reconstruction.[17]

Meanwhile, Hizbullah weathered Israeli military campaigns and adapted its strategy to counter its superior opponent and harass Israel's Lebanese auxiliary militia (the South Lebanon Army, or SLA). It adopted efficient insurgent tactics, forsaking suicide bombings in favour of well-prepared frontal and improvised explosive device (IED) attacks by well-trained fighters; it displayed shrewdness in its decisions to escalate, signalling to Israel its ability to hit a wider range of targets, including inside Israeli territory and abroad, but also its ability to exercise restraint; and it perfected the use of strategic communications, recording and disseminating propaganda to undermine Israeli morale and galvanise Lebanese and wider Arab support. This strategy of attrition eroded the morale and standing of the occupying forces and the SLA. In 2000, Israel retreated rapidly from the so-called 'security zone' it had occupied along its border with Lebanon. The Lebanese Armed Forces (LAF) played a marginal role: it was still weak and obedient to Syria, and could not withstand a direct confrontation with superior Israeli forces. Hizbullah itself saw no need for LAF involvement beyond information-sharing and cooperation on the group's terms. This allowed Hizbullah to claim sole responsibility for its military successes, and to establish itself on the same level as the armed forces in the national discussion.

Hizbullah delegates at a polling station in Beirut as Lebanon votes in the first parliamentary election in nine years, May 2018

2000s

After Israel's withdrawal from southern Lebanon, difficult questions arose concerning Hizbullah's ultimate purpose as an Islamist and Iranian project (which had heretofore been articulated as the defeat of Israel, perpetual resistance and reform of the political system in its favour), as well as the wisdom and costs of its strategy of resistance. The militant organisation insisted that a small band of territory on the edge of the Israeli-occupied Syrian Golan Heights, Shebaa Farms, remain under Israeli occupation in order to justify continued resistance, but the legal status of this area remains disputed, owing to long-standing unresolved border issues between Israel, Lebanon and Syria. At the same time, Hizbullah's insistence on remaining an armed standing force split Lebanon into two camps: one unconditionally supportive of Hizbullah, the other demanding that it commit to gradual disarmament and absorption into the state.

In 2004, France and the US sponsored UN Resolution 1559, which called for the disarmament of all militias in Lebanon (i.e., Hizbullah) and the departure of all foreign troops from Lebanon (i.e., Syria).[18]

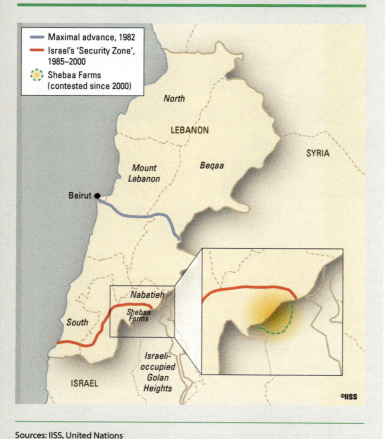

Map 2.1: **Israeli occupation of southern Lebanon, 1982–2000**

Sources: IISS, United Nations

Hizbullah, Iran and Syria saw the resolution as part of a broader scheme by the US and other countries to defeat the so-called Axis of Resistance on the back of the United States' invasion of Iraq in 2003. By then, Damascus, Hizbullah and Tehran were engaged in efforts to hamper US forces in Iraq, and to deter Washington from considering further military action by imposing prohibitive costs. Meanwhile, Hizbullah and Tehran were cooperating on shaping a new Iraqi political landscape dominated by Iran-aligned figures and militias.

The rift between Hizbullah's supporters and critics in Lebanon widened when Hizbullah was accused, alongside Syria, of the assassination of Rafiq al-Hariri, a former prime minister and the leader of the Sunni community, in February 2005 to prevent the implementation of UN Resolution 1559. Hariri, a critic of Syria, was preparing to challenge politically the Syrian occupation, thereby threatening Hizbullah's own position. Intense Lebanese popular mobilisation and international pressure forced Syria to withdraw its forces from Lebanon.

The reconfiguration of Lebanese politics in 2005 forced Hizbullah to adapt. Syria could no longer secure Hizbullah's armed status; instead, the organisation was now charged with protecting its own as well as Syria's interests. Although it gained political autonomy, Hizbullah became vulnerable to political attacks and public criticism as to its role and methods, including its reported part in the Hariri assassination.[19] Its logistical supply chain, once guaranteed, became more complicated, while its security infrastructure, previously shielded from the Lebanese security agencies, was now more important yet more exposed. To contain its opponents, Hizbullah deepened its involvement in domestic politics by reaching agreements with other factions and paralysing government activity and decision-taking through boycotts and the manipulation of the Lebanese sectarian system. Since 2005, when it obtained its first ministerial portfolio, it has at several junctures also used intimidation and, eventually, force against its opponents. These domestic challenges meant that the group had to consolidate its hold over the Shia community in order to build a sectarian buffer: as a result, the security and interests of this community were increasingly conflated with Hizbullah's armed status. The group was also compelled to invest more in its domestic infrastructure, including in supply and communications networks.

Hizbullah's main goal at this point was to obtain formal government acquiescence to its special status under the 'Army–Resistance–People' formula, which was designed to emphasise armed resistance as a national consensus, and a veto over government decision-making to help it neutralise Lebanese politics. However, the group met considerable opposition from a variety of factions, including the prime minister and government members. In May 2008, the government mounted a challenge to Hizbullah's security infrastructure, which the organisation decisively defeated in a swift and violent takeover of the central districts of Beirut. The ability of Hizbullah to deploy hundreds of well-armed and highly mobile troops, capture key points around the capital and defeat much weaker rivals – while deterring any response from the military or internal-security forces – starkly revealed the domestic military balance of power. In addition to targeted coercion, exemplified by a string of assassinations of political and media figures throughout the decade, Hizbullah demonstrated its ability to bend Lebanese politics and institutions to protect what it and Iran deemed most important to the group: its special armed status and its operational freedom. The Qatari-brokered deal that ended the violence, known as the Doha Agreement, delivered

Table 2.1: **Hizbullah: balance of power in government, 2005–19**

Date	Prime minister	Power balance within cabinet	Number of ministers	Ministerial positions	Main allies
1992–2005 (Syrian occupation)	Several	●	0	0	All parties
2005	Fouad Siniora	● ● ●	2	Minister of Energy and Water Minister of Labour	Amal Movement Small Christian parties
2008	Fouad Siniora	● ●	1	Minister of Labour	Amal Movement Major Christian party
2009	Saad Hariri	● ●	2	Minister of Agriculture State Minister for Administrative Development	Amal Movement Major Christian party Small Christian parties
2011	Najib Mikati	●	2	Minister of Agriculture State Minister for Administrative Development	Amal Movement Major Christian party Small Christian parties
2014	Tammam Salam	● ●	2	Minister of Industry State Minister for Parliamentary Affairs	Amal Movement Major Christian party Small Christian parties
2016	Saad Hariri	● ●	2	Minister of Industry Minister for Sports and Youth	Amal Movement Major Christian party Small Christian parties
2019	Saad Hariri	●	3	Health Minister State Minister for Parliamentary Affairs Minister for Youth and Sports	Amal Movement Major Christian party Small Christian parties Small Sunni bloc

Source: IISS   ● ● ● Against Hizbullah   ● ● Neutral (Hizbullah and allies with blocking power)   ● In favour of Hizbullah

the political returns Hizbullah had sought, by giving it and its allies the formal right to block government action, thereby neutering the opposition.

In this tense domestic context, Hizbullah faced its biggest military challenge to date. In July 2006, the militant organisation killed Israeli Defense Forces (IDF) soldiers in a cross-border attack designed to capture Israeli military personnel. What followed was a 34-day war with far-reaching consequences. Despite heavy human and infrastructure costs for Lebanon (over 1,200 killed and at least US$6 billion in damage),[20] the militant group denied Israel political and military victory by launching volleys of rockets and missiles into Israel and by hampering a poorly planned IDF ground invasion. This outcome, dubbed by Hizbullah 'al-Nasr al-Ilahi' (Divine Victory), solidified its regional standing. In the context of rising regional tensions and a potential war with Israel or the US over Iran's nuclear programme, Hizbullah's victory illustrated how a militarily superior opponent could be hindered and punished, and deterred from waging total war.

The 2006 war elevated Hizbullah on the regional stage. The organisation focused on rebuilding its infrastructure and upgrading its capabilities in anticipation of future conflict with Israel but also to serve Iran's deterrence needs. At the same time, it became more controversial inside Lebanon. This combination of prestige, military ambition and political vulnerability shaped the group's behaviour in the decade that followed. Its successes were made possible in part thanks to its leaders' enduring ties to Iran and an organisational structure adapted to its military needs.

Hizbullah's leadership structure

Hizbullah's leadership structure reflects the various facets of the movement. It seeks to propagate a culture of resistance sufficient to ensure the political and military viability of its ideological and security objectives. Although the group has outward-facing branches, such as its social services, Hizbullah is by nature and design secretive and segmented, in order to create plausible deniability and to shield its more sensitive assets and operations from domestic and foreign intelligence services.

The adherence of Hizbullah's senior-most leadership to *Velayat-e Faqih* and Iran's strategic outlook guarantees complete ideological and strategic alignment with Tehran, while the simultaneous personalisation and institutionalisation of the relationship ensures smooth communications and operational responsiveness. Indeed, Hizbullah's most senior political and security cadres have maintained strong, personal relations with Iran's top leadership

Figure 2.1: **The structure of Iran–Hizbullah relations**

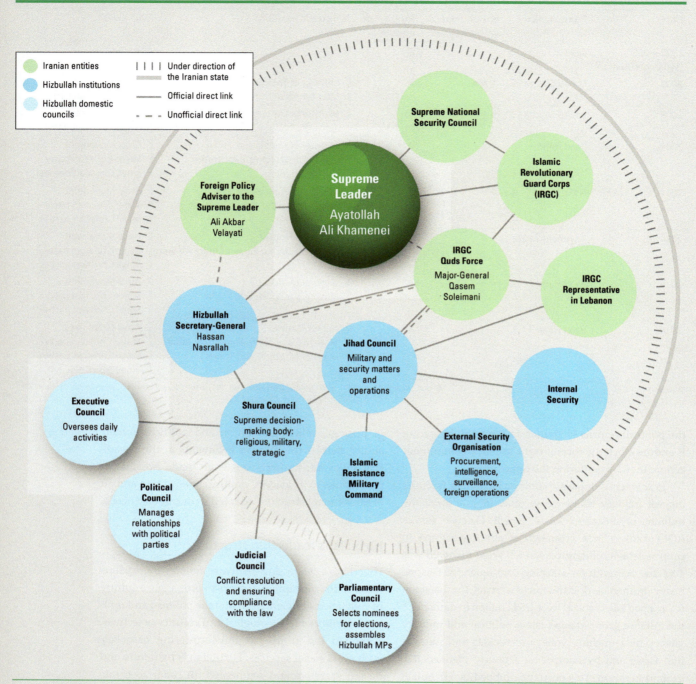

Sources: IISS interviews with Arab and Western officials; Ahmad Hamzeh, *In the Path of Hizbullah* (Syracuse University Press, 2004), p. 46; Magnus Ranstorp, 'Hizbollah's command leadership: its structure, decision-making and relationship with Iranian clergy and institutions', *Terrorism and Political Violence*, vol. 6, 1994.

since the 1980s. Members of the Shura and Jihad councils are among the closest to Iran, while senior commanders of the Islamic Resistance (the military command of Hizbullah) and the External Security Organisation (ESO) are organisationally linked to the IRGC's expeditionary wing, the Quds Force.

However, the opacity of Hizbullah's internal decision-making processes obscures how Iranian influence expresses itself, and the types of internal and institutional trade-offs the organisation has to make. This is particularly the case for foreign operations conducted by Hizbullah. While some appear to have been conducted to serve Hizbullah's interests, such as the bombing in 1992 of the Israeli consulate in Argentina in retaliation for the assassination of Abbas al-Musawi, others, including the bombing in 2012 of a bus carrying Israeli tourists in Bulgaria, appear to have been more in the service of Iran's priorities. The latter attack was probably designed as a response to Israel's assassination of Iranian scientists involved in the country's nuclear programme (though others see it as revenge for the assassination of Hizbullah commander Imad Mughniyah in 2008). In Bulgaria, Iran may have resorted to using *Hizbullahi* operatives rather than its own intelligence service in order to create deniability and avoid escalation. But how Iran and Hizbullah agree on such a division of labour remains unclear. Indeed, there may have been instances where Hizbullah resisted or even refused to conduct Iranian-ordered missions because of operational or political constraints.

Beyond dependence

Iran's relationship with Hizbullah has directly shaped the group's development and evolution. But what started as a straightforward proxy relationship with a clear power dynamic has developed into a more complex and reciprocal affiliation, and one which has not been immune to internal politics in Tehran. From the beginning, the ideologies and interests of Iran's various factions have influenced their perspectives on Hizbullah, and internal rivalries have sometimes affected resource allocations to Hizbullah.

Nevertheless, the overall effect of internal Iranian debates on Hizbullah has been limited, and ultimately the Supreme Leader has remained the ultimate decision-taker on the extent of Iran's support, overriding other players. Indeed, at no point has Tehran seriously considered disarming, defunding, downgrading or abandoning Hizbullah. The known fluctuations in material support were circumstantial and momentary rather than structural and permanent. For example, when Israel and the US expected Hizbullah's disarmament as part of Israel–Syria peacemaking in the 1990s, the little that is known about deliberations in Damascus and Tehran shows no Iranian inclination to accept or facilitate this.

Since the 1990s, Hizbullah has developed its own fundraising capabilities, supplementing Iranian assistance and even replacing it when Tehran's budget considerations required temporary cuts. However, after the 2006 war with Israel, when Hizbullah required significant support to jump-start a politically crucial reconstruction effort and rebuild its military capabilities, Iran provided large amounts of money, despite internal economic difficulties and international sanctions.

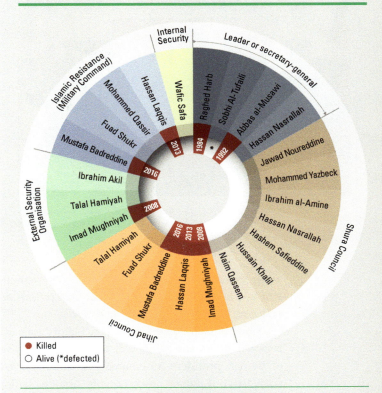

Figure 2.2: **Major Hizbullah leaders: status**

Note: individuals listed can have several affiliations simultaneously
Sources: Lebanese news reports; statements by the US State Department and Treasury

Most important to the dynamics of the relationship are Hizbullah's own performance, Iran's perception of the organisation's ideological and strategic utility, and the institutionalisation of the alliance. Hizbullah acquired ever-greater standing and value for Iran due to its military and political successes in the 1990s. These successes enabled Tehran – through its support for the group – to position itself as champion of the anti-Israel struggle and the foremost opposer of US hegemony, at a time when most Arab states assented to *Pax Americana*. For a Shia Persian power operating in a mostly Sunni and Arab Middle East, it also provided much-needed validation. This helped to transform the relationship from one of dependency on the part of Hizbullah to one of trust and reciprocity, as Hizbullah helped Tehran navigate and capitalise on the political turmoil of the Arab world.

Importantly, Iran has not imposed its preferences on Hizbullah within the Lebanese arena. Tehran accepts that Hizbullah is able to best identify and pursue its strategic and political interests as it navigates Lebanese politics. All the decisions made by Hizbullah – detailed above – have served the group's interests, as well as Iran's, and it remains difficult to identify any key political decisions where the two

Hizbullah supporters in front of a poster of Secretary-General Hassan Nasrallah in Beirut, September 2018

actors have diverged fundamentally. This demonstrates a level of trust and deference that reflects an enduring Iranian appreciation, and vice versa.

Much is made of the more conciliatory tone on regional affairs and religiously tolerant perspective of Iranian president Mohammad Khatami (served 1997–2005). Khatami was notable among senior officials for cultivating Lebanese political and religious relationships beyond Hizbullah, including with Shia clerics critical of the latter and Christian figures. In 2003, he was the first Iranian president to visit Lebanon, broadening his meetings to include non-Hizbullah individuals and emphasising the state-to-state character of his engagement. However, Khatami served as president when Hizbullah operatives allegedly assassinated Rafiq al-Hariri. Iran's role and input in this operation remain unclear, though its alleged mastermind, Mustafa Badreddine, was a central player in the Iran–Hizbullah relationship. As important, Hizbullah's post-2000 military build-up, notably the addition of large quantities of rockets and missiles to its inventory, occurred during the Khatami presidency.

This serves to illustrate the marginality of the Iranian presidency, the foreign ministry and other institutions in the supervision of Hizbullah, in contrast to the centrality of the Office of the Supreme Leader and the IRGC, which is best reflected by the special access and deference that Hassan Nasrallah enjoys in Tehran, most notably with Supreme Leader Khamenei. According to some observers, Nasrallah's influence matches that of IRGC Quds Force commander Major-General Qasem Soleimani in informing Khamenei's regional and security decision-making.[21] For example, Nasrallah's role in Iran's intervention in Syria was decisive.[22]

On an operational basis, Iranian ambassadors in Beirut and Damascus, who have generally been senior members or close associates of the IRGC, manage political relations between Hizbullah and Iran. Meanwhile, senior IRGC commanders (including most recently Brigadier-General Mohammad Zahedi) oversee security relations, as well as coordination over Syria. Senior *Hizbullahi* commanders, such as Imad Mughniyah, Hassan al-Laqqis and Mustafa Badreddine, are known to have had direct access to relevant officials in Tehran.

Intervention in Syria

As Lebanese politics were threatening to encroach on Hizbullah's strategic and operational autonomy by drawing the organisation into difficult domestic debates over its armed status, the need for a national-defence strategy and its role in the assassination of Hariri, a new challenge arose in the form of the Syrian civil war. The 2011 uprising, which quickly morphed into a multi-actor conflict, posed a potential existential threat to Hizbullah. It endangered the territorial hold and survival of the group's strategic ally, the Assad regime, and turned large numbers of previously supportive or passive Arabs and Sunnis against the Syrian regime; it exposed Hizbullah and the Shia community to potential attacks; it undermined the narrative of resistance and social justice that Hizbullah extolled; and it threatened supply lines and territorial access to Syria.

Hizbullah showed no enthusiasm to join the fight to save Assad; it was done out of obligation to an important strategic partner. In the early days of the civil war, Hizbullah politicians often decried in private the heavy-handedness of Assad's repressive strategy. On entering the war, its commanders seemed to have little respect for the weak discipline and performance of the Syrian security forces. The organisation was aware of the heavy costs of intervening in Syria, and while it achieved military successes along the Syrian–Lebanese border, rescuing Assad required military engagements deep inside Syrian territory, where Hizbullah would be more exposed and reliant on other security players. The Syria mission could also weaken its military preparedness against Israel. In addition, Hizbullah's own constituency had little affection for the Assad regime. Ultimately, however, the debilitating consequences of Assad's potential demise overrode these concerns.

Adapting to this new context required Hizbullah to again transform itself. Traditionally focused on

Lebanese President Michel Aoun with Iranian Minister of Foreign Affairs Mohammad Javad Zarif in Beirut, February 2019

Table 2.2: **Hizbullah: Lebanese elections, 1992–2018**

Election dates	Number of Hizbullah MPs (party members and affiliates)	Balance of power in parliament
1992 (Syrian occupation)	12	●
1996 (Syrian occupation)	9	●
2000 (Syrian occupation)	12	●
2005	14	●●●
2009	12	●●●●*
2018	13	●

Source: IISS ●●● Against Hizbullah ● In favour of Hizbullah *in favour after 2011

its southern flank (Israel), Hizbullah now needed to develop an eastern strategy. To intervene in Syria, it had to outmanoeuvre its Lebanese political rivals and neutralise any domestic challenge from its Christian, Druze and Sunni adversaries. This process began with denying, then understating, its growing involvement in Syria, before elaborating a narrative of communal self-defence, as well as a pan-Arab and strategic necessity. To do so, Hizbullah violated its commitment to the 2012 Baabda Declaration, a statement issued by the Lebanese presidency after national consultations meant to disassociate Lebanon from regional rivalries and conflict, notably the fighting in neighbouring Syria.[23] It also engaged in a campaign of domestic intimidation and punishment, including the attempted assassination of a critical Christian member of parliament.[24] In July 2015, Nasrallah justified Hizbullah's involvement in the Syrian theatre: 'the road to Al-Quds [Jerusalem] passes through Qalamoun, Zabadani, Homs, Aleppo, Deraa, Hassakeh and Swaida [sic], because if Syria was lost, Palestine would be lost too'.[25]

During this time, Hizbullah's Lebanese constituency came under jihadi attacks. Between 2012 and 2015, the Shia neighbourhoods of southern Beirut were targeted with bombs, killing dozens of civilians.[26] The Iranian embassy and cultural centres were also targeted. These vulnerabilities showed that Hizbullah's internal-security apparatus, primarily dedicated to protecting the party's leadership and infrastructure, and monitoring and coercing rivals, was facing a new challenge. Momentarily, Hizbullah demanded help from Lebanon's intelligence and military services to help secure these neighbourhoods. There were also signs of discontent in the Shia community concerning the costs of involvement in Syria, notably the increasing exposure to such attacks; however, such sentiments remained limited and were contained by community and *Hizbullahi* pressure.

By 2016, the success of the campaign to bolster the Assad regime began generating political returns in Lebanon for Hizbullah, meaning that it could recalibrate its military presence and shift its efforts in Syria to infrastructure building, alongside Iran. The political balance of power also moved in Hizbullah's favour. In late 2016, Michel Aoun, the group's main Christian ally and its favoured candidate, was elected as president after a two-year presidential vacuum and intense domestic brinkmanship. This was followed by political statements and security appointments, notably in the Lebanese armed forces, that consolidated Hizbullah's domestic position. In 2017, the organisation initiated several operations along the Lebanon–Syria border to defeat remaining rebel and jihadi forces in coordination with the Lebanese armed forces, in an uncomfortable division of roles for the latter. In 2018, Hizbullah obtained a large number of votes during the legislative elections, and, for the first time since 2005, its allies in other sects performed well. This was seen as the political dividend of Hizbullah's success in Syria.

Hizbullah's military evolution since 1980

The transformation of Hizbullah from a small guerrilla group into a hybrid force, combining conventional capabilities and non-state-actor tactics, is unprecedented in the Middle East. It now serves as a template for similar forces, as well as a benchmark for assessing other militias and their overall levels of performance.

A number of phases in Hizbullah's military history are identifiable. From 1982 to 1991, it operated as a rudimentary guerrilla movement against Israel's occupation of southern Lebanon; from 1991 to 2000, it evolved into a more sophisticated insurgency aimed at expelling occupation forces from Israel's

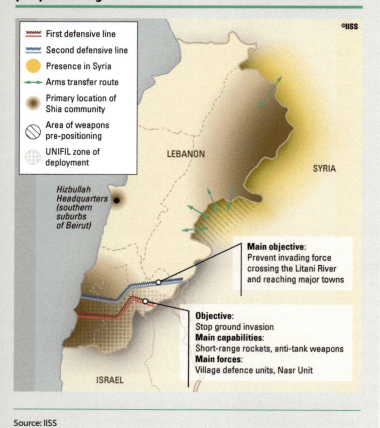

Map 2.2: **Hizbullah: defensive posture, supply lines and weapon pre-positioning**

Source: IISS

'security zone', that covered 10% of Lebanon's territory; from 2000 to 2011, it became a defensive force, designed primarily for deterrence; and from 2011, it quickly grew to meet the challenge of the Syrian conflict, developing counter-insurgency and conventional military capabilities. In each of these phases, it obtained essential and distinctively Iranian assistance.

Doctrine, capabilities and operations

In the 1980s, Hizbullah's battlefield performance was low or on par with that of other Lebanese militias. It lacked the organisation and firepower that the older and better-resourced militias possessed, and its military structure was overly centralised. It fielded around 500 core fighters engaged in a mix of guerrilla warfare and costly 'swarming' operations to capture territory from occupying Israeli forces. The group's main military innovation was honing the use of suicide attacks and IEDs, beginning with the 1983 bombings of French and US military and diplomatic installations, which ultimately led to the withdrawal of these foreign forces from Lebanon. It also mounted successful bombing and insurgent operations against Israeli forces, which retreated in 1985 to an 850-square-kilometre security zone in southern Lebanon.[27] In parallel, Hizbullah engaged in bombing and hostage-taking operations in Lebanon and in foreign operations in the Middle East and Europe on behalf of Iran.

The group's doctrine, capabilities and operations gained significant levels of sophistication throughout the 1990s. Syria–Iran alignment meant that Hizbullah could deploy across a much wider area, rely on secure and sustained logistical and material support, and obtain better and specialised training. Organisationally, the group's military command-and-control structure was flattened and local commanders given more operational latitude. Hizbullah proved to be a fast-learning organisation: its core fighters were battle-hardened and were accumulating experience, honing tactics, perfecting the use of armaments and adding new capabilities, such as anti-tank weaponry.

Indeed, Hizbullah's streamlined, flattened military structure has been vital to the organisation's performance. The empowerment of officers and non-commissioned officers on the battlefield breaks with the traditional operating methods of the Middle East's conventional armed forces. Instead, Hizbullah appears to have developed its own 'strategic corporal' concept, empowering every level of a fighting unit to ensure that a mission can be carried on regardless of the presence of a senior officer or losses during combat.[28] In essence, small units are afforded tactical autonomy within a broader operational concept and are thereby able to accomplish their missions with little oversight and to adapt to battlefield conditions and complications. This model, which proved successful in Lebanon, was later used in Syria.

A premium was put on eroding the morale of the occupying Israeli forces and their Lebanese allies, and to telegraph the futility of their venture. In parallel, Hizbullah increasingly deployed Iranian-supplied rockets to harass occupying forces and to reach into Israeli territory, thus imposing a new escalation paradigm. The targeting of Lebanese civilians or infrastructure could now trigger *Hizbullahi* retaliation beyond the front line and might include Israeli civilians and urban areas inside Israel. Conversely, Hizbullah would refrain from targeting Israeli civilians if Israel reciprocated. This strategy ultimately proved successful: the Ceasefire Understanding that ended the April 1996 war recognised indirectly Hizbullah's role and its right to conduct operations in Lebanon, giving it domestic and regional legitimacy. The war rallied many Lebanese around Hizbullah (especially after the Israeli bombing of a UN base in which more than 100 civilians were killed) and momentarily stilled domestic unease about the organisation.[29] Driving up the costs to the Israeli military and imposing new rules of escalation eventually led to the collapse of the Israeli-occupied security enclave in southern Lebanon in May 2000. By then, Hizbullah fielded a force of approximately 3,000 fighters, including an elite special force, supplemented by thousands of reservists.[30] It had reportedly lost 1,276 fighters since 1982.[31] By contrast, 256 Israeli soldiers and 450 Lebanese auxiliaries died between 1985 and 2000 (this number does not include the 1,200 Israeli soldiers killed during the invasion and the first phase of the occupation up to 1985, as the majority were killed in battles against Palestinian and non-*Hizbullahi* factions).[32]

Israel withdraws: 2000

The withdrawal of Israel from Lebanon, except from Shebaa Farms, compelled Hizbullah to adopt a new security posture – deterrence through the threat of punishment. From then, Hizbullah claimed to focus on countering Israeli violations of Lebanese sovereignty and creating a balance that the otherwise weak Lebanese armed forces could not establish. Crucial to this posture were rules that governed escalation.[33] For domestic and propaganda purposes, the group defended its claim of being a resistance movement by emphasising the unresolved status of Shebaa Farms. However, its priority was to build an infrastructure across southern and eastern Lebanon to ward off a potential Israeli ground invasion, as well as to deploy a growing missile capability to threaten IDF infrastructure and Israeli civilian centres.

This approach required a significant engineering and logistical effort, made possible by Syrian political and material support after the collapse of Israeli–Syrian talks in early 2000 and the coming to power of Bashar al-Assad in July of the same year. Indeed, the new Syrian president sought to acquire domestic and regional legitimacy by adopting a hardline position against Israel and aligning more closely with Hizbullah, breaking with his father's more cautious and primarily transactional relationship with the Shia movement. The qualitative upgrade of Hizbullah's infrastructure was also made possible by significant Iranian financial investment. The group's military success against Israel helped its advocates in Tehran justify the investment. The group's construction arm, Jihad al-Binaa, and associated companies built a network of command structures, bunkers, tunnels, weapons stores and other defensive buildings, linked by communications systems. Furthermore, there were credible allegations made in a US court that Hizbullah had received substantive North Korean support, including 'professional military and intelligence training and assistance in building a massive network of underground military installations, tunnels, bunkers, depots and storage facilities in southern Lebanon'.[34] This construction effort took place in a zone ostensibly patrolled by a United Nations peacekeeping force (UNIFIL) that had operated in southern Lebanon since 1978 under UNSC Resolution 425.

Preparedness, superior knowledge of the mostly undulating terrain and the backing of a largely supportive population in more than 200 villages and large towns, from which Hizbullah could recruit fighters, made territorial defence easier. Meanwhile, Israeli air superiority, as well as superior signals-

"FOR THE FIRST TIME, HIZBULLAH COULD PUT ISRAEL'S CIVILIANS, ECONOMY AND INFRASTRUCTURE AT SUSTAINED RISK DURING A CONFLICT"

and human-intelligence capabilities, compelled Hizbullah to pre-position IEDs, weapons caches (including anti-tank missiles) and other assets in order to minimise possible disruption to supplies during conflict.[35]

At this time, Hizbullah's missile force became a central element of its security posture.[36] The group's ability to threaten the northern third of Israel with its missiles and, according to Israeli officials, up to 13,000 short-range rockets,[37] with launchers deployed in layers across southern and southeastern Lebanon, had significant psychological and political implications for Israel. For the first time, Hizbullah could put Israel's civilians, economy and infrastructure at sustained risk during a conflict.

Another clash with Israel: 2006

This defensive strategy and military preparedness were put to the test in July 2006, when a standing order by its leadership to capture Israeli soldiers ignited a conflict after several were killed by Hizbullah in a cross-border operation. The human, infrastructure and economic costs to Lebanon were significant. In a rare sign of humility and self-reflection, Nasrallah acknowledged that 'We did not think, even one percent, that the capture would lead to a war at this time and of this magnitude. You ask me, if I had known on July 11 [the day before] that the operation would lead to

Figure 2.3: **Lebanon and Hizbullah: major events, 1975–2018**

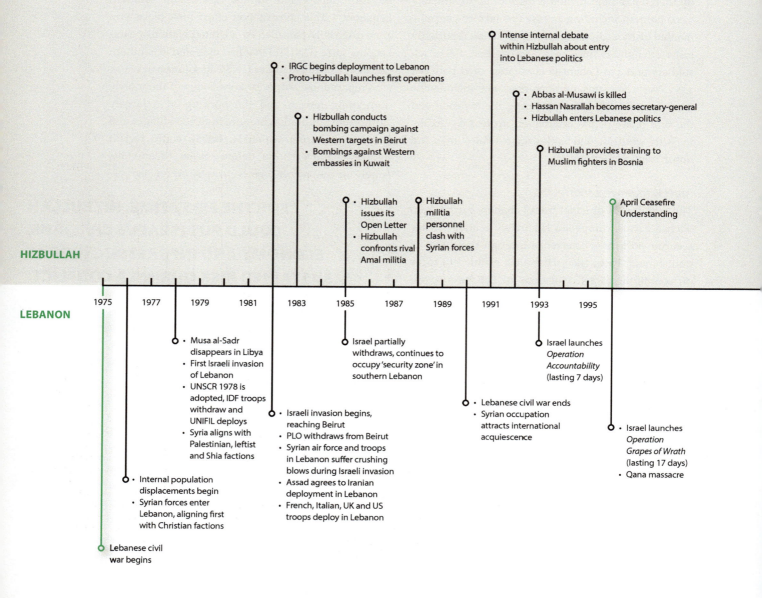

such a war, would I do it? I say no, absolutely not.'[38] Hizbullah's reading of Israel's willingness to escalate had failed. The group's trustworthiness was also put in question domestically, given that Hizbullah had early that year offered reassurances to its Lebanese counterparts that it would not start a war.

Strategically, Hizbullah's claim that its missile arsenal would deter any IDF attack came up against the reality that Israel had responded militarily. Furthermore, the group had caused a conflict, albeit unintentionally, at a sensitive time, as the international community pressured Iran over its nuclear programme, raising questions about Hizbullah's appreciation of the broader geopolitical context.

There is no open-source evidence and little probability that Iran encouraged Hizbullah to start

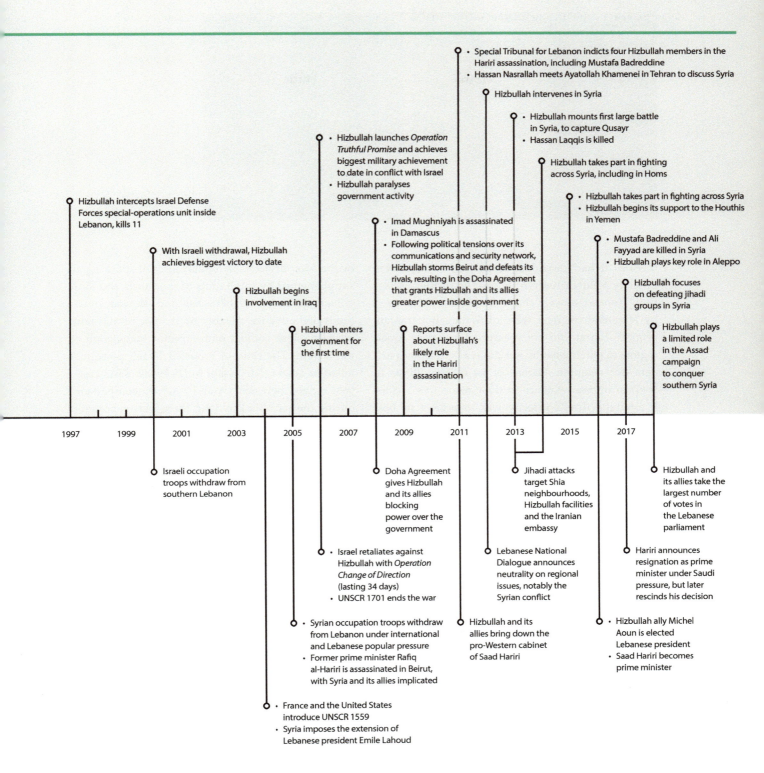

a conflict, or that it directed its conduct. At a time of rising tensions with Israel and the major powers over its nuclear programme, it is likely that Iran saw the accidental escalation as unwelcome and as unnecessarily risking its best regional security instrument. Tellingly, Tehran, including then-president Mahmoud Ahmadinejad, showed solidarity with Hizbullah by issuing supportive, though calibrated, statements. In July 2006, Ahmadinejad said: 'The real cure for the [Lebanon] conflict is elimination of the Zionist regime [Israel], but there should be first an immediate ceasefire.'[39]

IRGC officers were reportedly involved in logistical and command coordination in the 2006 war.[40] But Iran likely asked Hizbullah not to deploy against targets inside Israel territory the most advanced

Israeli Defense Forces personnel withdraw from southern Lebanon, August 2006

missiles it had provided, and *Zelzal* rockets were possibly held in reserve in case of further escalation.[41] Indeed, most of the rockets and missiles fired by Hizbullah in 2006 were of Syrian, not Iranian, origin.[42] Tehran did not pressure a reluctant Assad regime to join the battle, nor did it ask its other partners (for example, Hamas or its allied militias in Iraq) to initiate violence in their respective arenas. If anything, Iran's priority was to protect its best partner, an asset it had nurtured for more strategic purposes than an accidental and inconclusive war.

Though short of the 'divine victory' it proclaimed, and notwithstanding the cost to Lebanon and the Shia community, Hizbullah's military performance was significant.[43] Despite the near-total destruction of its medium-range missiles by the Israeli Air Force in the early days of the fighting, it managed to fire a continual volley of rockets into Israel (more than 100 per day, and around 4,000 in total), reportedly forcing more than 250,000 Israeli civilians to evacuate and another million to seek shelter.[44] Hizbullah also revealed a new capability: on an order given live on television by Nasrallah, it fired a *Noor* – an Iranian-made copy of the Chinese C-802 anti-ship cruise missile – at an Israeli naval corvette operating in Lebanese waters, killing four personnel and damaging the vessel. It was later alleged that Iran had directly provided this missile and that IRGC officers were present at its use.[45] Such battlefield surprises, which were widely broadcast and produced high political returns for Hizbullah, were made possible by Iranian technology and training.

During the 2006 war, Hizbullah also stopped a halting and delayed IDF ground invasion, conducted by a poorly trained force, by mounting a defence within the 15-km area south of the Litani River.[46] Its network of forward and underground defensive positions, in villages and across hills, manned by the Nasr Brigade – a regular force of about 1,500, supplemented by small units of specialists and local village defenders – harassed and slowed down the Israeli advance, notably by the use of anti-tank missiles, close combat and superior knowledge of the terrain. The ratio of reported Israeli personnel killed in action (KIA) (119) to *Hizbullahi* KIAs (250–700) ranged between 1:3 and 1:4.[47] By comparison, during the 1967 Six-Day War, there were reportedly 777 Israeli and 18,500 Egyptian–Syrian–Jordanian KIAs: a ratio of 1:23; during the 1973 Yom Kippur War, reported KIAs amounted to 2,569 and 18,500 respectively, a ratio of 1:7.[48]

For Hizbullah, the military lessons of the 2006 war were clear: its posture had succeeded. In addition to jump-starting a large reconstruction effort, it doubled down on developing both its defensive preparations and its missile arsenal. However, a new constraint on Hizbullah's materiel supply and operational latitude appeared in the form of UN Resolution 1701, which ended the war and mandated the deployment of a larger UNIFIL force in Lebanon than the one deployed since 1978, including a naval component. The resolution also demanded that Lebanon interdict the illegal supply of weaponry entering the country by securing its 375-km land border with Syria, deploy regular military units to southern Lebanon and – without naming Hizbullah – disarm non-government armed forces. In Arab and Western capitals, building up the LAF came to be seen as the best institutional way of weakening Hizbullah's claim to be the primary defender of Lebanese sovereignty, hurting its domestic standing and encouraging a domestic discussion about a national-defence strategy that would absorb or tame the organisation. More hawkish policymakers in Lebanon and abroad hoped that a stronger, more assertive LAF would eventually confront Hizbullah and disarm it forcefully.

The Israeli military displays an intercepted Iranian weapons shipment to Hizbullah at Port of Ashdod, Israel, November 2009

These restrictions meant that Hizbullah, which had long dismissed the LAF as a nuisance and had always relied on Syria for the prepositioning of weapons and as a logistic link to Iran, had to manoeuvre around the Lebanese Armed Forces. However, Hizbullah's defeat of its rivals in May 2008 and the LAF's paralysis opened political and military space for the group, enabling its swift recovery from the 2006 war. The senior LAF command was divided and risk-averse. Many officers were ostensibly sympathetic toward, or intimidated by, Hizbullah, and most were generally reluctant to take any action against the group that would lack broad political consensus in Lebanon and risk civil conflict. Indeed, the Lebanese border was never completely secured, despite external assistance and funding, and reports of weapons transfers through Beirut Hariri International Airport surfaced periodically. Western and Israeli sources suggest that Hizbullah was able to rebuild its supply routes within months of the end of the 2006 war.[49] Over time, it also bolstered its presence in the area bordering Israel, because of a mostly sympathetic local population, an ineffective UNIFIL force and a risk-averse LAF.[50] In later years, the relationship between the LAF and Hizbullah became even more complicated, as both sought to fight jihadi groups operating across the border from Syria. An uneasy relationship of cooperation and dependence developed in northeastern Lebanon, with the LAF deliberately ignoring Hizbullah's operations and materiel transfers inside Syria or within Lebanon, and the Shia organisation accepting the LAF's deployment along the border.

Involvement in Syria's civil war

The war in Syria became Hizbullah's biggest military challenge. Having dedicated its strategic and operational planning to the border with Israel, Hizbullah was not designed for expeditionary deployment and had limited knowledge of Syria geographically and socially. Yet securing its position there was crucial: its supply lines and strategic depth were exposed, the proliferation of anti-Hizbullah groups would become a threat to itself and its community, and regime change in Damascus would force difficult adjustments. While maintaining its domestic posture in Lebanon ('deterrence by punishment' against Israel), it had to develop quickly the military instruments and personnel to fight the Syrian insurgency, which began attracting Gulf Arab, Turkish and Western support in 2012.

Hizbullah rapidly developed the capability to operate successfully in Syria.[51] Within a couple of years, it was able to deploy a large force, combining light infantry, elite troops and specialists, such as sniper units and communications-interception teams. The ability to more than double the size of its forces in a short time suggests that Hizbullah's ongoing recruitment drive remained strong and well funded, that it could tap into a large pool of reservists and that it could, if needed, adjust its recruitment standards to bolster its personnel numbers.[52]

In Syria Hizbullah operated as a hybrid force. By combining counter-insurgency and conventional warfare tactics, partnerships with local militias and joint operations, it contributed to countering and eventually defeating the Syrian rebel, Islamist and jihadi forces. It also collaborated in the field for the first time with state militaries. Its work with Iranian and Russian officers to plan and conduct operations, and its operations as an equal alongside Syrian forces, transformed the group's sense of identity and capability. In November 2016, Hizbullah organised a military parade in the strategically important town of Qusayr in western Syria, near the border with Lebanon, where it displayed some of the capabilities at its disposal, including some that were unique

Table 2.3: **Hizbullah's Qusayr parade, 2016: observed military assets**

Type		Equipment	Number visible at parade	Weapon calibre (mm)	Likely origin
Main battle tank		T-54/55	7	100	Syria
		T-72AV	1	125	Syria
		T-72	1	125	Syria
Infantry fighting vehicle/armoured personnel carrier		BMP-1	6	73	Syria
		MT-LBu	1	n/a	Syria
		M113 with ZPU-2 air-defence gun	4	14.5	Lebanon (seized from other Lebanese militias)
Tracked self-propelled artillery		2S1 *Gvozdika*	3	122	Syria
		Improvised system based on a 2P25 chassis with KS-19 air-defence gun	1	100	Syria
		Improvised system based on a 2P25 chassis with KS-12 air-defence gun	1	85	Syria
Wheeled self-propelled artillery		Improvised system based on a truck chassis with KS-19 air-defence gun	2	100	Syria
		Improvised system based on a truck chassis with M-46 cannon	1	130	Syria
		Improvised system based on a truck chassis with D-30 cannon	1	122	Syria
Multiple-rocket launcher		*Grad* family	4	122	Syria/Iran
		Fadjr-5 mod	1	~330	Iran
All-terrain vehicle		Quad bike with *Dehlavieh* (Iranian licence-built *Kornet*) man-portable anti-tank system	5–6	n/a	Iran
Air-defence self-propelled gun		ZSU-57-2	2	57	Syria

Source: IISS

among Middle Eastern militia-style forces, such as T-72 main battle tanks.

Hizbullah entered the Syria conflict in part to secure its materiel supply routes. By 2016, Israeli and Western intelligence assessments reported that Hizbullah's missile arsenal included nearly 150,000 rockets and missiles, indicating that it had successfully augmented its munitions stock.[53] The reported presence of research and development, as well as production and assembly, workshops in Lebanon and Syria suggested a shift in *Hizbullahi* and Iranian thinking: the exposure of their supply lines to Israeli and US interdiction demanded that they create a local production and upgrading capability to ensure supply during conflict, rather than relying on weapons transfers across national boundaries.

Nevertheless, the war in Syria has imposed significant financial costs on Hizbullah. It has had to recruit, train, equip and sustain a much larger force; cover the health and pension costs of its fighters, including between 1,500 and 2,000 KIAs and 5,000 injured;[54] develop infrastructure within Syria; and pay the thousands of locally recruited Syrian fighters that joined one of the militia groups overseen by Hizbullah. Indeed, several Syrian groups aligned with Hizbullah reported delayed or unpaid wages in 2018 and 2019, when the organisation started facing financial difficulties.[55] Hizbullah was also forced to reduce social benefits to its constituency in Lebanon, suspending, for instance, free surgical operations and healthcare for civilians at its main hospital in Beirut, Al-Rasoul Al-Azam.[56] It remains unclear how Iran, Hizbullah and the Syrian regime have split the cost of this intervention, whether Hizbullah's financial difficulties are linked to Iran's and whether they can be mitigated by Hizbullah's other sources of income, such as its legal and illegal business activities in Latin America and Africa. Hizbullah's current financial woes have not significantly degraded its capabilities in Syria and elsewhere.

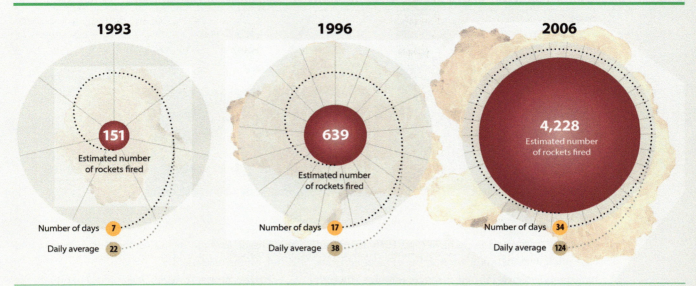

Figure 2.4: **Hizbullah rocket attacks on Israel: 1993, 1996 and 2006 conflicts**

Sources: Human Rights Watch, 'Civilian Pawns: Laws of War Violations and the Use of Weapons on the Israel–Lebanon Border', May 1996, www.hrw.org; Human Rights Watch, 'Operation Grapes of Wrath: The Civilian Victims', September 1997, www.hrw.org; Benjamin S. Lambeth, 'Air Operations in Israel's war against Hezbollah', RAND Corporation, 2011, www.rand.org.

Hizbullah's military capabilities

'The essence of Hizbullah is to be armed and equipped against the sworn enemy of the Lebanese nation, Israel, because the Israelis' first goal is the country of Lebanon ... It is natural that Hizbullah must be equipped with the best weapons for its security and this issue is non-negotiable.'[57]

IRGC commander Major-General Mohammad Jafari, 2017

Missiles

Rockets and missiles have been an integral part of Hizbullah's military successes, and Iran has been instrumental in the group's acquisition and development of these capabilities. Since the 1990s, Iran has provided to the group large numbers of rudimentary rockets and more sophisticated missiles, as well as the expertise and training to develop and deploy them. Deriving in part from Iranian technological input, Syria has also contributed to Hizbullah's arsenal, particularly since Bashar al-Assad became president in 2000.[58]

Hizbullah has articulated two missile strategies since its inception. During the 1990s, it followed a strategy of compellence, with the goal of imposing an escalation ladder on Israel and ultimately ending its occupation of southern Lebanon. The former goal was reached in 1996 with the signing of the Israel–Lebanon Ceasefire Understanding and the latter in 2000 with Israel's withdrawal from that territory. Since then, Hizbullah has embraced a strategy of deterrence, designed to avoid fully fledged war by quickly imposing heavy costs on Israel during a conflict. The continual firing of (even inaccurate) rockets is designed to achieve political and psychological goals: to saturate and overwhelm Israel's missile-defence systems (notably *Iron Dome* for short-range rockets and *David's Sling* for medium-range missiles); divert military, civil-defence and other resources; paralyse economic and human activity in the northern third of Israel and beyond; and ultimately erode Israeli morale and the will to fight. Hizbullah's investment in greater missile accuracy has forced Israel to deploy missile-defence systems to defend critical infrastructure and military installations. Being able to maintain and even increase the tempo of rocket and missile launches is a clear signal of Hizbullah's resilience and an illustration of the inability of Israel to deal it a decisive military blow. It is also used as a device to rally domestic support and draw international attention. This strategy proved successful in 2006, when Hizbullah's rocket barrage proved decisive in shifting Israeli public opinion against the war, forcing Israel to end its attacks and accept what to Tel Aviv were unsatisfactory terms.

Hizbullah's missile arsenal has grown considerably since the 2006 war; a resupply process that has involved both Iran and Syria. According to Western intelligence sources, its variants of the *Katyusha* rocket now number in the tens of thousands, while longer-range rockets, such as the *Fajr* and *Zelzal*, number in the low thousands.[59] Mindful of the poor accuracy and small payload of the *Katyusha*, Iran has assisted Hizbullah in developing a more advanced missile

(l) An Israeli Iron Dome short-range missile-defence system near Haifa, Israel, January 2013

(r) Iran tests its Fateh-110 missile, August 2010

capability.[60] Iran and Syria have reportedly equipped Hizbullah with an unknown number of more accurate road-mobile *Fateh*-110 short-range missiles (though these are thought of locally as medium range). These can be deployed further north in Lebanon, stretching Israeli reconnaissance and air capabilities in times of conflict. However, as demonstrated in 2006, rockets such as the *Fajr* and *Zelzal*, and missiles such as the *Fateh*-110, are vulnerable to Israeli air detection and attack because of their greater heat signatures, as well as their larger and more visible launchers.

Israel and some Western intelligence services assess that Hizbullah has built workshops in Lebanon to upgrade Syrian-sourced M-600 missiles into more sophisticated *Fateh*-110 missiles.[61] Such workshops are basic in terms of their outfitting, but require specialised technicians and reportedly receive quality-control and testing checks by Iranian personnel. Indeed, Tehran has established and oversees a cadre of Lebanese weapon technicians, some of whom trained in Russia in the 1990s. Hizbullah's Missile Accuracy Project, as it is dubbed by the Israeli government, has also benefited from Syrian support. In 2018, Aziz Asbar, a senior Syrian scientist believed to have been heading up a Syrian Scientific Studies and Research Center (SSRC) unit, was killed in a targeted air bombing in the town of Masyaf, which hosts an SSRC site. His unit was allegedly leading Iranian–Syrian–*Hizbullahi* missile-development cooperation.[62] Other assassinations or the targeting of Syrian scientists allegedly involved in such research programmes have taken place in the past, purportedly by Israel.

Nevertheless, the relatively easy method of firing the *Katyusha* rocket, including from multiple-rocket launching systems, has allowed Hizbullah to train thousands of fighters to operate this system, augmenting its strike options. Meanwhile, a specialised cadre operates Hizbullah's more advanced rocket and missile arsenal, including the *Fajr*, *Fateh*-110 and *Zelzal*, on the battlefield.[63]

At the strategic level, Iran and Hizbullah are agreed on the purpose and deployment of rockets and missiles. However, operational matters remain in the hands of Hizbullah's leadership, which has elaborated its own doctrinal and operational uses of this arsenal. Hizbullah decided the nature and tempo of rocket and missile use in 2006, while Iranian input in operational decision-making has been opaque.

Iran's missile capability constitutes a central pillar of Tehran's own deterrence and punishment strategy regarding Israel. So far, it has served the limited, defensive purposes of Hizbullah, but a full-scale regional war scenario would likely involve a wider use of this capability. Iranian officials have engaged in bombastic rhetoric against Israel, emphasising the use of missiles in future conflicts, and exaggerating the damage that Hizbullah's arsenal could inflict on the IDF and Israel's infrastructure. In 2016, then-IRGC deputy commander Brigadier-General Hossein Salami stated that

In Lebanon alone, over 100,000 missiles are ready to be launched. If there is a will, if it serves [our] interests, and if the Zionist regime repeats its past mistakes due to its miscalculations, these missiles will pierce through space, and will strike at the heart of the Zionist regime. They will prepare the ground for its great collapse in the new era … Tens of thousands of other high-precision, long-range missiles, with the necessary destructive capabilities, have been placed in various places throughout the Islamic world … They are just waiting for the command, so that when the trigger is pulled, the accursed black dot will be wiped off the geopolitical map of the world, once and for all.[64]

Table 2.4: Hizbullah's equipment inventory: observed and reported rockets, missiles, anti-tank guided-missile systems and uninhabited aerial vehicles

Type	Name	Base design	Calibre (mm)	Range (km)	Guidance system	Battlefield use	Origin	Research and development
Rockets	*Fajr*-1	PH-63	107	8	Unguided	2006	Iran	China
	Falaq-1/-2		240	10	Unguided	2006	Iran	Iran
	Grad	9M22	122	20–25	Unguided	2006	Syria	USSR
	Grad (enhanced range)		122	50	Unguided	2006	Syria	USSR
	Raad-2/-3	9M27	220	60–70	Unguided	2006	Syria	USSR
	Fajr-3		240	45	Unguided	2006	Iran	DPRK
	Fajr-5		330	75	Unguided	2006	Iran	Iran
	Khaibar-1 (M-302)	WS-1	302	~100	Unguided	2006	Syria	China
	Zelzal-1		616	160		2006 (one failed launch attempt)	Iran	Iran
	Zelzal-2/-3		616	200	Unguided	2006	Iran	Iran
Surface-to-surface ballistic missiles	*Fateh*-110 (M-600)		616	250	Inertial navigation system, with possible GPS	In small numbers	Iran or Syria	Iran
	Shahab-1	SS-1C *Scud*-B	885	300	Inertial navigation system	Doubtful	Iran or Syria	USSR
	Shahab-2	SS-1D *Scud*-C	885	500	Inertial navigation system	Doubtful	Iran or Syria	USSR
Anti-ship missiles	*Noor*	C-802	n/a	120–180	Inertial mid-course navigation with active radar homing	2006	Iran	China

Source: IISS

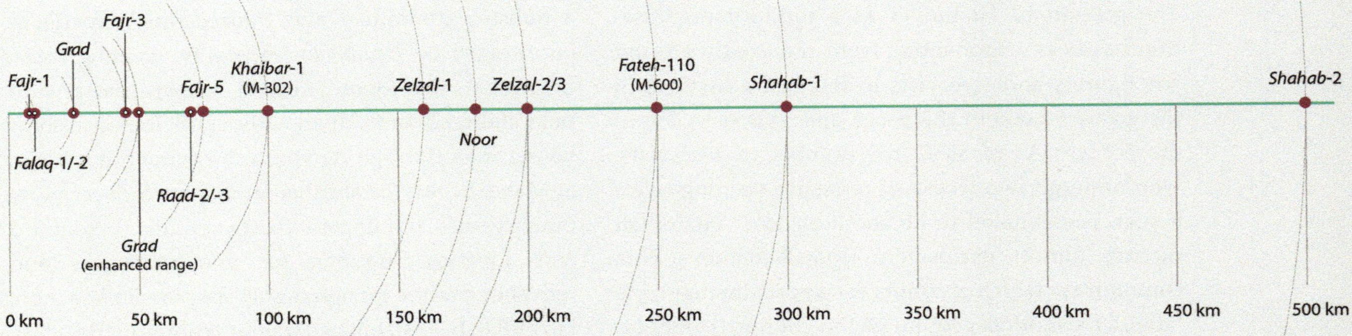

Man-portable anti-tank guided-missile systems	Surface-to-air missile systems	Uninhabited aerial vehicles
9M14 *Malyutka* (AT-3 *Sagger*)	9K32M *Strela*-2M (SA-7B *Grail*)	HESA *Karrar*
9M111 *Fagot* (AT-4 *Spigot*)	9K34 *Strela*-3 (SA-14 *Gremlin*)	HESA *Ababil*-2
9M113 *Konkurs* (AT-5 *Spandrel*)	9K310 *Igla*-1 (SA-16 *Gimlet*)	
9M131 *Metis*-M (AT-13 *Saxhorn*-2)	*Misagh*-1 (QW-1/CH-SA-7)	
9M133 *Kornet* (AT-14 *Spriggan*)	*Misagh*-2 (QW-18/CH-SA-11)	
Milan		
Toophan (BGM-71 TOW)		

Source: IISS

Anti-tank weaponry

Iran has provided Hizbullah with a wide range of anti-tank weaponry (including some of Russian design) that the latter put to use in 2006 against Israel and more recently during the Syrian civil war. In 2006, this capability proved essential in stalling Israeli ground advances into Lebanon and imposed a relatively high cost on the heavy and light armour capabilities of the IDF. Hizbullah's inventory includes wire- and laser-guided anti-tank missiles, such as the 9M131 *Metis*-M (AT-13 *Saxhorn*-2) and the 9M133 *Kornet* (AT-14 *Spriggan*).

(l) Hizbullah members in Beirut, October 2016

(r) An Imam al-Mahdi Scouts member in Nabatieh, Lebanon, October 2017

Hizbullah has trained specialist anti-tank units to fight alongside infantry and special forces. Its tactics in Syria have shown a high degree of sophistication. The anti-tank experience acquired in Syria by Hizbullah and allied militias, and the weaponry seized from Syrian rebels, including US-origin tube-launched, optically tracked, wireless-guided (TOW) missiles, has increased the group's military potency.

Recruitment, training and force development

The growth of Hizbullah as a military organisation has been exponential: from reportedly around 500 fighters and reservists in the 1980s, to 5,000 in the 1990s, 15,000 in the 2000s and 25,000–30,000 in the 2010s.[65] As of 2018, the number of reservists, who undergo two weeks of refresher training twice a year, is estimated to be about 25,000.[66] Hizbullah recruits almost exclusively from Lebanon's Shia community, which accounts for approximately 35% (about 1.5 million people) of the country's population of around 4.5m.[67]

At times, Hizbullah has partnered with non-Shia paramilitary forces in Lebanon for specific missions and to minimise its sectarian and political exposure. Since the 1990s, it has overseen the Lebanese Resistance Brigades (*Saraya al-Muqawamah al-Lubnaniyyah*). This is a small force composed of Christian, Druze and Sunni fighters, but its role has been marginal and symbolic.[68] Hizbullah has also provided basic training and political guidance to auxiliary forces, such as the Sunni Arab Movement Party militia, the secular Syrian Social National Party and the Druze Arab Tawhid Party.[69] From 2013, with the Syrian conflict ongoing, Hizbullah also helped to establish and train local Christian and Shia volunteer groups in the Bekaa Valley to defend their villages against Sunni rebel and jihadi militias. Such groups have been useful to Hizbullah in securing specific areas inside Lebanon, providing operational muscle, mobilising pro-Hizbullah elements in non-Shia communities, and challenging anti-Hizbullah leaderships within non-Shia communities. However, they are not integrated into Hizbullah's core force and are not expected to fight alongside it unconditionally.

Hizbullah's overall recruitment standards are high, and most fighters go through an ideological and cultural indoctrination process. The group has also sought to enshrine its 'culture of resistance', a holistic, communal and transcending experience encouraged by *Hizbullahi* leaders, by creating social institutions that identify, enroll, nurture and reward potential recruits from an early age.[70] It also grooms young men through its youth movement, the Imam al-Mahdi Scouts (established in 1985), which provides military-style training to young recruits.[71] Standard and advanced training for young recruits and refresher courses for reservists take place in Lebanon. Hizbullah has established training camps in the Bekaa Valley and along the border with Syria. Specialist training is provided both in Lebanon and Iran.

Since 2012, Hizbullah has adapted its training regime to the missions undertaken in Syria. Initially, for most recruits, it focused on defensive tactics and missile operations, while a small number of specialised units obtained offensive training. As the war progressed, it developed and honed a new range of fighting tactics and skills that were not part of its repertoire before, including urban and desert warfare, counter-insurgency, and joint operations with the Russian and Syrian commands, including their air forces. As a result, the organisation now offers urban-warfare and offensive training to many of its recruits. Several camps have been established in the Bekaa Valley, or existing ones upgraded, for this purpose, though Hizbullah's Syrian affiliates are trained mostly in Syria. Hundreds of Hizbullah officers and fighters

Table 2.5: **Hizbullah: military training and capabilities, 1982–2019**

Period	Main adversary	Posture	Training and tactics	Capabilities	Iranian input
1982–90	Israeli Defense Forces South Lebanon Army (IDF Auxiliaries)	Guerrilla warfare	Guerrilla warfare Improvised explosive devices Suicide bombings	Rocket-propelled grenades Small and light weaponry	Organisation Training Weaponry
1982–90	Amal militia Leftist groups Christian militias	Defence Offence	Guerrilla warfare Improvised explosive devices Urban warfare	Rocket-propelled grenades Small and light weaponry	Organisation Training Weaponry
1991–2000	Israeli Defense Forces South Lebanon Army (IDF Auxiliaries)	Compellence Guerrilla warfare	Guerrilla warfare Rocket attacks Improvised explosive devices	Anti-tank weapons Artillery Improvised explosive devices Rockets Small and light weaponry	Organisation Training Weaponry
2000–11	Israeli Defense Forces	Deterrence Defence	Fighting in rural environments Missile warfare	Anti-tank guided missiles Anti-ship missiles Artillery Rockets Short- and medium-range surface-to-surface missiles Small and light weaponry	Organisation Training Weaponry
2011–19	Israeli Defense Forces	Deterrence Defence	Fighting in rural environments Missile warfare	Anti-tank guided missiles Anti-ship missiles Rockets Surface-to-air missiles Surface-to-surface missiles Uninhabited aerial vehicles	Organisation Training Weaponry
2011–19	Syrian rebel groups	Deterrence Defence	Counter-insurgency Desert warfare Urban warfare	Anti-tank guided missiles Artillery Mechanised and armoured vehicles Rockets Short- and medium-range surface-to-surface missiles Small and light weaponry Uninhabited aerial vehicles	Organisation Training Weaponry
2011–19	Islamic State, otherwise known as ISIS or ISIL	Deterrence Defence	Counter-insurgency Desert warfare Urban warfare	Anti-tank guided missiles Artillery Mechanised and armoured vehicles Rockets Short- and medium-range surface-to-surface missiles Small and light weaponry Uninhabited aerial vehicles	Organisation Training Weaponry

Source: IISS

appear also to have received Iranian training, domestically and in Iran, in counter-insurgency operations based on Iran's experience in fighting the Baluchi, Kurdish and other insurgencies.[72]

However, the urgency of the Syrian civil war appears to have compelled the militant organisation to relax its standards in some areas. Hizbullah has increasingly recruited fighters motivated by the generous salaries and military victories it offers at a time of economic and social hardship in Lebanon.

Additionally, social pressure in the Shia community to join a party claiming to be defending its interests and security has helped recruitment. The speed at which Hizbullah was able to assemble and deploy new recruits is testament to its mobilisation capacity.

A key factor in Hizbullah's military performance are the strong ethics of its fighting force. Promotion often depends on merit; levels of corruption and brutality are relatively low; small units are tied by family or regional connections; and commanders

(l) A Hizbullah advert in the suburbs of Beirut, Lebanon, February 2018

(r) Jihad al-Binaa reconstruction work in Dahiya, Beirut, Lebanon, June 2006

are expected to lead in battle, as revealed by the *Hizbullahi* officers killed in Syria. In addition, Hizbullah imposes stringent operational-security measures. Its fighters avoid publicising their roles and missions on social media, and show an aversion to speaking to non-Hizbullah members, especially the media and academics.

Procurement and logistics

Hizbullah's procurement and logistics capability has been a critical element of its military success. As a non-state actor facing rivals with superior intelligence and military capacities, Hizbullah has had to operate in secrecy, secure and diversify its supply routes, and develop and tap into foreign procurement networks.

Specialised logistics units have sought to obtain weapons and technology worldwide, but Hizbullah has diversified its procurement strategy. At times, it has employed party members and networks specifically designed for this purpose; it has also used existing arms-smuggling networks or commissioned low-level entrepreneurs. Generally, it has sought to work with Lebanese citizens or members of the Lebanese diaspora in target countries.

Hizbullah's procurement networks span the world. For example, in 2006, Canada sentenced a Lebanese-Canadian businessman accused of trying to procure sensitive military equipment, including night-vision goggles, from US companies.[73] In 2014, several Hizbullah-linked businessmen in Lebanon were accused of trying to procure uninhabited aerial vehicle technology from as far away as China.[74] In the US, several men belonging to the same family were found guilty in 2016 of acquiring and shipping small-arms and ammunition to Lebanon.[75]

Inside Lebanon, Hizbullah's logistics branch serves several goals: the transfer of weaponry from Iran to Syria and pre-positioning it there; the transfer of arms from Iran to Lebanon and from Syria to Lebanon; the distribution and deployment of weaponry ahead of a conflict; the supply of arms during a conflict; and significant construction and engineering work.

Indeed, Hizbullah has excelled at construction. In the region south of the Litani River, Hizbullah's construction arm has reportedly built as many as 800 fortified positions, bunkers and tunnels, some at a depth of 40 metres.[76] In Beirut, it has built an extensive command and military infrastructure in the neighbourhoods it controls south of the capital. Hizbullah also possesses its own communications and IT infrastructure. Particularly revealing is the speed and efficacy of the Hizbullah reconstruction effort after the 2006 war. Branded '*Al-Waad*' (The Promise), this initiative was politically crucial in assuaging the Shia community after the devastating conflict.[77] Whether directly or through local contractors, Hizbullah was able to deploy significant capabilities to rebuild housing and infrastructure in areas under its control.[78] Lebanese politicians and media assert that Hizbullah received significant Iranian funding for this work. According to Waad officials, as much as US$400m was given for the reconstruction of Beirut's southern suburbs alone.[79] In February 2013, it was revealed that the senior Iranian reconstruction officer deployed to support Hizbullah's own effort was Hassan Shateri, a senior IRGC commander. He was killed during a journey from Damascus to Beirut on a mission for the IRGC as it escalated its role there.[80] This demonstrated the multiple roles that Iranian security officials undertake in favour of Hizbullah.

There have been several routes for weapons supplies to enter Lebanon, all facilitated by Syrian support.[81] The majority of weapons supplies have entered via the Lebanese border with Syria. Iranian-supplied weaponry has typically landed at Damascus's civilian and military airports or been

Map 2.3: **Major Hizbullah–Iran supply routes in Syria, 2019: observed and reported**

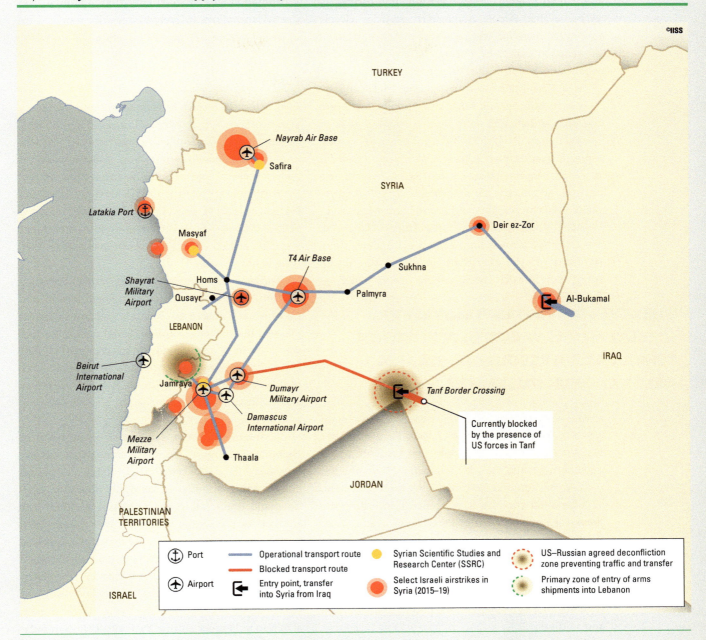

Source: IISS

shipped into the ports of Tartus and Latakia, before being either stored in Syria or transported by road into Lebanon.

The porous 375-km-long Syria–Lebanon border offers many entry points. In addition to the seven official border crossings, many informal routes exist, despite the rugged terrain, which local communities have reportedly used for legal and illegal activities. Conveniently, the Bekaa Valley, where Hizbullah possesses extensive infrastructure and can rely on a wide base of support, sits just across the main border crossing, Masnaa. Informal crossings east of the town of Nabi Chit have also served as primary entry points.[82]

Hizbullah has pre-positioned weapons in the Syrian regions of Zabadani and Western Qalamoun since the 1990s, accessing them as needed and when safe to bring into Lebanon. Until 2011, the pre-positioning of weapons in Syria had a strategic purpose: to shield its more advanced military capabilities from Israeli air attacks, while maintaining the latent threat of escalation. How these storage facilities were managed prior to the 2011 uprising remains unclear. A joint custodial arrangement between the Syrian authorities, the IRGC and Hizbullah is likely. It is also highly probable that Syria's intelligence agencies closely monitored these facilities to ensure that no movement of weapons, especially during conflict, would occur without the assent of the Syrian government.

UN Resolution 1701 mandated that Lebanon 'secure its borders and other entry points to prevent the entry in Lebanon without its consent of arms or related material'.[83] Limited LAF capacity and political tensions inside Lebanon, as well as continued border disputes between Lebanon and Syria, prevented a speedy and effective implementation of this requirement. To enforce this, and with the support of Western countries, notably the United Kingdom, the LAF has formed and deployed brigades along the border.[84] The European Union has funded an Integrated Border Management programme to

> **"THE LEVEL OF IRANIAN FUNDING FOR HIZBULLAH HAS VARIED DEPENDING ON TEHRAN'S OWN RESOURCES, STRATEGIC NEEDS AND CIRCUMSTANCES."**

assist 'border agencies to increase the security of citizens, secure and control borders for a smoother and safer movement of people, and facilitate trade, development and human interaction'.[85] In reality, the LAF has ignored Hizbullah's weapons transfers, as have other state security agencies, including the powerful General Security Directorate. This reflects the widespread aversion among the security agencies to impede Hizbullah's activities without a clear political mandate and popular consensus, as well as genuine sympathy towards and even cooperation with the Shia movement on the part of many officers and soldiers.

The key to Hizbullah's wartime resilience has been its preparedness and pre-positioned weaponry in strategic areas, both in dedicated structures and in civilian and other locations. In 2006, anti-tank missiles, IEDs, missiles and rockets, in addition to small-arms and other combat equipment, were all in-theatre before the start of the war with Israel. The management of the logistics and procurement department was the responsibility of senior-most Hizbullah commanders. Hassan al-Laqqis, a senior Hizbullah officer who served in several capacities and was rumoured to be a member of its Jihad Council, was head of research, development, logistics and procurement until his assassination in 2013.[86] Muhammad Qasir, who has played a key

coordination role between Hizbullah, the IRGC and the Syrian regime, is likely to have taken over some of Laqqis's tasks.[87]

Funding

Evaluating Hizbullah's annual budget, including Iran's contribution, is a difficult exercise. In June 2016, Nasrallah openly admitted the movement's financial and material dependency on Iran, and reassured his audience about the rumoured financial difficulties of the party: 'We are open about the fact that Hizbullah's budget, its income, its expenses, everything it eats and drinks, its weapons and rockets, are from the Islamic Republic of Iran ... So long as Iran has money, then we will have money.'[88]

The level of Iranian funding has varied depending on Tehran's own resources, strategic needs and circumstances. Estimates have ranged from US$40m per year in the 1990s to around US$1bn after the 2006 war, with most of the funds directed toward civilian and military reconstruction.[89] In 2010, US intelligence evaluated Iran's contribution at between US$100m and US$200m.[90] US estimates in 2018 hovered at around US$700m per year.[91]

Accounting for Iran's financial contribution to Hizbullah's military readiness and social-security activities is similarly complicated. Hizbullah's overall budget remains unknown, as do its allocation decisions and Iran's role in the process. How does Iran account for the weapons systems and training that it offers to Hizbullah? Are these expenses expressed as a direct cost in the Iranian budget or absorbed by an IRGC account, or does Hizbullah contribute a portion toward these costs? How have Iran and Hizbullah approached funding for the large number of Syrian militiamen during the conflict? Importantly, as a social-services provider, does Hizbullah seek or obtain guidance from Iran about this domestic spending allocation?

Another unknown is the extent to which Iran is directly involved in and benefits from Hizbullah's fundraising activities abroad. US Treasury officials assert that Iran and Hizbullah regularly cooperate in this, but that Hizbullah also conducts separate fundraising activities. The organisation has reportedly developed legal and illegal alternative sources of revenue that have supplemented and, at times, substituted for declining Iranian funding. In Lebanon, Hizbullah and its members operate as part of the formal and informal economies, producing and trading goods and services. Members and sympathisers, in Lebanon and abroad, donate *Khoms* (voluntary but expected religious contributions) to the group. They also run Hizbullah-owned or Hizbullah-linked companies that operate legitimately but which also serve as cover for other activities. Increasingly, Hizbullah benefits, like other political factions, by parasitising the Lebanese state. For much of its early history, the organisation was distrustful of and antagonistic toward Lebanese state institutions. From 1991 to 2005, Iranian and other external funding meant that, contrary to other Lebanese political actors, it could afford not to seek access to state resources to reward its base and fund its operations, thereby maintaining its reputation for integrity. From 2005, however, and more so in recent years, Hizbullah has sought to influence Lebanese state bureaucracies and budgetary decisions to compensate for its increasing spending needs and tight budget. This culminated in its decision to seek for the first time in its history a 'service ministry': since 2019, a Hizbullah member has headed the health ministry. With its large budget, control of this ministry allows Hizbullah to provide health services to its constituency and possibly cover the medical expenses of its fighters.

Hizbullah has been implicated in a wide range of illegal and criminal activities in Lebanon and abroad, including alleged money laundering, drug trafficking, smuggling, complex financial schemes, sanctions-breaking activities and illegal procurements in Europe, North and South America, Asia, Africa and the Middle East. In recent years, Hizbullah financiers or procurement managers have been operating or have been arrested in Western Europe, Brazil, the Czech Republic, Morocco, Nigeria, Paraguay and several other countries, indicating the global nature of the group's procurement and fundraising activities.[92]

Managing partners

An essential function that Hizbullah has performed on behalf of Iran is the management and mentoring of many of Tehran's Arab partners. Indeed, the organisation has become a central interlocutor for an array of Arab militias and political parties that have sectarian and ideological, or simply opportunistic, ties to Tehran. Its Arab identity and its political and military pedigree facilitate the rapport between Iran and these entities. Importantly, it manages and resolves some of the inevitable cultural tensions and political differences in these relationships. Significantly, Hizbullah lessens the stigma otherwise attached to any relationship with a non-Arab Shia power.

Using Hizbullah as an intermediary has helped Iran manage the expectations of these Arab partners and regulate interactions with them. Maintaining a degree of separation has allowed Tehran to structure its engagement with partners: Hizbullah conveys Iranian messages, including of dissatisfaction or conditionality; facilitates or denies access to the IRGC and the Iranian political leadership; and serves as a holding room when tensions exist between these partners and Tehran. Crucially, this dynamic also provides plausible deniability for all sides.

Hizbullah's prestige and intimate relationship with Iran's top leadership have political benefits for Arab non-state actors seeking association. For their domestic and regional audiences, the association with Hizbullah places them within the framework of the resistance against Israel and the US, thereby legitimising their

> ## "HIZBULLAH IS A CENTRAL INTERLOCUTOR FOR AN ARRAY OF ARAB MILITIAS AND POLITICAL PARTIES WITH TIES TO IRAN"

activities. In return, working with these actors places Hizbullah first among Iran's partners. Strategically, it affords Hizbullah regional legitimacy and operational depth, allowing it to more easily grow its military-mobilisation, fundraising, training and operations networks. In a conflict, this provides Hizbullah with the ability to threaten escalatory action and to expand the conflict to include more actors. In June 2017, Nasrallah raised this prospect in explicit terms for the first time:

> The Israeli enemy must know that if an Israeli war is launched against Syria or Lebanon, it is not known that the fighting will remain Lebanese-Israeli, or Syrian-Israeli. ... This doesn't mean there are states that might intervene directly. But this could open the way for thousands, even hundreds of thousands of fighters from all over the Arab and Islamic world to participate – from Iraq, Yemen, Iran, Afghanistan and Pakistan.[93]

Such a threat bolsters Hizbullah's strategy of deterrence. It also serves to inject purpose and coherence into its own network of partnerships.

To support Iran's allies, Hizbullah has over the years deployed a range of services, from hosting their leaders and families and providing basing in Lebanon, to financial assistance, military training and strategic communications.

A mural of Hizbullah commander Imad Mughniyah in Beirut, Lebanon, August 2008

To staff its and Iran's regional activities, Hizbullah has developed and deployed a cadre of experienced political–military officers who operate directly under the command of the Jihad Council and the ESO, and in coordination with the IRGC's Quds Force. Hizbullah has retained a generation of fighters from the 1980s and 1990s who rose through the ranks, filling military, command and logistical positions in Lebanon, and who later went on to play political and liaison roles. Organised into units dedicated to supporting regional partners and operations ('Unit 3800' is allegedly responsible for Iraq and Yemen and 'Unit 1800' for the Palestinian Territories), this pool of commanders distinguishes Hizbullah from other armed non-state actors in the Middle East. The group's strategy of promotion has created a sense of continuity, brotherhood and purpose among this generation of *Hizbullahi* commanders. Practically, this approach has produced a horizontal military-command structure that requires minimal operational guidance and guarantees responsiveness once strategic goals have been agreed. Commanders can also move across units depending on specific needs. Shared battlefield experiences and personal relationships simplify the group's communication protocols and increase operational safety. Additionally, this system facilitates recruitment from and the integration of clan and family members into the party's structures.

The tight-knit character of Hizbullah's security core (the Jihad Council, the Islamic Resistance and the ESO) can be illustrated by the family and command ties of senior Hizbullah leaders. Nasrallah lost a son, Hadi, in the war with Israel and another son, Jawad, is allegedly involved in the movement's Palestinian operations under Unit 1800.[94] Imad Mughniyah, Hizbullah's most famous security commander – and, until his death during an Israeli operation in Damascus in 2008, its second-most powerful member[95] – was a central player in Hizbullah's domestic resistance and regional activities. His cousin and brother-in-law, Mustafa Badreddine, took over his security and military roles, and headed Hizbullah's efforts in Syria until he died in Damascus in 2016.[96] Mughniyah also lost several brothers and a son called Jihad. The latter, who appeared several times in the presence of Qasem Soleimani after his father's death, was killed in 2015 while touring southern Syria, in close proximity to the Israeli-occupied Golan Heights, in the company of a senior IRGC commander, Brigadier-General Mohammad Allahdadi.[97] Another son, Mostafa, is reportedly serving as a commander in Syria. Another example is Muhammad Qasir, who plays a senior coordinating role in Syria and oversees procurement and logistics for the group and the IRGC. One of his brothers was an early *Hizbullahi* combatant who died fighting Israeli forces in 1982, while another is reportedly married to a relative of Hassan Nasrallah.[98]

Iraq

In line with Iran's strategy of deepening and diversifying its ties with the Iraqi Shia community, Hizbullah's engagement in Iraq since 2003 has helped Tehran nurture a wide range of non-state actors.[99] Hizbullah had its own reasons to be involved in Iraq: it saw itself as enabling a local resistance against an occupier (reflecting Hizbullah's own genesis); it fit its regional outlook against aggressive US imperialism; it gave the group regional depth and a popular cause to fight for, as the debate over its armed status intensified in Lebanon; and it built on long-standing ties between Lebanese and Iraqi Shia communities with shared narratives of oppression and resistance. Veteran commanders with established IRGC ties, such as Yousef Hashim, Ali Musa Daqduq, Mustafa al-Yakoubi and Muhammad Kawtharani, were reportedly put in charge of the effort.[100] They acted as military commanders, intelligence officers and political advisers, and at times were involved in Iraqi political deal-making and in reconciliation efforts between competing Shia parties. In 2018, a US official alleged that Kawtharani was involved in inter-Shia discussions about the formation of the Iraqi government, settled disputes and conveyed Iranian preferences.[101]

Hizbullah's role in Iraq remained subordinate to that of Iran, owing to the latter's geographical proximity to Iraq, overriding security priorities and long-time engagement of Iraqi Shia factions, notably through its primary partner, the Badr Organisation.[102] Hizbullah accordingly calibrated its involvement and deliberately avoided direct combat or front-line roles. Its Iraq training mission was small in size, adapting to the specific needs of the Shia insurgency against the US armed forces – primarily basic combat and insurgent tactics, artillery and mortar training, and IED production. These lessons were conducted chiefly in-country and often involved a small number of Lebanese trainers. Specialist training and the introduction of explosively formed penetrator warhead technology to Iraqi militia inventories were primarily conducted by Iranians, including in Iran. More significant was the mentoring assistance Hizbullah provided to its Iraqi partners. A hybrid political–military organisation itself, Hizbullah was well placed to help with recruitment, mobilisation, structuring and political engagement at a time of turmoil in Iraqi politics.

Early on, Iran and Hizbullah identified and courted Muqtada al-Sadr's Jaish al-Mahdi (JAM) as a prime vehicle for influence in Iraq. The young Shi'ite cleric's anti-US agenda, large following, family ties to Lebanon and avowed admiration for the Lebanese group facilitated the initial rapport. JAM obtained some training and support, but the relationship did not flourish as expected. Personal and ideological competition stood in the way: as a scion of one of Iraq's most prestigious clerical families, Sadr had fraught relations with his new partners. Tactical differences and organisational tensions between the well-established and disciplined Hizbullah and the confused and erratic Sadrist movement damaged the rapport. From 2007, Sadr suffered military and political setbacks following the defeat of his forces in southern Iraq by the US-backed Iraqi government. In the following years, he chose political retrenchment, abandoning military strategies in favour of popu-list approaches, which paid off in the 2018 elections, from which he emerged as kingmaker. This episode showed the limits of Hizbullah's engagement in Iraq. If Sadr and Hizbullah remain interlocutors with cour-teous relations, theirs is not a tight alliance that can be unconditionally leveraged by Tehran, but rather a partnership of convenience and limited value.

However, this setback did not reduce Hizbullah's influence in Iraq. Its engagement of JAM helped it identify dissatisfied or ambitious JAM commanders who would be interested in breaking with the Sadrist movement. Indeed, Hizbullah had invested early on in diversification strategies and long-term relationships with smaller, nimbler partners. In due time, Asaib Ahl al-Haq (AAH), Kataib Hizbullah (KH) and the associated Special Groups would become vehicles of *Hizbullahi* and Iranian interests in Iraq. The arrest in 2007 of senior Hizbullah opera-tive Ali Musa Daqduq, along with Qais al-Khazali, a former JAM commander who had established AAH, provides an insight into this approach. Khazali, who was freed in 2010, would end up becoming a reli-able Hizbullah favourite. Daqduq was freed in 2012 and reportedly became involved in militia training in Syria.[103] Though small in size and political influ-ence, AAH remained cohesive and operationally able. When Hizbullah required additional personnel in Syria in 2013, and again in 2015, it turned to AAH and other Iraqi militias, which provided combat-ants who fought battles from the Syria–Iraq border

"WHILE SMALL IN NUMBER, HIZBULLAHI COMMANDERS OPERATING ALONGSIDE IRGC OFFICERS ASSISTED THE PMU MILITIAS ACROSS SEVERAL BATTLEFIELDS"

against the Islamic State, otherwise known as ISIS or ISIL, to Aleppo against Syrian rebels.[104] Similar dynamics governed Hizbullah's relations with KH and its leader Abu Mahdi al-Muhandis, an Iraqi who began working with the IRGC in the 1980s and returned to Iraq in 2003. KH emerged as one of Iran's small but effective and reliable partners. In time, Muhandis rose to become the de facto commander of the Popular Mobilisation Units (PMU, or *al-Hashd al-Shaabi*), the conglomerate of militias that fought ISIS from 2014.

Hizbullah's credibility as an ally of these groups was demonstrated by its responsiveness to their own security interests. In summer 2014, it rushed the deployment of dozens of military advisers to help the Iran-aligned Shia militias fighting ISIS in northern and eastern Iraq.[105] The mission was motivated by Shia solidarity against a common '*takfiri*' (Sunni jihadi and rebel fighters) enemy, Iran's concerns about the Sunni jihadi threat approaching its borders, and a race with the US about who would shape the campaign against ISIS and ultimately determine Iraqi poli-tics.[106] While small in number, *Hizbullahi* commanders operating alongside IRGC officers assisted the PMU militias across several battlefields, including in Tikrit.

The return on Hizbullah's Iraq investment has been evident. Both AAH and KH deployed fighters along the border and inside Syria under IRGC and Hizbullah command, with their logistical support. On the Syrian battlefield, these militias often fought with their own insignia and under their own banners or the flags of their Syrian affiliates. Iraqi militias also supplemented pro-Assad forces in large battles such as those in Aleppo, Al-Bukamal, Damascus, Deir ez-Zor and Palmyra.

These groups also facilitate the supply network designed to ship weaponry from Iran to Syria via Iraq, and eventually into Lebanon. In June 2018, an Israeli airstrike against one such suspected shipment killed about 20 KH fighters in a joint KH–IRGC base in Iraq, close to the Iraq–Syria border.[107]

Importantly, Hizbullah's Iraqi partners have registered their readiness to contribute forces against Israel

"HIZBULLAH'S TRAIN-AND-ASSIST MISSION IN YEMEN APPEARS TO BE SMALL SCALE"

in the event of a future conflict. In December 2017, Qais Khazali visited the Lebanon–Israel border accompanied by Hizbullah commanders, announcing that:

> I'm at the Fatima Gate in Kafr Kila, at the border that divides south Lebanon from occupied Palestine. I'm here with my brothers from Hezbollah, the Islamic resistance. We announce our full readiness to stand as one with the Lebanese people, with the Palestinian cause, in the face of the unjust Israeli occupation, [an occupation] that is anti-Islam, anti-Arab, and anti-humanity, in the decisive Arab Muslim cause.[108]

Another Iraqi Shia militia leader, Sheikh Akram al-Kaabi, the founder of Harakat Hizbullah al-Nujaba (HHN), an AAH splinter group operating in both Iraq and Syria, announced the formation in 2017 of the 'Golan Liberation Brigade' to back the Syrian military in its attempts to 'free' the Israeli-occupied Golan Heights,[109] though there was no evidence that the unit had been fielded as of the end of 2018.

Regardless of whether AAH, HHN and similar Iraqi groups would mobilise in times of conflict, whether Hizbullah would demand they do so and whether it would make a military difference, the existence of this option affects the cost calculations of an Israeli ground war in Lebanon and raises the prospect of a regional war.

Yemen

As with Iran, Hizbullah's real interest in the Houthi movement started in earnest in 2009, evolved into limited support as Yemen entered a troubled transition period in 2011 and morphed qualitatively in 2014.

In May 2018, Nasrallah gave an emotional speech in which he stated that the 'most noble, best and greatest thing [I] have done in my life was the speech denouncing the Saudi intervention [in Yemen] on the day after it started [in 2015]'.[110] The symbolic importance given by Hizbullah to the war in Yemen belies the opportunistic rationale for its support to the Houthi insurgency.

Firstly, Hizbullah saw in Yemen an opportunity to broadcast a positive narrative of resistance and, in part, to redress negative perceptions linked to its role in Syria. The group's role had eroded its popularity across the Arab world, which had peaked after its 2000 and 2006 successes against Israel.[111] In Syria, Hizbullah was seen as intervening at the behest of a brutal dictator against a rebellion formed from the poor and rural socio-economic classes it purports to represent, in the process damaging its reputation. Yemen was a territory where it could restore, if only partly, its standing: it intervened in defence of a rural insurgency of deprived and repressed Yemenis that rose against a corrupt regime backed by Saudi Arabia, portrayed as the *takfiris'* sponsor. Yemen was also a place where it could hinder at minimal cost Riyadh, Iran's main regional rival, and gain a foothold in the Arabian Peninsula.

Operationally, Hizbullah's train-and-assist mission in Yemen appears to be small scale, owing to the limited needs of the already battle-hardened Houthi insurgents, who have access to weaponry and expertise from the Yemeni military units that joined them. Hizbullah's and Iran's risk calculations probably also demand restraint in Yemen: total victory for the Houthis is not a priority (while the continuation of the war is) and a greater footprint could lead to a regional escalation unwanted by both, while the returns on a small footprint and limited material investment have been significant. Senior *Hizbullahi* commanders such as Khalil Harb (a veteran from the 1980s) and Haitham Tabatabai head the effort; they also double as senior political officers.[112] Western intelligence agencies assess the size of the mission to be around 100 trainers and missile specialists.[113]

Hizbullah has also offered the Houthi movement a safe haven outside Yemen. Several insurgent leaders and their families reside around Beirut, living in neighbourhoods controlled by Hizbullah. The Houthi media and propaganda division, most notably the Al Massira television channel, is located in the Hizbullah media compound in the Lebanese capital. *Hizbullahi* influence on the Houthi message is evident in the visuals, themes, language and theatrics adopted by Massira. The nature of the relationship was best illustrated by the interview given by Houthi leader Abdul Malik al-Houthi to the pro-Hizbullah Lebanese *Al-Akhbar* newspaper in March 2018 – the first to the non-Yemeni media – in which he stated that he was ready to fight alongside Hizbullah against Israel.[114] Houthi himself has also increasingly adopted Hassan Nasrallah's way of speaking and rhetorical style.

Most significantly, Hizbullah could be a model for the Houthis to emulate, even if total replication is difficult. Indeed, Hizbullah has in many ways achieved goals that the Houthi leadership finds attractive: an armed status legitimised by a mix of coercion and political acquiescence; presence in state and security institutions; superior military capabilities, including missiles, and an autonomous supply line; good standing as a defender of its constituency; and a regional profile and international relevance. Such aspirations explain the deference that characterises Houthi engagement with Hizbullah.

However, upgrading the relationship between the Houthi movement and Iran to replicate the Tehran–Hizbullah affiliation would require a firm decision by Iran and considerably greater investment. For Iran, the primary value of the Houthi insurgency is limited to its rivalry with Saudi Arabia, its ability to shame its Arab and Western rivals and its disruptive power in the Bab al-Mandeb. The insurgency does not, however, compare to Hizbullah's sophistication, utility and reach, however. Lingering religious differences and the Houthis' own political calculations also militate against such a development. For Hizbullah, the Houthi insurgency is a convenient partner but, notwithstanding Nasrallah's emotional speech, ultimately secondary to its core interests.

Palestinian Territories: Hizbullah as sponsor

The Palestinian cause has been central to the respective outlooks of Iran and Hizbullah. Both parties have portrayed Israel as an oppressor of Middle Eastern people and as a critical enabler of US hegemony, and accused the Arab states of having reneged on the Palestinian cause to please their US protector. Politically and operationally, Hizbullah has given the struggle immense importance. It has justified ventures across the Middle East by framing them as necessary

to protect the effort to recover Al-Quds (Jerusalem). The fight against jihadists in Iraq and Syria has been portrayed as necessary to prevent the weakening of the resistance.

While Hizbullah has attempted operations inside Israel, instead of direct intervention the priority has been to empower Palestinian partners. This illustrates the operational limitations of the group, as well as its risk appetite: Hizbullah has sought to give select Palestinian partners the means to harass and kill Israeli forces and civilians but has mostly avoided direct involvement.

Hamas

Perhaps no group illustrates the vagaries of Iran's regional partnerships better than Hamas, the

> ## "HAMAS DOES NOT EXPECT DIRECT AND SUSTAINED IRANIAN ASSISTANCE DURING A CONFLICT"

Palestinian Islamist nationalist insurgent group. An affiliate of the Sunni Muslim Brotherhood, Hamas is a major political and security partner of Iran, but lacks an organic relationship with it. As a Sunni movement, it rejects the religious leadership of Tehran and, at times, adopts a chauvinist discourse against other sects, including Shia Muslims. As an Arab organisation, it is wary of accusations of bolstering Persian power, as Iran competes with other Middle Eastern powers and patrons. As a Palestinian faction, it is involved in domestic bargaining with other groups and maintains complex relations with Israel. Yet despite all these sources of tension, Iran and Hizbullah have become Hamas's main sponsors, seeing it as a powerful challenger of Israel, the Palestinian Authority and the US during the peace-process era, as a provider of political cover for their own political outreach in the Arab world, and as a military ally during a potential multi-front war. Tellingly, it took the Israeli assassination in 2004 of Hamas founder Sheikh Ahmed Yassin, who distrusted Iran and Shi'ites more generally, for the Hamas leadership to upgrade the relationship to a broad partnership with Iran.

Hamas does not expect direct and sustained Iranian assistance during a conflict, nor does it assume that Tehran would subordinate its interests to Hamas's as part of regional brinkmanship or dealmaking. During the Israeli operations *Cast Lead* in 2009, *Pillar of Defense* in 2012 and *Protective Edge* in 2014, and the 2018 confrontation in Gaza, neither Iran

Members of the Izz al-Din al-Qassam Brigades, Hamas's military wing, with an M-75 (Iranian Fajr-5) rocket in Gaza, December 2014

nor Hizbullah extended direct military assistance to Hamas, despite vociferous statements of support by Iranian and *Hizbullahi* leaders.

Hamas understands that Iran is more interested in its military activities and capacity for local nuisance-making than its state-building efforts in Gaza, and in maintaining the prospect of a multi-front war against Israel that would pin down Israeli forces. As a result, Hamas is engaged in balancing between competing local and regional constituencies. While it shares with Hizbullah a history of military resistance and a similar political outlook, the two organisations operate in different contexts and pursue different, if often overlapping, interests.

Despite these strategic limitations, Hamas's political and military development since the 1990s can be in no small part traced to Iranian and *Hizbullahi* patronage. The relationship flourished from 1992, when Israel expelled hundreds of Palestinians to Lebanon, including Hamas fighters and senior officials.[115] Among these militants, who spent months in a makeshift camp in the no-man's-land separating the Israeli-occupied zone in Lebanon and territory controlled by Hizbullah and the Lebanese authorities, was Yahya Ayash. The Hamas commander was identified and personally groomed by Imad Mughniyah in the use of explosives, including suicide bombings (which Hizbullah itself had forsaken). On his return to the West Bank in 1993, and until his assassination in 1996, Ayash led a bloody campaign against Israeli occupying troops, as well as civilians, which deeply shook Israeli society and contributed to the derailing of the peace process.[116]

Cooperation with Hizbullah became a central pillar of Hamas's own growth and resistance strategy: it learned from Hizbullah's political engagement, benefited from financial assistance and obtained military training. Since the 1990s, Hamas has established close political ties with the Iranian and *Hizbullahi* leaderships, opened offices in Beirut and Damascus, and vocally supported the Axis of Resistance.[117] Hamas fighters have trained in Hizbullah camps in Iran, Lebanon and Syria, and Hamas's operational leaders coordinate their military activities with their Iranian and Lebanese 'handlers'.[118] Operational similarities are numerous, from the kidnapping of Israeli soldiers to IED deployments and the use of rockets.

Iran and Hizbullah's material supply of Hamas has been primarily through the Sinai Peninsula and into Gaza, but also at times by sea, with weapons-carrying ships offloading materiel onto smaller boats sailing to Gaza. In 2008, the dismantlement by the Egyptian security services of a large Hizbullah cell operating under the ESO to supply arms to Hamas via the Sinai Peninsula revealed an element of the group's supply infrastructure.[119]

Seeking to emulate Hizbullah's successful use of rockets, Hamas has looked to develop its own missile force to deter and, when needed, fire at Israel. To this end, it has obtained missile expertise from Iran and Hizbullah. The IRGC commander Mohammad Ali Jafari boasted in 2012 that 'we are honoured to announce that we gave them the technology of how to make *Fajr*-5 missiles and now they have their hands on plenty of them'.[120] In 2017, Nasrallah publicly claimed that Hizbullah had 'transferred arms, including *Kornet* missiles, to Gaza'.[121] However, owing to the difficulty of supply and its own technical and military limitations, Hamas's arsenal is of considerably lower quality and size than Hizbullah's, consisting mainly of domestically designed and manufactured short-range *Qassam* rockets. Meanwhile, Tehran has concerns about the risk of unwanted escalation should sophisticated Iranian weapons cause significant damage in Israel. Nevertheless, the increased use since 2008 of *Katyusha* rockets, which have greater range and precision than the rudimentary *Qassam*, has been interpreted as the result of greater Iranian and *Hizbullahi* assistance to Hamas, and Hamas's improved technical skills.[122]

Yet the relationship has also produced unmet expectations and frustrations, and suffered setbacks. In contrast to its partners, Hamas has shown flexibility with Iran's adversaries, accepting indirect negotiations with Israel. It has also preserved relationships with both Turkey and Qatar, its other two sponsors, out of ideological alignment, as well as the need to balance the influence of Iran and Syria.

When Hizbullah or Hamas were engaged in direct conflict with Israel (in 2006 for the former, and 2009, 2012, 2014 and 2018 for the latter), the other party was not expected, nor apparently directed, to join the fighting, besides symbolic displays of solidarity. Indeed, both are highly mindful of the expectations and tolerance levels of their own constituencies, and the risks of unwanted regional escalation. However, this past behaviour does not necessarily mean that Hamas or Hizbullah would act similarly in the case of a full-blown regional conflict involving Iran.

The biggest indication of these complex calculations governing the relationship was the break between Hamas and its partners over the Syrian conflict, which demonstrated latent sectarian and political tensions. Hamas showed sympathy with the Syrian revolution in 2011: its Syrian Muslim Brotherhood counterpart was a key member of the rebellion and its two other patrons, Turkey and Qatar, became its main sponsors. In 2012, Ismail Haniyah, Hamas's then prime minister, endorsed the anti-Assad effort, as did Khaled Mashal, the Hamas chief in Damascus, thereby attracting the ire of Iran and Hizbullah.[123] Many Hamas fighters joined the radical Islamist Aknaf Beit al-Maqdis Brigade, and participated in the battles in Damascus against Assad and his allies alongside Syrian rebels.[124]

Despite close relations with Hamas, Hizbullah and Iran have never developed full command and control over the Palestinian movement and apparently did not attempt to splinter the organisation from within for its behaviour regarding Syria; instead, they imposed punishments on Hamas by decreasing and denying funding and other types of support while keeping the door open for future rapprochement. As a result, the Hamas office in Damascus was closed in 2012 and many Hamas leaders left Beirut in 2013; most settled in Qatar and Turkey. In 2013, Musa Abu Marzouq, a senior Hamas official, revealed the extent of the relationship: 'Iran used to be the most supportive state to Hamas in all aspects: money, arms and training. We don't deny this ... Our position on Syria affected relations with Iran. Its support for us never stopped, but the amounts [of money] were significantly reduced.'[125] In the same interview, Marzouq illustrated Hamas's delicate balancing act: 'We never for a moment considered withdrawing from our ties with Iran. On the contrary, we wanted to maintain ties which are in our best interest as well as Iran's.'[126]

Hamas's military wing, the Ezzeddine al-Qassam Brigades, was critical of the decision to part with Iran and Hizbullah, owing both to the material support it received and the deep relationship between their respective military and security cadres.[127] Osama Hamdan, a long-serving Hamas official in Beirut and the organisation's primary interlocutor with Hizbullah, was similarly opposed to this move.[128] Hamas's military officials understood that no other sponsor could provide the types and amount of military assistance that Iran and Hizbullah did.

This rupture with Iran ultimately weakened Hamas. It had wagered that the Muslim Brotherhood's victory in Egypt in 2012 would substitute Cairo as its patron and provide Hamas with an alternative source of strategic depth; this bet collapsed with the 2013 coup that unseated then-president Muhammad Morsi and brought to power the military, which considered Hamas a threat. While Turkish and Qatari political

"THE BREAK BETWEEN HAMAS AND ITS PARTNERS OVER THE SYRIAN CONFLICT DEMONSTRATED LATENT SECTARIAN AND POLITICAL TENSIONS"

and financial support replaced Iranian aid, it did not include military assistance. Both countries were also imperfect patrons: they had Western allies to placate and could not afford to fully antagonise Israel.

The 2013 coup in Egypt, the defeat of the Syrian insurgency and other regional shifts since 2016 have altered once again Hamas's strategic calculations. The Palestinian movement's Turkish and Qatari patrons de-prioritised the fight against the Assad regime and are engaged in competition with Saudi Arabia and the United Arab Emirates; as a result, Ankara and Doha have sought closer ties with Tehran. Consequently, Hamas has sought to rebuild ties with Iran and Hizbullah to restore previous levels of support, and asked for their help to repair relations with the Assad regime, which remains recalcitrant because of Hamas's disloyalty and its Muslim Brotherhood affiliation.

Tellingly, it took a reshuffle in the Hamas leadership to initiate the rapprochement, with Mashal, who endorsed the Syrian rebellion, being sidelined in 2016. The new leadership includes more radical military commanders, such as Yahya Sinwar and Saleh al-Arouri, with long-term and clear ties to Hizbullah. Mindful of its need to emphasise its pro-Palestinian credentials and demonstrate magnanimity, Hizbullah advocated for reconciliation with Hamas and opened the way to Tehran after years of estrangement.[129]

Table 2.6: **Hamas and Palestinian Islamic Jihad: relationship with Iran and assessment of strategic utility**

Group	Ideological affinity	Strategic convergence	Political expediency	Transactional value	Strategic value for Iran	Other 'patrons'	Assessment
Hamas	●●	●●	●●	●●	●●	Yes	Strategic ally
Palestinian Islamic Jihad	●●	●●●	●●●	●●●	●●	Yes	Strategic ally

Source: IISS   ●●● High   ●● Medium   ● Low

Hamas officials had consistently adopted a conciliatory line toward Hizbullah: Musa Abu Marzouq insisted in 2013 that 'there was never any real disagreement or crisis with Hizbullah'.[130] In August 2017, Sinwar, the leader of Hamas in Gaza, reported positively on progress: 'Relations with Iran are excellent and Iran is the largest supporter of the [Izz al-Din al-Qassam] Brigades with money and arms … The relationship today is developing and returning to what it was in the old days.'[131] A primary promoter of reconciliation within Hamas has been Arouri, a founding commander of the Izz al-Din al-Qassam Brigades and deputy political leader. In 2017, Arouri conducted a high-profile visit to Tehran, meeting with national-security and IRGC officials, in the hope of securing a resumption of assistance to Hamas.[132] *Hizbullahi* and, at a later stage, direct Iranian assistance, slowly resumed afterwards.

Palestinian Islamic Jihad

In contrast to Hamas, Palestinian Islamic Jihad (PIJ) has been an early and considerably more reliable partner of Iran and Hizbullah. The smaller, more radical Gaza-based organisation has eschewed Hamas's mass-movement, political-party and service-geared orientation to adopt a vanguard posture, prioritising the fight against Israel over domestic politics and regional engagement. Its founder, Fathi Shikaki, was an early Arab admirer of Ayatollah Khomeini and his brand of radical Islamist politics; in 1979, he authored a book entitled *Khomeini, the Islamic Solution and the Alternative*. Shikaki spent his years in exile in Damascus, building close relations with Hizbullah, Iran and the Syrian government before Hamas attracted their attention and active support. After his assassination in 1995, his successor Ramadan Shallah maintained the same course, living in Damascus and obtaining Iranian support for the PIJ's operations.

As such, the PIJ has more frequently embraced violent tactics against Israel and has refused to formally accept any indirect negotiations with the Jewish state or consider formal long-term ceasefires as alternatives to peace. This uncompromising rejectionist attitude and its loyalty regardless of regional developments have ingratiated the PIJ leadership with Hizbullah and Iran. Furthermore, PIJ leaders have lived in Damascus and in Hizbullah-controlled areas in Lebanon, and received training and funding from the group.

Practically, the PIJ obtains almost all the benefits extended to Hamas, though on a smaller scale. One difference is its rocket arsenal. The PIJ appears to have de-prioritised this capability, perhaps because of its limited capacity to maintain and deploy such weapons. Both Hizbullah and Iran see the PIJ as politically less valuable because of its low popularity, but operationally easier to manage, as well as a good check on Hamas.

Harakat al-Sabireen

Where Iran and Hizbullah lack organic alliances and operate in restrictive circumstances, they appear to conduct a diversification strategy driven by opportunism and the need to plan for contingencies. The emergence of Harakat al-Sabireen in 2014 provides a window into Iranian and *Hizbullahi* thinking. Hisham Salem, a disgruntled PIJ commander who reportedly converted to Shi'ism and recruited other converts, as well as Sunni fighters, leads the small Gaza-based movement and has obtained limited financial and material support from Hizbullah and Tehran.[133] According to Gaza-based sources, Iran and Hizbullah began supporting this new group in order to signal to Hamas and the PIJ their capacity to adapt and, if needed, diversify their alliances and support spoilers.[134]

Foreign operations: influence and punishment

A key capability Hizbullah has developed in the service of Iran is its foreign-operations arms. With the exception of global jihadi groups such as al-Qaeda and ISIS, Hizbullah's ability to operate worldwide and strike hard and soft Israeli, Saudi, US and other targets distinguishes it from other militant groups.

The importance given to this capability is reflected by the seniority of the leadership of the ESO, the unit

Table 2.7: Lebanese Hizbullah: relationship with Iran and assessment of strategic utility

Group	Ideological affinity	Strategic convergence	Political expediency	Transactional value	Strategic value for Iran	Other 'patrons'	Assessment
Lebanese Hizbullah	●●●	●●●	●●●	●●●	●●●	No	State organ/strategic and ideological ally

Source: IISS ●●● High ●● Medium ● Low

dedicated to this effort, which from 1982 to 2008 was headed by Imad Mughniyah, Hizbullah's de facto second-in-command. After his assassination, his brother-in-law Mustafa Badreddine took charge until his death in 2016, after which the portfolio was handed to Talal Hamiyah.[135] The ESO is understood to report directly to Hassan Nasrallah in Lebanon and to Qasem Soleimani in Iran.

Iran and Hizbullah have used this capability for common purposes, though at times the interests of one of the two parties have dictated its activities. Lebanese Hizbullah operatives have been implicated in Iranian-directed operations since the early 1980s. Hizbullah has operated as a subcontractor, either conducting the attacks or providing support for them. During this time, Iran's revolution-exporting agenda used Hizbullah to mobilise and recruit Shia citizens in Bahrain, Kuwait and Saudi Arabia. Much of its activities across the Gulf region in the 1980s were punishment for the Gulf states' financial support for Saddam Hussein during the Iran–Iraq War. This included, for instance, attacks against Western embassies in Kuwait and a failed attack on the Kuwaiti ruler in 1983.[136]

Hizbullah's hostage-taking, aircraft-hijacking and assassination activities in Lebanon and in Western countries were also designed to punish Western states for their political support for and arms sales to Iraq, as well as to settle scores. For example, Hizbullah's activities in France were reportedly tied in part to the Eurodif dispute, concerning a US$1bn loan made by the Shah to a French company that Tehran sought to recover.[137]

From the 1990s, reflecting both its and Iran's growth, Hizbullah became more strategic in its use of foreign operations. Over time, the implicit threat, based on the extensive if nebulous Hizbullah network, evolved into a deterrent. The knowledge that Hizbullah could hit soft and hard targets in countries abroad was believed by its and Iran's leadership to be an element of deterrence and a constraint on the calculations and behaviour of Israel and the US. Hizbullah's ability to strike Israeli targets abroad was a method used by the group to punish the Jewish state and force it to abide by Hizbullah's rules on the Lebanese battlefield. For example, in 1992, the bombing of the Israeli embassy in Argentina was likely retaliation for the assassination months earlier of Abbas al-Musawi, then-secretary-general of Hizbullah.[138]

Since the 1990s, Hizbullah has also served as subcontractor for several Iranian operations. In 1996, it provided training and logistical support for the suicide bombing in Khobar, Saudi Arabia.[139] The attack was reportedly ordered by the IRGC; its motives remain unclear, and include either an attempt to stymie an ongoing Saudi–Iranian rapprochement or retaliation for US sanctions passed in 1995. Its main architect, Ahmed al-Moghassil, a Beirut-based Saudi citizen who headed the military wing of Hizbullah al-Hijaz, a proxy outfit in Saudi Arabia, found refuge in Iran and later Lebanon, where he was arrested and delivered to the Saudi intelligence services in 2015.[140] More recently, Iran sought to employ Hizbullah to retaliate against the suspected Israeli assassination of Iranian scientists involved in the nuclear programme between 2010 and 2012, which culminated in the bombing in Bulgaria in 2012 of Israeli tourists.[141] Assassinations of Iranian scientists immediately ended, suggesting that Iran was able to deter Israel.

At times, however, Hizbullah's foreign operations have served its own objectives more than Iran's. After the assassination of Imad Mughniyah in 2008, Hizbullah reportedly sought retaliation and mounted several attempts against Israeli targets; most failed.[142]

Strategic assessment

As a rare, tangible regional achievement, the strategic and ideological value that Hizbullah represents for Iran is difficult to overstate. Hizbullah has allowed it to succeed where it would have likely failed on its own.

As detailed above, three sets of capabilities make the Lebanese Shia organisation a vital instrument of Iran's security policy: its missile arsenal, its regional expeditionary force, and its regional and foreign operations. All three efforts were funded, in full or in large part, and guided by Iran over four decades, and all three meet Iran's strategic requirements: deterrence against Israel, the mentoring and management of non-state partners across the Arab world as part of Iran's asymmetric toolbox, and the ability to strike against soft and hard targets abroad with plausible deniability and at low cost. This triad amounts to strategic depth unique among Middle Eastern states, regional relevance and negotiating tools as a new Middle Eastern balance emerges, and escalatory options against conventionally superior regional rivals.

Fundamentally, Hizbullah validates Iran's ideological outlook and narratives, bridging the gap with the Arab world, asserting anti-Israeli credentials and proving the inspirational influence of the Iranian revolution's ideals. As the embodiment of

"HIZBULLAH IS MORE AKIN TO A TRUSTED JUNIOR PARTNER AND A BROTHER-IN-ARMS FOR IRAN THAN A PROXY"

Muqawamah (Resistance), Hizbullah plays a central role in Iranian strategic designs. Though the Syrian civil war damaged the ideological self-portrayal of Hizbullah, its transformation into an expeditionary military force and its prioritisation of the war in Syria reveal the extent to which its security behaviour is shaped by Iran's own priorities.

The near-perfect alignment of their strategic objectives in the past and at present, and the certainty that Hizbullah would rise to Iran's defence during a regional conflict, mean that Tehran does not seek to increase its control over the group. In this sense, Hizbullah is more akin to a trusted junior partner and a brother-in-arms than a proxy.

Indeed, what matters beyond Hizbullah's capabilities is the nature of the relationship between Hizbullah and Iran. Their relations are reciprocal, and are based in ideology as much as mutual benefit. They are at once highly institutionalised, guaranteeing sustainability, and highly personalised, ensuring proximity and responsiveness. The long history and close ties between the two leaderships give Hizbullah, the junior partner, oversized influence in Iranian decision-making on Arab matters, as demonstrated by Hizbullah's role in the strategic planning and command and control of the intervention in Syria. Iran's main red line for Hizbullah seems to be that it is free to pursue its own interests as long as they do not contradict or clash with

Iran's: for example, Iran does not want to be led into a conflict with Israel or the US because of unwanted escalation initiated by Hizbullah.

Iran has shown respect and deference toward Hizbullah's domestic political choices intended to secure its armed status – the two partners' shared and ultimate priority. Iranian leaders have generally adopted a low profile in Lebanon, and have refrained from demanding that Hizbullah enact a formal takeover of the Lebanese state or pursue revolutionary and Islamist policies. Iran has accepted that Hizbullah, in order to navigate domestic politics and secure political support, will not try to enforce onto others Tehran's Islamist model and will not impose on Lebanese Shia Ayatollah Khamenei as the *marja al-taqlid* (source of emulation) to the detriment of other ayatollahs. A gradual approach, in which Hizbullah's domestic political participation and calibrated political coercion generate influence over Lebanese institutions, is seen as preferable, while a more assertive approach could jeopardise Hizbullah's armed status.

Divergences over tactics and resources have emerged, however. At times, Iran and Hizbullah have parted on regional, albeit secondary, issues. Hassan Nasrallah condemned the coup in 2013 against Egyptian president Morsi, a member of the Muslim Brotherhood, while Khamenei welcomed it. Nasrallah later apologised for parting with the ayatollah.[143] In Syria, Hizbullah is alleged to have been sceptical about Iran's encouragement of Russian intervention but ultimately assented to Tehran's decision. During the early stages of the battle for Aleppo in 2016, Mustafa Badreddine reportedly resisted a demand by Qasem Soleimani to send 1,000 troops, sending instead 500 because of limited resources and competing priorities. Hizbullah also resisted working with the Syrian armed forces out of contempt and distrust borne of a contentious history and clashing cultures and ethics, again against Iran's wishes.

Ultimately, however, Hizbullah is a product of its Lebanese environment as much as it is an Iranian creation. The weakness of Lebanese institutions, the country's exposure to Israeli military action and the strategic calculations of the Syrian regime all guarantee that Hizbullah will remain a potent actor, regardless of the level and nature of Iranian support. Hizbullah has grown considerably militarily and politically, to the extent that it does not need Iranian support to dominate Lebanese politics and security, or to preserve its strategic and operational autonomy. That said, without Iranian political impetus, funding and resupply, its regional position and capabilities would be more difficult to sustain and, from a domestic perspective, to justify.

For Iran, there are also limits to Hizbullah's utility. Ironically, the Shia movement has become such a high-value organisation that Iran carefully weighs the risk of involving it in conflict. The stronger Hizbullah becomes, the better its deterrence value, but the greater the cost of defeat in war. Indeed, an accidental war would damage an instrument carefully groomed both to deter but also to fight in a regional contingency. For Iran, the decision to use Hizbullah militarily against Israel or the US, and beyond the mentoring and advisory role it currently plays in the region, would be a high-stakes choice, and would depend on the nature of the threat: it would have to be existential to the regime in Tehran or to the territorial integrity of Iran.

The close alignment between Hizbullah and Iran also means that both are intimately aware of how their relationship can be perceived and interpreted. Caught by surprise by the 2006 war, Tehran was reportedly concerned that Israel would interpret the use of Iranian rockets and missiles by Hizbullah as escalation on its part, as tensions also worsened over its nuclear programme. Accordingly, an overwhelming number of the rockets and missiles fired by Hizbullah were instead sourced from Syria, suggesting that Tehran and Hizbullah have an understanding about the use of major military capabilities.

It is difficult to imagine realistic scenarios that would profoundly change the Iran–Hizbullah relationship in the foreseeable future. Hizbullah's leaders show no concern about Iran's loyalty and commitment, and Iran's support has always been commensurate with Hizbullah's needs and Iran's own requirements. Indeed, Iranian regional policy does not correlate with oil revenues, sanctions and nuclear negotiations; instead, it has a logic and momentum of its own, and Iran has shown a consistent ability to sustain and justify support to Hizbullah. Furthermore, a change in political orientation or regime in Tehran, whether driven by domestic dynamics or foreign intervention, is highly unlikely in the short to medium term.

A test of the relationship might come when there is a change in the leadership in Tehran. Relations between Khamenei and Nasrallah are notoriously strong, and are sustained institutionally and ideologically in both countries by their subordinates. Only a few in the Iranian system consider that the reputational, political and financial cost of supporting Hizbullah generates unacceptable domestic and regional backlash. However, it cannot be assumed that Khamenei's successor will view and value the

relationship in the same manner. A bigger test would be the collapse of the Iranian regime, an unlikely scenario at this point. Even so, the resulting loss of funding and political sponsorship would substantively weaken the Lebanese movement and force it to redefine its own priorities. Hizbullah's survival and political relevance would probably not be affected, but its standing would.

In Lebanon, Hizbullah faces constraints on its activities. Its involvement in the Syrian civil war and its regional activities have been controversial and deeply damaging to its domestic standing. Hizbullah is blamed by its political rivals for the worsening political and economic situation inside Lebanon, and for tensions with traditional Arab and Western partners, who have underwritten the country's economic stability and extended political assistance to Beirut. Criticism has

> ## "IT IS DIFFICULT TO IMAGINE REALISTIC SCENARIOS THAT WOULD PROFOUNDLY CHANGE THE IRAN– HIZBULLAH RELATIONSHIP IN THE FORESEEABLE FUTURE"

also emerged from within Hizbullah's Shia community, which has been the target of Sunni jihadi attacks, feels alienated from other Lebanese constituencies and has suffered significant human wartime losses. Indeed, the cost for Hizbullah of covering the health and pension benefits of the veterans and of the families of the combatants killed in action in Syria reportedly surpasses US$50m per year.[144]

Yet Hizbullah has been able to manage, subdue and dismiss such criticism. It has repressed dissent from within its community, used its military successes in Syria to retrospectively validate its engagement there and silence its critics, and used its political engagement to avoid any political pressure. Indeed, the May 2018 national elections demonstrated Hizbullah's continuing hold over the Lebanese Shia community and illustrated the political weakening of its rivals. In such conditions, Hizbullah does not see an organised threat within Lebanon anymore. Its rivals have been weakened and state institutions are either penetrated, complicit or unable to constrain it.

Nevertheless, Hizbullah is not insensitive to the perceptions of its Lebanese environment. It has demonstrated awareness of the wide popular and political rejection of another war with Israel, refraining from retaliating against Israeli attacks against Hizbullah and Iranian targets in Syria to avoid a full-blown war.

Military considerations are also at play: still recovering from its intervention in Syria, Hizbullah is not yet ready for a two-front war, and is instead focusing on building military infrastructure in southern Syria and on regenerating its forces inside Lebanon.

Much will depend on how Iran and Hizbullah decide to organise and manage their presence inside Syria. With Assad's position currently unthreatened, it is likely that both would prefer to draw down a sizeable number of troops, leaving in place senior commanders and trainers to oversee the network of militias that they already sponsor and the new supply routes they are putting in place. Such calculations are made more complex by the need to adapt to and manoeuvre around Moscow's preference to rebuild Syria's conventional military under Assad's command, as well as by the priority given to countering the explicitly anti-Iran posture of US forces in northeastern Syria.

A significant question is whether the much-discussed Hizbullah 'model' can be replicated elsewhere. The distinctive features of this model are:

- a well-armed militia operating alongside, as well as separate from, state institutions;
- a mix of persuasion and coercion that enshrines its armed status in national frameworks;
- maintaining total autonomy on decisions of war and peace;
- pursuing its own force development and operational plans.

Iranian officials such as the IRGC's late Major-General Hossein Hamadani stated their intent to apply this model in Syria, and Shia organisations across the Middle East have shown rhetorical interest in adopting it. However, specific circumstances have allowed Hizbullah to attain its current status in Lebanon: a weak state lacking legitimacy and reach; a large, mostly homogenous and highly mobilised Shia community; a sectarian distribution of power that allows a united sect to block policymaking; a clear and proven threat in Israel; and committed external backers with a common agenda.

These conditions do not exist elsewhere at present. In Syria, the reassertion of power by the Assad regime, Russia's security interests, the small size of the Shia community, and the high costs of building and sustaining a Hizbullah-like organisation combine against this aspiration. A looser network, such as the one Iran has established in Syria since 2016, is a more realistic, more flexible and less costly approach. In Iraq, the fragmented nature of Shia politics is an obstacle to a Hizbullah-like model, but Iran has been able to diversify its investment in Shia militias and political factions in a way that secures its influence there. Ultimately, Iran's strategies have been opportunistic and country-specific, recognising that the Hizbullah model is an exception that is unlikely to succeed elsewhere – and that it is not necessarily needed in order to secure its interests in other regional arenas.

Hizbullah has become a fully fledged regional actor, offering a valuable range of services to Iran. However, mobilising, directing and supporting logistically and operationally a Shia 'foreign legion',[145] an often-discussed concept that has been referred to by none other than Nasrallah himself,[146] remains beyond Hizbullah's capacity at this point and would require active IRGC supervision, funding and logistical capabilities. Nevertheless, Hizbullah and the IRGC are likely studying the feasibility of such a semi-permanent, multinational force, which they have the capability and experience to deliver.

Notes

1   Fawwaz Traboulsi, 'The Crisis of the Politics of Mumana'ah: Statehood and Participation', Heinrich Böll Stiftung, 3 March 2014, https://lb.boell.org/en/2014/03/03/crisis-politics-mumanaah-statehood-participation.

2   'Kuchaktarin tahdidi alayh-e iran "ta'm-e talkhi" baraye motajavezan khahad dasht' [The smallest threat against Iran will leave a bitter taste for the aggressors], Fars News, 16 November 2008, https://www.farsnews.com/news/8708260065.

3   H.E. Chehabi, Distant relations: Iran and Lebanon in the last 500 years (London: I.B. Tauris, 2006).

4   Arash Reisinezhad, The Shah of Iran, the Iraqi Kurds, and the Lebanese Shia (Basingstoke: Palgrave Macmillan, 2018), pp. 143–312.

5   Joseph Alagha, Hizbullah's Documents: From the 1985 Open Letter to the 2009 Manifesto (Amsterdam: Amsterdam University Press, 2011), pp. 39–62.

6   Fouad Ajami, The Vanished Imam: Musa al Sadr and the Shia of Lebanon (London: I.B. Tauris, 1986), pp. 52–152; Reisinezhad, The Shah of Iran, the Iraqi Kurds, and the Lebanese Shia, pp. 143–312; Augustus Richard Norton, Amal and the Shi'a: Struggle for the Soul of Lebanon (Austin: University of Texas, 1987), pp. 37–83; Chehabi, Distant relations: Iran and Lebanon in the last 500 years, pp. 180–98.

7   Mohammad Ataie, 'Revolutionary Iran's 1979 Endeavor in Lebanon', Middle East Policy Journal, vol. 20, no. 2, 2013,

https://www.mepc.org/revolutionary-irans-1979-endeavor-lebanon.

8 Haleh Vaziri, 'Iran's Involvement in Lebanon: Polarization and Radicalization of Militant Islamic Movements', *Journal of South Asian and Middle Eastern Studies*, vol. 16, no. 2, Winter 1992, p. 4.

9 Chehabi, *Distant relations: Iran and Lebanon in the last 500 years*, p. 216.

10 Magnus Ranstorp, *Hizballah in Lebanon: the politics of the Western hostage crisis* (London: Macmillan Press, 1997), pp. 79–80.

11 'Bitter rivals: Iran and Saudi Arabia', PBS Frontline, 20 and 27 February 2018, https://www.pbs.org/wgbh/frontline/film/bitter-rivals-iran-and-saudi-arabia/transcript.

12 Alagha, *Hizbullah's Documents: From the 1985 Open Letter to the 2009 Manifesto*, pp. 39–40.

13 Ranstorp, *Hizballah in Lebanon: the politics of the Western hostage crisis*, pp. 116–30.

14 Jason Wimberly, 'Wilayat al-Faqih in Hizballah's Web of Concepts: A Perspective on Ideology', *Middle Eastern Studies*, vol. 51, no. 5, pp. 687–710.

15 Melani Cammett, *Compassionate Communalism: Welfare and Sectarianism in Lebanon* (Ithaca, NY: Cornell University Press, 2014), pp. 58–114; Chehabi, *Distant relations: Iran and Lebanon in the last 500 years*, pp. 259–86.

16 Eric Lob, 'Construction Jihad: state-building and development in Iran and Lebanon's Shi'i Territories', *Third World Quarterly*, vol. 39, no. 11, May 2018, pp. 2103–25.

17 Kamran Taremi, 'At the Service of Hizbollah: The Iranian Ministry of Construction Jihad in Lebanon, 1988–2003', *Politics, Religion and Ideology*, vol. 16, nos. 2–3, 2015, pp. 248–62.

18 United Nations Security Council, 'Resolution 1559', 2 September 2004, http://unscr.com/en/resolutions/1559.

19 Ronen Bergman, 'The Hezbollah Connection', *New York Times Magazine*, 10 February 2015, https://www.nytimes.com/2015/02/15/magazine/the-hezbollah-connection.html.

20 'Facts and figures about 2006 Israel–Hezbollah war', *Deutsche Presse Agentur*, 12 July 2007, https://reliefweb.int/report/lebanon/background-facts-and-figures-about-2006-israel-hezbollah-war.

21 Interview with Western intelligence official, October 2018.

22 See Chapter Three, 'Syria'.

23 UN Security Council, 'Baabda Declaration issued by the National Dialogue Committee', 11 June 2012, https://www.securitycouncilreport.org/atf/cf/%7B65BFCF9B-6D27-4E9C-8CD3-CF6E4FF96FF9%7D/Lebanon%20S%202012%20477.pdf.

24 'Man Accused of Attempt on Harb's Life "Killed in Syria"', Naharnet.com, 26 May 2014, http://www.naharnet.com/stories/en/132315.

25 'Sayyed Nasrallah: The Road to Al-Quds Passes through Qalamoun, Zabadani, Homs…', *Almanar*, 10 July 2015, http://syriatimes.sy/index.php/news/regional/18686-sayyed-nasrallah-the-road-to-al-quds-passes-through-qalamoun-zabadani-homs.

26 Ben Hubbard and Anne Barnard, 'Deadly Bombing in Beirut Suburb, a Hezbollah Stronghold, Raises Tensions', *New York Times*, 2 January 2014, https://www.nytimes.com/2014/01/03/world/middleeast/Beirut-Hezbollah-explosion.html.

27 Nicholas Blanford, *Warriors of God: Inside Hezbollah's Thirty-Year Struggle Against Israel* (New York: Random House, 2011), pp. 64–70.

28 General Charles C. Krulak, 'The Strategic Corporal: Leadership in the Three Block War', *Marines Magazine*, January 1999, http://www.au.af.mil/au/awc/awcgate/usmc/strategic_corporal.htm.

29 Amnesty International, 'Unlawful Killings During Operation Grapes of Wrath', July 1996, https://www.amnesty.org/download/Documents/168000/mde150421996en.pdf.

30 Interview with former Arab officials, July 2018.

31 Blanford, *Warriors of God: Inside Hezbollah's Thirty-Year Struggle Against Israel*, p. 281.

32 Gal Luft, 'Israel's Security Zone in Lebanon – A Tragedy?', *Middle East Quarterly*, September 2000, https://www.meforum.org/70/israels-security-zone-in-lebanon-a-tragedy.

33 Daniel Sobelman, 'New Rules of the Game. Israel and Hizbollah after the Withdrawal from Lebanon', Jaffee Center for Strategic Studies, Memorandum 69, January 2004, pp. 67–82, http://www.inss.org.il/publication/new-rules-of-the-game-israel-and-hizbollah-after-the-withdrawal-from-lebanon.

34 'Chaim Kaplan et al. v. Hezbollah', Memorandum Opinion, US District Court for the District of Columbia, 23 July 2014, https://ecf.dcd.uscourts.gov/cgi-bin/show_public_doc?2010cv0483-54.

35 Blanford, *Warriors of God: Inside Hezbollah's Thirty-Year Struggle Against Israel*, pp. 301–71.

36 Uzi Rubin, 'Hizballah's Rocket Campaign against Northern Israel: A Preliminary Report', Jerusalem Center for Public Affairs, *Jerusalem Issue Brief*, vol. 6, no. 10, 31 August 2006, http://jcpa.org/article/hizballahs-rocket-campaign-against-northern-israel-a-preliminary-report.

37 'Lessons of the 2006 Israeli–Hezbollah War', 14 November 2007, p. 12, https://csis-prod.s3.amazonaws.com/s3fs-public/legacy_files/files/publication/120720_Cordesman_LessonsIsraeliHezbollah.pdf.

38 Rory McCarthy, 'Hizbullah leader: we regret the two kidnappings that led to war with Israel', *Guardian*, 28 August 2006, https://www.theguardian.com/world/2006/aug/28/syria.israel.

39 'Ahmadinejad's solution: "elimination" of Israel', *Daily Star Lebanon*, 4 August 2006, http://www.dailystar.com.lb/News/Middle-East/2006/Aug-04/72227-ahmadinejads-solution-elimination-of-israel.ashx.

40 Frank Gardner, 'Hezbollah missile threat assessed', BBC News, 3 August 2006, http://news.bbc.co.uk/1/hi/world/middle_east/5242566.stm.

41 Mark William Pontin, 'The Missiles of August', *MIT Technology Review*, 16 August 2006, https://www.technologyreview.com/s/406282/the-missiles-of-august.

42 Rubin, 'Hizballah's Rocket Campaign against Northern Israel: A Preliminary Report'.

43 Steven Erlanger and Richard Oppel, 'A Disciplined Hezbollah Surprises Israel With Its Training, Tactics and Weapons', *New York Times*, 7 August 2006, https://www.nytimes.com/2006/08/07/world/middleeast/07hezbollah.html.

44 Rubin, 'Hizballah's Rocket Campaign against Northern Israel: A Preliminary Report'.

45 Frank Gardner, 'Hezbollah missile threat assessed'.

46 Benjamin Lambeth, 'Air Operations in Israel's War Against Hezbollah: Learning from Lebanon and Getting it Right in Gaza', RAND Corporation, 2011, pp. 49–69, https://www.rand.org/content/dam/rand/pubs/monographs/2011/RAND_MG835.pdf.

47 'Costs of war and recovery in Lebanon and Israel', Reuters, 9 July 2007, https://www.reuters.com/article/us-lebanon-war-cost/factbox-costs-of-war-and-recovery-in-lebanon-and-israel-idUSL0822571220070709.

48 'Casualties of Mideast Wars', *Los Angeles Times*, 8 March 1991, https://www.latimes.com/archives/la-xpm-1991-03-08-mn-2592-story.html.

49 Interview with Western intelligence source, November 2018.

50 'Lebanon – Tour of Hezbollah Frontlines', AP News, 21 July 2015, https://youtu.be/dtziCgcF7I4.

51 Interview with Arab military source, July 2018.

52 Michael Eisenstadt and Kendall Bianchi, 'The ties that bind: Families, clans, and Hizballah's military effectivess', War on the Rocks, 15 December 2017, https://warontherocks.com/2017/12/ties-bind-families-clans-hizballahs-military-effectiveness.

53 Donna Abu-Nasr and Jonathan Ferziger, 'What's Next for Hezbollah After its Syria Adventure?', Bloomberg, 11 December 2018, https://www.bloomberg.com/news/articles/2018-12-11/what-s-next-for-hezbollah-after-its-syria-adventure-quicktake.

54 Interviews with Western and Arab officials and analysts, July 2018, November 2018.

55 Interviews with Syrian militia commanders, September–November 2018.

56 Liz Sly, 'Trump's sanctions on Iran are hitting Hezbollah, and it hurts', *Washington Post*, 18 May 2019, https://www.washingtonpost.com/world/middle_east/trumps-sanctions-on-iran-are-hitting-hezbollah-hard/2019/05/18/970bc656-5d48-11e9-98d4-844088d135f2_story.html?utm_term=.e50f72991958.

57 Parisa Hafezi, 'Iran Guards ready to help rebuild Syria, Hezbollah will not disarm – TV', Reuters, 23 November 2017, https://uk.reuters.com/article/uk-mideast-crisis-iran-guards/iran-guards-ready-to-help-rebuild-syria-hezbollah-will-not-disarm-tv-idUKKBN1DN0RL; 'Piruziha-ye akhir beh ma'na-ye nabudi-ye kamel-e da'esh nist' [The recent victories do not mean the complete destruction of Da'esh], *Fars News*, 22 November 2017, https://www.farsnews.com/news/13960902000221.

58 Blanford, *Warriors of God: Inside Hezbollah's Thirty-Year Struggle Against Israel*, pp. 337–38.

59 Interviews with Western government sources, October–November 2018.

60 Adam Entous, Charles Levinson and Julian E. Barnes, 'Hezbollah Upgrades Missile Threat to Israel', *Wall Street Journal*, 2 January 2014, https://www.wsj.com/articles/hezbollah-upgrades-missile-threat-to-israel-1388707270.

61 Jonathan Lis and Amos Harel, 'Syria Gave Advanced M-600 Missiles to Hezbollah, Defense Officials Claim', *Haaretz*, 5 May 2010, https://www.haaretz.com/1.5116165.

62 David M. Halbfinger and Ronen Bergman, 'A Top Syrian Scientist Is Killed, and Fingers Point at Israel', *New York Times*, 6 August 2018, https://www.nytimes.com/2018/08/06/world/middleeast/syrian-rocket-scientist-mossad-assassination.html.

63 Interview with Western government official, October 2018.

64 '100,000 Qaem missiles in Lebanon trained on Israel: Iran cmdr.', Press TV, 1 July 2016, https://www.presstv.com/Detail/2016/07/01/473c99/Iran-Lebanon-Israel-Hossien-Salami-Qaem-IRGC-Palestinian-Quds-Day; 'Tens of thousands of long-range missiles from different parts of the Muslim world ready to destroy Israel', Mashregh News, 11 July 2016, https://www.mashreghnews.ir/news/597328.

65 Interviews with Arab and Western analysts and officials, November 2006, November 2018.

66 Interviews with Arab officials, November 2018.

67 'Lebanon', CIA World Factbook, https://www.cia.gov/library/publications/the-world-factbook/geos/le.html.

68 Chris Zambelis, 'Hizb Allah's Lebanese Resistance Brigades', *CTC Sentinel*, vol. 7, no. 11, November–December 2014, https://ctc.usma.edu/hizb-allahs-lebanese-resistance-brigades.

69 Interviews with Lebanese analysts and politicians, 2007–10.

70 Naim Qassem, *Hizbullah: The Story from Within* (London: Saqi Press, 2005); Shawn Flanigan and Mounah Abdel-Samad, 'Hezbollah's Social Jihad: Nonprofits as Resistance Organizations', *Middle East Policy*, vol. 16, no. 2, Summer 2009, pp. 122–37, http://www.mepc.org/hezbollahs-social-jihad-nonprofits-resistance-organizations; Joseph Daher, 'Hezbollah, the Lebanese Sectarian State, and Sectarianism', Middle East Institute, 13 April 2017, https://www.mei.edu/publications/hezbollah-lebanese-sectarian-state-and-sectarianism.

71 Blanford, *Warriors of God: Inside Hezbollah's Thirty-Year Struggle Against Israel*, pp. 104–06.

72 Interviews with Western government and Arab sources, July 2018, November 2018.

73 'Lebanese-Canadian gets 5-year term for helping Hezbollah', CBC News, 3 February 2006, https://www.cbc.ca/news/world/lebanese-canadian-gets-5-year-term-for-helping-hezbollah-1.607340.

74 US Department of the Treasury, 'Treasury Sanctions Procurement Agents Of Hizballah Front Company Based In Lebanon With Subsidiaries In The UAE And China', 7 October 2014, https://www.treasury.gov/press-center/press-releases/Pages/jl2562.aspx.

75 US Department of Justice, 'Third Person Sentenced in Scheme to Smuggle Guns to Lebanon is Ordered to Serve 342 Months in Federal Prison', 31 October 2016, https://www.justice.gov/usao-ndia/pr/third-person-sentenced-scheme-smuggle-guns-lebanon-ordered-serve-342-months-federal.

76 Blanford, *Warriors of God: Inside Hezbollah's Thirty-Year Struggle Against Israel*, pp. 331–36.

77 John Kifner, 'Hezbollah Leads Work to Rebuild, Gaining Stature', *New York Times*, 16 August 2006, https://www.nytimes.com/2006/08/16/world/middleeast/16hezbollah.html.

78 Hana Alamuddin, 'Wa'd: The Reconstruction Project for the Southern Suburb of Beirut', in Howayda al-Harithy (ed.), *Lessons in Post-War Reconstruction: Case Studies from Lebanon in the Aftermath of the 2006 War* (London: Routledge, 2010), pp. 46–70.

79 Hanin Ghaddar, 'Hezbollah's Extreme Makeover', *Foreign Policy*, 17 March 2010, https://foreignpolicy.com/2010/03/17/hezbollahs-extreme-makeover-2; Carine Torbey, 'Hezbollah heartlands recover with Iran's help', BBC News, 12 June 2013, https://www.bbc.co.uk/news/world-middle-east-22878198.

80 Torbey, 'Hezbollah heartlands recover with Iran's help'.

81 Magnus Ranstorp, 'The Role of Hizbullah in the Syrian Conflict', in Maximilian Felsch and Martin Wählisch (eds), *Lebanon and the Arab Uprisings: In the eye of the hurricane* (London: Routledge, 2016), pp. 32–49.

82 Interviews with Arab officials, November and December 2018.

83 United Nations Security Council, Resolution 1701 (2006), 11 August 2006, http://unscr.com/en/resolutions/doc/1701.

84 'Land Borders Regiments', Lebanese Army Command, https://www.lebarmy.gov.lb/en/content/land-borders-regiments; British Embassy Beirut, 'Minister Burt lays first stone for a new Lebanese Army Border Training Centre', 29 June 2018, https://www.gov.uk/government/news/minister-burt-in-lebanon-a-new-training-center-for-the-army.

85 European Union External Action, 'Strengthening Lebanon's Border Management for Safety and Security', 29 May 2018, https://eeas.europa.eu/headquarters/headquarters-homepage/45718/strengthening-lebanons-border-management-safety-and-security_en.

86 Matthew Levitt, *Hezbollah: The Global Footprint of Lebanon's Party of God* (London: Hurst and Company, 2013), pp. 165–67; Martin Chulov and Harriet Sherwood, 'Hezbollah suffers heaviest blow in years as commander is shot dead in Beirut', *Guardian*, 4 December 2013, https://www.theguardian.com/world/2013/dec/04/hezbollah-commander-shot-dead-beirut-shia-israel-sunni.

87 US Department of the Treasury, 'Treasury Designates Illicit Russia–Iran Oil Network Supporting the Assad Regime, Hizballah, and HAMAS', 20 November 2018, https://home.treasury.gov/news/press-releases/sm553.

88 'Nasrallah fi arba'in badr al-din amwaluna kasawarikhina tasiluna min iran' [Nasrallah at the forty-day ceremony for Mostafa Badr al-Din: Our money, like our rockets, come from Iran], https://youtu.be/m9ITEu1OObc.

89 'A regional security official with access to current intelligence assessments put Hizbullah's annual income at between US$800 million and US$1 billion, with 70–90% coming from Iran, the amount partly depending on the price of oil.' Samia Nakhoul, 'Special Report: Hezbollah gambles all in Syria', Reuters, 26 September 2013, https://www.reuters.com/article/us-syria-hezbollah-special-report-idUSBRE98P0AI20130926.

90 US Department of Defense, 'Annual Unclassified Report on Military Power of Iran', April 2010, https://fas.org/man/eprint/dod_iran_2010.pdf.

91 Joyce Karam, 'Iran pays Hezbollah $700 million a year, US official says', *National*, 5 June 2018, https://www.thenational.ae/world/the-americas/iran-pays-hezbollah-700-million-a-year-us-official-says-1.737347.

92 Matthew Levitt, *Hezbollah: The Global Footprint of Lebanon's Party of God* (Washington DC: Georgetown University Press, 2013); Matthew Levitt, 'Attacking Hezbollah's Financial Network: Policy Options', Testimony submitted to the House Foreign Affairs Committee, Washington Institute for Near East Policy, 8 June 2017, https://www.washingtoninstitute.org/uploads/Documents/testimony/LevittTestimony20170608.pdf.

93 'Hezbollah says future Israel war could draw fighters from Iran, Iraq, elsewhere', Reuters, 23 June 2017, https://uk.reuters.com/article/uk-mideast-crisis-hezbollah-idUKKBN19E1X6.

94 'Sayyed Hadi Nasrallah: From Birth to Martyrdom', Alahed News, https://english.alahednews.com.lb/44574/385; US Department of State, 'State Department Terrorist Designations of Jawad Nasrallah, al-Mujahidin Brigades, and Hizballah', 13 November 2018, https://www.state.gov/r/pa/prs/ps/2018/11/287318.htm.

95 Ronen Bergman, *Rise and Kill First* (New York: Random House, 2018), pp. 595–609.

96 'Israel: Hezbollah commander Mustafa Badreddine "killed by own men"', BBC News, 21 March 2017, https://www.bbc.co.uk/news/world-middle-east-39339368.

97 'Hezbollah fighters killed in Israeli attack', Al-Jazeera,

19 January 2015, https://www.aljazeera.com/news/middleeast/2015/01/israeli-air-raid-kills-hezbollah-commander-201511816323696o984.html.

98 Matthew Levitt, 'Hezbollah's Procurement Channels: Leveraging Criminal Networks and Partnering with Iran', *CTC Sentinel*, March 2019, https://ctc.usma.edu/hezbollahs-procurement-channels-leveraging-criminal-networks-partnering-iran.

99 James Risen, 'A Region Inflamed: the Hand of Tehran; Hezbollah, in Iraq, Refrains From Attacks on Americans', *New York Times*, 24 November 2003, https://www.nytimes.com/2003/11/24/world/region-inflamed-hand-tehran-hezbollah-iraq-refrains-attacks-americans.html.

100 'The Qayis al-Khazali Papers', Tactical Interrogation Reports 28, 48 and 54, American Enterprise Institute, http://www.aei.org/spotlight/qayis-al-khazali-papers.

101 Interview with US official, October 2018.

102 Michael Knights, 'The Evolution of Iran's Special Groups in Iraq', *CTC Sentinel*, vol. 3, no. 11, November 2010, https://ctc.usma.edu/the-evolution-of-irans-special-groups-in-iraq.

103 Michael R. Gordon, 'Against US Wishes, Iraq Releases Man Accused of Killing American Soldiers', *New York Times*, 16 November 2012, https://www.nytimes.com/2012/11/17/world/middleeast/iraq-said-to-release-hezbollah-operative.html.

104 Babak Dehghanpisheh, 'Special Report: The fighters of Iraq who answer to Iran', Reuters, 12 November 2014, https://www.reuters.com/article/us-mideast-crisis-militias-specialreport/special-report-the-fighters-of-iraq-who-answer-to-iran-idUSKCN0IW0ZA20141112.

105 'Hezbollah man dies on "jihad duty" in Iraq', Al Jazeera, 31 July 2014, https://www.aljazeera.com/news/middleeast/2014/07/hezbollah-man-dies-jihad-duty-iraq-20147302029917675.html.

106 Liz Sly and Suzan Haidamous, 'Lebanon's Hezbollah acknowledges battling the Islamic State in Iraq', *Washington Post*, 16 February 2015, https://www.washingtonpost.com/world/middle_east/lebanons-hezbollah-acknowledges-battling-the-islamic-state-in-iraq/2015/02/16/4448b21a-b619-11e4-bc30-a4e75503948a_story.html.

107 Sune Engel Rasmussen and Felicia Schwartz, 'Israel Broadens Fight Against Iran', *Wall Street Journal*, 15 July 2018, https://www.wsj.com/articles/israel-broadens-fight-against-iran-1531684841?redirect=amp#click=https://t.co/Z6IrXjcs7X.

108 Jonathan Spyer, 'Behind the Lines: Who is Qais al-Khazali, and why should you care?', *Jerusalem Post*, 15 December 2017, https://www.jpost.com/Arab-Israeli-Conflict/Behind-The-Lines-Who-is-Qais-al-Khazali-and-why-should-you-care-518131.

109 'Amadegi-ye "Nojaba" baraye azadsazi-ye Joulan-e Suriyeh; behtar ast e'telaf-e Arabestan soragh-e Iran nayayad' [Harakat al-Nujaba stands ready to liberate Syria's Golan Heights; it would be unwise for Saudi Arabia's coalition to try to attack Iran], *Fars News*, 8 March 2017, https://www.farsnews.com/news/13951218001601.

110 'Hassan Nasrallah za'im milishya "hizb allah" ya'tarifu: a'tham amr fa'altuh fi hayati laysa moharabat isra'il…!' [Hassan Nasrallah, the leader of the Hizballah militia, admits: the greatest thing I've done in my life is not the fight against Israel…!], Radio Sawt Beirut, 27 May 2018, https://twitter.com/SawtBeirut/status/1000880573014052865.

111 Pew Research Center, 'Concerns about Islamic Extremism on the Rise in the Middle East: Negative Opinions of al Qaeda, Hamas and Hezbollah Widespread', 1 July 2014, p. 7, http://assets.pewresearch.org/wp-content/uploads/sites/2/2014/06/PG-2014-07-01-Islamic-Extremism-Full-Report.pdf.

112 US Department of State, State Department Terrorist Designation, 20 October 2016, https://www.state.gov/j/ct/rls/other/des/266473.htm.

113 Interview with Western intelligence official, October 2018.

114 Da'a Suwaydan, Khalil Kawtharani and Ili Hana, 'al-Huthi: mosta'iduna lil-qital ila janib hizb allah did isra'il' [al-Houthi: we are ready to fight alongside Hezbollah against Israel], *Al-Akbar*, 23 March 2018, https://al-akhbar.com/Yemen/246826.

115 Clyde Haberman, 'Israel Expels 400 From Occupied Lands; Lebanese Deploy to Bar Entry of Palestinians', *New York Times*, 18 December 1992, https://www.nytimes.com/1992/12/18/world/israel-expels-400-occupied-lands-lebanese-deploy-bar-entry-palestinians.html.

116 Bergman, *Rise and Kill First*, pp. 420–23.

117 Rola El Husseini, 'Hezbollah and the Axis of Refusal: Hamas, Iran and Syria', *Third World Quarterly*, vol. 31, no. 5, September 2010, p. 811.

118 Rafael Frankel, 'Keeping Hamas and Hezbollah out of a war with Iran', *Washington Quarterly*, vol. 35, no. 4, October 2012, https://doi.org/10.1080/0163660X.2012.725018.

119 Joshua L. Gleis and Benedetta Berti, *Hezbollah and Hamas: A Comparative Study* (Baltimore, MD: Johns Hopkins University Press, 2012), pp. 65–66.

120 Saeed Kamali Dehghan, 'Iran supplied Hamas with Fajr-5 missile technology', *Guardian*, 21 November 2012, https://www.theguardian.com/world/2012/nov/21/iran-supplied-hamas-missile-technology.

121 Jack Khoury and Reuters, 'Nasrallah Admits: Hezbollah Smuggled Advanced Arms Into Gaza', *Haaretz*, 20 November 2017, https://www.haaretz.com/middle-east-news/nasrallah-admits-hezbollah-smuggled-advanced-arms-into-gaza-1.5467043.

122 Mark Mazzetti, 'Striking Deep Into Israel, Hamas Employs an Upgraded Arsenal', *New York Times*, 31 December 2008, https://www.nytimes.com/2009/01/01/world/middleeast/01rockets.html.

123 'Hamas prime minister backs Syrian protests against Assad', *Guardian*, 24 February 2012, https://www.theguardian.com/world/2012/feb/24/hamas-pm-backs-syrian-protests.

124 Nicholas Blanford, 'Hamas switches sides to train Syrian rebels', *Australian*, 6 April 2013, https://www.theaustralian.com.au/news/world/hamas-switches-sides-to-train-syrian-rebels/news-story/6265b0676c034bfff18c8b14f8de6bfd.

125 Elhanan Miller, 'Iran slashed Hamas funding, senior official admits', *Times of Israel*, 16 October 2013, https://www.timesofisrael.com/iran-slashed-hamas-funding-senior-official-admits.

126 *Ibid*.

127 Maren Koss, 'Flexible Resistance: How Hezbollah and Hamas Are Mending Ties', Carnegie Endowment for International Peace, 11 July 2018, https://carnegieendowment.org/2018/07/11/flexible-resistance-how-hezbollah-and-hamas-are-mending-ties-pub-76782.

128 Interview with Arab politician close to Hamas, February 2013.

129 Yasser Okbi and Maariv Hashavua, 'Strengthening alliances: Deputy Hamas chief meets with Nasrallah', *Jerusalem Post*, 16 June 2017, https://www.jpost.com/Arab-Israeli-Conflict/Strengthening-alliances-Deputy-Hamas-chief-meets-with-Nasrallah-497010.

130 Miller, 'Iran slashed Hamas funding, senior official admits'.

131 Nidal al-Mughrabi, 'After Syria fall-out, Hamas ties with Iran restored: Hamas chief', Reuters, 28 August 2017, https://www.reuters.com/article/us-palestinians-hamas-iran/after-syria-fall-out-hamas-ties-with-iran-restored-hamas-chief-idUSKCN1B81KC.

132 'Hamas deputy leader says to continue Iran ties, armed fight', *National*, 23 October 2017, https://www.thenational.ae/world/mena/hamas-deputy-leader-says-to-continue-iran-ties-armed-fight-1.669510.

133 US Department of State, 'State Department Terrorist Designations of Ismail Haniyeh, Harakat al-Sabireen, Liwa al-Thawra, and Harakat Sawa'd Misr (HASM)', 31 January 2018, https://www.state.gov/r/pa/prs/ps/2018/01/277792.htm.

134 Interview with Palestinian politician from Gaza, September 2018.

135 US Department of State, 'Reward Offer for Information on Hizballah Key Leaders Talal Hamiyah and Fu'ad Shukr', 10 October 2017, https://www.state.gov/r/pa/prs/ps/2017/10/274722.htm.

136 Robin Wright, 'The Demise of Hezbollah's Untraceable Ghost', *New Yorker*, 13 May 2016, https://www.newyorker.com/news/news-desk/the-demise-of-hezbollahs-untraceable-ghost.

137 David Styan, *France and Iraq: Oil, Arms and French Policy-Making in the Middle East* (London: I.B. Tauris, 2006), pp. 147–62.

138 Levitt, *Hezbollah: The Global Footprint of Lebanon's Party of God*, pp. 98–102.

139 *Ibid.*, pp. 181–87; Neil A. Lewis, 'Judge Links Iran to '96 Attack in Saudi Arabia', *New York Times*, 23 December 2006, https://www.nytimes.com/2006/12/23/world/middleeast/23khobar.html.

140 Levitt, *Hezbollah: The Global Footprint of Lebanon's Party of God*, pp. 181–207; David D. Kirkpatrick, 'Saudi Arabia Said to Arrest Suspect in 1996 Khobar Towers Bombing', *New York Times*, 26 August 2015, https://www.nytimes.com/2015/08/27/world/middleeast/saudia-arabia-arrests-suspect-khobar-towers-bombing.html.

141 Levitt, *Hezbollah: The Global Footprint of Lebanon's Party of God*, pp. 354–55.

142 Anne Barnard, 'Hezbollah Appears to Acknowledge a Spy at the Top', *New York Times*, 5 January 2015, https://www.nytimes.com/2015/01/06/world/middleeast/hezbollah-appears-to-acknowledge-a-spy-at-the-top-.html.

143 Parvaneh Masoumi, 'The Khamenei–Hezbollah Rift over Egypt's Mohamed Morsi', IranWire, 16 March 2018, https://iranwire.com/en/features/5230.

144 Interviews with Arab politicians, July and December 2018.

145 In 2016, IRGC Brigadier-General Ali Falaki, formerly a commander of one of the Fatemiyoun units in Syria, was the first to refer to this force as the 'Shia Liberation Army', but tellingly this label failed to gain traction inside Iran or abroad. See Fatemiyyun pishgharavol-e nabard-e suriyeh budand [The Fatemiyoun were at the forefront of the battle in Syria], *Fars News*, 18 August 2016, https://www.farsnews.com/news/13950528000439.

146 'Hezbollah says future Israel war could draw fighters from Iran, Iraq, elsewhere'.

CHAPTER THREE

SYRIA

- The Quds Force has played a crucial role in organising and directing a vast array of foreign and domestic militias to save Bashar al-Assad's regime during the Syrian civil war
- Iran is embedding itself in the evolving Syrian government and informal security structures, making its posture flexible, deniable and affordable
- Iran's security investment in Syria is designed to enhance its threat to Israel, counter the presence of the United States there, hedge against Russian policy and ensure a lasting role regardless of the fate of the Assad regime

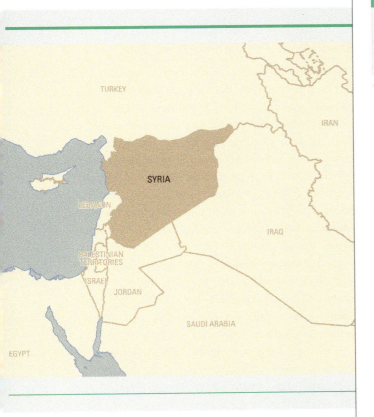

The alliance between Iran and Syria has been one of significant durability and stability, and one that has generated considerable strategic and political returns for both countries. Forged in the 1980s over shared enmity with Saddam Hussein's Iraq, the relationship developed more relevance as Damascus and Tehran sought to challenge a Middle Eastern region shaped and dominated by the United States and its Arab allies.[1] They also used this alliance to face Israel: Syria for advantage in complex negotiations over a potential diplomatic settlement and Iran as part of an ideological commitment against the Jewish state.

While the two countries at times diverged on political preferences, and even engaged in competition, the fact that the alliance has survived American, Arab and Israeli attempts to break it through coercion and enticements strongly suggests deep commitment among Iranian and Syrian security elites. While Iran was always the larger power, its political isolation gave Syria a strong hand in the relationship, allowing it to maintain contact with other Arab and Western states and engage in negotiations with Israel, despite Iranian reservations. Moreover, through its engagement with Tehran, Syria was able to monitor and regulate Iran's involvement in the Levant, and leverage it for its own purposes. In Damascus, the Iranian file was directly

Figure 3.1: **Syria: major events, 1976–2018**

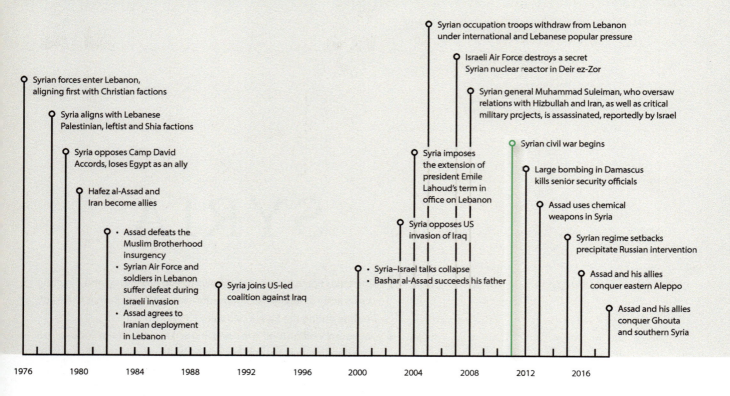

managed by the presidency, with long-serving figures such as Maher al-Assad (the president's brother and commander of the 4th Division and the Republican Guard), Deputy Vice-President for Security Affairs Muhammad Nasif Kheirbek, Hisham Ikhtiyar (a national-security adviser) and Muhammad Suleiman (a special presidential adviser) playing key coordination and logistical roles over decades.

Importantly, Iranian-sponsored Lebanese Hizbullah rose to become a fully fledged pillar of the Iran–Syria alliance, and the Shia militant organisation became a joint project of both countries. Under president Hafez al-Assad (1970–2000), Syria's commitment to Hizbullah was more opportunistic than ideological, seeking to constrain the group at several junctures during Syria's occupation of Lebanon. However, Bashar al-Assad, his son and successor, deepened the relationship during the 2000s as he sought to legitimise his rule in the face of regional headwinds. Syria's withdrawal from Lebanon in 2005, and Hizbullah's military performance against Israel in 2006, proved transformative for the alliance. Syria increasingly depended on Hizbullah to secure its Lebanese interests, while Hizbullah continued to rely on Syria for military supply and strategic depth. Iran's role in the relationship grew in parallel.

Saving Assad, establishing a new front

The Syrian uprising of 2011 and subsequent civil war became the most significant strategic and political challenge for the Iranian-led 'Axis of Resistance' since its inception. It eroded the narrative of unconditional Arab popular support for the Resistance, introduced weaponised sectarianism into an already volatile geopolitical landscape, and pitted Iran and its allies against powerful and wealthy regional actors. The stated intention of the rebellion's leaders was to cut ties with Iran and fundamentally reorient Syrian foreign policy.[2] The insurgency also threatened the supply lines and the strategic depth that Hizbullah depended on. Importantly, it diverted Hizbullah and Iran from their Israel-first focus, resulting in significant reputational and political costs in the Arab world.[3]

Demonstrating a level of embarrassment, but also their initial underestimation of the potency and popularity of the anti-Assad challenge, both Iran and Hizbullah originally denied any military involvement in Syria. In May 2012, a Hizbullah leader stated that the movement 'did not and will not fight in Syria'.[4] Even when Iranian leaders began to acknowledge the presence of Iranian military units in Syria in September 2012, they publicly stressed their non-combatant role.[5]

In fact, Iranian planning for an active counter-insurgency role in Syria started in early 2012. Major-General Qasem Soleimani, the commander of the Quds Force, the expeditionary wing of the Islamic Revolutionary Guard Corps (IRGC), reportedly conducted assessment visits to Lebanon and Syria in late 2011 and early 2012, and is believed to have left concerned about the capacity of the Assad regime to face the revolutionary surge and insurgent pressure. At his request, Brigadier-General Hossein Hamadani, a senior IRGC commander with experience in counter-insurgency and domestic repression, visited Syria and prepared a strategy for how Iran could come to the rescue of the Assad regime and preserve its interests there. He was assisted by Hassan Shateri, an IRGC general serving in a covert capacity in Lebanon. The deployment of small advisory teams, as well as train-and-assist units, followed promptly. The size and nature of this mission became public when 48 IRGC personnel, newly arrived in Damascus and posing as pilgrims, were kidnapped by Syrian rebels in August 2012 (they were later freed as part of a prisoner exchange).[6]

In parallel with Iran, Hizbullah escalated its presence in Syria, although quietly at first in order to manage the domestic fallout of this decision, as well as to expedite its combat role there, concentrating on securing important roads, towns and facilities along the Syria–Lebanon border. 'Since the first day of the crisis in Syria, Sayyed Mustafa Badreddine [senior Hizbullah commander, in charge of the group's Syria operations] was working hard to confront the Takfiris there', noted Hassan Nasrallah, Hizbullah's secretary-general, in 2018.[7] There are reports of Hizbullah casualties as early as 2011, though in small numbers;[8] their identities are difficult to ascertain because of Hizbullah's decision to mask its early involvement in the campaign. By early 2012, *Hizbullahi* commanders and fighters were regularly visiting Syria on reconnaissance, intelligence and liaison missions. The effort was qualitatively significant but relied on small numbers and a targeted approach. There is no evidence that Hizbullah was involved in the direct repression of anti-Assad protesters, but IRGC teams, having contributed to the quashing of the Green Movement in Iran in 2009, offered guidance and support in anti-uprising tactics to the Syrian government.[9]

By mid-2012, the extent and potency of the revolution required a different approach. The dire state of the Syrian armed forces, the growing military organisation of the rebellion and the escalation of Arab, Turkish and Western support for the uprising compelled a joint Iranian–*Hizbullahi* decision to devote considerable resources. President Assad's military forces, ill-prepared for a large-scale domestic revolt, quickly lost territory across the country. The regime's weakness was revealed in full in July 2012, when a bomb exploded during a meeting of Assad's top security leadership, killing several senior officials, including the defence minister, the deputy chief of staff and the chief of the National Security Bureau, and wounding others.[10]

Syrian president Hafez al-Assad receives Iranian minister of foreign affairs Ali Akbar Velayati in Damascus, May 1997

The consultations that led to Tehran and Hizbullah's decision to intervene reveal the dynamic between the Iranian and the *Hizbullahi* leaderships, with the strategic and operational planning intimately coordinated by the two actors. Soleimani informed Hamadani (as he related in his biography) that, per Supreme Leader Ayatollah Ali Khamenei's instruction, 'comprehensive policies of the Resistance Axis in Syria [were] to be under the supervision of Sayyed Hassan Nasrallah', who 'managed all issues related to Syria'.[11] In turn, during a visit to Beirut at an undisclosed date, Nasrallah advised Hamadani that 'Right now, we have to drag [the Assad regime] out of the swamp ... This is the first, and most important strategic step.'[12]

Several Lebanese and Iranian observers and officials credit Nasrallah, in tandem with Qasem Soleimani, for swaying an initially cautious Khamenei and a split Iranian Supreme National Security Council in favour of intervention in Syria.[13] The Supreme Leader was said to be wary about the high costs of a large ground operation and the risks of entrapment in Syria.[14] Nasrallah and Soleimani together argued that the stakes were existential for Hizbullah and that Assad's ouster would considerably weaken Iran's regional reach. Mohammad Esmail Kousari, a former member of parliament and former IRGC general, reported in 2013 a conversation with Nasrallah:

> Sayyed Hassan Nasrallah said that it was about eight or nine months since the Syria issue had started when we went to meet the Supreme Leader in Tehran and we reported that the Syria matter and Bashar Assad's rule was finished. Sayyed Hassan Nasrallah said the Leader at first listened to our reports and finally added: 'Go and do your duty well and both Syria and Assad will remain.'[15]

"AS IRAN AND HIZBULLAH GEARED TOWARD LARGE-SCALE INTERVENTION IN 2012, THEY SHARED ALMOST IDENTICAL POLITICAL AND MILITARY OBJECTIVES"

However, there are reports of operational divergences between Nasrallah and the IRGC. The former allegedly resisted Iranian requests for the deployment of large Hizbullah units until Khamenei made a direct appeal.[16]

Iranian and *Hizbullahi* goals in Syria

As Iran and Hizbullah prepared large-scale intervention in 2012, they shared almost identical political and military objectives. The first set of mostly overlapping goals was primarily, from their standpoint, of a defensive nature: the survival of the Assad regime and control of major urban centres; the military containment and ultimate defeat of the insurgency; the protection or recapture of existing supply lines and the development of alternative ones; and, from 2014, the defeat of the Islamic State, also known as ISIS or ISIL, as it expanded in Iraq and Syria. Another goal was derivative of the others: the defeat of the ambitious Syria projects of Iran's two rival axes in the Middle East: namely, the Qatar–Turkey alliance that supported Sunni political Islamism (and whose stance against Iran mellowed in 2017) and the Saudi–United Arab Emirates partnership, which led the Arab effort to weaken Iran's regional reach. Two immediate objectives were also agreed: the protection of Shia communities inside Syria and securing the Syria–Lebanon border.

In parallel, and as Iran and Hizbullah secured the first sets of goals, they pursued more offensive, if complementary, objectives. The first was the devel-

opment of a network of loyal militias inside Syria to operate alongside and, if needed, independently from the Assad regime; should the regime collapse or act against Iran's own interests, or if its future were subject to negotiations, this capability would ensure Iran's autonomous relevance and centrality. The second was to develop a new defensive and deterrent posture against Israel and the US by investing in the creation of a front against the Jewish state in southern Syria.

Operationally, for Hizbullah these goals translated into four complementary and overlapping war efforts:

- the defence of the Lebanon–Syria border and control over areas inside Syria within its proximity;
- the containment then defeat of Syrian rebel groups in the first phase, and, as Sunni jihadi groups emerged, their defeat even if it meant operating deep inside Syrian territory;
- the concomitant development of a network of allied Syrian militias; and
- the development of a new military infrastructure and new supply routes.

Building a 'Syrian Hizbullah'?

Iran and Hizbullah's initial approach to defeating the insurgency was to identify, organise and direct the array of local communal self-defence militias that had sprung up across Syria. In response to the withdrawal of the Syrian armed forces from numerous regions as a result of military setbacks, loss of personnel or deliberate retrenchment, armed groups of varying size and potency from loyalist as well as minority communities emerged out of fear and the rejection of the revolutionary and Islamist character of the rebellion. In the early years of the war, these groups primarily focused on territorial control and support missions, alongside the Assad regime's security and conventional forces.

These militias developed in a chaotic context, but maintained formal and informal links to the regime's security agencies for legitimacy, guidance and resources. By 2012, a framework emerged to manage these militias: the National Defence Forces (NDF).[17] While united in purpose, the groups lacked unity of command, centralisation of resources, clear definition of mission and delineation of territory. As such, they represented an opportunity for an external patron willing to entice, nurture and shape them. Iran initially relied on its experience in Iraq and Lebanon, where it developed influence primarily outside formal state structures and only later focused on the penetration of state institutions. Indeed, the NDF has never been formally integrated into the Syrian armed forces. Instead, the NDF's status is best understood as a 'civilian' volunteer network. (In this context, a 'civilian' means a person not required for compulsory or reserve military service, who joins an armed group ostensibly subordinate to the state.) In operational terms, the NDF has primarily served as one of many local auxiliary forces across Syria.

It is in this context that Iran and Hizbullah sought to recruit and mobilise partner forces. This joint effort was organic where possible (in ideologically or religiously aligned communities) and opportunistic elsewhere (in politically aligned communities). IRGC Brigadier-General Hamadani was most explicit in what he sought to achieve. In May 2014, reflecting on the progress made in building up local militias loyal to Iran and Hizbullah (which comprised 70,000 Syrian fighters in 128 NDF units), he went as far as declaring that Iran had 'created a second Hizbullah in Syria'.[18] This claim was bombastic given the realities and circumstances of the Syrian civil war, but it reflected the aspirations of some Iranian commanders involved in the war effort, who saw Lebanese Hizbullah – Iran's most capable and paramount ally – as the best template.

In an interview republished after his death in 2015, Hamadani described himself as Qasem Soleimani's representative in Syria, saying that Soleimani had tasked him with transferring knowledge and expertise to the Syrian regime, an objective that would inevitably see him embedded at the highest level of the Assad regime's command structures.[19] However, as Hamadani reported in the same interview, the first two months of his mission in early 2012, which he carried out alongside two Lebanese 'friends', appeared to meet with resistance among Syrian officers. He described the Ba'ath Party personnel that he encountered as having built 'an iron door and steel wall' with Syrian society, eroding their knowledge of local communities. At the time of Iranian intervention, Hamadani described Syria (the Assad regime) as being 'like a sick person who does not know they are ill', and assessing that, at the time of his intervention, '80% of Syria had fallen into the hands of armed groups'.[20] Hamadani prescribed Iran as the cure to Syria's ills.[21] This tension reflected clashing cultures, and pushback in Syrian military circles against a dominant Iranian role, one that Assad himself had reluctantly come to accept. The weakening security forces did not have, however, the latitude, power or resources to counter or shape Iranian intervention.

Hamadani's stated objective in Syria was not only to assert influence inside the regime but also to build forces, modelled on the Iranian Basij ('Mobilise')

IRGC Brigadier-General Hossein Hamadani, who was killed in Syria in 2015

paramilitary militia, to bolster popular support for Assad and, relatedly, form fighting units deeply interconnected with the IRGC command. Mohsen Rezai, a former IRGC commander-in-chief, stated that Hamadani's role in Syria was similar to that of IRGC commander Ahmad Motevasselian's role in Lebanon, saying 'in the same way that Motevasselian in 1982 went to Syria and then to Lebanon to transfer knowledge to form waves against occupation from which Hizbullah emerged, Hamadani's knowledge organised tens of thousands of Syria's young generation'.[22]

Hamadani himself acknowledged that the creation of militia groups modelled on the structure of the Basij was a major goal of Iran's presence in Syria. His refusal to allow the Syrian Army to integrate these units into the regular military strongly indicates that this strategy was not only to build support for Assad in the short term, but in the long term to create a clear constituency for Iranian influence by creating its own networks outside of regime control. Hamadani said in his final interview that in forming a popular front, Iran was 'accused of trying to create another army'. He added that Iran was 'asked to place [these groups] under the control of the regular army', but that 'we told [the Syrian government and military] that it wouldn't be a good move, and that they should strengthen the army through regular recruitment. We argued that what made the Basij force special was the fact that it was comprised solely of volunteers. It is also a cost-effective and efficient force. They were clueless about all of this until they saw the results.'[23]

Hamadani's ambitious project, though primarily meant to help Assad win the war, was intended to secure lasting Iranian influence regardless of his fate or preferences. The network of militias could be used to secure objectives – such as control of strategic territory or assets – in case Assad himself were weakened,

Syrian pro-regime forces fire a heavy machine gun mounted on a technical vehicle, during the advance towards rebel-held positions west of Aleppo, November 2017

ousted or killed. It would be flexible enough to adapt to changes on the battlefield and to regional politics, growing or shrinking as required. It could be used to pursue objectives that ran counter to the interests of Assad and Russia, his other patron. And it would guarantee political and diplomatic relevance for Iran during negotiations over Syria's future.

Developing militias

Early on, Iran and Hizbullah approached communities that shared their communal and ideological affiliations. In the first instance, this meant, in particular, the small and scattered Syrian Twelver Shia community (which amounted to less than 2% of the Syrian population). Shi'ites mostly lived in small towns and villages along the Syria–Lebanon border, outside the cities of Aleppo, Damascus, Deraa, Homs and Idlib, and in small settlements of mostly recently converted Shi'ites in Deir ez-Zor and Raqqa.[24] Given their exposure and geographical dispersal, these communities quickly became vulnerable to rebel and, later, jihadi attacks. For example, the isolated village of Hatla in Deir ez-Zor governorate suffered a massacre of Shi'ite residents by Islamist rebels in June 2013.[25] Such threats and Shia community pressure compelled Hizbullah to dedicate substantial resources to defending them. Culturally and politically aligned with Hizbullah even before the uprising, Syrian Shi'ites welcomed this assistance as the Syrian state unravelled or withdrew. This made inroads into the community relatively easy for Hizbullah. Hizbullah had begun recruiting, training and organising fighters from these villages in 2012, often exporting its own institutions to do so. The Imam al-Mahdi Scouts, the Jihad al-Binaa construction arm and various Hizbullah social providers and charities opened branches in or extended services to many of these villages.[26] This soft-power appeal, combined with Hizbullah's military build-up, amounted to a kind of 'whole-of-government' approach, rather than the more low-key, opportunistic ways adopted in more challenging or hostile areas. Many Syrian Shi'ites primarily joined Hizbullah itself or militias intimately tied to it; a smaller number of more secular Shi'ites joined either the regime's armed groups or allied militias, such as the Syrian Social Nationalist Party's Eagles of the Whirlwind.[27]

Of the several Syrian military factions, Liwa al-Baqir stands out because of its size, reach and institutional links to Iran. This militia, founded in 2012 by Khalid Ali al-Hassan and his siblings in the Aleppo governorate, grew to include 3,000–5,000 fighters, recruited primarily from the Baqara and Aqidat tribes. Reflecting tribal complexity, its fighters are both Sunni and Shia, including recent converts to Shi'ism. However, its leadership is mostly Shia and its spiritual reference is Mahmoud al-Jubouri, a senior cleric who serves as the director of the Imam Mahdi Center in Sayyida Zainab, in the southern suburbs of Damascus. Liwa al-Baqir has emerged as a serious military actor in northern Syria, taking part in battles in Aleppo and Deir ez-Zor provinces alongside the IRGC and Hizbullah. Indeed, its leadership has privileged relations with both: it has been courted by senior Iranians, such as Ali Akbar Velayati (senior adviser to the Supreme Leader) and Qasem Soleimani, has appeared in the presence of senior Hizbullah commanders and has made high-profile visits to Iran.[28] It also plays a central role in facilitating Iranian outreach to other Syrian actors, including non-Shia groups. It notably played a key role in organising large meetings of tribal figures in 2017 and 2018 to enroll them in the effort to oppose the US and Western presence in Syria.[29] In April 2018, it issued a formal call for jihad against US and Turkish troops. The militia has played a front-line role in this: in May 2017, dozens of its fighters were killed during an advance toward the US base of Tanf

(l) Declaration of jihad against the US and allied forces in Syria by the Baqara tribe and Liwa al-Baqir, April 2018

(r) Iranian Senior Adviser Ali Akbar Velayati meeting Syrian Ambassador to Iran Adnan Mahmoud, Governor of Aleppo Hussein Diab and Iran's ambassador to Syria Jawad Turk Abadi, Aleppo, November 2017

in southern Syria.[30] In February 2018, several hundred of its fighters accompanied a Russian mercenary force that confronted US troops on the outskirts of Deir ez-Zor.[31] Dozens of Liwa al-Baqir fighters were reportedly killed in the subsequent fighting.

Another privileged target for recruitment and organisation were Iraqi Shia living in Syria prior to the uprising. Hundreds of thousands of these, many having fled the Saddam Hussein regime and the 2003 war, as well as some longer-term Iraqi residents, lived in neighbourhoods in and around Damascus, close to Shia holy shrines, but also in proximity to the areas where the insurgency emerged. These Iraqis, including a large number of underemployed young men, carried the scars of Iraq's own sectarian war and were predisposed to seeing the conflict in Syria as its continuity and to therefore join the fight.

From this fertile milieu emerged several Shia militias with an Iraqi identity, notably Liwa Abu al-Fadl al-Abbas (LAFA), an umbrella organisation that would over time integrate Iraqi as well as Syrian Shia fighters. LAFA traces its origins to two founders: Hussein Ajeeb Jazza, a Syrian Shi'ite from Nubl, and Ahmad Kayara, an Iraqi living in Syria prior to the outbreak of the civil war.[32] Its leadership in Syria was originally predominantly Iraqi, but over time included more Syrians. From its inception, LAFA closely cooperated with Hizbullah and served as an early partner of the IRGC in protecting Damascus against rebel attacks, and later in besieging and retaking rebel-held areas.

However, reflecting the chaotic and competitive nature of the conflict, and also the difficulty of the IRGC and Hizbullah to fully control their partners, LAFA quickly weakened, with several disgruntled or entrepreneurial commanders founding their own militias. Liwa Zhulfiqar, Quwat Abu al-Fadl al-Abbas (distinct from LAFA) and other armed groups emerged from this competition over leadership, resources and prestige. Commanders and fighters often moved to other groups for opportunistic reasons. The lack of consolidation of these forces also reflected their local identities and the number of fronts in the war. All sought and many obtained Iranian patronage, though they maintained working relationships with the Assad regime and often deployed alongside its forces under the NDF banner. LAFA was mainly present in and around Damascus and in southern Syria. In western and northern Syria, Shia groups operated primarily under Hizbullah and IRGC command. Estimates for these groups vary from 5,000 to 8,000 fighters, mostly equipped with light weaponry provided by the Syrian regime or the IRGC.[33]

As the Assad regime weakened, Iraqi Shia militias began deploying in Syria at the behest of the IRGC and with Hizbullah facilitation. The most prominent groups were Asaib Ahl al-Haq, Harakat Hizbullah al-Nujaba and Kataib Hizbullah. From late 2012, established Shia militias obedient to Iran began deploying large numbers of fighters, who took part in most of the large battles across Syria under IRGC command. They were notably present in Al-Bukamal, Aleppo, Deir ez-Zor and Homs, and in southern Syria. Western intelligence services and Syrian rebels allege that the militias' logistical and transportation needs were arranged by the IRGC.[34] While battle-hardened, these forces were not well equipped or trained, and they faced other obligations. Indeed, the capture by ISIS of the northern third of Iraq in 2014 compelled Iraqi militias to return there to fight the jihadi organisation. This reduction in personnel contributed to the weakening of the Assad regime in 2015, illustrating the importance of such auxiliary forces. Since 2017, Iraqi militias have deployed persistently along the main roads that link the Syria–Iraq border to the Syrian capital and western regions, and taken part in the fight against ISIS in eastern Syria.

Transactional relationships

Interviews provide important insights into the transactional nature of the relationships between NDF groups and the IRGC/Hizbullah. An NDF official in Deir ez-Zor speaking in 2018 noted, for example, that Hizbullah had initially offered salaries for NDF personnel; those payments were subsequently cut off, meaning that NDF fighters in that governorate rely on the NDF leader in Deir ez-Zor for remuneration.[35] In 2018, another NDF official in the primarily Druze governorate of Suwayda praised the advisory role of Iran and Hizbullah in the establishment of the NDF and the training they offered to fighters.[36] He further noted Hizbullah's role alongside the NDF in the 2018 Suwayda desert offensive against ISIS. On the subject of salaries, he stated that funds had not been disbursed for the past ten months, which he attributed in part to Hizbullah's financial problems. He nevertheless expressed hope that ties could be strengthened between the NDF in Suwayda and Hizbullah.

The IRGC and Hizbullah also appealed to non-Shia communities, with limited success. Alawite, Christian, Druze and Sunni militias operating under the NDF banner sought or accepted mainly transactional relationships with the IRGC in order to secure resources and organise their defences. These militias were mostly opportunistic, welcoming the material assistance and political support, while remaining concerned about Iran's ideological and religious message, and preferring to deal with the Syrian military and intelligence agencies. Hizbullah appears to have conducted much of the engagement with these factions: its image as a resistance movement, its Arab identity and its experience in dealing with non-Shia communities in Lebanon made it more appealing to local Syrian factions than Iran's Persian identity. The failure to make significant inroads in the Alawite community demonstrates the limits of Iranian appeal. The Alawite community, the largest minority group, which serves as the security core of the Assad regime and its main source of personnel, is culturally distinct from and religiously less pious than Iran's revolutionary commanders. Throughout the civil war, Alawites have individually preferred to join NDF units or conventional forces, such as the Quwwat al-Nimr (Tiger Force), the Liwa Suqur al-Sahara (Desert Hawks), the 4th Division and the Republican Guard, instead of Iranian-dominated groups. Senior Alawite military and security officers have, however, maintained very close ties to the IRGC, notably Maher al-Assad, the president's brother and effective commander of the 4th Division and the Republican Guard. Battlefield coordination between these units and IRGC-backed groups has been observed across Syria. The Russian intervention and attempt to reorganise Syria's conventional armed forces from 2017 disrupted relations between a number of Alawite-dominated units and IRGC-backed ones.

Adapting to the failure of the Syrian Hizbullah project

By mid-2015, the weakness and possible collapse of the Assad regime, despite foreign Shia support deployed by Iran, had alarmed the leaderships in Tehran and Moscow. Setbacks in northwest Syria, where an alliance of jihadi and Islamist groups conquered important territory, led to an admission by Assad in July 2015 that his military's performance suffered from a lack of personnel and that difficult decisions to abandon areas had been made as a result.[37] In response, a series of secret assessments and negotiations starting in the spring of 2015, including visits to Moscow by Qasem Soleimani, culminated in the Russian intervention in Syria. This was accompanied by a parallel Iranian military escalation (which mobilised Artesh and IRGC units and also included large numbers of Afghan and Pakistani fighters organised as the Fatemiyoun and Zainabiyoun brigades) that September.

The Russian intervention

The joint Russian–Iranian decision to cooperate strategically and operationally in Syria was extraordinary and unprecedented. It brought together two countries that had fraught relations and different military cultures and capabilities against a wide range of enemies on a complex battlefield. While both governments shared important immediate interests in Syria, notably the survival of the Assad regime, their preferences for the future shape of the Syrian security structure differed considerably. Indeed, Russia sought to rebuild a centralised state and strong armed forces, while Iran focused on its militia-building strategy that contradicted Moscow's preferences. For Russia, its involvement meant operating in concert with Iranian-backed militias, notably Hizbullah. This was an uncomfortable position for a great power deeply opposed ideologically to political Islam and a partner of Israel.

According to an account in a pro-Iranian newspaper in Lebanon, corroborated by other sources, the effort was conducted at the initiative of Iran.[38] It involved joint assessments and operational planning over several months by Soleimani and the Russian ministry of defence. While reservations in Tehran were probably intense, given a deep-seated distrust of Moscow, the fact that Soleimani spearheaded the effort and that public criticism was muted indicated that Ayatollah Khamenei had given the initiative full backing. Tehran was likely wary of sending more Iranian troops, thereby becoming more entangled, against Khamenei's preferences. Iran lacked the crucial airpower and intelligence, surveillance and reconnaissance capabilities that Moscow provided, and which ultimately destroyed the insurgency. Russia also brought its ability, as a great power, to shield Iran against a counter-escalation by the US or regional rivals. Crucially, however, Iran would contribute personnel in the form of Shia militias from Afghanistan, Iraq, Lebanon and Pakistan that would prove essential to capturing and holding terrain across Syria.

Russia's intervention was itself an indication of the failure of the 'Syrian Hizbullah' project pursued under the NDF banner. For a start, direct Iranian support for a multitude of Syrian and non-Syrian groups and the provision of foreign Shia fighters had not been enough to restore Assad's authority or deal a decisive defeat to the insurgency. Demographic limitations, the difficulty of managing a disparate array of pro-regime militias, competition over prestige and resources, and resistance by the Assad regime, as well as the intensity of the civil war, stood in the way of the development of a large, consolidated and effective Basij- or Hizbullah-like force.

Moreover, Moscow's intercession and desire to rebuild Syria's military capability and state along a centralised, statist model changed the landscape for Iran and Hizbullah. They had to both accommodate and compete with Russia for the attention and loyalty of the Syrian officer corps and militias. Together with the eventual recovery and new-found assertiveness of the Assad regime, it made the continued pursuit of a 'Syrian Hizbullah' project as envisioned by the likes of Hamadani unrealistic. Without a change in strategy, Iran's intervention in Syria risked becoming an expensive venture, with no clear prospect of recouping its investment.

Iranian Senior Adviser Ali Akbar Velayati and President Vladimir Putin, Russia, July 2018

Local Defence Forces

What followed revealed the ability of Iran to demonstrate flexibility and be responsive to changing local and strategic conditions, in terms of both strategic planning and operations. Instead of vesting itself in the NDF model, it identified ways to secure influence through other means. In 2017, a new framework, the Local Defence Forces (LDF), was adopted by the Syrian government in order to organise and integrate pro-regime militias, including NDF units, into a tighter structure, and when required dissolve them. Substantively, the LDF differs from the NDF in that the LDF is on the register of the Syrian armed forces and is not a civilian volunteer group. LDF units recruit personnel who are considered 'civilians', but also draft dodgers or deserters (including former insurgents) seeking to reconcile with and reintegrate into the Syrian state system.[39]

The IRGC and Hizbullah have deep links with many militia units, but not all units that are administratively part of the LDF have direct relationships with Iran. The status of LDF units defined as working with the IRGC and Hizbullah was formalised in a series of decisions issued in April 2017, agreed by Bashar al-Assad himself as commander-in-chief of the armed forces and by the defence minister. The decisions categorised LDF units 'working with the Iranian side' by governorate, defining their personnel as draft evaders, deserters or civilians. Draft evaders and deserters could have their status regularised and change their 'party of summoning' from the regular armed forces to the LDF, thereby allowing them to complete their military service within LDF units. Importantly, the burden of combat and provi-

Local Defence Forces: command structure

An examination of the higher command levels of the LDF shows how it has been conceived as a joint and hybrid project between the IRGC and the Syrian armed forces. The LDF's chief of staff is Syrian, and is likely to remain so. The first chief of staff was Brigadier-General Haitham Abd al-Rasul al-Nayef, originally from the Shia village of Fua in Idlib governorate, and who died in a traffic accident in May 2018.[40] According to a social-media post, he was reportedly succeeded by General Yousef al-Hassan, who was appointed to the position by Bashar al-Assad himself.[41]

LDF units are organised by region and governorate, each headed by an overall LDF commander. In several instances, Iranians have been identified as LDF regional and governorate commanders, though it is generally not possible to know their real names. According to a representative from an Idlib-sector LDF unit, an Iranian commander known as 'al-Hajj Asghar' oversees Hama, Idlib and the 'northern region as a whole'. Previously, this Iranian also served as the 'deputy commander of the forces of the northern region'.[42]

Other Iranians have served in the LDF command structure: the Aleppo region is commanded by 'Sayyid Salman' and the Latakia region by 'al-Hajj Ayoub'. In turn, these Iranian commanders in the northern LDF sectors are likely linked to 'Sayyid Javad', who has been identified as the IRGC's Ahmad Madani.[43] In fact, according to the leader of the 313 Force, a prominent Syrian Shia militia, Sayyid Javad is the overall leader of the LDF and the overall leader of the IRGC's presence in Syria.[44]

Syrians also play local leadership roles: in the governorate sector of Homs, the LDF leader is the Syrian Army's Colonel Ali Yunis. In Hama, General Ali al-Hamo was reportedly promoted to the governorate leadership of the LDF in February 2018.[45]

The Idlib-sector LDF-unit representative offered a more comprehensive view of the functioning of LDF commands: each governorate sector has a Syrian Army officer assigned to it, but the project as a whole is under the supervision of 'the friends' (i.e., the Iranians).[46] The reason for assigning Syrian Army officers to the LDF was explained as follows: 'There has to be a Syrian officer as an officer of connection [liaison officer] in order to coordinate between the Hujjaj [Iranian officers], Iranian officials and the Syrian army.'[47]

In fact, at the individual-unit level, Syrian Army officers can sometimes be found in direct command. For example, the Aleppo LDF unit Saraya Fursan al-Basil, which has deployed in the Manbij area in proximity to the Syrian Democratic Forces and the US presence, is reportedly led by Basil Ali Abdullah, a Syrian Army first lieutenant originally from Latakia.[48]

It is also possible to identify Iranians in command positions at the individual-unit level. The two most notable cases are in the militias Faylaq al-Mudafieen an Halab and Fawj al-Sayyida Zainab. The former was established following the Syrian government's recapture of rebel-held eastern Aleppo city at the end of 2016. Its commander is 'al-Hajj Mohsen' from the IRGC, though Syrian military personnel operate in lower command positions. Fawj al-Sayyida Zainab was founded by a Syrian (Fadi Dahduh) but subsequently taken over by an Iranian going by the name of 'al-Hajj Mahdi'.[49]

However, other units within the LDF instead have direct relationships with Hizbullah. This may be because the IRGC wants their Lebanese client to share the burden of the financial and administrative management of Syrian forces, because of specific personal relationships or because of agreed-on geographic zones of responsibility. This is the case for the Special Force, which is based in the Sayyida Zainab area of Damascus and primarily recruits Syrian

sioning, as well as material entitlements and benefits for 'martyrs' and those wounded and missing, was placed on Iran. The decisions also stipulated that the LDF units were to remain affiliated with Iran and coordinate at the same time with the Syrian military command 'until the crisis ends' or new decisions are made. In effect, this amounted to Iran embedding itself in the Syrian state structure, to an extent that exceeded even Hizbullah's own penetration of the Lebanese state.

The April 2017 decisions are a mutually beneficial arrangement for the Syrian government, Iran and Hizbullah. For the IRGC and Hizbullah (who are often referred to in the context of the LDF as 'the friends' (al-asdiqa), the decisions resolve the problem that Syrian personnel working with them might still be arrested for draft evasion or desertion, and that friendly militias may be constrained for arbitrary or competitive reasons. For the Assad regime, logistical and salary costs associated with

Shi'ite personnel (though it has at least one Iraqi in its ranks).[50] The group was created in 2013 by Hizbullah commander Ali Shabib Mahmoud (also known by the *nom de guerre* Abu Turab Ruways), who was killed in November of that year near Sayyida Zainab. Since the group's inception, it has been commanded, trained, armed and financed by Hizbullah. Indeed, one member of the group rejected the idea of a distinct 'Syrian Hizbullah', instead seeing the Special Force as an organic part of Hizbullah itself.[51] The same source claimed that the Special Force had no direct relations with the IRGC. In his recounting, LDF units working with the Iranians receive their salaries consistently from them, whereas the Special Force has seen delays in receiving salaries from Hizbullah.

Similar to the Special Force is Quwat al-Ridha, which is based in the Homs area. Like the Special Force, the group should be seen as an organic extension of Hizbullah with a direct affiliation to its command. A key figure behind the establishment of Quwat al-Ridha was the Hizbullah commander Hamza Ibrahim Haidar (Abu Mostafa), who was killed in fighting in Homs city in 2013. Similarly, another Lebanese Hizbullah figure of note in Quwat al-Ridha was Hassan Najib Madlaj (Ali al-Ridha), originally from the Baalbek area, who was an officer in the group's artillery and missile intervention force. Madlaj was killed in December 2016 during combat in the Homs desert.[52]

As a source in Quwat al-Ridha noted, LDF identification cards have been issued for Syrian rank-and-file members of the group, but the leadership has not received such cards. The reason for this is clear: if the command of the group is with Lebanese Hizbullah, it has no need for identification cards issued for the purpose of regularising the LDF's status, and avoiding arrest for draft evasion or desertion. In terms of salaries, the Quwat al-Ridha source – himself wounded – said that he had been receiving his monthly salary without a problem, but that LDF members who were fighting have seen delays.

It should also be noted that while some LDF units proudly proclaim an affiliation with the IRGC, it is uncertain whether all have direct contact. For example, one of the leaders of Liwa Ashbal al-Hussein – a Homs LDF unit that claims association with the IRGC, and has deployed in the desert area in proximity to the US presence at Tanf in southeastern Syria – asked during a conversation whether his interviewers knew someone at the Iranian embassy he could contact in order to set up a new LDF formation.[53] Indeed, developing a direct relationship with Tehran rather than the Syrian regime demands more than forming a group and proclaiming an ideological affinity with Iran. Rather, as stated by an Iraqi veteran of the war in Syria based in Damascus, it also requires good introductions (*wasta*), such as with the Iranian *Hujjaj* (Iranian commanders) in Syria or Ayatollah Khamenei's office in Iran.[54]

In other cases, the formation of a new group or structural changes can be traced to an IRGC order. The leader of the 313 Force, for instance, explained that his group was ordered to separate from Liwa al-Sayyida Ruqayya (which itself originated in the NDF and was once affiliated with the Iraqi group Kataib Sayyid al-Shuhada) in the interests of 'the resistance'.[55] When asked, he clarified that it was the IRGC who gave this order. More recently, the wider grouping of which the 313 Force is a part – Liwa al-Rasul al-Akram (The Most Noble Messenger Brigade) – changed its name to Liwa al-Abbas (Abbas's Brigade) as per a directive from Sayyid Javad, the LDF chief-of-staff.[56]

All of this illustrates the competitive nature of the LDF project: ambitious or dissatisfied local commanders have sought Iranian, *Hizbullahi* or regime protection and patronage to support new or re-composed militia units.

supporting these units are reduced and transferred to its foreign allies, even as the state is ostensibly strengthened and its control of all armed groups in theatre nominally assured. Many of the groups described by familiar monikers such as 'Syrian Hizbullah' and 'The Islamic Resistance in Syria' now come administratively under the LDF. For Assad, this poses the risk that foreign-supported elements in the state structure could over time undermine its cohesion and loyalty.

The basis of affiliations

On what basis do groups proclaim affiliation with Iran and Hizbullah or have actual links with them? In many cases, the proclaimed affiliation and relationship are of an ideological and religious nature. This point is most apparent in the groups whose foundations lie in Twelver Shia communities in Syria, especially more recent converts to the faith.

A representative case is that of the Liwa al-Baqir militia, whose leadership consists of Baqara tribesmen

Table 3.1: Syrian militia groups: relationship with Iran and assessment of strategic utility

Militia	Ideological affinity	Strategic convergence	Political expediency	Transactional value	Strategic value for Iran	Other 'patrons'	Assessment
101 Battalion	Medium	High	High	High	Medium	Yes	Strategic ally
313 Force	High	High	High	High	High	No	Proxy
Fawj al-Imam al-Hujja	High	High	High	High	High	No	Organ of Hizbullah and Iran
Fawj al-Nayrab	Medium	High	Medium	Medium	Medium	n.k.	Partner
Fawj al-Sayyida Zainab	High	High	High	High	Medium	No	Proxy
Fawj Raad al-Mahdi	Medium	High	High	Medium	Medium	n.k.	Ideological ally
Fawj Sheikh al-Jabal	Medium	High	Low	High	Medium	n.k.	Proxy
Faylaq al-Mudafieen an Halab	Medium	High	High	High	High	Yes	Strategic ally
Liwa Ahrar	High	High	Medium	Medium	Medium	No	Proxy
Liwa al-Baqir	High	High	High	High	High	Russia, Syrian government	Ideological and strategic ally
Liwa al-Doushka	Medium	High	Medium	Medium	Medium	n.k.	Partner
Liwa al-Safira	Medium	Medium	Medium	Medium	Medium	Yes	Partner
Liwa al-Sayyida Ruqayya	High	High	High	High	High	No	Proxy
Liwa al-Shahid Zain al-Abideen Berri/Liwa Ali Zain al-Abideen	Medium	High	Medium	Medium	Medium	n.k.	Partner
Liwa Ashbal al-Hussein	High	High	Medium	Medium	Medium	n.k.	Proxy
Liwa Usud al-Hussein	Medium	High	High	Medium	Medium	Yes	Strategic ally
Mahrada LDF	Low	Medium	Medium	Medium	Medium	Yes	Partner
Majmuat al-Ghadab	Low	Medium	Medium	Medium	Medium	Yes	Partner
National Ideological Resistance	High	High	Medium	High	Medium	n.k.	Proxy
Quwat al-Ridha	High	High	High	High	High	None	Organ of Hizbullah
Saraya al-Arin	Medium	High	High	Medium	Medium	Yes	Strategic ally
Saraya al-Muqawama	Medium	High	Low	Medium	Medium	Yes	Strategic ally
Saraya al-Raad	Medium	High	Medium	Medium	Medium	n.k.	Proxy
The Special Force	High	High	High	High	High	No	Organ of Hizbullah

Ideological affinity: the level of ideological alignment and the corresponding loyalty it generates; **Strategic convergence:** the level of strategic alignment (i.e., of visions and interests regarding the shape of the regional order, the nature of the threats and enemies, and the strategies deployed to that effect); **Political expediency:** the level of the political benefits generated by the relationship; **Transactional value:** the level of the mutual security, military, political and economic returns created by the relationship.

Source: IISS

●●● High   ●● Medium   ● Low

from Aleppo governorate, who had converted to the Twelver faith from Sunnism prior to the outbreak of the war. The conversions had arisen during the previous decade as the result of Iranian proselytism, which tied the Baqara tribe to descent from the Shi'ite Imam Mohammad al-Baqir. In fact, the two brothers who founded Liwa al-Baqir – al-Hajj Khalid and al-Hajj Hamza – reputedly had links to Hizbullah that well predate the war: the group claims that they both participated in Hizbullah's 2006 war against Israel.[57] Liwa al-Baqir's religious and ideological affinities with Iran are illustrated in social-media posts, which refer to both Bashar al-Assad and Ayatollah Khamenei as 'leader' (i.e., Assad as the political leader of Syria and Khamenei as the supreme religious authority).[58] The ties between Liwa al-Baqir and Iran are further illustrated by an 'official' visit to Iran that members of

the group undertook in March 2018.[59] Other converts have also played a role in Iran's war infrastructure: the first leader of the Ghaliboun militia, Rami Yousef (Abu al-Meqdad), is an Alawite from Latakia who converted to Shia Islam before the war and also reputedly participated in the 2006 war against Israel.[60]

Occupying an intermediate position in terms of religious/ideological affinities with Iran are LDF units of a distinctly Alawite origin. The civil war has seen the espousal of sectarian identities on all sides, including among Alawites, many of whom are not acquainted with the detailed intricacies of their faith. Among these Alawites, a proclaimed affinity with figures such as Imam Ali and Imam Hussein, seventh-century revered relatives of the Prophet Muhammad, as well as Alawite shrines, are observed. While there has been some resemblance in imagery on banners and other visual displays to that used by Shia groups during the war, the distinct Alawite identity is still very much apparent. In this content, two Latakia-based LDF groups are of note: Saraya al-Arin (Brigades of the Den) and Liwa Usud al-Hussein (Lions of Hussein's Brigade), both of which are based around Qardaha and are led by members of the extended Assad family. Saraya al-Arin uses the number 313 in its imagery, which refers to the number of soldiers who fought at the seventh-century Battle of Badr and also the number of the companions of the religious figure Imam al-Mahdi, the ultimate saviour, according to Shia Twelver Muslims. Liwa Usud al-Hussein's name, meanwhile, can be interpreted as having a double meaning: referring to the group's leader Hussein Tawfiq al-Assad, as well as Imam Hussein. When both of these groups were initially established, they were not affiliated with the LDF: Liwa Usud al-Hussein worked with the al-Bustan Association of Rami Makhlouf, Bashar al-Assad's cousin, while Saraya al-Arin began as an independent group. Only later did they acquire an affiliation with the LDF. At the time, these groups developed social-media presences with distinct imagery.[61]

At the other end of the spectrum are groups affiliated with the LDF that have no religious or ideological affinity with Iran. The clearest examples are LDF groups based in the Christian towns of Suqaylabiya and Mahrada. In the town of Mahrada, the LDF is led by a member of parliament from the Ba'ath Party.[62]

More generally, Syrian Twelver Shia are still a very small minority in Syria – no more than 2% of the population. To build an effective native Iran- and Hizbullah-linked network in Syria, Syrian Shi'ites alone cannot be its components, even as both likely hope that in the long term they can convert more Syrians to Shia Islam and thereby increase their proportion in Syria. Indeed, Iran is a state that has engaged in proselytism for its brand of Shia Islam. A former member of the Ghaliboun militia, himself of Syrian Shia origin, characterised one of the goals of Iran and Hizbullah in Syria as converting people to Shia Islam, and noted that it could happen through more subtle means, such as the provision of salaries and books on the faith for recruits to groups such as Ghaliboun.[63] The recruitment efforts of Liwa al-Baqir have also been reportedly tied to proselytism efforts. Conversely, Ghaliboun changed its recruitment policy: initially open only to Syrian Shi'ites, or those intending to convert to the faith, the group subsequently came to accept non-Shi'ite recruits into its ranks, even if they did not wish to convert. This was reflected in its change of imagery, dropping 'Islamic Resistance Brigades in Syria' from its name and becoming 'The National Resistance Brigades in Syria'. Druze recruits in Hizbullah-affiliated group Quwat al-Wad al-Sadiq (Forces of the True Promise), based in the Sayyida Zainab area of Damascus, have remained Druze in their identity and clearly do not intend to convert to Shia Islam.[64]

Typology of Iranian-backed militias in Syria

'Syrian Hizbullah' is better understood as a franchise that combines core Hizbullah and IRGC partners, as

> ## "THE RELATIONSHIPS BETWEEN THE MILITIA GROUPS, IRAN AND HIZBULLAH HAVE BEEN HIGHLY VARIED AND DYNAMIC"

well as groups with looser ties. Iran and Hizbullah have pursued a multifaceted strategy in Syria, reflecting both operational pragmatism and complex realities on the ground. In places deemed strategic, they have sought to nurture and deploy loyal local forces. Elsewhere, the approach was more opportunistic and flexible.

The relationships between the militia groups, Iran and Hizbullah have been highly varied and dynamic. But all can be defined with reference to five principle features: ideological affinity, strategic convergence, political expediency, transactional value and strategic value for Iran. A sample of groups tabulated against these criteria is given in the adjacent table (see Table 3.1). From this, it is clear that Iran and Hizbullah have been pragmatic in terms of the levels of each feature shown by these groups; not, for example, insisting on a high level of ideological affinity or strategic value, and even in some cases acknowledging other patrons. The overall breadth of the network and the efficacy of groups on the battlefield have mattered more than alignment with Iranian strategy and values. Against that, Iran has insisted on a basic level of sympathy and strategic alignment, but has not allowed this to deny it access to potentially effective groups.

Iran and Hizbullah: multifaceted engagement strategies

In their attempts to attract and nurture partners across Syria, Iran and Hizbullah have deployed a toolkit that combines coercion, political and economic incentives, soft power and services.

Map 3.1: **Selected Iranian and *Hizbullahi* 'soft-power' activities in Syria, 2015–18**

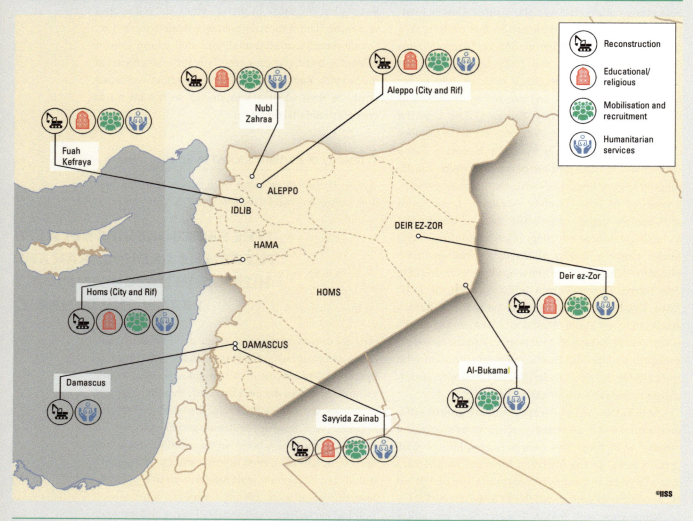

Source: IISS

The core tool has been to embed their presence in local communities. This strategy has combined military recruitment and presence with soft-power projection in the form of social and educational services, as well as reconstruction and economic projects. The approach has included the provision of services, more to obtain local goodwill and incentivise and reward particular constituencies than as part of a holistic strategy of overall stabilisation. Iran has opened a number of schools and expanded its cultural influence in strategic areas of Damascus and eastern Syria.[65] Meanwhile, state-backed Iranian political and cultural associations have helped organise events throughout Syria to raise the profile of the Islamic Republic of Iran, including the celebration of the anniversary of the Islamic Revolution.[66]

The joint Hizbullah–Iran approach also has a religious and sectarian dimension. Many Sunnis originating from areas south of Homs have complained about demographic-engineering attempts, with Hizbullah expelling Sunni residents and preventing the return of refugees and internally displaced persons, instead allowing Shi'ite settlers (many of whom have fled their own villages) to create a Shia-friendly area stretching from the Bekaa Valley into northwestern Syria.[67]

Iran and Hizbullah have engaged in outreach even in communities that supported the insurgency. Across Syria, they have offered those willing to surrender and join their forces preferential terms, including conscription deferrals and amnesty for some who served in rebel forces in southern Syria. This has helped Iran and Hizbullah co-opt local non-state actors, thereby creating an indirect presence and infrastructure in regions where it is difficult to operate in the open, such as southern Syria.[68]

Building a new front against Israel in southern Syria

'Syria is a path for the resistance [against Israel] and a bridge of communication between the Resistance and Iran.'[69]

Hassan Nasrallah, 2012

In January 2015, the Israeli Air Force bombed a convoy in the northern sector of Syria's Quneitra governorate, killing IRGC Brigadier-General Mohammad Allahdadi, as well as several Hizbullah commanders, including Jihad Mughniyah, the son of famed Hizbullah security chief Imad Mughniyah.[70]

The presence of such senior figures revealed Hizbullah and the IRGC's interest in developing a military presence in southern Syria along the Israeli-occupied Golan Heights. The possibility of developing a second front against Israel, from which a missile arsenal could threaten the northern third of the country, has strategic importance for Tehran and Hizbullah. It would increase Iran's deterrence against Israel, which has so far been reliant on Lebanon. Indeed, calibrating deterrence on two separate fronts against state and non-state actors with a sophisticated missile arsenal would complicate Israeli defence planning. Moreover, missiles of greater range and precision-fired simultaneously from the Lebanese and Syrian fronts could possibly overwhelm Israeli missile defences and overstretch its air force as it seeks to destroy launchers.

Prior to the Syrian uprising, Israel saw the Assad regime as weak, predictable, easy to penetrate and deter, and unable to countenance a conventional escalation. Importantly, Bashar al-Assad was seen as unwilling to allow his Iranian and *Hizbullahi* allies to develop a presence close to the Golan Heights. The rebellion and the rapid weakening of the Assad regime changed this set of assumptions. Southern Syria became a more complex environment, where Sunni insurgent and jihadi groups, as well as regime troops and Shia militias, operated. This meant that the IRGC and Hizbullah could develop a covert presence near the Golan Heights with or without the regime's approval.

Between 2013 and 2018, Israel reportedly conducted hundreds of airstrikes against alleged Iranian and *Hizbullahi* targets in Syria, 200 between 2016 and 2018 alone.[71] In doing so, Israel signalled it would reject any attempt to impose in Syria the strategic reality governing Hizbullah's operations in Lebanon. Instead, Israel sought to deny through air dominance and superior intelligence-gathering an IRGC and *Hizbullahi* presence along the Golan Heights, and to destroy suspected missile shipments and other advanced military technology throughout

Table 3.2: Iranian and *Hizbullahi* entities and companies operating in Syria, as of 2018

Iranian entities
Al-Thaqlin Charity Center
Astan Quds Razavi Foundation
Iranian Reconstruction Authority
Irano Hind Shipping Company
Iran Powerplant Repair Company
Islamic Azad University
Islamic Culture and Relations Organization
Khatam al-Anbiya Construction Headquarters
MAPNA Group
Mazarat Ahl al-Bayt Authority
Mobile Telecommunication Company of Iran
Tehran Construction Engineering Organization
The Imam Khomeini Relief Foundation
Hizbullahi entities
Jihad al-Binaa
Imam al-Mahdi Scouts

Source: IISS

Syria.[72] Iran's persistence despite regular attacks indicates that while effective, the airstrikes have not deterred the IRGC.

To keep IRGC and Hizbullah forces at bay, Israel opportunistically supported Syrian rebel forces in the southern governorates of Deraa, Quneitra and Suwayda, providing ammunition, food, medical supplies and other kinds of assistance.[73] These forces served as a buffer until they collapsed in summer 2018 under regime military pressure.

From Israel's perspective, dealing with this threat demanded that it maintain full air superiority and autonomy over Syrian skies. However, Russia's military presence in Syria from 2015 complicated this requirement. Israel insisted on conducting operations across the Syrian theatre of war, and at times carried out attacks against air bases where Russian forces were located next to Iranian weapons inventories and personnel, such as in April and July 2018 in strikes on the T-4 military airport in central Syria. For Moscow, such operations were deemed both reckless and provocative, but manageable as long as they did not threaten Assad's survival or harm Russian troops.[74] Russian displeasure with Israeli activity was mostly confined to private discussions between Russian President Vladimir Putin and Israeli Prime Minister Benjamin Netanyahu, who reportedly met ten times between September 2015 and early 2019 to discuss Syria. However, when a Russian surveillance aircraft was mistakenly shot down by Syrian air defences

(l) IRGC soldiers in Tehran carry a banner during the funeral of IRGC Brigadier-General Mohammad Allahdadi, who was killed in southern Syria, January 2015

(r) Jihad Mughniyah, son of Hizbullah commander Imad Mughinyah, who was killed in Syria in 2008, speaks at a Hizbullah rally in Beirut, February 2008

aiming at an attacking Israeli bomber in Latakia in September 2018, Putin and Russian defence officials issued stern condemnation.[75]

With the collapse of the rebellion in southern Syria in summer 2018, the role and presence of Iranian-allied forces in southern Syria became a major topic of concern for Israel in its dealings with the US and, more importantly, Russia. Moscow came under pressure to prevent the deployment of such forces within a 60-kilometre radius of the Israel–Syria armistice line.[76] Intense Israeli–Russian diplomacy led to agreements that stipulated that only regime and Russian forces would deploy in the area. In reality, there is evidence that Iranian-allied troops participated in the battle for southern Syria.[77] To circumvent the Russian–Israeli understanding, Hizbullah and the IRGC recruited former Syrian rebels to serve as local auxiliaries.[78] For example, one resident of a southwest Deraa locality on the border with Jordan claimed that Hizbullah has a presence in Tel al-Hara in Deraa, facing the Israeli-occupied Golan Heights, and has been recruiting locals via the Syrian Army's 4th Division, aiming to gain influence at the expense of Syria's Russian-backed V Corps.[79]

Iran has been accused by Israel of using Syrian military bases to store weaponry and train local militias. A military base in Kiswah, south of Damascus and less than 50 km from the Golan Heights, has featured prominently in this regard.[80] A target near Kiswah was bombed by the Israeli Air Force in December 2017.[81] In May 2018, it conducted its largest bombing operation to date, *House of Cards*, hitting dozens of suspected IRGC facilities, including Kiswah and Damascus's civilian and military airports and other facilities in and around the capital.[82]

As Iran developed its military infrastructure in Syria, it faced two additional challenges from Russia and the Assad regime. Despite Moscow's recognition of Iran's instrumental military contribution in securing Assad's survival, it still viewed a potential Iranian conflict with Israel as endangering this hard-won success and remained suspicious of Iran's regional agenda. Russia tried to moderate Iranian ambitions by brokering tactical arrangements that demanded Iranian concessions on ground deployment, such as no-go zones in southern Syria. Ultimately, this put Moscow in an uncomfortable position. It proved unable to constrain Iranian deployments seriously, to stop Israeli attacks and to enforce its own preferences. Competition with Iran over the future shape of the regime also factored in Russian calculations: the two countries differed over the end goal, resources, economic assets, the structure of the military and other issues.

The Assad regime also faced a dilemma. Iranian military activities in Syria, including logistics, were not necessarily coordinated with the Syrian government, which Israel nevertheless held responsible for this activity. Iranian attempts to retaliate against Israel in 2018, whether with missiles or uninhabited aerial vehicles, invited more Israeli operations that struck Syrian facilities and embarrassed the Syrian government; indeed, just as it claimed victory in the civil war, the Syrian government remained unable to counter Israeli violations of its airspace, promising instead retaliation in an undefined future.[83]

The land bridge

Achieving territorial continuity from Iran to Lebanon (a 'land bridge') has always been an aspiration for Tehran and Hizbullah, though not an active pursuit nor, for decades, a priority. Indeed, the reliable trans-shipment role played by Syria and the reliance on tightly controlled military airports over decades made it unnecessary, however desirable.

Map 3.2: **Iran's main transport routes to Syria**

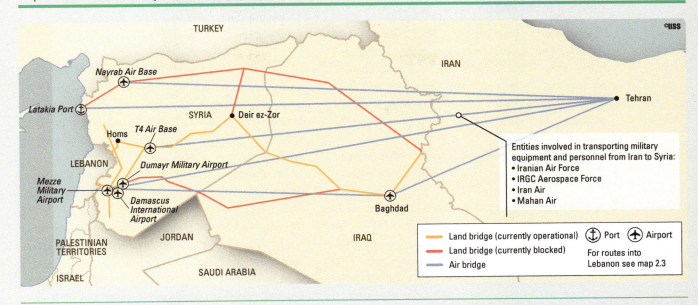

Source: IISS

Nonetheless, the rise since 2003 of Iraqi political and military actors sympathetic to or allied with Iran offered new possibilities. The realisation in Beirut and Tehran that the Shia community, while a minority in the Arab world, represented, together with associated sects, a majority in the northern Middle East – and had achieved full or semi-political control in Iraq, Iran, Lebanon and Syria – generated new geopolitical ambitions. Until 2011, these ambitions were frustrated by the US military presence in Iraq; after 2011, the Syrian rebellion and, later, the capture of eastern Syria and western Iraq by ISIS, stood in the way of Shia territorial continuity. However, the escalation of regional conflict from 2011 and the rise of rival Sunni forces, threatening the regime in Damascus and its territorial control, reinvigorated the strategic thinking behind a land bridge.

There has been debate between those who believe that Iran's quest for a land corridor is a driver of its Syria campaign and those who see it as an ancillary benefit. However, uninterrupted land transport has objective merit relative to air transport. Logistically, territorial continuity and an uninterrupted supply corridor from Iran to Lebanon have numerous advantages for Tehran and Hizbullah. Compared to air transport, land transport of weaponry is cheaper and accommodates larger volumes, is more convenient and easier to hide, and can be concealed by legitimate transportation methods. In times of conflict, air flights are also easier to detect and interdict.

However, at present the 700-km land bridge from Al-Bukamal in Iraq to Damascus crosses difficult, dangerous and inhospitable territory. The infrastructure along it is also of low quality: aside from the main highways, most roads are in poor condition, while the surrounding desert makes it difficult to hide trucks. Convoys would also require heavy security. Furthermore, in times of conflict, Israeli and US intelligence capabilities and air dominance jeopardise the safe supply of advanced military capabilities and the movement of personnel along the bridge.

The behaviour of Iran and its allies since 2016 lends credence to the pursuit of a land bridge in parallel with other strategic objectives, such as the recovery of Syrian territory for the benefit of the Assad regime and control over the Syria–Iraq border. The methodical reconquest since 2016 of ISIS territory in eastern Syria by a group of Iraqi Shia militias, Lebanese Hizbullah, the Afghan Fatemiyoun militia, IRGC forces and the Syrian military and its own allies supports this conjecture. Iran-affiliated groups have invested in local recruitment, reconstruction and services in key towns along the Syrian–Iraqi border and along the Euphrates River Valley to cultivate local support. For example, the small Iraqi groups Harakat Ansar al-Awfiyah and Kataib Sayyid al-Shuhada are deployed on the Iraqi side of the Syrian–Iraqi border. The November 2017 capture of Al-Bukamal from ISIS received intense coverage in the Axis of Resistance-affiliated media, highlighting the importance of this moment for them,[84] as it re-established control over a border crossing with Iraq.

Selling the intervention: ideological and political mobilisation

'The enemy has been targeting Syria's security and stability. During the sedition of 2009 in Iran the enemy shouted the slogan "Not Gaza, not Lebanon, sacrifice my life for Iran" and now in the events in Deraa they have shouted the slogan "Not Hezbollah, not Iran". This shows that the slogans come from the same source.'[85]

Ahmad Mousavi, Iranian ambassador to Syria, April 2011

Further illustrating their commonality of views and interests, Iran's and Hizbullah's rationale for and messaging on their intervention in Syria was mutually reinforced. The narrative in Beirut and Tehran was strikingly similar: the Syrian rebellion was a

> # "THE NARRATIVE IN BEIRUT AND TEHRAN WAS STRIKINGLY SIMILAR: THE SYRIAN REBELLION WAS A WESTERN-, SAUDI- AND QATARI-ENGINEERED CONSPIRACY"

Western-, Saudi- and Qatari-engineered conspiracy, as well as the continuation of prior efforts to break the Axis of Resistance and denude it of its Islamic and Arab legitimacy. From the very early days of the uprising, Ayatollah Khamenei affirmed that 'In Syria, the hand of America and Israel is evident',[86] an assessment often echoed by Hizbullah's Nasrallah, who said in 2013: 'If Syria falls into the hands of America, Israel and the takfiris, the people of our region will go into a dark period.'[87]

Along the same lines, the uprising was also described as Western and Israeli punishment of Bashar al-Assad for his steadfast partnership with Iran and Hizbullah. Nasrallah justified in July 2012 Hizbullah's support for the Assad regime as follows: 'There is a US–Israeli project against Syria. The US and Israel consider Syria as a problem, because Syria is a true supporter of the resistance.'[88]

He further illustrated the importance of Assad's support to his group, declaring in 2012:

> Israel, today, is afraid of Gaza and afraid for Tel Aviv. Who gave [Gaza fighters] the rockets? The Saudi regime? The Egyptian regime? No. They were rockets from Syria and transferred through Syria. The Syrian leadership was risking its interests and existence in order for

the resistance in Lebanon and Palestine to be strong. Show me one Arab regime that does the same.[89]

In May 2013, Nasrallah credited Hizbullah's performance to his allies: 'Israelis know that the source of strength of resistance in Palestine and Lebanon is Syria and Iran.'[90] Loyalty to a dependable ally required unconditional commitment to his survival.

In Beirut and Tehran, the thinking was that, ultimately, failure to confront Syria's insurgency and, later, foreign jihadis, would inevitably bring the fight to Iran and Lebanon, causing instability at home. Nasrallah publicly disclosed his 2011 interventionist argument to Khamenei: 'If we don't fight in Damascus, we will have to fight in Hermel, Baalbek, Dahieh, Ghazieh, western Bekaa Valley, and southern Lebanon.'[91] Iranian ideologues such as cleric Mehdi Taeb, adviser to Supreme Leader Khamenei, echoed this argument: 'Syria is the 35th province [of Iran] and a strategic province for us. If the enemy attacks us and wants to appropriate either Syria or Khuzestan [in southern Iran], the priority is that we keep Syria.'[92]

Another potent narrative had a strong religious dimension. In both Hizbullah's and Tehran's view, the Syrian rebels were both instruments of foreign agendas and promoters of a *takfiri* – or a Sunni Salafi exclusivist and chauvinist – world view that would inevitably endanger the very existence of the Shia community. Indeed, all Syrian rebels were portrayed as Sunni extremists, intent on destroying Syria's religious diversity and eradicating its small Shia community, including religious sites.

The radicalisation of the Syrian insurgency validated this messaging retrospectively. The growth of anti-Shia slogans even among mainstream rebel groups, the besieging of Shia villages in northwest Syria and the genocidal campaign of ISIS (including its alleged intention to destroy the holy Shia cities of Karbala and Najaf) contributed to the strengthening of this perception. The '*takfirisation*' of the rebellion allowed Hizbullah and Iran to ignore or understate the profound political and social roots of the insurgency, and address it as a purely ideological security threat. At the same time, portraying their enemies as *takfiris* allowed Hizbullah and Tehran to distinguish between 'good' and 'bad' Sunnis. The strategy proved effective in a number of places in co-opting or reassuring Sunnis opposed to the *takfiris* or the rebels.

Table 3.3: **Liwa Fatemiyoun and Liwa Zainabiyoun: relationship with Iran and assessment of strategic utility**

Group	Ideological affinity	Strategic convergence	Political expediency	Transactional value	Strategic value for Iran	Other 'patrons'	Assessment
Liwa Fatemiyoun	●●●	●●●	●●●	●●●	●●●	No	State organ
Liwa Zainabiyoun	●●●	●●●	●●●	●●●	●●●	No	State organ

Source: IISS   ●●● High   ●● Medium   ● Low

Liwa Fatemiyoun and Liwa Zainabiyoun

Iran has deployed increasing numbers of Afghan and Pakistani Shia fighters, organised into two separate fighting units, between 2012 and 2018 in support of the Assad regime. Officially announced in 2013, the Afghan Liwa Fatemiyoun and Pakistani Liwa Zainabiyoun have been specifically raised by the IRGC for this mission in Syria and are under the IRGC's direct command. Designed to bolster the number of pro-Assad fighters in light of shortfalls in the regime's own recruitment, these two militias have provided crucial personnel for territorial control and operations, fighting rebel groups as well as jihadi organisations across Syria.

The enabling role of the IRGC in recruiting, organising, deploying and directing Liwa Fatemiyoun and Liwa Zainabiyoun has been unique, conducted in a mostly unconcealed manner. Of all Iranian partner militias in Syria, these forces are the most directly answerable to and dependent on the IRGC. Since these forces would not have come into existence or been able to operate abroad without active IRGC sponsorship, Liwa Fatemiyoun and Liwa Zainabiyoun can be considered de facto subordinate parts of the IRGC, a hybrid between an auxiliary force and a 'Foreign Legion'.

The recourse to these foreign fighters has helped Iran lessen the exposure of its own personnel, thus reducing the associated human and domestic political cost of its overall intervention. Indeed, Supreme Leader Ayatollah Ali Khamenei and other high-ranking officials were concerned from the outset of the Iranian involvement about Iranian casualties and their impact on the population's support for the war. They therefore capped the number of Iranian deployments into Syria and required IRGC commanders to tap into non-Iranian manpower. This strategy has also limited the financial cost of the operation, with the cost of recruiting and deploying non-Iranian fighters a fraction of that required for Iranian personnel.

Recruitment and training

Iran's cultural and political reach into Afghan and Pakistani Shia communities – amplified since 1979 by the Islamic Revolution, continuous turmoil in Afghanistan and sectarian strife in Pakistan – has facilitated the recruitment and indoctrination of significant numbers of fighters from both countries. Pakistan has the second-largest number of Shia Muslims after Iran, estimated at approximately 10–15% (21–31 million) of Pakistan's population. Estimates of Afghanistan's Shia population vary considerably between official ones of 10–20% and non-official estimates of 25–30% of the country's total population (approximately 36m).[93]

Domestic conflicts and the growing closeness of Pakistani and Afghan clerics to Iran's powerful clergy during the 1980s created enduring links and networks. Afghanistan's historically repressed Hazara Shia minority has been a significant recipient of Iranian overtures. In the 1980s, small numbers of Hazara fighters joined Iran's defence during the war with Iraq. Tehran also supported a variety of Afghan groups (including the Hazara) that fought the Soviet-backed regime and later vied for power in the country. Iran's involvement in Afghanistan has been primarily a matter of security and necessity, given their shared border and the large number of Afghans seeking refuge in Iran, but also the avowed hostility of the Taliban and other Sunni extremist forces to Iran. Since 2012, intensifying conflict and economic hardship have compounded Shia disenfranchisement in Afghanistan. Similar dynamics have played out in Pakistan, where Sunni sectarian ascendancy during the rule of General Zia-ul-Haq (1977–88) was met with increased organised resistance among Shia citizens.

Recruitment

Iran has employed a combination of ideological propaganda and material enticements to attract recruits.[94] Just as it has done elsewhere, Iran has propagated a message of Shia religious duty to defend sacred sites in Syria threatened by Sunni extremists. The names of the two militias have clear religious references: Zainab and Fatima are sacred figures for Muslims, and especially Shias. An intense messaging campaign, deploying Shia imagery and themes, celebrated Afghan and Pakistani fighters as 'defenders of shrines' along with Iranian and other Shia fighters, creating a unified sense of identity and purpose.

Iran has enrolled Afghan men from two distinct pools: from the Afghan refugee and migrant population (numbering up to 3m) that lives in Iran in precarious legal and economic circumstances, and, in smaller numbers, directly from inside Afghanistan itself. Iranian and Afghan recruiters offer a mix of monetary incentives and legal promises to Afghans who are residing in Iran, often without the necessary residency and work permits. Indeed, easing their and their families' precarious circumstances appears

> **"IN EFFECT, PAKISTANI SHIA FIGHTERS HAVE BEEN FIGHTING NOT FOR IRAN'S NATIONAL-SECURITY INTERESTS BUT RATHER FOR THE CAUSE OF THE ISLAMIC REVOLUTION"**

to have been a prime motivation for thousands of Afghan men living in Iran to join Liwa Fatemiyoun.

According to a senior Afghan contact, recruitment has taken place through local offices of the IRGC or Afghan clerical and cultural centres located in Iranian cities such as Tehran, Qom, Mashhad and Zahedan.[95] Afghan immigrants, due to poverty and unemployment, approach these offices for employment only to be recruited for the Fatemiyoun. Many unemployed immigrants and refugees, including teenagers as young as 14 years old, choose recruitment over imprisonment or deportation.[96]

Recruitment of Pakistani fighters has taken place primarily inside Pakistan.[97] The majority of the Zainabiyoun militia are of Punjabi origin, but the militia also includes Turi Shias (Pashtuns from Parachinar) as well as Shias from Gilgit-Baltistan and ethnic Hazaras (from Balochistan). In the context of decades of Shia persecution in Pakistan, the powerful narrative of exploitation and oppression, as well as the Sunni jihadi threat to Shia religious identity, have served as fundamental motives for the recruitment of fighters.[98] In effect, Pakistani Shia fighters have been fighting not for Iran's national-security interests but rather for the cause of the Islamic Revolution.[99]

Growing profile

In the early years of the Syrian conflict, Iran's deployment of Liwa Fatemiyoun and Liwa Zainabiyoun was mostly kept hidden, owing both to the secret nature of Iran's involvement and to Iran's reluctance to admit to any reliance on mercenary forces. Growing casualties and social-media coverage made this approach unsustainable. Ultimately, the rise of Sunni jihadi forces (which validated the idea of Shia resistance) and the need for further recruitment led to a growing political and religious acknowledgement of this reality. In 2015, senior Iranian officials began extolling the Afghan and Pakistani contribution to the war effort in Syria. This included pronouncements by Khamenei, who even met the families of deceased Afghan fighters.[100] In November 2016, a statement appeared on the Supreme Leader's official English website: 'Convey my greetings to the Pakistani defenders of the holy shrines. The Zainabiyoun fight so courageously ... Convey my greetings to their fathers, mothers and families.'[101]

Command, organisation and operations

Leadership

Both Liwa Fatemiyoun and Liwa Zainabiyoun operate under the command of the IRGC. A senior Afghan intelligence source stated that the Fatemiyoun is fully funded, trained and equipped by the Quds Force, the manager of the IRGC's network of partners.[102] Liwa Fatemiyoun is entirely subordinated to Iranian command on the Syrian battlefield, and its forces have fought under the direction of embedded senior Iranian officers, with subordinate Afghan officers filling staff and tactical roles. The same command structure also applies to the Zainabiyoun militia. Iranians inserted into these forces were killed in combat and were acknowledged in Iranian media as tactical commanders, even if their IRGC affiliation was often masked to stress the voluntary nature of their combat mission. This was the case of Mostafa Sadrzadeh, a young IRGC commander, who died in battle in southern Aleppo in October 2015 while leading the Amar Battalion of the Fatemiyoun.[103] Among the Iranian officers with oversight of these forces was Brigadier-General Mohammad Ali Falaki, who had ostensibly retired from the IRGC and volunteered to command Fatemiyoun units.[104]

The trajectory of Ali Reza Tavassoli's career highlights Liwa Fatemiyoun's closeness and subordination to the Quds Force, as well as the fact that some Afghan and Pakistani commanders have histories fighting for

Rebel weapons surrendered to Assad regime forces in Dumayr, to the northeast of Damascus, April 2018

(Louai Beshara/AFP/Getty Images)

Iran. Tavassoli, an Afghan veteran of the Iran–Iraq War and long-time resident in Iran, became Liwa Fatemiyoun's most prominent commander, before being killed in action in 2015.[105] He was pictured on the Syrian battlefield alongside Qasem Soleimani, the head of the Quds Force, who attended his funeral alongside other Iranian clerics and officials.[106] Other Fatemiyoun commanders have similar profiles.

On the battlefield

Both militias have nominally maintained their base in the district of Sayyida Zainab, south of the Syrian capital of Damascus, where Shia shrines are located and in close proximity to the Damascus civilian and military airports. Their known areas of operations extend across Syria. Among their key deployments were the 2015 battles in the southern province of Deraa; the 2015–16 operation to retake the rebel-held parts of Aleppo; the battle for Palmyra in 2015 and its recovery followed by the eastern campaign to conquer ISIS-held territory from Deir ez-Zor to Al-Bukamal in 2017; the siege of rebel-held areas surrounding Damascus from 2013 and the ultimate battle over eastern Ghouta in 2018; and the offensive to seize southern Syria in 2018.

Assessments of the size of the two militias, which are among the least well-known pro-Assad forces, vary considerably, especially as fighters are deployed inside Syria on rotations of differing length. Upper estimates have put the total number of Fatemiyoun fighters alone as high as 50,000.[107] However, most estimates, including from Western and Arab government sources, place the range of Fatemiyoun forces deployed in theatre between 4,000 and 8,000 at the height of the Syrian conflict (2013–18).[108] Estimates for Liwa Zainabiyoun are considerably lower, reaching at most 1,000 fighters at any one time. A former Pakistani government official has offered an estimate of 8,000–10,000 for the total number of Pakistani personnel having rotated into Syria.[109]

Liwa Fatemiyoun and Liwa Zainabiyoun have fielded mostly low-skilled, lightly equipped and mostly inexperienced infantry forces rather than specialist units.[110] They have primarily been deployed in static positions to hold territory or in support of other, often better-equipped, light mechanised units. There have been no reports of either militia manning a front, operating independently of other allied militias or leading a campaign. Their military value seems to have been in the additional numbers they have provided on the battlefield for assault operations rather than in the quality or expertise of their fighters.

Casualties

Zohair Mojahed, a media officer for Liwa Fatemiyoun, stated that more than 2,000 members of the Afghan militia had been killed in Syria and more than 8,000 injured as of January 2018.[111] A study based on Iranian and Afghan media sources recorded at least 895 confirmed dead Fatemiyoun fighters between January 2012 and July 2018, more than Iranian fighters (558) and second only to Lebanese fighters (1,232).[112] Such numbers suggest that the Fatemiyoun have been deployed in front-line positions; indeed, former Fatemiyoun fighters believe that the Iranians have used them as expendable forces, ill-equipped and recklessly deployed in battle.[113]

Strategic assessment

Contrary to other theatres where Iran has exerted power primarily through non-state partners it supports, it has so far refrained from using Shia militias for influence inside Afghanistan and Pakistan.

Pro-government forces at the Sayyida Zainab mosque, Damascus, April 2017

The reported downsizing of the two militias – which began in late 2017 after the Assad regime recovered most of the territory in Syria and major fighting ended – suggests that these units are deployed on a need-basis and are not central to Iran's post-conflict presence in Syria.

Two questions remain unanswered: could Iran deploy these forces, in similar or greater numbers, for other military operations in the Middle East, and would it mobilise them to gain influence inside Pakistan and Afghanistan as it did elsewhere with local partner forces? Worried about the ramifications, both Afghan and Pakistani intelligence agencies have closely monitored and complained about Iranian recruitment of their nationals, but political sensitivities have often overtaken such concerns. At present, it appears that Afghan fighters have been returning to Afghanistan or Iran. In Iran they appear to remain loosely organised, taking part in activities such as relief efforts in the country.[114] In Afghanistan, however, their reintegration into local communities is raising concern from the government as well as Shi'ites worried about being targeted by the Taliban or ISIS.

Shia combatants who fought in Syria were accordingly presented as 'defenders of the shrines', fulfilling a holy mission to protect the dozens of shrines in Syria.[115] The most prominent was the tomb of Sayyida Zainab, a granddaughter of the Prophet Muhammad, located in the southern suburbs of Damascus. Sayyida Zainab's tomb has served as a fulcrum of Shia mobilisation since the 1980s, attracting pilgrims from the Gulf states, Iran, Iraq and Lebanon. The site hosted religious centres, recruitment offices and other nodes in a network that would serve to quickly recruit and sustain fighters. The ubiquitous 'Labayke ya Zainab' ('At your service, Zainab') served as a rallying cry, and was displayed on flags, uniform insignias and other forms of propaganda. Other revered sites include Sayiddah Ruqayya mosque and Bab al-Saghir cemetery in Damascus, and Al-Nuqtah mosque in Aleppo. In time, Sayyida Zainab, as well as several lesser-known Shia shrines in Damascus and as far as Jisr al-Shughour and Raqqa, would come under attack, whether by car bombs or mortars, fuelling Shia resentment. This was the case of the Hajar Ben Adi al-Kundi shrine east of Damascus, which was desecrated by Islamist rebels in May 2013 and provoked outrage among Shia clerics, including Khamenei and Nasrallah.[116]

This sacralisation of the war effort, both genuine and manufactured, legitimised the military mobilisation and political violence that ensued. Indeed, the messaging that married ideological duty with the necessity to protect the Shia sect was also essential in recruiting new fighters and creating a common sense of purpose and identity among the various nationalities joining the armed movement. Afghan and Pakistani fighters, culturally different from Arab fighters, were socialised into this jihad through such experiences and exposures.

This aggressive communications strategy was essential in securing domestic support in Iran and Lebanon for costly and controversial operations abroad, and in containing the inevitable dissent they would generate. Indeed, in both Iran and Lebanon, some dissatisfaction over the resources and lives dedicated to the war in Syria, and concerns about an escalation of regional violence, were evident.[117] However, Hizbullah's de facto hegemony over the Shia community in Lebanon and its power to compel

Map 3.3: **Hizbullah: main deployments and operations in Syria, 2012–18**

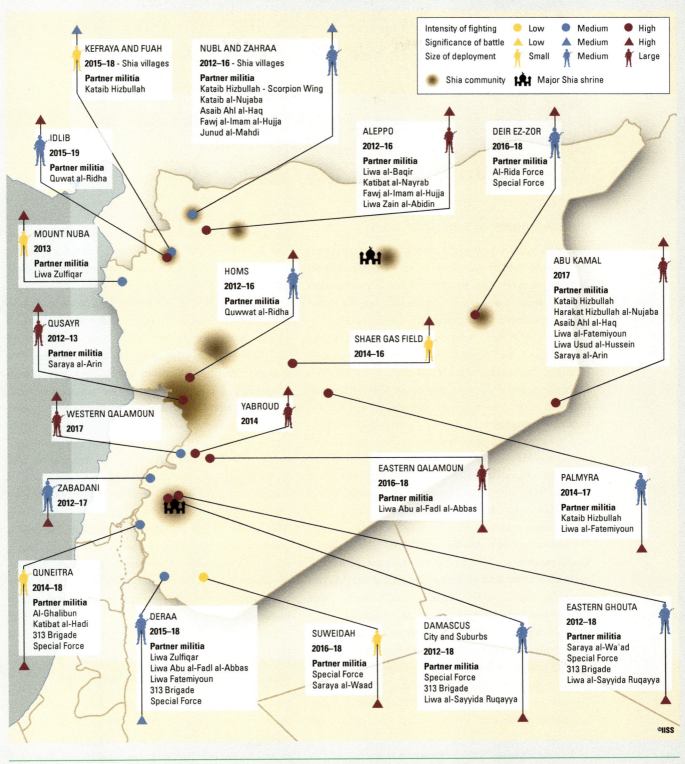

Source: IISS

solidarity contributed to the containing of such expressions of discontent; later, jihadi attacks on Shia shrines in Syria and on Shia neighbourhoods in Lebanon itself, as well as the rise of ISIS, resulted in overwhelming support for the intervention. A poll conducted by a non-governmental organisation in 2015 found that 78.7% of the Lebanese Shia community surveyed supported Hizbullah's involvement in Syria.[118]

SYRIA 107

(l) Syrian and Hizbullah forces, Qara, Syria, August 2017

(r) A Hizbullah camp on the Lebanese side of the Qalamoun Mountains, on the border with Syria, May 2015

Hizbullah on the Syrian battlefield

The alignment of strategic goals in Syria between Iran and Hizbullah translated into a mostly smooth division of roles and territory, as well as seamless coordination. However, operational tensions did appear, mostly centring on resources and prioritisation. This was notably the case in the battle for Aleppo, which lasted for almost two years and required significant numbers of ground forces. The IRGC demanded in 2015 and 2016 that Hizbullah dispatch troops to support the offensive, but the Lebanese movement stalled as it prioritised the fight over western Qalamoun and faced personnel shortages, growing discontent in the Shia community and jihadi attacks in Beirut.[119] Such divergences did not escalate into disputes, however, as both Iran and Hizbullah were able to deploy other militias from Afghanistan and Iraq.

Hizbullah was present militarily across Syria. Media reports, social-media posts and witnesses mark its presence in almost every significant battle. The group has displayed the capacity to calibrate its presence to the local context, resourcing material needs and its own priorities. It has proved able to deploy small train-and-assist units to the besieged villages of Nubl and Zahraa, as well as to Fuah and Kefraya, where a small unit of six troops was deployed for the duration of the three-year siege.[120] Hizbullah has also fielded light-infantry units of about 1,000 troops for large battles.

Its first sizeable battle in Syria was in spring 2013 in Qusayr, a city near the border with Lebanon and close to Shia villages inside Lebanon and Syria. It mobilised as many as 2,000 personnel, including fighters and logistics units.[121] In places such as southern Damascus, it took a less active role, but deployed allied LDF and NDF forces, notably LAFA and other Shi'ite groups. In Aleppo, it played an essential part in the campaign to capture important ground around the city; during the fight for eastern Aleppo, it played an important role in urban fighting (as it did in Homs), but adopted a low profile to allow regime forces to claim victory.

Much of Hizbullah's military efforts focused on the Lebanon–Syria border, from the region around Homs all the way to the Beirut–Damascus highway and along the M5 highway, in turn revealing the group's priorities. Preventing rebel and, later, jihadi forces from establishing bases close to Lebanese territory from which they could operate in Lebanon and outflank Hizbullah was an urgent task, especially as jihadi attacks had targeted the group's Beirut neighbourhoods in 2012–15. Of equal importance was the recovery of significant supply routes in Syria's western Qalamoun and Zabadani regions. Hizbullah operated in these areas, often in the lead, organising NDF units and sometimes dealing with the Syrian military as an auxiliary force. At several junctures, Hizbullah was clearly in overall charge, such as in Maaloula in 2013, Yabroud and Zabadani from 2013 to 2015, and throughout the battle around Arsal, which ended in 2017.

Hizbullah and Iran on the battlefield: the campaign to retake eastern Syria

One of the most complex operations mounted by Syrian government forces, Iranian forces and the mostly Shia militias they both supported was that to re-capture eastern Syria from ISIS, *Operation Fajr*, which took place in 2017.

A spring offensive spearheaded by the same actors retook large parts of the Badiya (central Syrian desert), areas around Palmyra and the town of Sukhna. The Damascus–Palmyra highway was secured, as was most of the Palmyra–Deir ez-Zor M20 highway. The towns of Palmyra and Sukhna served

(l) Pro-government fighters hold up a Syrian flag in Sukhnah, Syria, as they clear the area after taking control of the city from ISIS, August 2017

(r) Russian Air Force Su-25 and Su-34 at Hmeimim Air Base, January 2016

as staging points for the autumn campaign toward Deir ez-Zor. These operations had proved logistically challenging, as the regime and its allies had to extend their supply lines long distances, through desert and in hostile territory. In previous years, regime forces and Iranian-backed militias had struggled to fend off rebel and ISIS attacks in the eastern desert, losing key battles in Palmyra, the Shaer gas fields and elsewhere because of the difficulty of supplying units, protecting advancing forces and dedicating adequate numbers of personnel.

The campaign culminated in late 2017 with *Operation Fajr 3*. The objective was to seize ISIS-held territory in Deir ez-Zor governorate and restore Assad regime control over key cities, infrastructure and routes in the southern Euphrates River Valley, and ultimately border crossings into Iraq. The three key urban areas to be recovered were the ISIS-controlled parts of the city of Deir ez-Zor, the town of Mayadin and the border town of Al-Bukamal, which sits across from the Iraqi town of Qaim. Importantly, Iraqi Security Forces and Shia Popular Mobilisation Units (PMU, or *al-Hashd al-Shaabi*) mounted a concomitant assault on ISIS-held Qaim, liberating the Iraqi town in November 2017.[122]

The spring and autumn 2017 operations benefited from large numbers of fighters drawn from a variety of conventional and militia forces, as well as from air dominance and, crucially, the input of Russian military advisers. These advisers offered strategic planning and operational coordination, and also served in combat missions.[123] The dispatch to Syria of Russian military-bridging equipment suggests that the operation had required considerable effort during 2017 to plan and prepare, before the final phase began in September that year. News reports and social-media postings by all the main actors involved, including ISIS, allow the reconstruction of the operation.

The spring and autumn operations were commanded from a Russian-led field headquarters (HQ), where IRGC and Syrian command and liaison teams were established. The death in September 2017 of a Russian flag officer, Lieutenant-General Valery Asapov, who commanded the Syrian Army's 5th Corps, illustrates the multidimensional nature of the operation.[124] There was extensive cooperation between the multinational allied ground forces and Russian and Syrian aircraft, as well as armed Iranian uninhabited aerial vehicles (UAVs).[125] This appears to have been coordinated by a Russian air-component HQ, which also used an air-deconfliction communications channel with US-led *Operation Inherent Resolve* air forces.

Management of this complex battlespace – including artillery, aircraft, helicopters and UAVs – was coordinated at the Russian HQ. Russian military-communications teams and fire-support coordination teams established themselves at artillery positions, assisting both Syrian Army and Iranian-sponsored formations, while Russian special forces operated alongside partner forces. Iranian IRGC personnel were also deployed in front-line roles, leading to publicised deaths in their ranks.[126]

Order of battle

In the final phase of the campaign, which started in September, Iran appears to have deployed a land tactical HQ (equivalent to a NATO brigade HQ). Apparently commanded by an IRGC Quds Force general reporting to Major-General Qasem Soleimani, who made several appearances on the battlefield,[127] this HQ oversaw a brigade-sized force with the following assessed composition:

- Lebanese Hizbullah light infantry and elements of its mechanised battlegroup;
- tanks and artillery from the Syrian Army's

Syrian government forces backed by Russian air support hold a position on the southwestern outskirts of Deir ez-Zor, September 2017

- 4th Division;
- elements of the following Iranian-sponsored militia units:
  - Hizbullah-backed Saraya al-Arin (an Alawite LDF unit)
  - Hizbullah-backed Syrian Shia fighters from Nubl and Zahraa
  - 313 Force
  - Iraqi Shia Kataib Imam Ali militia
  - Afghan Shia Fatemiyoun militia – a company-sized unit with supporting tanks, former Iranian Army M101 howitzers, armoured bulldozers and large numbers of armed 'technicals' (flat-bed utility vehicles)

Hizbullah

The Lebanese Hizbullah mechanised battlegroup (equivalent to a US Combined Arms Battalion) was a new capability for Hizbullah, whose infantry had been observed to be dependent on armour and artillery support from Syrian forces. It is assessed to have comprised:

- at least 600 Hizbullah fighters;
- at least one tank company using T-72 and T-55 tanks;
- at least one mechanised company using M113 and MTLB armoured personnel carriers and BMP infantry fighting vehicles;
- Kornet anti-tank missiles mounted on quad bikes;
- civilian SUVs mounted with heavy machine guns;
- an artillery battery equipped with a mixture of weapons (a total of at least 14), which were observed to be capable of forming at least two fire-support groups. This weaponry included rocket launchers, self-propelled guns, improvised self-propelled guns mounted on M113s and self-propelled anti-aircraft guns;
- an engineer element with armoured bulldozers.

A small detachment of Syrian Army T-90 tanks was observed moving and fighting with the Hizbullah battlegroup, which was also assigned some Syrian self-propelled guns to augment its artillery.

Operation Fajr 3

The campaign required the brigade-sized formation to move 200 km from Palmyra, the nearest Syrian/Russian base, and from Sukhna toward Deir ez-Zor. As the desert terrain was empty and devoid of any usable resources, logistical support, operating at range, was essential. This was provided by civilian vehicles, a mixture of trucks and large heavy-equipment transporters, observed to carry up to five pallets of artillery ammunition each.

Once the battle for Deir ez-Zor, in which Russian officers played a significant role, was won in October, the focus turned to Mayadin and Al-Bukamal, where the IRGC played the central role. Soleimani was widely reported to be in overall command of the force, travelling in an SUV fitted with multiple radios.[128] He was seen not only personally addressing groups of fighters, but also directing the final assault on Al-Bukamal from a command post.[129]

The advancing formation, comprising several Iranian-backed units, including Fatemiyoun militia fighters[130] and significant numbers of Hizbullah fighters, moved eastward from the T-2 Pumping Station towards Al-Bukamal in November. Units of the Syrian Army's 5th Corps attacked from the north while the Tiger Force pro-government militia advanced from the southwest along the bank of the Euphrates. Just across the Iraqi border, Iranian-supported Shia militias moved westward in parallel along a road that lead to Qaim. The crucial factor was a well-planned attack mounted by elements of the Hizbullah mechanised battlegroup employing combined-arms tactics, integrating tanks, mechanised infantry, self-propelled artillery and armoured bulldozers.[131]

By 9 November, the formation had approached the western outskirts of Al-Bukamal, supported by missile strikes on ISIS defensive positions from Iranian *Shahid* UAVs launched from within Syria. ISIS defenders destroyed several Hizbullah vehicles with anti-tank missiles. The town was then subjected to nearly a week of artillery fire and air and missile strikes.

On 16 November the formation began attacking Al-Bukamal from west to east. The command and coordination of the attack was aided by commanders from Soleimani down, reportedly using photo-graphic maps of the town, on which buildings were given a unique number, which made coordinating supporting fire by artillery and aircraft simpler and faster, and reduced the chances of accidents. At least one Hizbullah commander was seen viewing these maps on a smartphone.[132]

The leading role in the urban battle, in which house-to-house fighting took place, was assumed by Hizbullah, with the militias playing supporting roles. In addition, Iraqi PMU attacked north from across the Iraqi border into the south of the town.[133]

About 30 Hizbullah fighters were reportedly killed in this campaign. IRGC officers were also killed, some of whom had previously commanded IRGC forces in Iran.[134] Some died in the intense street fighting, while others were killed in ISIS raids on lines of communi-cations or by ISIS mortar, artillery or rocket fire. There is no evidence that these casualties slowed down the pace of the advance or had any significant effect on Hizbullah or IRGC personnel, indicating high levels of morale, motivation and training.

The capture of Al-Bukamal was hailed as a major victory for Iran, with an IRGC-affiliated newspaper proclaiming: 'The liberation of this city [Al-Bukamal] will mean the completion of the final link in the resist-ance's land corridor, by which, for the first time, Tehran has land access to the Mediterranean coast and Beirut, an unprecedented achievement in Iran's several-millennia-long history.'[135]

Hizbullah: impact of the Syria campaign

Hizbullah's military intervention in Syria has trans-formed the militant organisation. It is there that it waged and supported logistically its biggest battles to date, conducted complex offensives and joint-forces operations, and lost the most fighters. It is also

in Syria that Hizbullah commanders organised and led non-*Hizbullahi* troops in battle for the first time. Since 2013, Hizbullah has reportedly deployed at any one time over 4,000 fighters across Syria, with peaks of 7,000 during the major battles in Aleppo in 2015 and 2016 and the push against ISIS in eastern Syria in 2017.[136]

Significantly, Hizbullah has done this while also maintaining force levels along the front line with Israel. There are strong suspicions that Hizbullah did not alter the posture or reduce the numbers of the Nasr Unit, which is stationed south of the Litani River along the Lebanon–Israel border, and which together with village volunteers is the first line of defence against an Israeli ground incursion. Similarly, Hizbullah's missile force remained untouched, to

"HIZBULLAH'S MILITARY INTERVENTION IN SYRIA HAS TRANSFORMED THE MILITANT ORGANISATION"

preserve its deterrence posture against Israel. Instead, Hizbullah mobilised at first veterans and small units drawn from its Badr Unit, as well as its reserves, and later recruited specifically for its Syria mission.

The human toll for Hizbullah has, however, been considerable: estimates of combat casualties range from 1,500 to 2,200 over the 2011–18 period (the low esti-mate is almost equal to the total number of Hizbullah fighters killed in action against Israel between 1982 and 2006).[137] In addition, nearly 6,000 *Hizbullahi* have suffered battle injuries of differing levels of gravity, requiring medical treatment and rehabilitation.[138]

As revealing as the total Hizbullah death toll is the profile of its senior officers killed in Syria. Many senior commanders who rose through the ranks in the 1980s and 1990s and were killed in action in Syria had front-line or command roles. These include Hamza Ibrahim Haidar in the Homs region, Wissam Sharafeddine in eastern Ghouta, Hassan al-Hajj in Idlib, Muhammad Issa in Quneitra, Ali Fayyad, a commander in the Radwan Unit (Hizbullah's special forces), in Aleppo and Fawzi Ayyoub in an unreported location.[139] The highest-ranking Hizbullah casualty was Mustafa Badreddine, the overall military commander in Syria, who was killed in Damascus in May 2016.[140]

The seniority of Hizbullah's casualties reveals that Hizbullah deployed high-ranking and experi-enced commanders, who often played a front-line role rather than a headquarters staff-command one. Indeed, the group's doctrine and ideology required

Hizbullah's relations with the Syrian high command

Despite decades of strategic partnership, ties between *Hizbullahi* forces and the Syrian military were limited by design. The two organisations had different cultures, competitive relations and condescending views of each other. This reflected initial Syrian scepticism about Hizbullah, which was considered an Islamist instrument of convenience. For its part, Hizbullah was concerned about being exposed to Syrian intelligence penetration and feared that weak Syrian security protocols would endanger its secretive organisation. Recriminations between Hizbullah and the Assad regime over the assassination in 2008 of Imad Mughniyah in Damascus and over the ability of Israeli intelligence to operate in Syria were reportedly intense.[142] Moreover, Hizbullah's domestic constituency, like many Lebanese, had a dim view of Syria's excesses and heavy-handedness during its occupation of Lebanon in 1976–2005. As a result, prior to the Syrian uprising, only a few senior commanders on each side were in charge of the Lebanon–Syria military relationship, while troops were largely insulated from each other.

The Syrian conflict only exacerbated these feelings. Hizbullah commanders developed a poor opinion of Syrian regime troops. The speed at which the Syrian military contracted from 2011, its weak performance on the battlefield, the unreliability of its recruits, its low levels of morale and its professionalism clashed with Hizbullah's ethos.[143]

Western sources claim that Hizbullah preferred not to embed senior commanders in the Syrian high command and operations room.[144] Instead, the coordination of strategic objectives was made at senior level and through the IRGC, while operational decisions were made on the ground.

that senior commanders were embedded at the front for operational and motivational reasons.

Looking at the patterns of those killed in action, the lack of correlation between Hizbullah's and allied forces' battlefield casualties suggests that for the most part, the two coordinated their efforts strategically but did not necessarily fight together; instead, they divided the battlefield so that each actor could prioritise its own interests.[141]

Strategic assessment

Iran's involvement in the Syrian civil war to secure the survival of President Bashar al-Assad has been, to date, the costliest and most controversial of Iran's regional endeavours. It has also tarnished Tehran's regional and global standing. Iran has been involved in large battles, has overlooked Assad's use of chemical weapons and has used brutal military tactics that have generated immense human suffering.[145]

For a long time it seemed that, on its own, Iran would be unable to prevent the collapse of the Assad regime. From 2012, it deployed its own forces, enrolled Hizbullah, and appealed to Afghan, Iraqi and Pakistani fighters. Even with this influx of military power, the weakening of the Syrian regime seemed irreversible: reluctantly, in 2015 Iran was forced to appeal to Russia, a traditional rival, for additional personnel, crucial airpower and political cover.

Ultimately, Iran's commitment to saving Assad and defeating the insurgency proved crucial. It provided the personnel, organisation and material support that shored up Assad's depleted and battered forces. The intervention has also been essential in securing Iran's strategic depth in the Middle East and its reach to the eastern Mediterranean. Furthermore, Tehran's risk-taking and reliance on militia partners have both been rewarded, at a financial cost that is certainly high but at a limited human cost to itself. With a smaller force in Syria than other powers active in Syria, and the discipline to prevent an unnecessary direct expansion, it has secured its key objectives, become a prime shaper of Syria's future, dealt setbacks to its regional rivals and began to establish another front against Israel. Its contribution to the fight against ISIS in Iraq since 2014 and later in Syria has repaired some of the reputational damage of supporting Assad.

Iran has successfully orchestrated two approaches: it mobilised its regional non-state partners and it recruited and organised Syrian militias. Unwilling to commit a large number of its own personnel, and in line with its doctrinal principles, Tehran has deployed a limited number of commanders, trainers and fighters to oversee and at times accompany this effort. The presence on the battlefield of IRGC Quds Force commander Qasem Soleimani has conveyed commitment to the multinational militia deployed against Syrian rebels and jihadis. By early 2018, the estimated number of Shi'ite fighters from Afghanistan, Iraq, Lebanon, and Pakistan to have rotated through Syria ranged between 30,000 and 60,000, with most fulfilling front-line fighting roles.[146] In comparison,

CHAPTER THREE

the assessed number of Sunni foreign fighters who joined the ranks of ISIL up to 2018 was 33,000.[147]

Defeating the Syrian insurgency proved to be a difficult undertaking, one that IRGC and Hizbullah commanders conducted jointly. The wide variety of missions, from the local defence of villages with small units to large, joint operations involving armour, airpower and formations of different cultures and qualities, has created a sense of accomplishment, purpose and comradeship among a significant number of allied fighters. This complex military effort, large in size and relatively low in cost, required senior Iranian supervision but comparatively few junior Iranian officers and soldiers. It produced experienced and hardened fighters who have developed new skills and institutionally learned to work together in combat. For Iran, the emergence of this transnational generation of veterans is an unintended benefit of the Syrian civil war.

However, the next phase of the civil war will be as complex and possibly more dangerous for Tehran. Securing its influence in Syria will require navigating a complicated political landscape, as well as the calculations of international, regional and local powers with considerable interests and influence.

The Assad regime is intent on re-establishing full territorial and political control over the country. To do so, it has to attract, temper and reintegrate the vast array of militias that rose to its defence but that developed specific identities, interests and regional affiliations. Many of those militias have associations with Iran, and may resist this effort. In order to obtain regional and international acquiescence for Assad and financial assistance for reconstruction, the regime also has to decrease its dependency on Iran, or at least the perception of it. Bringing these militias under nominal and possibly even effective Syrian control will be the main and ultimate evidence of this.

Similarly, Iran has a complex, ambivalent partnership with Russia, one defined simultaneously by cooperation and competition, dependence and mistrust. To declare victory and decrease over time its military and political contribution in Syria, Moscow is already building up the conventional military capabilities of the Assad regime, by reorganising the armed forces and the integration of militias into newly formed units, and diluting where possible their ties to Iran and Hizbullah. This has been the case for several Alawite militias, such as the Tiger Force and the Desert Hawks. This puts Iran and Russia at odds in terms of their influence strategies. Simultaneously, Russia must manage the security concerns of Israel,

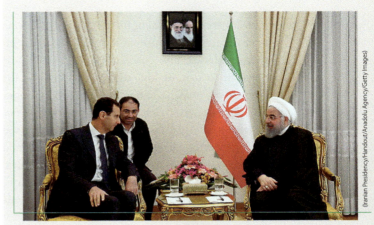

Iranian President Hassan Rouhani meets Syrian leader Bashar al-Assad in Tehran, Iran, with Hizbullah's Muhammad Qasir, February 2019

which centre on Iran's network and infrastructure building in Syria. Moscow is an uncomfortable arbiter of Iranian–Israeli competition over Syria, eager to ensure that its fallout does not endanger the recovery of the Assad regime.

Iran's supply and partner network in Syria also faces Israel and the US, and their stated desire to counter its presence. The US maintains a significant presence in northeast Syria in support of its Kurdish partners and a smaller one in Tanf, both backed by significant airpower and intelligence, surveillance and reconnaissance capabilities that outmatch what Iran can deploy. Israeli and US airpower can identify and interdict movement along the Al-Bukamal–Deir ez-Zor–Palmyra route, while US control of Tanf cuts off an important road that could otherwise be used to transfer fighters and weapons from Iraq into Syria.

Iran's appeal in Syria therefore remains limited by resource availability, competition with its ostensible allies, and distrust of its ideology by secular and non-Shia forces. Iran has, however, found ways to manage and work around all three constraints.

Faced with two militarily superior enemies, Israel and the US; an ambivalent partner, Russia; and a calculating ally, the Assad regime, Iran is seemingly on a weak footing in Syria. Yet it has over the years demonstrated an impressive ability to adapt quickly to significant changes on the Syrian battlefield. When the limitations and costs of building an autonomous, Basij-like structure in Syria became clear in 2015 and 2016, Iran downgraded the NDF model, then reversed course and sought instead to embed its allies inside Syrian regime security and militia structures through the LDF framework. It chose to acquire a stake in existing and emerging frameworks rather than develop a new and separate one, thereby extending its influence into Syrian state structures. This approach provides Iran political cover, deniability, cost-sharing and flexibility, allowing it to test, at low cost and indirectly, the resolve of its rivals. Challenging the US presence through Liwa al-Baqir, countering Russian influence from within security institutions, reminding Assad of its role through Iranian officers in the LDF and using Syrian partners to expand its military infrastructure are all more viable and realistic options for long-term success than pursuing an autonomous and expensive approach.

By accompanying personnel deployments with small but targeted soft-power and reconstruction activities in the communities it operates in, and by providing political incentives to former insurgents and regime militia fighters, Iran has sought to build local support among sympathetic communities and recruit locally, as it has done in southern, eastern and central Syria. And, where necessary, Iran has proven oppor-

tunistic, supporting directly, or through Hizbullah, partners with no ideological or organic ties. It has expediently supported pro-regime militias from the Alawite, Christian and Sunni sects, and reached out to local community leaders. To work around Russian constraints in southern Syria, Hizbullah has recruited small numbers of former Sunni rebels, offering them amnesty in exchange for their assistance.

Ultimately, Iran's comparative advantage has been its ability to adapt to challenging conditions. Its current set-up in Syria is flexible, responsive, adjustable and deniable. The militias that Iran has trained are not a standing force. For example, Liwa Fatemiyoun and Liwa Zainabiyoun, respectively composed of Afghan and Pakistani recruits, have been downsized since late 2017, once strategic objectives were achieved. By embedding itself in the Syrian security structure, Iran is well placed to compete for loyalty among Syrian officer elites and militia commanders brought into the state forces.

Notes

[1] Jubin M. Goodarzi, *Syria and Iran: Diplomatic Alliance and Power Politics in the Middle East* (London: I.B. Tauris, 2006).

[2] Jay Solomon and Nour Malas, 'Syria Would Cut Iran Military Tie, Opposition Head Says', *Wall Street Journal*, 2 December 2011, https://www.wsj.com/articles/SB1000142405 2970204397704577070850124861954.

[3] Pew Research Center, 'Iran's Global Image Mostly Negative', 18 June 2015, http://www.pewglobal. org/2015/06/18/irans-global-image-mostly-negative.

[4] 'Lebanon's Hizbollah Turns Eastward to Syria', *International Crisis Group Middle East Report*, no. 163, 27 May 2014, p. 1, https://www.files.ethz.ch/isn/180517/153-lebanon-s-hizbollah-turns-eastward-to-syria.pdf.

[5] Farnaz Fassihi and Jay Solomon, 'Top Iranian Official Acknowledges Syria Role', *Wall Street Journal*, 16 September 2012, https://www.wsj.com/articles/SB1000087239639044372 0204578000482831419570.

[6] Farnaz Fassihi, 'Tensions Rise Over Iranian Hostages', *Wall Street Journal*, 8 August 2012, https://www.wsj.com/articles/ SB10000872396390443792604577575221903873222.

[7] Marwa Haidar, 'Sayyed Nasrallah: Syria, Allies Shattered Zionist Entity's Prestige', *Almanar*, 16 May 2018, http://english.almanar.com.lb/506332.

[8] '7 Hezbollah fighters killed in Syria', *Yalibnan*, 2 September 2011, http://yalibnan.com/2011/09/02/7-hezbollah-fighters-killed-in-syria.

[9] Reza HaghighatNejad, 'Outspoken Guards Commander Killed in Syria', *IranWire*, 9 October 2015, https://en.iranwire. com/en/features/1390.

[10] Neil MacFarquhar, 'Syrian Rebels Land Deadly Blow to

Assad's Inner Circle', *New York Times*, 18 July 2012, https:// www.nytimes.com/2012/07/19/world/middleeast/suicide-attack-reported-in-damascus-as-more-generals-flee.html.

[11] Gol Ali Babai, *Peigham-e mahiha: sargozasht nameh-ye sardar-e shahid hossein hamadani* [Message of Fishes: Memoir of the Martyr General Hossein Hamadani] (Tehran: 27 Besat Publications, 2015).

[12] Tony Badran, 'Hezbollah Calls the Shots in Iran's Syria Policy', Foundation for Defense of Democracies Cipher Brief, 11 October 2017, https://www.fdd.org/analysis/2017/10/11/ hezbollah-calls-the-shots-in-irans-syria-policy.

[13] Wafiq Qansouh, 'Nasrallah: naktub tarikh al-mantiqah … la lubnan' [Nasrallah: we are writing the history of the region … not only Lebanon], 12 September 2017, *Al-Akhbar*, https:// www.al-akhbar.com/Politics/237618.

[14] International Crisis Group, 'Iran's Priorities in a Turbulent Middle East', *Middle East Report*, no. 184, https://www. crisisgroup.org/middle-east-north-africa/gulf-and-arabian-peninsula/iran/184-irans-priorities-turbulent-middle-east.

[15] 'Esma'il Kousari: Iran dar suriye kamtar az 20 nafar niru darad' [Esmail Kousari: Iran has fewer than 20 soldiers in Syria], Khabar Online, 26 November 2013, https://www. khabaronline.ir/news/324700.

[16] Matthew Levitt, *Hezbollah: The Global Footprint of Lebanon's Party of God* (Washington DC: Georgetown University Press, 2013), p. 383.

[17] Reinoud Leenders and Antonio Giustozzi, 'Outsourcing state violence: The National Defence Force, "stateness" and regime resilience in the Syrian war', *Mediterranean Politics*, vol. 21, no. 3, 2017, https://www.tandfonline.com/doi/abs/10.

18 Arash Karami, 'Former IRGC Commander's Comments on Syria Censored', *Al-Monitor*, 6 May 2014, http://www.al-monitor.com/pulse/originals/2014/05/former-irgc-commander-syria-comments-censored.html; 'Farmandeh-ye arshad-e Sepah: Iran Hezbollah-ye dovvom ra dar Surieh tashkil dad' [Senior IRGC Commander: Iran created a second Hizbullah in Syria], BBC Persian, 5 May 2014, http://www.bbcpersian.com/persian/iran/2014/05/140407_l45_Hamadani_syria_iran_war; Hossein Bastani, 'Iran quietly deepens involvement in Syria's war', BBC News, 20 October 2015, https://www.bbc.co.uk/news/world-middle-east-34572756.

19 Kristin Dailey, 'Thousands gather to mourn Iranian general Hamadani', Middle East Eye, 11 October 2015, https://www.middleeasteye.net/news/thousands-gather-mourn-iranian-general-Hamadani. Mohsen Rezai, former commander-in-chief of the IRGC, reported that Hamadani had been involved in 80 high-level operations in Syria since 2011. He also mentioned that Hamadani had 'established the Zeinab headquarters in Damascus and Roghayye headquarters in Aleppo'.

20 'Akharin goftogu-ye sardar-e shahid Hossein Hamadani' [The last conversation with the martyred general Hossein Hamadani], Mizan Online, 9 October 2015, https://www.mizanonline.com/fa/news/85605.

21 *Ibid.*

22 Dailey, 'Thousands gather to mourn Iranian general Hamadani'.

23 Reza Parchizadeh, 'U.S. Aims To Thwart IRGC's Plans in the Middle East', Kayhan Life, 14 November 2017, https://kayhan-life.com/news/u-s-aims-thwart-irgcs-plans-middle-east.

24 The Shia community of Hatla consists of converts from 2003 onwards, whereas the Shia of Busra al-Sham in Deraa can trace their origins to around 100 years ago, from migrations from southern Lebanon. For more on the distribution of Syrian Shia Muslims, see Fabrice Balanche, 'Sectarianism in Syria's Civil War: A Geopolitical Study', Washington Institute for Near East Policy, February 2018, https://www.washingtoninstitute.org/policy-analysis/view/sectarianism-in-syrias-civil-war.

25 'Syria rebels "kill Shia residents of eastern village"', BBC News, 12 June 2013, https://www.bbc.co.uk/news/world-middle-east-22870776.

26 Rick Gladstone and Anne Barnard, 'U.S. Accuses Hezbollah of Aiding Syria's Crackdown', *New York Times*, 10 August 2012, https://www.nytimes.com/2012/08/11/world/middleeast/us-officials-say-hezbollah-helps-syrias-military.html.

27 Nour Samaha, 'The Eagles of the Whirlwind', *Foreign Policy*, 28 March 2016, https://foreignpolicy.com/2016/03/28/the-eagles-of-the-whirlwind.

28 'Iran has the strongest influence in eastern Syria, the "al-Baqir Brigade" and details of its forming', 27 February 2018, https://www.nso-sy.com/Details/954/Iran-has-the-strongest-influence-in-eastern-Syria,-the-%22al-Baqir-Brigade%22-and-details-of-its-forming-in-a-special-report-of-NSO/en.

29 'Ma hiya al-dowal al-lati istahdafaha tajammu shuyukh kabael wa ashaer souriya?' [What are the countries that were targeted by the meeting of the sheikhs of Syria's clans and tribes?], *Al-Alam*, 30 June 2018, http://www.alalam.ir/news/3598316/ما-الدول-التي-استهدفها-تجمع-شيوخ-قبائل-وعشائر-سوريا؟.

30 Phil Stewart and Suleiman Al-Khalidi, 'U.S. strikes Syria militia threatening U.S.-backed forces: officials', Reuters, 18 May 2017, https://www.reuters.com/article/us-mideast-crisis-syria-usa-idUSKCN18E2JU.

31 Thomas Gibbons-Neff, 'How a 4-Hour Battle Between Russian Mercenaries and U.S. Commandos Unfolded in Syria', *New York Times*, 24 May 2018, https://www.nytimes.com/2018/05/24/world/middleeast/american-commandos-russian-mercenaries-syria.html; Gregory Waters, 'Inside the U.S. coalition attack on Syrian forces in Deir-ez-Zor', International Review, 10 February 2018, https://international-review.org/inside-u-s-coalition-attack-syrian-forces-deir-ez-zor.

32 'Liwa Abu al-Fadl al-Abbas and the Republican Guard', Aymenn Jawad Al-Tamimi's Blog, 29 March 2018, http://www.aymennjawad.org/2018/03/liwa-abu-al-fadl-al-abbas-and-the-republican-guard.

33 Interviews with Western intelligence officials, October 2018.

34 Interview with Western intelligence official, October 2018.

35 Interview with a founder of the NDF unit in Deir ez-Zor, August 2018.

36 Interview with NDF official, September 2018.

37 Maher Samaan and Anne Barnard, 'Assad, in Rare Admission, Says Syria's Army Lacks Manpower', *New York Times*, 26 July 2015, https://www.nytimes.com/2015/07/27/world/middleeast/assad-in-rare-admission-says-syrias-army-lacks-manpower.html.

38 'Al-qusa al-kamila li-qarar al-tadakhol al-askari al-russi fi suriya: moufad li-Khamenei ila Moscow wa al-Assad lina-jdat saria't wa Putin yastajib' [The full story of the Russian decision to intervene in Syria: Khamenei's emissary goes to Moscow and Assad for an urgent saving and Putin responds positively], *As-Safir*, 20 October 2015, http://assafir.com/Article/5/451301.

39 Aymenn Jawad Al-Tamimi, 'Administrative Decisions on Local Defence Forces Personnel: Translation & Analysis', 3 May 2017, http://www.aymennjawad.org/2017/05/administrative-decisions-on-local-defence-forces.

40 'Local Defense Commander mysteriously Killed in Aleppo', *Nedaa Syria*, 3 May 2018, https://nedaa-sy.com/en/news/5902.

41 Social-media post by Liwa al-Baqir media official Mohamad Hendawi, 6 June 2018, https://justpaste.it/hendawi6june2018.

42 Interview with Idlib sector LDF representative, August 2018.

43 Social-media post by Fawj al-Nayrab media activist Abu Wanas Nashar, 20 April 2018, https://justpaste.it/abuwanas-bashar20april2018.

44 Interview with leader of 313 Force, January 2019.

45 Social-media post by Salmiya News Network, 14 February 2018, https://justpaste.it/salmiyanewsnetwork14feb2018.

46 Interview with Idlib sector LDF representative, August 2018.

47 *Ibid.*

48 Aymenn Jawad Al-Tamimi, 'Saraya Fursan al-Basil: Aleppo Local Defence Forces Unit', 12 December 2018, http://www.aymennjawad.org/2018/12/saraya-fursan-al-basil-aleppo-local-defence.

49 Social-media post by Fawj Sayyida Zainab, 25 February 2018, https://justpaste.it/fawjsayyidazainab2018.

50 Interview with member of the Special Force, July 2018.

51 *Ibid.*

52 Al-Ghad al-Souri, 'Hizbullah yashi'u ahad 'anasirihi al-mokhdarimin mima laqu masrafahum fi Homs mo'akhkhiran' [Hizbullah pays tribute to one of its veteran members who recently died in Homs], 14 December 2016, https://www.alghadalsoury.com/2016/12/14.

53 Interview with a Liwa Ashbal al-Hussein commander, July 2018.

54 Interview with Iraqi veteran, August 2018.

55 Interview with 313 Force leader, March 2017.

56 Interview with 313 Force leader, January 2019.

57 Social-media post by Mohamed Hendawi, 14 June 2016, https://justpaste.it/mohamadhendawibaqir.

58 Social-media post by Mohamed Hendawi, 5 February 2019, https://justpaste.it/mohamadhendawi5feb2019.

59 'What advantages did Khamenei give to the "Shiite regime militias"?', Orient Net, 8 March 2018, https://www.orient-news.net/ar/news_show/146543.

60 Aymenn Jawad Al-Tamimi, 'Al-Ghalibun: Inside Story of a Syrian Hezbollah Group', 16 April 2017, http://www.aymennjawad.org/2017/04/al-ghalibun-inside-story-of-a-syrian-hezbollah.

61 Saraya al-Arin also has an affiliation with the 223 branch of Syrian military intelligence. Interview with a member of the group, December 2018.

62 Post by Mahrada News on Facebook, 24 January 2019. Posts by various local Mahrada pages. See https://justpaste.it/maherqawarmamp.

63 Interview with former member of Ghaliboun militia, May 2017.

64 Interview with a Druze member of Quwat al-Wad al-Sadiq, August 2017.

65 Sada al-Sham, 'The Cultural Frontlines for Russia and Iran in Syria', *Syrian Observer*, 9 August 2018, https://syrianobserver.com/EN/features/19709/the_cultural_front-lines_russia_iran_syria.html; Al-Hal, 'Iran and Shi'ite Islam Spread in Old Damascus', *Syrian Observer*, 16 August 2018, https://syrianobserver.com/EN/features/45096/iran_Shi'ite_islam_spread_old_damascus-2.

66 'Bargozari-ye jashn-e piruzi-ye enghelab-e islami dar "Haleb"' [Holding a celebration of the victory of the Islamic Revolution in Aleppo], Tasnim News, 11 February 2017, https://www.tasnimnews.com/fa/news/1395/11/23/1324597.

67 Martin Chulov, 'Iran repopulates Syria with Shi'ite Muslims to help tighten regime's control', *Guardian*, 14 January 2017, https://www.theguardian.com/world/2017/jan/13/irans-syria-project-pushing-population-shifts-to-increase-influence.

68 Sune Engel Rasmussen and Suha Ma'ayeh, 'Iran Ally Hezbollah Pays Syrian Rebels to Switch Sides', *Wall Street Journal*, 1 November 2018, https://www.wsj.com/articles/iran-ally-hezbollah-pays-syrian-rebels-to-switch-sides-1541073600.

69 Alistair Lyon, 'Analysis: Syria's implosion worries neighbors', Reuters, 20 July 2012, https://ca.reuters.com/article/topNews/idCABRE86J0TO20120720.

70 Saeed Kamali Dehghan, 'Top Iranian general and six Hezbollah fighters killed in Israeli attack in Syria', *Guardian*, 19 January 2015, https://www.theguardian.com/world/2015/jan/19/top-iranian-general-hezbollah-fighters-killed-israel-attack-syria.

71 Dan Williams, 'Israel says struck Iranian targets in Syria 200 times in last two years', Reuters, 4 September 2018, https://www.reuters.com/article/us-mideast-crisis-israel-syria-iran/israel-says-struck-iranian-targets-in-syria-200-times-in-last-two-years-idUSKCN1LK2D7.

72 Amos Harel, '"Aerial and Intelligence Superiority": Army Chief Reveals How Israel Beat Iran's Soleimani in Syria', *Haaretz*, 13 January 2019, https://www.haaretz.com/israel-news/army-chief-reveals-how-israel-beat-iran-s-solei-mani-in-syria-1.6830387.

73 Elizabeth Tsurkov, 'Inside Israel's Secret Program to Back Syrian Rebels', *Foreign Policy*, 6 September 2018, https://foreignpolicy.com/2018/09/06/in-secret-program-israel-armed-and-funded-rebel-groups-in-southern-syria.

74 'Russia says "arbitrary" Israeli air strikes on Syria must stop', Reuters, 23 January 2019, https://www.reuters.com/article/us-mideast-crisis-syria-israel-russia/russia-says-arbitrary-israeli-air-strikes-on-syria-must-stop-idUSKCN1PH1K5.

75 Barbara Starr, 'Syria accidentally shot down a Russian military plane', CNN, 18 September 2018, https://edition.cnn.com/2018/09/17/politics/syrian-regime-shoots-down-russian-plane/index.html.

76 Jack Khoury, 'Israel and Russia Agree to Remove Iranian Forces From Syrian Border, Report Says', *Haaretz*, 1 June 2018, https://www.haaretz.com/israel-news/report-israel-and-russia-agree-to-remove-iranian-forces-from-syrian-1.6137601.

77 'The Special Force: Syrian Hezbollah Unit', Aymenn

Jawad Al-Tamimi's Blog, 29 July 2018, http://www.aymennjawad.org/2018/07/the-special-force-syrian-hezbollah-unit; Caleb Weiss, 'Confirmed: First evidence of Iranian-controlled militia involvement in southern Syria', Long War Journal, Threat Matrix blog, 27 June 2018, https://www.longwarjournal.org/archives/2018/06/confirmed-first-evidence-of-iranian-controlled-militia-involvement-in-southern-syria.php.

78 Rasmussen and Ma'ayeh, 'Iran Ally Hezbollah Pays Syrian Rebels to Switch Sides'.

79 Interview with resident of Deraa locality, January 2019.

80 Gordon Corera, 'Iran building permanent military base in Syria – claim', BBC News, 10 November 2017, https://www.bbc.com/news/world-middle-east-41945189.

81 'Israeli missiles hit military post near Damascus: Syrian state TV', Reuters, 2 December 2017, https://www.reuters.com/article/us-mideast-crisis-syria-attack/israeli-missiles-hit-military-post-near-damascus-syrian-state-tv-idUSKBN1DW081.

82 Amos Harel et al., 'Israel Launches Most Extensive Strike in Syria in Decades After Iranian Rocket Barrage', Haaretz, 11 May 2018, https://www.haaretz.com/israel-news/israel-launches-extensive-syria-strike-after-iranian-rocket-barrage-1.6073938.

83 'Syria complains Israeli airstrikes violated international law', Times of Israel, 17 March 2017, https://www.timesofisrael.com/syria-complains-israeli-airstrikes-violated-international-law.

84 'Tour of the liberated Al Bukamal', November 2017, https://youtu.be/jtGebs4f1Hg.

85 'Asr Iran, 'Safir-e Iran: Havades-e Suriyeh noskheh-ye dovvom- fetneh-ye 88 Iran ast' [Iranian Ambassador: The events in Syria are the second version of the 2009 sedition in Iran], Asr Iran, 3 April 2011, https://www.asriran.com/fa/news/161184.

86 'Amrika ba shabihsazi-ye havades-e mantagheh beh donbal-e ijad-e moshkel dar Suriyeh ast' [By simulating regional events America is looking to create a problem in Syria], Fars News, 30 June 2011, https://www.farsnews.com/news/9004090228.

87 'Hezbollah leader vows to stand by Syrian regime in fight against rebels', Guardian, 25 May 2013, https://www.theguardian.com/world/2013/may/25/hezbollah-leader-syria-assad-qusair.

88 'Syria Connects Iran, Resistance: Nasrallah', PressTV, 20 July 2012, http://iqnanews.ru/en/news/2372581/syria-connects-iran-resistance-nasrallah.

89 'Sayyed Nasrallah Speech on 6th Anniversary of Divine Victory: "Israel's" Operation Was Qualitative Illusion', Alahed News, August 2012, https://english.alahednews.com.lb/20509/444.

90 'Text of Nasrallah's May 9 speech', 9 May 2013, https://now.mmedia.me/lb/en/lebanonnews/hezbollah-leader-sayyed-hassan-nasrallah-speaks-live.

91 Ahmad Madijyar, 'Hezbollah Leader Declares Victory in Syria, Recalls Meeting with Khamenei', Middle East Institute, 12 September 2017, https://www.mei.edu/publications/hezbollah-leader-declares-victory-syria-recalls-meeting-khamenei.

92 Paul Iddon, 'Iran doubles down in Syria', New Arab, 12 January 2017, https://www.alaraby.co.uk/english/indepth/2017/1/13/iran-doubles-down-in-syria.

93 Clément Therme, 'The Shi'a Afghan Community: Between Transnational Links and Internal Hurdles', Iranian Studies, vol. 50, no. 4, April 2017, p. 2, http://dx.doi.org/10.1080/00210862.2017.1295537.

94 Saeed Kamali Dehghan, 'Afghan refugees in Iran being sent to fight and die for Assad in Syria', Guardian, 5 November 2015, https://www.theguardian.com/world/2015/nov/05/iran-recruits-afghan-refugees-fight-save-syrias-bashar-al-assad.

95 Interview with Afghan intelligence official, October 2018.

96 Human Rights Watch, 'Iran: Afghan Children Recruited to Fight in Syria', 1 October 2017, https://www.hrw.org/news/2017/10/01/iran-afghan-children-recruited-fight-syria.

97 Interview with a former Pakistani government official, November 2018.

98 Babak Dehghanpisheh, 'Iran recruits Pakistani Shi'ites for combat in Syria', Reuters, 10 December 2015, http://www.reuters.com/article/us-mideast-crisis-syria-pakistan-iran-idUSKBN0TT22S20151210.

99 Interview with a Shia cleric at the Mohammadi Shia mosque in Lahore, Pakistan, January 2018.

100 'Didar-e khanavadeh-ye shohada-ye Afghanestani-ye modafe'-e haram-e Lashkar-e Fatemiyun' [Meeting with the families of martyred Afghan fighters of the Fatemiyoun Division], Khamenei.Ir, 27 March 2016, http://farsi.khamenei.ir/video-content?id=33070.

101 'Convey my greetings to the Zeynabiyoun of Pakistan: Imam Khamenei', Khamenei.Ir, 6 December 2016, http://english.khamenei.ir/photo/4411/Convey-my-greetings-to-the-Zeynabiyoun-of-Pakistan-Imam-Khamenei.

102 Interview with Afghan intelligence official, October 2018.

103 'Shahid-e modafe'-e haram dar kenar sardar Soleimani' [A martyred Holy Shrine defender alongside commander Qasem Soleimani], Jahan News, 25 October 2015, http://www.jahannews.com/gallery/451742/1/-شهید-مدافع-حرم-درکنار-سردارسلیمانی.

104 'Fatemiyun pishgharavol-e nabard-e Suriyeh budand' [The Fatemiyoun were the vanguard in the Syrian War], Fars News, 18 August 2016, https://www.farsnews.com/news/13950528000439.

105 '"Fatehan-e farda" az farmandeh-ye Fatemiyun miguyad' ['Tomorrow's victors' talks about the Fatemiyoun commander], Fash News, 20 February 2016, http://fashnews.ir/fa/news-details/43055/ «فاتحان فردا» از فرمانده فاطمیون میگوید.

106 Golnaz Esfandiari, 'Increasing Number Of Afghans,

Pakistanis Killed In Syria Buried In Iran', RFE/RL, 2 April 2015, https://www.rferl.org/a/persian-letters-afghans-pakistanis-killed-fighting-in-syria-for-iran/26977907.html.

107 Ahmad Shuja Jamal, 'The Fatemiyoun Army: Reintegration into Afghan Society', United States Institute of Peace, Special Report no. 443, March 2019, https://www.usip.org/sites/default/files/2019-03/sr_443-the_fatemiyoun_army_reintegration_into_afghan_society-pdf_0.pdf.

108 A senior Afghan contact assessed that there were approximately 6,000 Fatemiyoun fighters in Syria at any one time. Interview with Afghan intelligence official, October 2018.

109 Interview with former Pakistani government official, November 2018.

110 'Afghani kesafat-e diruz va razmandegan-e Fatemiyun emruz mosahebeh-ye seda-ye mohajer ba yeki az farmandehan' [Afghan is yesterday's dirt and the Fatemiyoun fighters are today's; The Voice of Refugees' interview with one of the commanders], Voice of Refugees, 23 November 2017, https://www.facebook.com/vorefugee/videos/%D8%A7%D9%81%D8%BA%D8%A7%D9%86%DB%8C%DA%A9%D8%AB%D8%A7%D9%81%D8%AA-%D8%AF%DB%8C%D8%B1%D9%88%D8%B2-%D9%88-%D8%B1%D8%B2%D9%85%D9%86%D8%AF%DA-%AF%D8%A7%D9%86-%D9%81%D8%A7%D8%B7%D9%85%DB%8C%D9%88%D9%86-%D8%A7%D9%85%D8%B1%D9%88%D8%B2%D9%85%D8%B5%D8%A7%D8%AD%D8%A8%D9%87-%D8%B5%D8%AF%D8%A7%DB%8C--%D9%85%D9%87%D8%A7%D8%AC%D8%B1-%D8%A8%D8%A7-%DB%8C%DA%A9%DB%8C-%D8%A7%D8%B2-%D9%81%D8%B1%D9%85%D8%A7%D9%86%D8%AF%D9%87%D8%A7%D9%86-/1512565795463276/.

111 'More Than 2,000 Iran Backed Afghans Killed In Syria', Radio Farda, 7 January 2018, https://en.radiofarda.com/a/afghan-casualties-in-syria/28959545.html.

112 The Arab Gulf States Institute in Washington, 'Using Syria as a training ground: The case of the Pakistani Zainabiyoun Brigade', 17 July 2018, http://www.agsiw.org/using-syria-as-a-training-ground-the-case-of-the-pakistani-zeinabiyoun-brigade.

113 Fariba Sahraei, 'Syria war: The Afghans sent by Iran to fight for Assad', BBC News, 15 April 2016, https://www.bbc.co.uk/news/world-middle-east-36035095.

114 'Hozur-e janbaz-e Fatemiyun "Sayyed Ali Asghar Hosseini" dar Lorestan bara-ye emdadresani beh mardom-e seil zadeh' [Sayyid Ali Asghar Hosseini, a disabled Fatemiyoun fighter, visits Lorestan to provide assistance to those affected by the floods], Fatemiyoun's official Twitter page, 23 April 2019, https://twitter.com/Fatemiyoun1434/status/1120586369410260992.

115 Benjamin Isakhan, 'The Islamic State Attacks on Shi'ite Holy Sites and the "Shrine Protection Narrative": Threats to Sacred Space as a Mobilization Frame', *Terrorism and Political Violence*, January 2018, https://doi.org/10.1080/09546553.2017.1398741.

116 Thomas Erdbrink and Hania Mourtada, 'Iran Warns Syrian Rebels After Report of Shrine Desecration', *New York Times*, 6 May 2013, https://www.nytimes.com/2013/05/07/world/middleeast/iran-warns-syrian-rebels-after-report-of-shrine-desecration.html.

117 Randa Slim, 'Hezbollah's Plunge into the Syrian Abyss', *Foreign Policy*, 28 May 2013, https://foreignpolicy.com/2013/05/28/hezbollahs-plunge-into-the-syrian-abyss; Rakan al-Fakih, 'Baalbek Figures Urge Hezbollah to Stop Fighting in Syria', *Daily Star Lebanon*, 25 February 2013, http://www.dailystar.com.lb/News/Politics/2013/Feb-25/207786-baalbek-figures-urge-hezbollah-to-stop-fighting-in-syria.ashx.

118 '15 Questions for the Lebanese Shi'ite Community', Shi'iteWatch, July 2015, http://www.Shi'itewatch.com/article/623.

119 Interview with Arab sources, July 2018.

120 'Lebanon Welcomes 6 Hezbollah Fighters Liberated from Fua, Kefraya', *Alahed News*, https://english.alahednews.com.lb/44135/390.

121 Interviews with Western intelligence sources, October 2018 and January 2019; interviews with Arab interlocutors, July 2018 and December 2018.

122 'Al-Husseini yaqul inna al-bukamal al-suriyyah wa al-qa'im al-'iraqiyyah jabhah wahidah' [Hosseini says that Syrian Al-Bukamal and Iraqi Qaim are one front], Al Mayadeen, 4 November 2017, https://youtu.be/JX-KuqMpcjk; 'IS loses Deir al-Zour in Syria and al-Qaim in Iraq on same day', BBC News, 3 November 2017, https://www.bbc.co.uk/news/world-middle-east-41856330.

123 'Palmira: Boitsi SSO VC RF ne astavili terroristam shansa' [Palmyra: Russian Special Operation Forces left no chance for terrorists], Russia 24, 5 March 2017, https://youtu.be/dn_XTbkFnVc.

124 'Russia says general killed in Syria held senior post in Assad's army', Reuters, 27 September 2017, https://www.reuters.com/article/us-mideast-crisis-syria-russia-general/russia-says-general-killed-in-syria-held-senior-post-in-assads-army-idUSKCN1C22TW.

125 'Iran Says Its Drones Attacked IS Convoy', Radio Farda, 25 August 2017, https://en.radiofarda.com/a/iran-drone-syria-isis/28697039.html.

126 'Iranian Martyr Hojaji's Funeral Procession to Be Held in Tehran Saturday', Tasnim News Agency, 31 August 2017, https://www.tasnimnews.com/en/news/2017/08/31/1507156/iranian-martyr-hojaji-s-funeral-procession-to-be-held-in-tehran-saturday.

127 'Iran's General Soleimani spotted with Iraqi fighters in Syria', New Arab, 20 November 2017, https://www.alaraby.co.uk/english/news/2017/11/20/irans-general-soleimani-

128 'Mushahid li-liwa' Soleimani wa howwa yukhattit wa yuwajjih al-'amaliyyat al-'askariyyah 'ala al-ard' [Scenes of Major-General Suleimani planning and directing military operations on the ground], Al Mayadeen, 30 November 2017, https://youtu.be/GlxaXyV-N8o.

129 'Al-janral Qasim Suleimani qa'id faylaq al-quds qada binafsih ma'rikat al-bukamal' [General Qasem Soleimani, commander of the Quds Force, personally directed the battle for Al-Bukamal], Al Mayadeen, 20 November 2017, https://youtu.be/Cx613Aq1tUY.

130 'Mufakhkhakhah wa aliyat mudammirah qurb al-bukamal wa maqtal qadah Afghan' [Car bomb and explosive devices near Al-Bukamal and the death of Afghan commanders], Step News, 8 November 2017, https://stepagency-sy.net/2017/11/08/مفخخة-وآليات-مدمّرة-قرب-البوكمال-ومقت.

131 'Shahid Hizbullah bi-musa'idat al-jaysh al-suri yaqum bi-tahrir badiyat al-bukamal min tandhim da'ish muwajihat 'anifah' [Watch Hizbullah liberate the Al-Bukamal desert from ISIS with the help of the Syrian Army, violent confrontations], 16 January 2019, https://youtu.be/kBAwsw3Gsos.

132 *Ibid.*, 9:16.

133 'Inside Albu Kamal: Will the collapse of IS in Syria strengthen the Iranian influence?', BBC News, 20 November 2017, https://www.youtube.com/watch?v=JKPYVNYC8aw.

134 'Two Senior Officers and Three Other IRGC Personnel Killed In Syria', Radio Farda, 20 November 2017, https://en.radiofarda.com/a/iran-casualties-syria-irgc-soleimani/28863973.html.

135 'Do rahi-ye Amrika dar Suriyeh ba payan-e Da'esh' [America's two possible paths in Syria after the end of ISIS], Javan Online, 14 November 2017, https://www.javanonline.ir/fa/news/881269/دو-راهی-امریکا-در-سوریه-با-پایان-داعش.

136 Interviews with Western intelligence sources, October 2018 and January 2019.

137 Interviews with Western intelligence sources, October 2018 and January 2019; interviews with Arab interlocutors, July 2018 and December 2018.

138 *Ibid.*

139 'Hezbollah recovers body of senior commander Ali Fayyad killed in Syria', *Arab News*, 29 February 2018, http://www.arabnews.com/middle-east/news/888096.

140 Anne Barnard and Sewell Chan, 'Mustafa Badreddine, Hezbollah Military Commander, Is Killed in Syria', *New York Times*, 13 May 2016, https://www.nytimes.com/2016/05/14/world/middleeast/mustafa-badreddine-hezbollah.html.

141 Ali Alfoneh, 'The Heavy Price of Lebanese Hezbollah's Military Engagement in Syria', Arab Gulf States Institute in Washington, 11 October 2018, https://agsiw.org/the-heavy-price-of-lebanese-hezbollahs-military-engagement-in-syria.

142 Ronen Bergman, *Rise and Kill First* (New York: Random House, 2018), p. 603.

143 Interview with Arab sources, July 2018.

144 Interviews with Western intelligence sources, October 2018 and January 2019.

145 'Both ISIL and Syrian Government responsible for use of chemical weapons, UN Security Council told', UN News, 7 November 2017, https://news.un.org/en/story/2017/11/570192-both-isil-and-syrian-government-responsible-use-chemical-weapons-un-security.

146 Interviews with Western and Arab officials, 2018 and 2019.

147 Joana Cook and Gina Vale, 'From Daesh to "Diaspora": Tracing the Women and Minors of Islamic State', International Centre for the Study of Radicalisation and Political Violence, July 2018, https://icsr.info/wp-content/uploads/2018/07/Women-in-ISIS-report_20180719_web.pdf.

CHAPTER FOUR

IRAQ

- Iran's paramount goals are to shape Iraq's domestic trajectory and security policy, and to deter or counter any hostile action by the United States
- Since 2003, Iran has empowered several militia groups that are now crucial players in the state-endorsed Popular Mobilisation Units (PMU), providing Iran with unique depth and leverage within Iraqi society and institutions
- Iran's partners in Iraq are in competition with each other and vie for institutional power as well as resources, requiring the Quds Force to manage these rivalries and exposing Iran to political and popular criticism

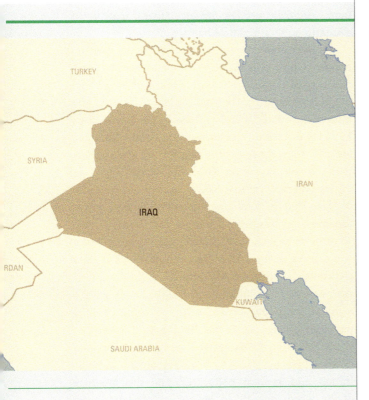

Iraq is Iran's single most important foreign-policy brief. For Iranian policymakers, Iraq is a more critical – and therefore more sensitive – theatre of operation than other countries in which Iran supports local militant groups. History has shown that events in Iraq can have important consequences for Iran's stability. Iraq continues to pose a threat to Iranian national security, which is why Iran is intent on shaping Iraq's domestic politics and strategic orientation. Since 2003, Iran has skilfully penetrated Iraq's Shia population, taking advantage of its long shared border and cultural, religious and economic ties. Iran's influence is multifaceted and has included outreach to a broad spectrum of political and social actors. Iran has even attempted to influence the Hawza' (Iraq's Shia clerical seminaries).

Iran's two key concerns are countering the presence of US military forces and shaping the re-emergence of the Iraqi state. To do so, Iran has invested its strategic capital in a broad portfolio of Iraqi political and militant groups, many of which are in direct competition with each other. Tehran's tactical and strategic approaches to managing its militia relationships are similar to its approach in the political sphere. Indeed, there is now significant

(l) Grand Ayatollah Ali al-Sistani with Iranian President Hassan Rouhani and Iranian Foreign Minister Mohammad Javad Zarif, Najaf, Iraq, March 2019

(r) Faleh al-Fayadh, Iraqi national security adviser and PMU chief, at the organisation's command headquarters in Basra, March 2018

overlap between the two, as an increasing number of militia members have graduated into Iraq's mainstream politics. Iran generally does not seek to dictate the outcome of Iraqi political disputes, but instead is focused on ensuring that whoever becomes pre-eminent is a friend. Iran also capitalises on existing domestic rivalries to help facilitate long-term Iranian influence in Iraq.

Iran's relationship with Iraqi militant groups in its sphere of influence is often more one of mentorship than of direct command and control. Tehran recognises that Iraq's political context will affect the style and mechanism by which it projects influence there, and is content in the short term for these militia groups to compete – as long as they do not attack and undermine each other and thereby reduce the overall influence of the Iran-backed camp.

The operations and deployment of the Iranian-backed militias across Iraq have served several purposes: countering real threats (such as the Islamic State, also known as ISIS or ISIL), entrenching the militias and meeting Iran's security objectives. Often these objectives have aligned with those of the Iraqi state, and at times overlapped with the United States' goals. By embedding themselves in the emerging security structure of the Iraqi state, these militias provide Iran with significant security and political benefits beyond the neutralisation of rivals. These include the capacity to bog down the US at low cost, create a territorial corridor between Iran and Lebanon, and ensure that Iraqi territory will not be used to threaten Iran's sovereignty.

Iran and the PMU programme

Since 2014, the Popular Mobilisation Units (PMU, or *al-Hashd al-Shaabi*) has been the foremost conduit for Iranian influence in Iraq. The PMU has become a formal Iraqi government programme, with ostensible ideological grounding in a 2014 fatwa by Iraq's most senior Shia cleric, Grand Ayatollah Ali al-Sistani.[1] The programme organises and funds the salaries of paramilitary volunteers fighting ISIS, while providing them with weapons and the imprimatur of state legitimacy. Nominally a branch of the security forces subordinate to the prime minister's office, the PMU is in practice a collection of independent militias (many of whom predate Sistani's fatwa), answerable primarily to their political patrons.

Fighters operating under the PMU framework are diverse, with a Shia majority complemented by large numbers of Sunni Arabs and a range of ethnic and religious minorities. The Shia can be subdivided into multiple groups, including those aligned with Iran, those loyal to Sistani and those that fall under Muqtada al-Sadr. They are present in every Iraqi governorate, with the exception of the Kurdistan region.

Iran-aligned groups likely constitute a minority of the PMU's total number of fighters, which according to Iraq's 2018 budget law is more than 100,000.[2] However, several factors give Iran an influential stake in the PMU. The organisation's deputy chairman, Jamal Jaafar Mohammad al-Ibrahimi (aka Abu Mahdi al-Muhandis), an Iraqi militant who is a fluent Farsi speaker and who has spent most of his adult life in Iran, is the dominant administrator in charge of coordinating the various factions, and of handling logistics, supply, personnel administration and general policy. Despite the presence of the word 'deputy' in his title, Muhandis is the most powerful single actor in the PMU programme. He is also widely understood to be the effective commander of PMU militia Kataib Hizbullah (KH). The PMU's nominal chairman in 2014–18, Faleh al-Fayadh, never exercised as much authority over day-to-day matters as Muhandis, and was removed from his largely symbolic post by President Haider al-Abadi in August 2018, leaving the chairman spot empty and Muhandis as the top-ranking PMU figure. Designated a terrorist by the US for his role in an Iran-sponsored 1983 attack targeting US forces in Kuwait,[3] Muhandis is construed by many domestic and international observers as acting on behalf of the Iranian government. Iran-backed factions idolise him and he has faced criticism from some elements of the PMU for supposedly favouring such factions at the expense of others.[4]

While in US detention in 2008, Asaib Ahl al-Haq (AAH) militia leader Qais al-Khazali described Muhandis as 'well trusted by Iran', portraying him as a direct and important proxy for enacting Iranian interests,[5] and tied to the Islamic Revolutionary Guard Corps (IRGC).[6] At that time, Khazali believed Muhandis's purchase on Iraqi affairs to be limited. By assuming effective control of much of the PMU, and overtly pitting himself against Prime Minister Abadi in the 2018 post-election environment,[7] Muhandis has made it clear those limits no longer apply.

Beyond Muhandis, many of the PMU staff are former exiles who spent time in Iran and have ties to Tehran. Within the PMU, Iran-backed militant factions are generally thought to be the best equipped, and many of them have also deployed fighters in Syria, under Iranian direction and without the formal permission of the Iraqi government.

Iran maintains a policy of deliberate public ambiguity about its role in the PMU, as it does in general regarding its intervention in Iraq. Militia fighters are salaried employees of the Iraqi state, and at least some of the weapons they possess – including those made in Iran – are purchased and provided by Baghdad.[8] This saves Iran the cost of sustaining such groups without any erosion of its authority over those elements most important to its interests. Iran also has extra-legal and undocumented relationships with many of these factions, at least with regard to supporting their fighting in Syria but probably also inside Iraq. IRGC Quds Force commander Major-General Qasem Soleimani and other Iranian military advisers regularly made conspicuous appearances alongside PMU officials during the anti-ISIS military campaign.[9]

Beyond the direct value of Iranian material support, the fact that some PMU factions are favoured by Iran empowers them to ignore the Iraqi authorities, and makes Iraqi security and political officials reluctant to impede them. Some of the most grievous abuses of power by PMU militias,

IRGC Quds Force Major-General Qasem Soleimani in Tikrit, Iraq, March 2015

from severe military abuses during the anti-ISIS campaign, to kidnapping-for-ransom and profiting from oil smuggling, have reportedly been perpetrated by Iran-backed factions.

Categorising PMU groups and their relationship to Iran

Iran-linked PMU groups can be usefully divided into four broad categories, from the closest to the most tenuously tied to Tehran.

Ideological militants

Some Iran-backed PMU groups define themselves primarily as ideological militants that adhere to *Velayat-e Faqih* (supreme religious jurisprudence). For them, the fight against ISIS is but one chapter in a broader struggle against Sunni powers and against the Anglo-American world order, a struggle in which the Islamic Republic of Iran is the champion of the oppressed and leader of the Axis of Resistance. Abu Mahdi Muhandis's KH is the foremost group of this type. KH defines itself as a 'resistance' force, priding itself on its role in attacks on US and allied targets in Iraq in the years leading up to 2011, and openly boasting of its Iranian ties.[10] The group has been implicated in a series of attacks on foreign targets (including high-profile mass kidnappings),[11] but does not claim public credit for such operations. KH is widely respected and feared in Iraq as the country's most potent Shia militant force, and as the militia closest to Iran. It has made no apparent effort to merge with the Iraqi security state beyond taking allocations from the PMU programme. In contrast to many other PMU groups, its leaders maintain a low media profile and do not run in elections, but they occasionally issue statements threatening US targets

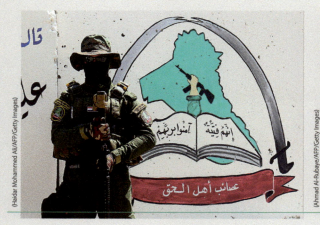

(l) An Asaib Ahl al-Haq fighter in Basra, May 2015

(r) Badr Organisation head Hadi al-Ameri, during the advance of Iraqi forces to recapture Hawija from ISIS, September 2017

or condemning the government for its continued relations with Washington.[12]

A second militant group, Kataib Sayyid al-Shuhada (KSS), appears to have split from KH at some point in the past decade. The details of the split and its causes are unclear. When asked about this in a television interview, KSS leader Abu Ala al-Walai suggested the founding of KSS was not based on any ideological differences with the mother movement, saying 'splits among us are a sign of vitality'.[13] Under Walai's leadership, KSS has in some ways established a higher profile than KH. It is not a mass political movement but remains primarily a militant group trading off the caché of its Iranian ties. In an interview with Iraq's Beladi TV, Walai said of his and KSS's relationship to Iran: 'to be clear, we are a resistance faction supported by the Islamic Republic of Iran'.[14]

For either of these groups, breaking with Iran or defying its orders would necessitate a radical reinterpretation of the group's identity and purpose, and such a scenario seems highly unlikely. The upshot for Tehran is that these groups are the most reliable of their Iraqi allies, and least likely to defy Tehran's orders.

Political movements

Still very close to Iran – albeit with more distance than the ideological militants – are a cluster of (well-armed) political movements that generally embrace Iran's ruling ideology, but seek to adapt it to Iraqi conditions. The largest and most important of these is the Badr Organisation, originally an auxiliary military force of Iraqi Shia volunteers that fought on the Iranian side of the Iran–Iraq War. Although an Iraqi organisation, the group's deep Iranian roots are undeniable. Hadi al-Ameri, its head, and its other top leaders spent much of their professional lives in Iran. It was there that they received much of their academic education and military training. The Badr Organisation does not flaunt its Iranian ties the way some other factions do – though its leader is effusive in his praise of Quds Force commander Soleimani[15] – and its leaders at times take pains to emphasise their Iraqi identity and belonging.

More than any other Iran-aligned group, the Badr Organisation and its armed component, previously known as the Badr Corps, has progressively gained access to Iraqi politics and state institutions, while retaining its separate militia capacities. The group has entrenched itself within Iraq's government. Ameri served as Iraq's transport minister in 2010–14, and the Badr Organisation has a long-standing presence in Iraq's powerful Ministry of Interior, including the Federal Police force. Qasim al-Araji, a senior member of the group, was arrested by US forces in January 2007 for involvement in the 'smuggling and distribution of explosively formed projectiles (EFPs)'[16] used by Iran-backed Shia forces against US-led coalition forces in Iraq, but later repositioned himself as a politician, serving as minister of interior in 2017–18. Araji's predecessor in this post, Mohammad al-Ghabban, was also a Badr Organisation official, with the group's leader, Ameri, believed to ultimately be in control.[17]

The Badr Organisation's militia is probably the largest faction in the PMU. Relative to other PMU militias, the group is generally observed to have a relatively high level of technical proficiency and professionalism – although its fighters have been accused by Kurds and Sunnis of oil smuggling[18] and have also been implicated in extra-judicial detentions.[19] The group's leaders and cadres see themselves not so much as servants of Iran, but rather as Iraqis trying to adapt components of the ideology of Iran's Islamic Revolution to their own local context. Nevertheless, even if the organisation does not seek out Iranian instruction on every detail of its operations, it remains a trusted affiliate of the Iranian regime inside Iraq. The Badr Organisation retains deep organic ties to Iran.

A tank flying the Asaib Ahl al-Haq flag advances with Iraqi forces through Anbar governorate, in the desert bordering Syria, November 2017

The Badr Organisation's closest rival is AAH, which both complements and competes with it to fill more or less the same political space. Originally a Sadrist militant group that split off from Muqtada al-Sadr's Office of the Martyr Sadr because of disagreements between Sadr and Qais al-Khazali,[20] AAH is an anti-American militant group, which turned to politics after the United States' military withdrawal from Iraq in 2011.

As with other militant Sadrists and Iran-aligned groups, AAH received weapons training, substantial weapons supplies and cash from Iran from 2005 through the 'Special Groups' programme organised by the IRGC's Quds Force in order to bolster Iraqi resistance to the coalition occupation.[21] Training was conducted by Iran and Lebanese Hizbullah in at least three camps inside Iran,[22] and weapons and supplies were smuggled across the border from Iran to equip them.[23]

Even though it is now represented in parliament, AAH's approach to politics is less disciplined and less institutionalised than the Badr Organisation's, and AAH militants have often been implicated in kidnappings and other abuses.[24] For AAH, what began as an opportunistic acceptance of Iranian support has now become an integral part of the group's own identity, and one with which it cannot easily part. AAH activity in Syria, including a visit by Khazali to the Syria–Israel border in December 2017,[25] indicates the group's ideological transition from Sadrist-style Iraqi nationalism to the Iranian belief in a global Shia Islamist Axis of Resistance.

Meanwhile, there are other less influential groups within the PMU that follow the AAH/Badr Organisation model. Saraya Ashura, for example, is a militia associated with the Islamic Supreme Council of Iraq (ISCI). Although ideologically the political party has drifted away from Iran's revolutionary rhetoric, the ISCI was based in Iran for many years and its leaders still have close ties with Tehran. Groups like this are somewhat dependent on Iranian support, but they may be interested in changing their approaches. For example, Ammar al-Hakim, ISCI's former leader who split off with many former ISCI supporters to run in the 2018 elections under the newly created National Wisdom Movement, has taken a relatively independent line from Iran in recent years. Still, historic Iranian ties and a shared Shia Islamist ideology may make it difficult for Saraya Ashura or its political backers to ever fully break free of Iran's orbit.

A collection of predominantly Iran-aligned PMU militias/political parties ran in the 2018 national parliamentary elections under the Fatah coalition, headed by the Badr Organisation leader Ameri. The coalition won 48 seats, coming in second behind Muqtada al-Sadr's Sairun Alliance, and ahead of former prime minister Abadi's Nasr Alliance. While the Badr Organisation, with 22 seats, has a plurality of Fatah's MPs in Iraq's parliament, that figure was in line with their 2014 election result. AAH on the other hand saw its seat count spike from one in 2014 to 14 in 2018. While Fatah's broad success (particularly relative to the Nasr Alliance) suggests that the Iran-aligned militia brand still has significant popular appeal in Iraq, that the Badr Organisation's popularity has lessened while AAH's has increased points to the latter's anti-establishment appeal. Evidence of this anti-establishment trend can also be found in the Sadrists' success, as they increased their bloc's parliamentary seat count to 54 in 2018, a big increase from the 34 seats the bloc won in 2014.

A shared trait of the ideological militants and political movements is their respective groups' senior leaderships' exile in Iran in the 1980s and 1990s. In addition to a belief in Khomeinism, many of these former Iraqi exiles – through their experience of being persecuted by the Ba'ath regime and fighting against Saddam Hussein's military forces – share the

Figure 4.1: **Iraqi parliamentary elections, 2018: seats**

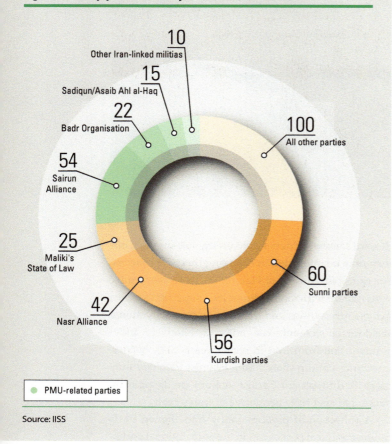

Source: IISS

view held by many senior Iranian political and military officials of the potential threat posed by a secular nationalist Iraqi state, or at least by the potential for a secular nationalist Iraqi state to move quickly in what they deem to be a dangerous direction. For Iran, there is no easy substitute for Iraqis who were exiled in Iran, and particularly those that were there during the formative years of the Islamic Republic. As that older generation disappears over the coming decade or two, replicating the relationships that exist between Qasem Soleimani and other senior IRGC leaders on one side, and Iraqis like Ameri and Muhandis on the other, will become more difficult.

While these groups are reliable partners for Iran, they also have their own priorities and responsibilities in Iraq's domestic affairs and governance. Unlike ideological militants – which can be used against Iran's enemies with little downside – the political movements must navigate the domestic fallout of being perceived as too willing to advance Iran's priorities.

Mercenaries and opportunists

The establishment of the PMU in 2014 brought to prominence a series of small, pre-existing Iraqi militant groups that are essentially parasitic in nature.

Organisations including Jund al-Imam, Saraya al-Khorasani, Harakat al-Nujaba and others organised the flow of Iraqi Shia volunteers fighting under Iranian tutelage in Syria in 2012–13. Although generally left unmentioned in Iraqi sources, the command role of Iranian officials in Iraq's fight against ISIS was openly celebrated in the Iranian press.[26] Harakat al-Nujaba is an AAH splinter group led by former Jaish al-Mahdi and AAH commander Akram al-Kaabi, while most of the others had no existence as political or military forces prior to the Syrian conflict. These groups appear to be highly reliant on Iran, displaying an ideological commitment that is probably opportunistic rather than intrinsic. Their leaders loudly profess their dedication to Iran's Supreme Leader Ayatollah Ali Khamenei, a posture that they may believe enhances their own profiles and intimidates potential opponents.

There is little indication that the leaders of and spokesmen for this cadre of militant groups have significant constituencies of their own. They appear to have been plucked from relative obscurity for the task, and they owe everything to Iranian support. The language they use in public appearances suggests they have little formal education and only a casual familiarity with Shia religious traditions,[27] an indication that their allegiance to Khamenei is more a matter of opportunism than conviction. The level of education and ideological fervor among their standard fighters is probably lower still. These factions were particularly notorious for looting and other wartime abuses in the 2014–15 period, but their profile has since decreased, perhaps as the need for reinforcements in the fight against ISIS has ebbed.

These factions would probably not exist without Iran. However, if Iranian support ended, their members would no doubt seek alternative employment in any organisation willing to hire them, even if this required them to adopt a new ideological orientation.

Affiliates

Within the PMU, there are a variety of party-based militias, Sunni groups and others that receive some Iranian logistical support, but whose relationship with Tehran seems to be entirely contingent on military or political circumstances. In some cases, these groups are effectively the subordinates of Iran's militias.

For example, Liwa Salahaddin (51st Brigade) is a Sunni group based in northern Salahaddin governorate, led by Yazan al-Jabouri, the son of long-time MP and sometime Ba'athist insurgent leader Mishan al-Jabouri. The 51st Brigade works closely with

A poster memorialising an Asaib Ahl al-Haq fighter killed in Syria, Sadr City neighbourhood, eastern Baghdad, June 2014

(Scott Nelson for The Washington Post via Getty Images)

Iranian-affiliated Shia PMU militias, and claims to have received weapons and intelligence support from Iran.[28] This relationship is based on Jabouri's need for outside support and Iran's desire for Sunni political allies, not on any ideological affiliation. Another example of this is the recruitment of local Sunni Arab members of the Karawi tribe in northern Diyala governorate by Iran-aligned AAH, effectively creating a local franchise. This local AAH affiliate is dependent on AAH for material support and, just as critically, the political legitimacy that comes with being able to identify as a PMU-affiliated entity.[29] Iran and its ideological Shia Islamist allies in Iraq probably have several interrelated reasons for wanting to cultivate Sunni Arab allies:

- It helps expand their influence into geographic areas where neither Iran nor its close Shia allies previously had reach (including areas like Baiji in Salahaddin, home to what was once Iraq's largest oil refinery);
- It diversifies Iraqi political actors that are beholden – to varying degrees – to Iran and Iran's closest Iraqi allies;
- It allows Iran to compete with its regional and international adversaries (Saudi Arabia, Turkey, the US and others) for influence among Iraq's Sunni Arab political elite.

However, some Shia PMU groups that are not politically aligned with Tehran have at times received Iranian support, directly or indirectly. For example, militias affiliated with the Sistani-affiliated Imam Ali and Imam Hussein shrine administrations in Najaf and Karbala are not politically aligned with Iran, but some of their members participate in PMU training courses conducted in Iraq by Badr Organisation veteran trainers operating on orders from Muhandis.[30] Providing limited support to groups outside its ideological orbit helps Iran normalise its role in Iraq, while at the same time granting it cover to export training functions to Iraq under the PMU banner. This may soften affiliated groups' attitudes towards Iranian influence, but it does not turn them into reliable allies, nor does it instill an ideological connection.

These groups do not represent long-term reliable surrogates for Tehran. Rather, they are seen as something akin to short-term hires. Such groups can be useful for Tehran as long as both parties hold convergent interests and can be of mutual assistance to each other for overlapping short-term objectives. Tehran is also likely to outsource management of these relationships to Shia militia groups that fall into the political-movement or ideological-militant categories.

Non-PMU groups

Beyond the PMU, Iran also has strong ties to elements within Iraq's traditional security forces. After 2003, many Badr Corps officers were integrated directly into the army or police force, retaining their ranks and often experiencing rapid promotions due to their good political ties. The Federal Police, the Ministry of Interior's Emergency Response Division, and the Iraqi Army's 5th and 8th Divisions are the units thought to have the greatest Badr influence,[31] but there are other Badrists and other exiles returned from Iran scattered throughout the security forces and the Ministry of Interior's bureaucracy. The perception in Iraq that Iranian influence has grown since 2014 may give these personnel greater clout in their organisations than they previously enjoyed or than their ranks entitle them to, even without any direct Iranian assistance. The presence of officers with strong Iranian ties inside the security forces also helps PMU fighters avoid prosecution for abuses, provides access to intelligence regarding unit sizes and the locations of US

(l) Members of the Badr Organisation stand guard outside the Kadamiya mosque in Baghdad, March 2004

(r) A Popular Mobilisation Units fighter trains fellow members on weapons use in Qaim, November 2018

forces and their allies, and gives their militia units better access to government resources. The last of these includes armoured vehicles and air support, training courses for advanced military skills, and logistical support or basing rights.[32] Furthermore, the line between some of these Iraqi Security Forces (ISF) units and PMU-affiliate groups can appear blurred, at least when viewed from the outside.[33] Sources in some urban areas in Anbar have claimed that in the immediate aftermath of the city's liberation from ISIS, PMU members put on Federal Police uniforms so as to remain in the city despite orders from Baghdad that they withdraw to the outskirts.[34]

In the Kurdistan Region, Iran has at times provided tactical military support to Peshmerga units fighting ISIS.[35] Kurdish leaders have openly acknowledged that Iran shipped weapons and ammunition to Peshmerga forces in 2014, particularly before ground-level Western military support arrived.[36] In interviews, Peshmerga personnel have discussed the presence of Iranian advisers and even of Iranian artillery units embedded with Peshmerga forces in some areas, especially in Patriotic Union of Kurdistan (PUK)-controlled territory.[37] The decision to provide tactical assistance to the Peshmerga in 2014 was in direct service of Iranian interests, as it would forestall a possible jihadi advance through Kurdish territory toward the Iran–Iraq border. However, it may have had the added benefit of easing Kurdish forces away from a reliance on US advisers, and of softening Kurdish opposition to the role of Iran-backed PMU militias in the terrain that both the Kurdistan Regional Government (KRG) and Iraq's central government lay administrative claim to (referred to locally as 'disputed territories').

For Tehran, the strong presence of the Badr Organisation and other Iran-aligned militia groups in the conventional ISF is a hedge against those forces ever embracing a strong Iraqi-nationalist position that would oppose the idea of Iranian influence in Iraq. Tehran may never exert the type of influence within conventional ISF units that it does in most Iran-aligned Shia militia groups, but it can work to ensure that ISF units never emerge at the forefront of anti-Iran currents.

Iran-aligned militias: geographic deployment

The deployments of Iran-affiliated militia groups inside Iraq reflect Tehran's regional geopolitical ambitions as much as, or even more than, its military goals. In some cases, militia deployments appear to be guided by a long-term strategy to place Iranian-backed groups in control of key political sites, especially along Iraq's national borders and the disputed internal boundaries of the Kurdistan Region. However, such deployments also seem to be driven by the local concerns of Iranian-affiliated militias, including competition for distinction in the fight against ISIS, attempts to gain access to various kinds of economic resources and efforts to cultivate new constituencies among ethnic and religious minorities.

In addition, the Iraqi media has often reported on alterations being made to militia deployments in response to domestic or international political pressure. For example, Ahmad Abdullah al-Jibouri, governor of Salahaddin, described an agreement he had reached with government officials and PMU leaders to withdraw PMU forces from the governorate's population centres after allegations of abuses in 2018.[38] The PMU militias' responsiveness to such pressure is an indication both of their vulnerability and of their political survival skills.

Interviews with officers in various PMU militias suggest redeployment orders typically come from the PMU's central command, and specifically from

(l) Kataib Hizbullah members near Ramadi, May 2015

(r) Popular Mobilisation Units fighters secure the border with Syria in Qaim, November 2018

Muhandis.[39] According to one officer, relocations are effected by transfer of a unit from one regional command to another. This order will originate with Baghdad.[40] Once a PMU unit is deployed to a specific location under a regional command, it may be moved within that sector by a joint operations room that includes both ISF and PMU personnel.

Anbar

One of the most strategically decisive militia deployments has been the heavy PMU presence in the Iraq–Syria border areas of Anbar governorate. Knowledgeable local sources say that PMU checkpoints are present along key highways in the Qaim area, with KH clearly the leading force, although other groups are also deployed in the area.[41] Local reports say that KH has established an 'Imam Ali Border Crossing' – an unofficial intersection used to move Iran-backed fighters and supplies between Iraq and Syria.[42]

Iran-backed militia deployments in western Anbar governorate are a notable achievement for Tehran's regional strategy. They help to facilitate unrestricted land access to Syria from areas of Iraq in which Tehran's Iraqi allies have a firmer foothold (i.e., Baghdad and southern Iraq). Anbar governorate is relatively sparsely populated and marked by difficult terrain, and as recently as July 2018 there were occasional roadside bombings by ISIS.[43] Anbar's restive history also suggests that local insurgent groups – either with a transnational jihadist ideology, or driven by other grievances and resentment of the state – are likely to remain active in Anbar for the foreseeable future.

Deploying to these areas requires a combination of a serious investment in logistical and engineering resources and maintenance of durable ties with ISF units deployed to the area, so that Iran-aligned PMU groups benefit from the ISF's logistics and supply chain. The militias must spend these resources (or political capital) with little immediate political or economic pay-off. As Iraq's most heavily Sunni-populated governorate, Anbar presents few obvious local allies for the PMU, and any attempt to insinuate themselves into local politics would be challenging for the militias. Indeed, the deployment of Iran-backed PMU forces to the Iraqi–Syrian border reflects the loyalty and strategic obedience of groups such as KH to broader Iranian interests.

In addition to their presence in western Anbar, local political and security officials claim that a number of PMU militias – mostly Iran-aligned – have had a presence in the eastern and central part of the governorate.[44]

The deployment of Iran-aligned PMU militias includes:

- Kataib Hizbullah (western Anbar; Fallujah–Ramadi corridor)
- Abbas Combat Division (western Anbar)
- Harakat al-Nujaba (western Anbar)
- Badr Organisation (Fallujah district)
- Asaib Ahl al-Haq (Hit district; Rutba district)
- Kataib Imam Ali (Fallujah district)

The PMU presence in eastern and central Anbar enables militia elements to transit highways between the Anbar–Baghdad and Anbar–Karbala borders and the western part of the governorate near the Syrian border.

Disputed territories: an opportunity to cultivate new constituencies

Another notable success for Iran-affiliated militias in Iraq has been a series of deployments to and recruitment drives in the disputed territories (areas of central-northern Iraq claimed by both the autono-

Map 4.1: **Iran-aligned PMU militias: operational zones and installations, in Iraq**

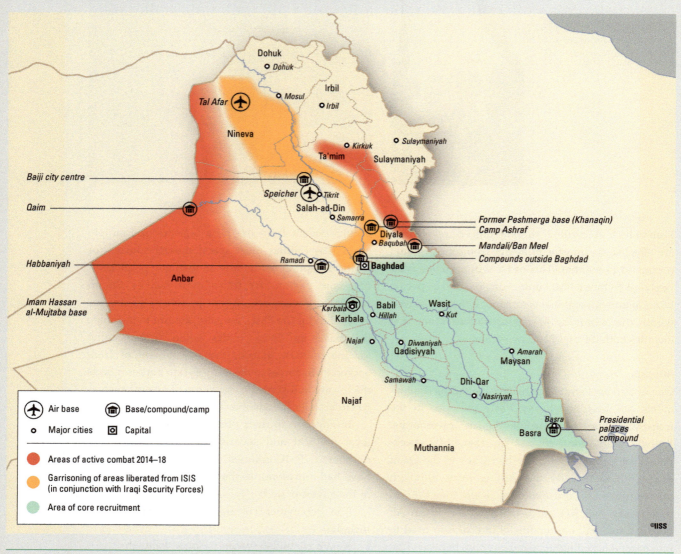

Sources: IISS; Interviews and assessment of PMU promotional material

mous Kurdistan Region and the federal government in Baghdad). Iran-backed groups have persistently pursued a strategy of minority engagement in this area.

Shia Turkmen and Shia Kurds (often referred to as Faili Kurds) have been natural targets for militia recruitment, particularly in the disputed territories in Diyala, Kirkuk and Salahaddin governorates. In the past, political activism in these communities was centred on ethnic identity, with Kurdish and Turkmen parties having both Sunni and Shia activists. Substantial PMU recruitment, in response to ISIS's anti-Shia violence, has resulted in a hardening of Sunni–Shia divides among Turkmen,[45] and in a renewed emphasis on Shia identity among some Faili Kurds. Faili Kurdish activists claim their community provided some 5,000 volunteers for the PMU – if true, this would be a heavy over-representation compared to their demographic weight in Iraq.[46]

The PMU has heavily recruited in Nineva governarate from the Shabak community, who speak a Kurdish dialect and some of whom identify as Shia. According to local sources, Badr Organisation MP Hanin al-Qaedu initiated and led the Shabak Brigade's recruitment campaign.[47] The Christian and Yazidi communities in Nineva have also been the target of recruitment efforts by Iran-aligned PMU groups – albeit to a lesser degree than the Shabak and Turkmen. This has resulted in the creation of militias from these communities that are reliant on Iranian proxy groups for political and logistical support. These minority PMU militias compete with KRG-aligned Christian and Yazidi militias for power within their respective communities, which have become players in the Baghdad–Erbil contest over the disputed territories.[48] In addition to the Badr Organisation, Iran-aligned groups including AAH, Kataib Imam Ali, Kataib Sayyid al-Shuhada and Saraya al-Khorasani are believed to have been based in and recruited from the disputed territories since 2014.

The disputed territories are important targets for Iran-affiliated militias. They provide a way for PMU groups to raise their own political profile – as well as Tehran's – in Iraq. Protecting small Shia groups in places like Amerli or Tal Afar also helps militias portray themselves as defenders of the Shia community against persecutors. Such a role could enhance the PMU's standing and legitimacy in intra-Shia debates about whether or not to disband the organisation once ISIS is finally defeated. The presence of Iran-backed groups on the fringes of Kurdistan also gives them – and thereby Iran – a point of leverage over the KRG.

The spread of Iran-backed militias in the disputed territories has been successful, but their impact has not always cast them in a good light. Repeated bouts of violence between Turkmen Shia militias and Kurdish forces in Tuz Khurmatu effectively divided the city into sharply defined sectarian enclaves. A series of failed truces in 2016–17 undermined the impression of the PMU as a unified force. The Badr Organisation's Ameri led the truce efforts, but his inability to enforce his will on other factions was damaging both to him personally and to the reputation of Iran-backed militias in general.[49]

Diyala: an example of overreach
If deployments in Anbar and the disputed territories show the Iran-backed militias' strengths, other deployments have shown their weaknesses. Hadi al-Ameri won responsibility for Diyala governorate's security affairs in 2014, but the Badr Organisation-led war on ISIS there was not wholly successful, with periodic insurgent attacks continuing.[50] Diyala is Ameri's home governorate, and his struggle to defeat ISIS there was a major blow to the narrative that local volunteers motivated by religious zeal can do a better job than traditional security forces. The Badr Organisation's struggles in Diyala have been noted by the movement's political rivals, indicating that Iran-backed militias can become vulnerable when they overextend militarily.[51]

Despite these struggles, Iran-backed militias have managed their deployments in ways that build their

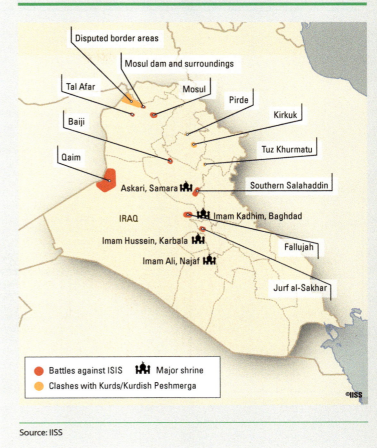

Map 4.2: **Major battles involving the PMU, 2014–18**

Source: IISS

political influence while avoiding direct conflict with competing forces. Militias largely avoided the battle of Ramadi in 2015–16, allowing US airstrikes and formal security forces to dominate the fight. However, there were claims made by local residents that Badr Organisation forces were present, wearing Federal Police uniforms.[52] The militias also largely avoided the battle of Mosul in 2016–17, focusing instead on rural areas around the city, some of which had Shia or other minority populations. After the fighting ended, a number of Shia militias reportedly opened offices inside Mosul, ostensibly to build political support among the city's residents. This proved controversial, and most of these offices were eventually closed.[53]

Key infrastructure
Critical to Iran's long-term plans for its Iraqi proxies are a series of large logistical and support bases scattered across the country. Many of these are co-located with the Iraqi Army at existing military bases. Beyond the utility of any existing infrastructure, using Iraqi military bases is a way for Iran-backed proxies to complicate any possible future US airstrikes on them.

Figure 4.2: **Iran-aligned militia groups: major events, 1970–2019**

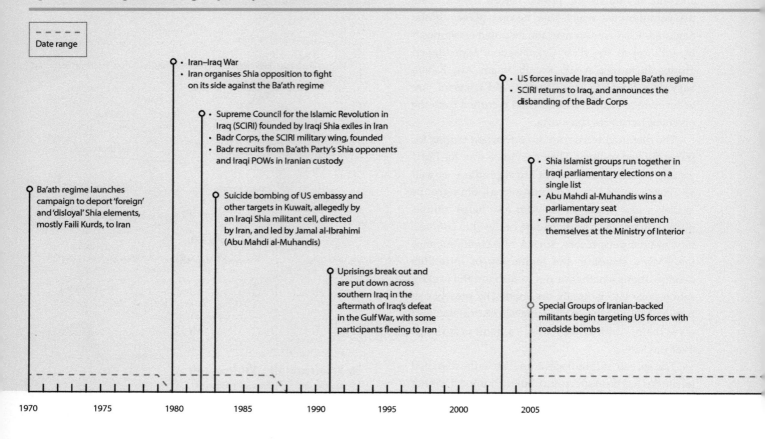

Deployments in southern Iraq

Iran-backed militia deployments in southern Iraq are generally more discreet, partly due to the decreased threat from ISIS. A militia presence in the Shia heartland would also potentially incite Shia-on-Shia conflict between competing armed groups. Muhandis has said that the PMU plans to move all of its bases out of urban areas, which might go some way towards forestalling such tensions.[54] However, Iran-backed militias maintain at least some forces in predominantly Shia areas, especially in Baghdad, that could deploy quickly in the event of a crisis. A possible dress rehearsal for such action was seen in spring 2016, when, as anti-government protests gathered pace, fighters from Iran-backed Saraya al-Khorasani deployed on the streets of central Baghdad in a show of force.[55] PMU groups also reportedly maintain weapons stockpiles in Baghdad and southern Iraq.[56] Even if militias typically do not have large units on standby in predominantly Shia governorates, the large number of fighters from these areas would facilitate the ability to mobilise quickly.

Southern Iraq also represents the heartland for Shia militia recruitment. Tens of thousands of lower-rank fighters among the Iran-affiliated Shia militias are from that area, with an especially large number from Basra.[57] Provincial governments typically have a PMU liaison committee run by a member of the provincial council, and the PMU commission has branch offices in many governorates. Public-works teams operating under the auspices of regional PMU offices have also engaged in engineering and public works in Basra and Dhi Qar.[58] However, the burning of Iran's Basra consulate and the Basra political offices belonging to several Shia Islamist groups that operate militias are a clear reminder of the limitations of Iran's popularity in southern Iraq, as well as the limit of the popular goodwill won by Shia political parties/militias for their role in the fight against ISIS. Indeed, as these groups become increasingly enmeshed in politics, they might face the same resentment over poor service provision and stunted non-oil economic growth that the rest of Iraq's political class has had to address.

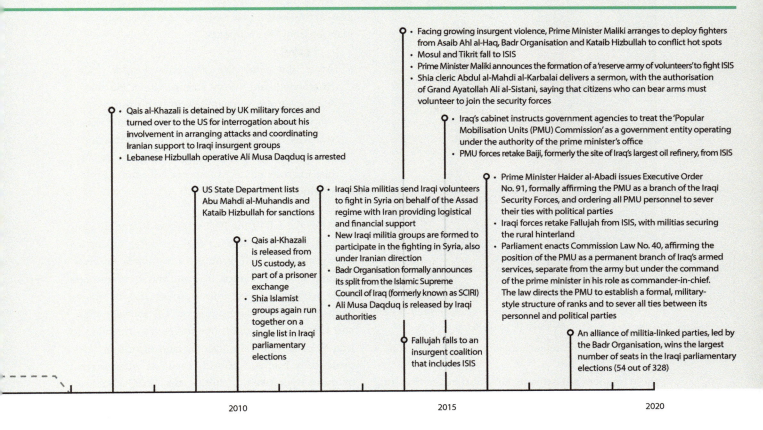

Expeditionary deployments and training of non-Iraqi militias

Syria

Local administrative and security officials based in western Anbar governorate – and Western observers – believe that many Iraqi Shia militia groups aligned with Iran frequently cross the border into Syria.[59] Militias listed as having access to the border area – and being involved in cross-border traffic – include Harakat al-Nujaba and KH.[60] Vehicles allegedly cross the border carrying goods and fuel, and possibly fighters as well.[61]

ISF officers based in western Anbar claimed in mid-2018 that Iranians continue to play an operational role with Iraqi militias engaged in cross-border activity.[62]

Yemen

In 2015 and 2016, Houthi representatives travelled to Baghdad[63] to strategise with Iraqi officials, including PMU-affiliated representatives politically and/or ideologically aligned with Iran.[64] This may have included Abu Mahdi al-Muhandis. Around this time, the Houthis began using language that in many ways mirrored that used by the PMU in Iraq. At the same time, groups including AAH, KH and Saraya al-Khorasani began calling for mobilisations to Yemen. In the 2015–16 period, Western diplomats in Yemen were reportedly tracking what were believed to be small, albeit politically significant, deployments of Iraqi Shia militiamen to Yemen. However, there is no agreement among Western officials as to whether this actually happened.

Bahrain

Bahraini militants have reportedly received training in Iraq, and possibly in Iran, from Iraqi militia groups, including KH,[65] though the number of trainees and scope of the training remains unclear.

Training and evolution of Iran-aligned militias to 2014

There have been a number of phases in Iran's training and equipping of Iraq-based militias. Iranian decision-makers have repeatedly adjusted their relationships with Iraqi militias to reflect changing political and military realities, and these flexible relationships have allowed Tehran to remain relevant. However,

Popular Mobilisation Units deputy head Abu Mahdi al-Muhandis, Basra, January 2018

these frequent adjustments have also meant that Iraqi militias have not been able to build and maintain competence in a variety of military skills.

The Islamic Republic of Iran's training of Iraqi armed factions goes back to at least the early 1980s, when opponents of Saddam Hussein's regime sought refuge in Iran. Iraqi exiles gained experience on conventional battlefields and in clandestine operations. Beneficiaries of such training and support included Muhandis, who helped establish the Badr Organisation, and Ameri,[66] head of the present-day Badr Organisation. The Supreme Council for the Islamic Revolution in Iraq (SCIRI) was also established in Iran at this time. It initially incorporated the Badr Organisation and has been the progenitor of a variety of Shia militias and political groups with Iranian ties. SCIRI rebranded in 2007 as the Islamic Supreme Council of Iraq.[67] In 2017, the party further fractured, with ISCI's head taking much of the party's resources and personnel to form a new group, Hikma.

Iraqi Shia militants failed to have a decisive impact on the course of the Iran–Iraq War, and their cross-border raids – which continued throughout the 1990s – failed to inflict any real damage on the Ba'ath regime. Although ineffective at securing military objectives, Iran's training of Iraqi affiliates in the 1980s had significant consequences. It created a generation of Iraqi Shia militants comfortable with Iranian interlocutors, and familiar with Iranian methods of organisation and management.

A telling anecdote from Muhandis suggests that even at the time, it was clear that Iran had a long-term plan for Iraqi Shia militants:

> After the war, the Supreme Leader [Ali Khamenei] said a very strange thing. He said, 'Badr will play a major role in Iraq's future' … We were amazed, what role did he mean? The war was over, Saddam was still in Baghdad, and we were refugees. But today we can see Badr's historic role: the most important leaders of this Hashid [PMU] are Badrists.[68]

After the fall of the Ba'ath regime in Iraq in 2003, Iranian support shifted to anti-American insurgent organisations. Small groups of militants received training at IRGC camps in Iran, and Iranian-made EFPs were smuggled into Iraq for use by insurgents in roadside ambushes on US forces.[69] IRGC and Lebanese Hizbullah operatives also travelled to Iraq to provide on-site training and direction. Their presence in Iraq was publicly revealed when several of these operatives, including the IRGC's Mohsen Chizari[70] and Hizbullah's Ali Musa Daqduq,[71] were captured by the US military in a wave of raids in 2006–07. At this time, Muqtada al-Sadr's Jaish al-Mahdi militia was a primary recipient of Iranian support and training, including via Lebanese Hizbullah – a fact Sadr publicly acknowledged in 2007.[72]

In a cache of interrogation reports declassified by the US in April 2018, dating from his capture in March 2007 to 2009, AAH leader Khazali describes the formation and support of the 'Special Groups' in detail. Khazali's account reveals a concerted Iranian effort to mount a Shia insurgency in Iraq using almost exclusively Iraqi fighters from as early as summer 2003, when Sadr, Khazali and others visited Tehran.[73]

The mix of Iraqi groups receiving Iranian support shifted over time in response to Tehran's political needs, as did the level of support provided. Iranian-backed insurgent groups were diffuse and disorganised, apparently by design, as a means of maximising dependency on Iran.[74] The basic training in Iran for Special Group fighters reportedly lasted a month and covered light weapons, heavy weapons, crew-operated weapons and improvised explosive devices (including EFPs).[75] Specialisation was optional for recruits who showed aptitude, and would involve more training in Iran. IRGC trainers taught conventional-warfare tactics, while Lebanese Hizbullah trainers took the lead on insurgency tactics,[76] having become more adept than Iranian forces at those.

Hizbullah training reportedly covered small arms, mortars, rocket-propelled grenades (RPGs) and EFPs.

Weapons provided by Iran came from depots in Ahvaz in Iran and were supplied free of charge once smuggled across the marshlands in Maysan governorate. They reportedly included AK-47s, machine guns, mortars, RPGs, explosives and *Katyusha* rockets.[77] Within a few months of the battle of Najaf in summer 2014 between US forces and Sadr's Mahdi Army, a regular stream of weapons was flowing from the IRGC to Special Groups via Maysan-based smuggling networks. In this period, Iranian-backed Special Groups were just one of many armed, clandestine actors in a chaotic environment, filled with insurgents, local political party-backed militias and organised-crime groups.

Jaish al-Mahdi, the largest of the militias, stood down after being defeated in a series of clashes with government forces in early 2008. A December 2008 US–Iraq agreement to withdraw US forces by the end of 2011 further reduced the insurgent campaign's urgency. At the same time, perceived Iranian support for militias was hurting Iran's image among Shia Iraqis, who wished to see the restoration of state order. Iranian support did not stop completely, but was scaled back to a smaller number of more elite insurgent groups, including KH and some Sadrist splinter groups.

However, Iranian sponsorship increased as the Syrian civil war intensified in 2012. Veteran Iraqi groups such as the Badr Organisation[78] and new ones such as Kataib Jund al-Imam and Saraya al-Khorasani began recruiting Shia volunteers to fight in Syria under IRGC direction. Increases in materiel supplies and funding revived some militias, reversing their post-2008 decline. After Fallujah fell to ISIS-linked Sunni militants in January 2014 and insurgent attacks increased elsewhere, some of these militias began to operate inside Iraq again, this time at the request of Nouri al-Maliki's government.[79] Although kept secret at the time, the role of Iran-backed Iraqi militias months before the formal founding of the PMU is now openly acknowledged by PMU leaders.[80]

Tehran and the PMU experience

Iranian support for Iraqi militants has proceeded along multiple channels, and Tehran's relations with its proxy militias are not uniform. Since 2014, the PMU structure has provided an effective means to nurture sympathetic militias, promote key leadership figures, deepen Iran's infiltration of Iraqi political and security

Iraqi Shia cleric Muqtada al-Sadr, Najaf, April 2015

institutions, and support Iran's regional objectives. It has also come at extremely low cost, given that the Iraqi state supports the programme financially, while the broad popular legitimacy the PMU enjoys would be extremely hard for Iranian-aligned militias to generate directly.

Nevertheless, generally speaking, the level of training and military readiness of Iran-backed Iraqi PMU groups is low, though within some, pockets of more advanced capabilities exist. In interviews, PMU personnel describe being sent into battle in 2014 after training courses of 15 days.[81] In some cases, training was limited to just three days, or none at all for personnel with prior military experience.[82] Video footage of Iranian-backed militias in combat, even when released for propaganda purposes by these same groups, confirms their low level of professionalism: for example, fire discipline and radio protocols are generally weak or non-existent, and equipment is often clearly inadequate or unavailable.[83]

The need to speedily recruit and deploy fighters against ISIS after the fall of Mosul is only a partial explanation of the PMU militias' amateur character. A deeper issue is that each militia conducts its own training programmes.[84] Some personnel may have been through Iranian training courses as part of the Special Groups or as members of the Badr Corps in the 1980s, but since 2014 most PMU training has been carried out inside Iraq. Moreover, according to PMU members who have been through training with multiple militia groups, there is no standard basic-training programme. Nor is there evidence of standardised performance benchmarks, whether for enlisted personnel or officers. Since PMU groups are generally linked to political actors, professional procedures are difficult to establish or enforce, even within a single faction – and commanders with political aspirations likely need to prioritise smooth relationships over performance considerations. Moreover, PMU leaders seem to pride themselves on its nature as a volunteer group rather than a professional army.[85]

Iran and its closest PMU militias have made efforts to create areas of professionalism, apparently with the primary goal of providing combat support to the various factions' volunteer formations. By summer 2014 the PMU had a small tank force. Its commander, Abu Thanun Khaledi, was personally selected by Muhandis and, according to Khaledi, the force received 'equipment and advisers' from Iran.[86] An artillery directorate, led by Badr Organisation

"IRAN AND ITS CLOSEST PMU MILITIAS HAVE MADE EFFORTS TO CREATE AREAS OF PROFESSIONALISM"

veteran Abu Majid Basri, was set up before the fall of Mosul in early 2014 at the behest of Ameri, and later integrated into the Muhandis-led PMU that formed in June that year. According to Basri, the PMU artillery force has 1,400 personnel, some of whom have received training in Iran on the use of a computerised targeting system.[87] He added that Muhandis was the key driver in creating specialised service-branch elements for the PMU:

> I think that it is important to transmit the heroism of the Hashid al-Shaabi [PMU], and to give out a clear sense of their efforts and of their technical and practical achievements, so that people won't think that they are just a group of folks who showed up just as they were, to bare their chests and fight. Yes, that was part of it, but there was also a lot of preparation and support from the leadership, represented by the Haj Abu Mahdi al-Muhandis, may God reward him. He showed great attention to the military specialties, including the artillery.[88]

These armoured-vehicle and artillery units are presented by their commanders as specialist military formations, attached to the PMU umbrella itself rather than to specific militias. Control of such assets by the

PMU is a small step towards turning the organisation from a collection of independent militias into a common military force. However, other PMU militias with little to no Iranian support also operate heavy weapons of this type. These create the potential for conflict or an arms race between Iranian-backed and non-Iranian-backed PMU militias.[89]

Over the 2015–17 period, Iran's provision of heavy weapons and associated training was tailored to the needs of the PMU in the fight against ISIS. This fits a broader pattern in which Iran trains its external militia allies based on specific operational needs at a given time, as well as when Tehran believes group identity and loyalty warrant the additional support. Particularly important in this regard were a military-engineering directorate, added to create berms and perform roadworks,[90] and an anti-armour directorate, added to combat ISIS's armoured-vehicle bombs.[91] The anti-tank directorate has been observed to use *Kornet* and TOW anti-tank guided missiles (presumably Iranian copies of the respective Russian and US designs).[92] Iran has also likely provided some uninhabited aerial vehicle training to militia groups in Iraq, and elsewhere, based on perceived operational need. Some of this training may have come from Lebanese Hizbullah operatives.[93]

The provision and use of heavy weapons does not mean that the PMU has become a fully professional force. Even in advanced units, the level of training and professionalism likely falls far below the level of most conventional militaries. In general terms, PMU fighters and officers are drawn from the lower socio-economic strata of Iraqi society.[94] This appears to be true even in specialist or supposedly elite formations. For example, personnel in the PMU's anti-armour directorate in late 2017 reportedly undertook a programme to combat illiteracy, held at the former US base at Camp Speicher. This suggests that personnel were assigned to the anti-armour directorate, which operates sophisticated guided-missile systems, without regard for their educational qualifications – or that few personnel with minimal education were available for the mission.

To close the remaining gaps in PMU capabilities, Iran has deployed advisers embedded into the ranks of local units. For example, sources in Diyala governorate reported seeing Iranian advisers, deployed either as individuals or in pairs, regularly embedded with Badr Organisation units since 2014. These Iranian officers are reportedly experts in plotting artillery fires, and in identifying and clearing mined areas. They also helped to collect intelligence

Popular Mobilisation Units fighters gather at Tal Afar's airport during an operation to retake the city from ISIS, August 2017

about ISIS's movements and suspected intentions.[95] PMU members deployed in the Tal Afar district of Nineva governorate during the anti-ISIS campaign also said their units had embedded Iranian personnel providing advisory support.[96] The roles ascribed to such Iranian advisers are similar to those filled by US and other Western special-forces units partnered with local armed forces in Iraq and elsewhere; some of these Iranian advisers have reportedly died in action in Iraq, suggesting front-line roles.

Command and control will remain a core concern for the PMU's leadership. To assert itself as a cohesive force, the PMU needs a way to unite its various factions around common policies. This is an immense structural challenge, but the PMU's discipline in avoiding attacks on US forces is an indication that the group has some ability to implement consensus decision-making. Throughout the fight with ISIS, even as PMU-aligned propaganda channels accused the US of supporting ISIS, PMU groups never fired on US troops. Whether PMU leaders had political concerns about undermining the fight against ISIS or feared retaliation, they were clearly able to restrain fighters from all factions in the field.

That there were no rogue attacks on US forces by splinter cells during the ISIS conflict could suggest a high degree of discipline within the PMU, with all factions accepting the dictates of Iran-backed leaders. The absence of attacks on US forces could also be read as a sign of relative military professionalism. However, given reports of PMU looting and racketeering, the absence of such attacks most probably stems not so much from tight discipline as from a mercenary mindset among many field commanders, more interested in financial gain and political power than pursuing ideological aims. In any case, the PMU's structure as an umbrella group for competing militias suggests that its factions' political and military discipline will face future challenges, and that strong leadership will be needed to preserve its cohesion.

Between two models: the PMU as Hizbullah and as Basij

Rather than establishing the PMU as a military force with clear professional standards, Tehran – perhaps limited by what is deemed attainable in the Iraq context – aims to create and organise a reservoir of military skills among Shia groups that harbour a range of pro-Iranian sentiments. Trainees also describe a haphazard process of selection, in which personnel with prior military experience (including in the Ba'ath-era Iraqi Army) can quickly attain high ranks.[97]

Several PMU fighters have described receiving training inside Iraq from Lebanese Hizbullah personnel in the post-2014 period; several claimed to have heard stories of Iranian trainers as well, and a smaller number confirmed that they received training from Iranians inside Iraq.[98] Muhandis confirmed the presence of IRGC and Lebanese Hizbullah support staff in a 2017 interview. Speaking to Iraq's Afaq TV, Muhandis said that the initial deployment of Iranian and Lebanese trainers in 2014 numbered in the hundreds, but that the number had dropped to a few dozen, as the PMU's need for them had declined over time.[99] Muhandis explained in the same interview that his policy is not to identify the PMU's Iranian or Lebanese Hizbullah advisers by name while they are still alive. Other PMU leaders and media outlets seem to follow this policy. Those who have been 'martyred', usually senior officers, may be named but are often only identified by code names.

Some elite PMU personnel have received Iranian training on a scale far beyond that of the average volunteer.[100] As in the heyday of anti-US Shia insurgent groups in 2005–08, Iran seems to be providing both broad support for a mass of fighters, who can be a strong and visible public presence, and more specialised training for secretive militants who can carry out pinpoint raiding operations.[101] How much of this training is provided in Iran, and how much in Iraq by militants with prior Iranian training (the 'train the trainer' model), is open to question – although, given several decades of Iranian backing for Iraqi proxies, it should be borne in mind that in 2014 Iraqi militants had some semblance of capability.

The large gaps in the level of training provided to different groups appear to be a deliberate choice by PMU planners and Iranian advisers. This system fits the model of how Iran treats other surrogates throughout the region. The PMU, and especially its

"THE LARGE GAPS IN THE LEVEL OF TRAINING PROVIDED TO DIFFERENT GROUPS APPEAR TO BE A DELIBERATE CHOICE BY PMU PLANNERS AND IRANIAN ADVISERS"

former insurgent factions, is in some ways modelled on Lebanese Hizbullah. At times, PMU militias even refer to themselves as 'resistance' movements. But the PMU also appears in other ways to have more in common with Iran's domestic ideological militia, the Basij – a large mass of men and women united more by a shared religious zeal than by military discipline, and whose purpose is less to fight opposing military forces and more to protect the existing political order from domestic threats. For example, the 2014–15 period saw intensive recruitment of young people in some areas of Iraq for short-term training programmes that did not lead directly to recruitment as full-time fighters.[102] The roles of elite resistance movement and people's army are difficult to combine in a single force; separating the PMU into mass and elite elements is at least a partial solution to this dilemma.

In the long term, decisions about how the PMU is structured, trained and equipped may provide clues as to the role it will play in Iraq's political life in the future. On the one hand, there has been a trend towards professionalisation: the addition of service branches, the decision in 2017 to refer to PMU units by brigade numbers rather than faction names in official communications, and a March 2018 executive order that imposes military-style rank structures and disciplinary courts, or at least instructs the PMU leadership

to establish such features.[103] On the other hand, there are signs of an expanding Basij mentality: after the liberation of Mosul, PMU military-engineering assets were employed in a well-publicised public-works campaign in Basra and other southern governorates, apparently an effort to win a permanent role as an economic and social force in civilian life.[104] Likewise, multiple officials in Basra confirmed plans, launched in late summer 2018, to recruit at least ten units (size unknown) of unpaid local volunteers, who would be available both to defend the city in an emergency and to engage in educational and propaganda activities under the direction of the PMU.[105] That this plan was announced shortly after a wave of anti-government protests in Basra suggests an attempt to use the PMU against domestic unrest, along the lines of the Basij's role in Iran.

PMU leaders and Tehran are no doubt aware that they cannot simply copy the Basij's role in Iran – or Hizbullah's role in Lebanon – into the Iraqi context. Asked whether the PMU takes the IRGC as its model, Muhandis replied: 'No, each country has its own circumstances … the Hashid [PMU] is not the Guards, Iraq's situation is different.'[106] The AAH's Khazali has argued that the PMU must be careful not to 'militarise society';[107] his and other militias implemented this advice by eschewing military parades during the 2018 parliamentary election campaign.

The frequency with which Iran's Iraqi PMU proxies present ideas that seem drawn from the Basij, Hizbullah and IRGC experiences suggests that, protests aside, they see these groups as their model. Ameri, Khazali and Muhandis each appear to be trying to find a formula for an Iraqi expression of Khomeinism – the drive for a well-organised bureaucratic system, but one led by revolutionaries who are empowered to use extra-legal violence to 'protect' Shia society from division, moral decay and outside interference. Finding a viable Iraqi version of this model is the key challenge for Iran's Iraqi militias, and it takes priority in their planning over the implementation of conventional military capabilities or force structures.

Limits of a semi-clandestine programme

The secretive and compartmentalised nature of Iran's relationships with its Iraqi groups has important implications for their training and operational readiness. The PMU is not a single entity or movement, but rather a collection of competing groups, many of which have histories of splits and defections. Furthermore, although Muhandis is in essence an Iranian agent, the PMU contains within it a variety of factions that are neutral or even hostile to Iran's agenda in Iraq. In the immediate term, turning any one of the PMU militias into a truly competent and professional military force, adequately staffed and supplied, would make it a threat to the other factions, and perhaps even to the Iraqi political system itself. A backlash – between Iraqi militia groups, and against Iran – would be probable.

However, the PMU's military effectiveness is also limited by the domestic political context. Among the PMU, there is a great deal of resentment over which factions or units have received particular training or support. The perception that groups close to Iran obtain preferential access to weapons, training and logistical provision is widespread, both in the Iraqi media and among the PMU.[108] This perception undermines inter-faction cooperation, and damages efforts by the PMU leadership to portray the organisation as a unified, popular expression of Iraqi Shia identification. Even the factions most loyal to Iran are organised as independent political–military groups, competing with each other for resources, popular support and power. Additionally, with the entry of PMU militias into Iraq's political system, they now vie for votes and support as well as materiel: this political dynamic has given rise to a new set of means by which militias compete, including elections, traditional and social media, and social programmes. From Iran's perspective, competition between groups is a nuisance, but as long as it does not jeopardise or complicate its own interests inside Iraq, these squabbles are tolerable.

Operating within the framework of the PMU, Iran has used training and support to revive and expand its portfolio of militias in Iraq. However, this success has come at the cost of accepting a low level of military performance among the militias, and a high degree of friction in their relationships with each other and with outside actors, including the Iraqi government. The PMU's battlefield successes against ISIS have been considerable, but there are structural factors that limit its further military development, at least in the existing Iraqi political environment.

While the PMU has been given official permanent status as a security institution parallel to the police and conventional armed forces, it also lacks any coherent role in the post-ISIS environment in Iraq. As such, the popular enthusiasm afforded to key leaders such as Ameri and Muhandis by PMU victories, led by the Badr Organisation and other pro-Iran militias, may fade over time.[109] Protests in Baghdad and southern Iraq in summer 2018 saw protesters chanting slogans denouncing Iran, indicating Iraqi resentment of mili-

tarised Iranian influence.[110] Furthermore, protests in Basra culminated in the the the burning of the offices of Iran-aligned militias alongside those of other political parties. The PMU's transition, in the eyes of many of its supporters, from a band of patriotic volunteers to an entrenched part of the country's ruling order, has cost it popular support.

Financing

PMU militias, including those closely aligned with Iran, are primarily financed and equipped by the government of Iraq, via a budgetary allocation controlled by the organisation's headquarters in Baghdad. This formal, legally codified funding source is augmented by a variety of other mechanisms, some

> **"THE PMU'S TRANSITION FROM A BAND OF PATRIOTIC VOLUNTEERS TO AN ENTRENCHED PART OF THE COUNTRY'S RULING ORDER HAS COST IT POPULAR SUPPORT"**

legitimate and some clearly unsanctioned or illegal. Militia groups ideologically aligned with Iran dominate both the legitimate and illegitimate sources of PMU funding, significantly reducing Iran's need to provide direct material aid itself.

Formal and semi-formal Iraqi government support

Iraq's 2018 budget law allocated just over US$1.4 billion to the PMU programme.[111] This formal allocation is just over 10% of the amount the government was anticipated to spend on forces operating under Iraq's Ministry of Defence and Ministry of Interior in 2018.[112] If the 2018 budget law's assumption that there are 122,000 salaried PMU personnel is accepted, it is likely that approximately half of the PMU's state budget goes towards salaries. In his capacity as deputy PMU chairman, Muhandis almost certainly has significant discretionary authority over how this money is directed within the PMU programme, including the relative share allocated to component militias. However, the ability of Iran's allies in the PMU to control the allocation of state resources is not limited to Muhandis. Regional and local PMU officers in areas with substantial deployments often come from Iran-aligned militias,[113] and these commanders are reported to have some discretionary authority in how they allocate funds within their sectors.[114]

Figure 4.3: **Popular Mobilisation Units: official budget, 2016–19 (US$ billions)**

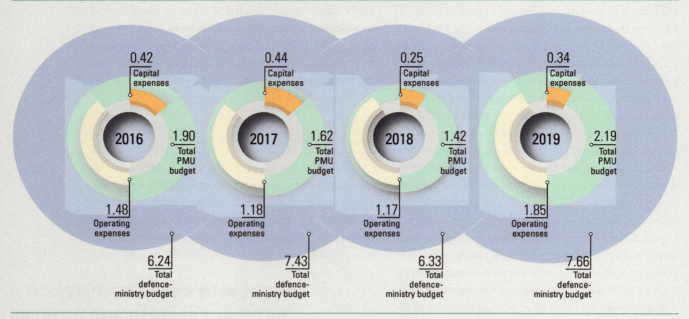

Sources: IISS; Iraqi 2018 budget law

Access to substantial state resources via the PMU budgetary allocation allows Iraqi groups aligned with Iran to project influence in areas where they might not otherwise have purchase. This has enabled the AAH, the Badr Organisation, Saraya al-Khorasani and others to use state funds to recruit and return Shia Turkmen, and Shia Kurdish and Shabak populations in Iraq's disputed territories or predominantly Sunni areas of central Iraq over the past several years, in active units.[115]

The promise of a steady salary has been an important driver for the recruitment of non-Shia groups into the PMU, with evidence that the PMU headquarters has found funds to allocate to such groups in territories liberated from ISIS, even as Shia militias in other areas have complained of delayed payments. This fits an observed Shia majoritarian approach to Iraqi governance, in which non-Shia groups are incentivised to accept patronage,[116] even if they do not receive the same level of support as Shia groups in the PMU. Sunni tribal fighters in Nineva governorate, for example, reportedly received regular salaries from the PMU but only minimal small-arms supplies, creating dependency without threatening the emergence of these groups as rival security actors.[117]

The PMU headquarters also controls assets outside its formal budgetary allocation. This includes the allocation of weapons seized from ISIS, which since at least 2016 have been distributed by the PMU in Baghdad to component militias.[118]

In addition to formal, legally codified support through the PMU headquarters, the organisation enjoys semi-formal support from various government entities. This largely includes support programmes such as donation drives or set-aside jobs for the families of deceased fighters, but also includes technical assistance aimed at supporting PMU operations. For example, Iraq's Ministry of Oil has a 'Hashid [PMU] Support Committee', which is primarily focused on providing medical and social services to wounded PMU fighters, and the families of deceased fighters.[119] During the campaign against ISIS, PMU militia units also often shared bases and accommodation with government forces, particularly the Federal Police, saving on costs.[120] However, many of the PMU support programmes were launched in 2014–15, in an atmosphere of national mobilisation to support the war effort.

Muhandis and the PMU wield material influence beyond the US$1.4bn formal 2018 budget allocation. Support from government entities defrays costs that would otherwise have to come out of the PMU budget. The PMU also accrues non-monetary material assets by seizing weapons and vehicles.

State allocations to the PMU programme increased significantly in the 2019 budget. Under a different set of circumstances, growing Iraqi state funding for the PMU that diminished the relative significance of Iranian funding could reduce Tehran's influence among the militias, even those that have an ideo-

Iraqi Prime Minister Haider al-Abadi with Iranian President Hassan Rouhani, Tehran, June 2017

logical overlap with Iran. However, so long as Iraqi officials – pre-eminent among them Muhandis – with deep personal and ideological ties to Iran control the allocation of Iraqi state resources within the PMU, Tehran's influence is unlikely to wane in line with the diminished importance of direct Iranian funding. This is particularly true given the limited influence of the Iraqi prime minister over the PMU. Attempts by Abadi to curtail Muhandis's authority and to remove Faleh al-Fayadh, the national security adviser and nominal head of the PMU, have failed.[121] Fayadh retained his position under Prime Minister Adil Abdul-Mahdi.

Donors

Numerous PMU sources talk of the role played by external donors in funding the militias.[122] In many cases, these donors are clearly private Iraqi individuals, and result from organic popular support for the PMU. In addition to cash donations from individuals or charities, disbursed from specific fundraising or the general coffers of religious or charitable institutions, volunteers have provided in-kind donations (food, clothing, etc.) to PMU fighters.[123] In other cases, the nationality of the donors is unclear, though there is no hard evidence that they were Iranian. For example, a member of Muqtada al-Sadr's Saraya al-Salam militia said that wealthy individuals that look to Muqtada's late father, Muhammad Sadiq al-Sadr, as their source of emulation (*marja al-taqlid*) are a significant source of support – via donations – to the militia.[124] This support most likely decreased once Saraya al-Salam formally joined the PMU programme. Other militias affiliated with the Imam Ali Shrine in Najaf and the Imam Hussein Shrine in Karbala receive donations from the administrators of these religious sites, which are major pilgrimage centres in Shia Islam, built around the tombs of Shia imams. The administrators, who are appointed by Grand Ayatollah Sistani, collect donations from the faithful, which are spent on the shrines' upkeep, but also on charitable and religious projects, one of which is support for specific PMU factions that are under the shrine administrators' control. The largest of these is the Abbas Combat Division.

Individuals and militias closely aligned with Iran enjoy preferential access to PMU funding mechanisms. It is possible that donations are more critical for Shia militias outside or on the periphery of Iran's sphere of influence (for example, Saraya al-Salam) and those militias such as the Abbas Combat Division that are close to the Najaf establishment, which works to keep Iranian influence at bay. Supporting this hypothesis is an August 2018 order by Muhandis instructing all militias to cease receiving donations from 'groups, parties, holy shrines and others'. The order said that any units failing to comply would cease to be considered PMU elements.[125] Given Muhandis's history of using his position to strengthen Iran-backed groups at the expense of others, this order suggests a competition between Muhandis and the Najaf Hawza' for the loyalty of militias, with the non-Iran-backed militias more dependent on donations.

Illicit fundraising

Individual PMU militias engage in a number of extra-legal activities that generate funds. In most of these cases, it is impossible to distinguish whether these are fundraising activities ordered by either the senior PMU leadership or the leadership of the militia in question, or whether this activity reflects lower and mid-tier personnel seizing opportunities for personal enrichment. Any reductions in state-budget allocations to the PMU or financial strain in Iran may incentivise PMU militias to turn to illicit activities to sustain their payroll. More hardline sectarian units in Sunni areas may also hold a 'to the victor, the spoils'

Popular Mobilisation Units fighters from the Abbas Combat Division fire a rocket towards ISIS positions northwest of Mosul, March 2017

attitude in conducting post-conflict looting, smuggling and ransom activities. Such activities tend to be concentrated in predominantly Sunni Arab or heterogeneous areas; the ongoing ISIS threat provides cover for arbitrary or unjust uses of force. Sunni communities also have relatively little political power with which to push back against such abuses.

Oil smuggling

Multiple Iran-aligned militias have been implicated in oil-smuggling activities. Officials in Salahaddin governorate say that following the area's liberation from ISIS, local Badr Organisation officials have been involved in smuggling from oilfields near the Hamrin Mountains (where the Ajil, Allas and Hamrin oilfields are clustered).[126] Such activity was reported as far back as 2016,[127] and has continued intermittently, with other sources describing the activity as ongoing as recently as August 2018.[128] The Iran-aligned militia group Kataib Imam Ali was also implicated in oil smuggling from the Qayara oilfield south of Mosul in summer 2017.[129]

Order issued to PMU regional commands by Abu Mahdi Muhandis, 18 August 2018

In all the above cases, the operations were described as being run on basic business principles. One local observer familiar with smuggling in Salahaddin noted: 'It is purely business and money. Nobody asks about political, ethnic, or religious backgrounds.'[130] Similarly, a source in Qayara said that where the oil ended up – Baghdad, Kurdistan or elsewhere – depended on viable routes, and who would pay the most.[131]

Checkpoints and looting

From 2015 through to at least 2017, PMU militias often charged extra-legal fees to allow commercial vehicles to pass through checkpoints under their control. For instance, several militias demanded funds from trucks delivering cement blocks produced in Tuz Khurmatu to central and southern Iraq. Numerous competing militias charged tolls at a series of checkpoints that were previously the purview of the ISF:

> Under government control, the checkpoints' ostensible purpose was to prevent the free movement of terrorists, arms, and explosives. For the militias, they became profit centers. Trucks were no longer just paying bribes to feather the nests of individual inspectors. Now they were paying internal tariffs used to fund militia operations.[132]

Militias – including Iran-aligned groups – were also engaged in systematic looting for the purpose of generating revenue. Perhaps the highest-profile case of this is the dismantling of the Baiji oil refinery after it was retaken from ISIS in 2015. Baiji was garrisoned by multiple ISF units, as well as several PMU militias, following its recapture. While the refinery was badly damaged during fighting, it was subsequently ransacked by militia groups.[133] Components of the refinery were then sold off in a process reportedly overseen by the AAH and possibly other militia groups.[134] From an illicit-financing standpoint, the PMU militias' worst excesses took place while the fight against ISIS was at its most intense, creating chaotic conditions and impeding media scrutiny.

Though smuggling and checkpoint-extortion activities have continued, they seem to be well below their peak levels in the 2014–16 period. However, the need to financially sustain PMU militias despite uncertainty about the future of allocations from the PMU headquarters (or from the federal budget to the PMU grouping) may drive an increase in criminal activity and the splintering of existing groups into smaller units less amenable to centralised edicts regulating

(l) Popular Mobilisation Units fighters approach Baiji to retake the town from ISIS, October 2015

(r) Popular Mobilisation Units fighters recapture a refinery complex from ISIS near Baiji, Iraq, October 2015

their behaviour. Nevertheless, there is a recognition among some PMU leaders that criminal behaviour harms their collective reputation, which they are especially eager to maintain given that numerous militia groups are engaged in national and regional-level politics. To this end, in August 2018 Muhandis released an edict ordering all PMU groups to 'cease political and economic work' or risk being ousted from the grouping.[135] The political component of the order is clearly impossible for groups like the AAH, the Badr Organisation or the Sadrists to comply with, and therefore can be read as an effort at image control rather than a serious initiative to restrict militia activities to security matters. However, the economic aspect of the order likely reflects an understanding that the PMU's numerous elements are at times dangerously out of control, in large part because of their exponential growth during the 2014–16 period (the fight against ISIS), and because PMU militias enjoy the imprimatur of the state without any accountability. As one former PMU administrator noted:

> The Hashid [PMU] opened the door to everyone to join without any background checks of any types. This caused many problems for Hashid itself. Some [members] are just brutal and violent, and came to enjoy the killing of Sunnis, or to steal and loot whatever they can. Their leaders are aware of that, but it is something that is very hard to control.[136]

A return on investment

Just over a decade ago, AAH leader Khazali told his US interrogators that, during the insurgency, the US spent 'billions on the war while Iran spends millions. And even though [the US] spends so much more, Iran is able to be much more effective.'[137] Although circumstances are different, there are parallels to the PMU's competition with US-backed Iraqi armed forces in the fight against ISIS. Despite being less instrumental – and often peripheral – to victory in the conventional military campaign against ISIS, relative to more costly contributions from conventional Iraqi forces and the US-led coalition, the PMU reaped a disproportionate dividend in terms of public support and political legitimacy, as have its constituent Iran-aligned groups and senior figures. Unlike the Special Groups, which obtained a large part of their funding directly from the IRGC, the PMU has largely paid for itself via the Iraqi state. By contrast, the coalition forces' political dividend for large-scale military assistance has been relatively low.

Though a degree of direct Iranian financial support for some PMU militias exists, access to Iraqi state resources lets Iran-aligned groups flourish without much direct funding. Additionally, Iran-aligned militias/political parties such as the Badr Organisation can plunder state resources through senior positions in government external to the PMU programme.[138] In essence, organic ideological allies of Iran inside the PMU have direct access to Iraq's financial resources, greatly mitigating – although not totally negating – the need for direct Iranian financial support.

Order issued to PMU formations, commanders and departments by Abu Mahdi Muhandis, 2 August 2018

Iran's engagement with militia groups

Iran takes a varied approach to the command and control of armed groups in its sphere of influence. By and large, when it comes to domestic security operations in Iraq carried out by Shia militias close to Tehran, Iran is relatively distant. Rather than try to dictate to groups such

Tuz and 'Agha Eghbali'

Tuz Khurmatu, a town of about 80,000 people in a district of the same name in northern Salahaddin governorate, sits on intersecting highways that link Baghdad, Kirkuk, Tikrit and the Iranian border. The population comprises three major groups, each bearing their own territorial claims and broader affiliations. The minority Sunni population had largely fled after a spate of kidnappings and killings, leaving Kurds and Shia Turkmen to face off across fortifications separating their respective areas. Its position, and its Shia Turkmen population, gives Tuz strategic importance to the IRGC.

In June 2014, ISIS laid siege to around 12,000 lightly defended civilians in the town of Amerli south of Tuz. The breaking of the siege by PMU militias (with US airdrop support) became a galvanising moment for Shia Turkmen in the area. Tuz was now the epicentre of an assertive, militarised Shia Turkmen resurgence in response to the ISIS invasion and Kurdish irredentism, which Iran-linked PMU militias sought to foster and co-opt. The town became a hub for PMU offices and recruitment. While the Badr Organisation predominated, intra-PMU competition for Shia Turkmen support arose among AAH, Imam Ali Brigades and KH, as well as Shahid al-Sadr and other smaller Da'wa Party-backed militias.

Tuz itself was never taken by ISIS, but the war turned the town into a theatre for the most violent and overt second-order contest for control in Iraq's post-ISIS environment. The two populations segregated into separate geographic enclaves and acquired more

weapons from their patrons, exacerbating existing tensions. While the Kurdish and Turkmen sides were both heavily backed by broader outside forces (PUK-aligned Kurdish forces on one hand and PMU militias on the other), violence more than once broke out spontaneously from tensions arising at a local level. Since 2015, fighting has not only been between Kurdish Peshmerga and Shia militias, but also between heavily armed Kurdish and Shia Turkmen residents not formally part of any Peshmerga units or Shia militias respectively.

Since the ISIS takeover in 2014, IRGC operative Mohammad Hajji Ali Eghbalpour (referred to locally simply as 'Agha Eghbali') has found uncommonly prominent status as a widely respected and effective power broker in and around Tuz Khurmatu. While generally referred to as the 'Iranian representative in Tuz Khurmatu', local PUK administrative and security officials who claimed to be familiar with Eghbali since the 1980s stated he is a senior officer in the IRGC.[139]

The volatility and importance of Tuz have both raised the profile of Eghbali and suggest he is a significant IRGC operative, making him a case study for how the IRGC manages its interests across Iraq's volatile patchwork of contested northern territories. The IRGC may station other officers in key locations in Iraq. It is unclear if Eghbali enjoys a uniquely prominent role because of Tuz's special circumstances, or if other equivalent Iranian liaison officers operate more discreetly in other areas of Iraq.

as the AAH, the Badr Organisation and KH, Iran appears content to let them make their own decisions based on their understanding of the local context.

Their commanders take the lead on navigating inter-group relations and directing relations with Iraq's security and political establishment. However, at times some senior Iranian officials will step in, playing a mediation or facilitation role.

A prime example of a senior Iranian official playing an influential role in Iraq's security and political sphere is the case of a presumed IRGC operative long based in the area of Tuz Khurmatu, a disputed territory southeast of Kirkuk (see text box above).

Tactical support

Iran has provided tactical-level support to a number of Iraqi militia groups during combat operations

against ISIS.[148] For most Iraqi combatants in the PMU militias, the precise rank and identity of the Iranians is not clear, in part because nothing on their uniforms – often identical to what is worn by Iraqi fighters – gives away name or rank.[149] Sources describe embedded Iranians providing logistical and surveillance support, and advice on target identification and other aspects of fire support during combat operations. Iran also augmented the PMU's limited armour capability with Iranian equipment and officers in 2014 in the period immediately following Sistani's fatwa.[150]

While generally described positively, Iran's support for its allies in the PMU programme has at times been criticised by those receiving it. In one such episode, Iran reportedly provided faulty intelligence to a close Shia militia ally in northern central Iraq, leading to a fatal ambush by ISIS.[151] However, there

Now seemingly in his late 50s or early 60s, Eghbali – who speaks Kurdish – has been known to Kurdish officials in the area since the IRGC embedded operatives with PUK-aligned Peshmerga to assist with guerrilla operations against the Iraqi Army around Kirkuk in the 1980s, and was present with Kurds when the Ba'athist regime conducted the Anfal campaign in reprisal. He does not operate with any security or directly command any military force.[140] Save for a few photos on PMU social-media pages, he shuns media attention.

In this febrile environment, Eghbali has played an overt role as a mediator, while seemingly enforcing IRGC prerogatives and acting as a PMU military adviser and strategist. In the absence of effective Iraqi state policing or political representation, Eghbali's long-standing connection to the area has allowed him to broker agreements between senior Kurdish (primarily PUK) and PMU figures, and gain in stature in an environment of continual crisis.

Eghbali's apparent goals have been to coordinate PMU military operations against ISIS and reduce Kurd–Turkmen violence. In addition, Eghbali sought to ensure that Iran-affiliated PMU groups, particularly the Badr Organisation, gained control in Tuz and in the southern Kirkuk governorate as a means of projecting IRGC influence in the area. Where fighting has receded, Eghbali has reportedly mediated agreements over policing, checkpoints and troop deployments in Tuz district.[141]

In 2014, Eghbali remained in Tuz when ISIS was nearby, helping to coordinate Kurdish and Turkmen forces and their troop movements in defending southern Kirkuk and northern Salahaddin governorates (including the besieged Shia Turkmen village of Amerli) from the jihadi group.[142]

After the ISIS threat receded, Eghbali worked on security and political stabilisation, brokering security agreements on checkpoints and troop deployments around Tuz,[143] going so far as to issue instruction letters on individual checkpoints and roadblocks.[144]

The multiplicity of actors in Tuz made local rivalries difficult to control. Eghbali struggled to tame Kurdish–Turkmen violence, illustrating the limits of his power.

Outbursts of fighting inside the town in November 2015, April 2016 and June 2016 escalated into deadly fighting for several days before Eghbali brokered prisoner swaps and eventual ceasefires[145] with PMU and PUK officials. However, in June 2016, simultaneous ISIS attacks around Tuz triggered fighting between the Peshmerga and PMU militias, demonstrating the limits to Eghbali's ability to secure the area and reconcile Kurdish and PMU actors.[146]

While Eghbali was able to coordinate effectively with Badr Organisation leadership, elements of the AAH and KH militias in the Tuz area have proved harder to control. This further demonstrated the limitations of Eghbali's influence – and perhaps also deficiencies of command and control inside even ideologically pro-Iranian Shia militias.[147]

is no indication that, beyond resentment harboured by those involved, this episode or others like it have done anything to damage fundamentally Iran's relationship with its local allies.

Iraqi interlocutors with the IRGC and Iran: Qais al-Khazali's testimony

The manner in which Iran interacts with the militia groups in its sphere of influence is opaque. Some insight in the form of recent historical context is provided by information conveyed by Qais al-Khazali. While it is crucial to note that Khazali was likely engaged in a good deal of self-preservation in his interrogation by US operatives, and his claims should be treated with some scepticism, the insights show how Iran approached the management of Iraqi militias in the post-2003 period.

According to Khazali, the Special Groups era began with a trip to Iran in 2003 by a small group of Sadrists led by Muqtada al-Sadr, with Qais al-Khazali. They met Ayatollah Khamenei, Quds Force commander Soleimani and Abdul Reza Shahlai (Hajji Yousef), the IRGC Quds Force 'point man' for weapons procurement for what became the Special Groups.[152] This was apparently part of Iran's strategy to diversify its support for the anti-coalition insurgency.

The Special Groups worked under decentralised regional commands (Baghdad, Central and Southern), with minimal communication between officers in different commands. Each command liaised independently with the Quds Force and associated contacts for advanced training,[153] weapons supplies and financial support, and had their own liaisons to preserve separate lines of communication.[154] Trainers in Iran reportedly included Iranian[155]

(l) Popular Moblisation Units fighters with portraits of Grand Ayatollah Ali al-Sistani and PMU leader Abu Mahdi al-Muhandis, Basra, December 2017

(r) Asaib Ahl al-Haq leader Qais al-Khazali, Tikrit, March 2015

and Lebanese Hizbullah operatives.[156] Khazali identified Muhammad al-Tabatabai and Akram al-Kaabi (later of the Harakat al-Nujaba militia) as Special Group leaders with access to Iranians[157] in whom he placed absolute trust.[158] The groups also operated internal decision-making councils, and a 'legislative committee', which provided some management functions and, together with Khazali, religious guidance on the legitimacy of larger attacks.[159]

The training and support effort ran separately but in parallel with Iranian support for what Khazali dubbed 'Khamenei's Groups' (such as the Badr Organisation and KH), between which there were strong ideological tensions[160] and differences in weapons provision and training.[161] Group unit leaders would reportedly sign up via senior Special Groups officials, who would then broker passage to Iran for 10–20 fighters at a time through a single Iranian contact, with communications strictly on a one-to-one basis for operational security.[162] Recruits crossed the border singly, or in pairs.[163]

Maissan governorate-based smuggler Abu Sajjad Gharawi was a primary conduit for donated weapons[164] transfers to the Special Groups, according to Khazali.[165] Gharawi's interlocutors in Iran were Hajji Yousef[166] and officials from the Quds Force and Iran's Ministry of Intelligence and Security.[167] Gharawi sought to maintain operational independence and did not have strong ideological ties to Tehran, though he once resided there and remained on the Quds Force payroll as a valued asset.[168]

Special Group commanders' main point of contact in Amarah, a city near the Iranian border, was Abu Dhar, an Iraqi associate dating back to the 1980s.[169] There was a 'constant need' for weapons, which regional Special Groups commanders communicated to Abu Dhar. Just-in-time supply[170] and direct liaison with regional commands[171] obviated the need for weapons caches,[172] and prevented the network from failing if one part of it was compromised. The network appears to have been designed to ensure Iranian exposure would be minimal.[173] Gharawi also reportedly ran guns to the Badr Organisation, which operated its own smuggling networks. Iran's goal in working through the Gharawi network was to channel 'as many weapons as possible to reach the hands of Shia Muslims in Iraq'.[174]

Khazali claimed that the 'Khamenei Group' militias (for example, the Badr Organisation) obtained support through a network independent of the Special Groups, led by Abu Mustafa al-Shaibani,[175] an Iraqi who, also according to Khazali, had lived in Iran since the Iran–Iraq War and who served as an IRGC intelligence commander.[176] In a separate statement, Khazali describes Shaibani as in control of the AAH, the group he would go on to lead.[177]

Khazali's testimony describes – post-2003 – a series of siloed, superficial contacts with middlemen and lower-tier operatives, intended to maintain individual groups' operational security and dependence on the IRGC. He details only a few meetings with Soleimani and other Iranian officials of similar rank since the introduction in Iran in 2003. Senior officials are not mentioned as taking part in any operational aspect of the weapons, training or cash-support programmes, instead leaving them to deputies or tertiary-level operatives. The result was a diffuse set of networks that afforded Iran operational resilience and plausible deniability.[178]

Iran has much less need to act in a clandestine manner than it did when it was supporting Special Groups engaged in conflict with US and coalition forces in Iraq, and its current set of militia allies in Iraq are legally codified through the PMU programme. Moreover, though rhetorically hostile to the US, kinetic activity by these groups aimed at American and Western targets is rare.[179] The compartmentalised, cell-like engagement between

Strategic communications

An ancillary benefit to Iran of its wide-ranging set of Shia Islamist political and militia allies is the ability this confers to communicate messages, both to these groups and to their constituents. There are several examples of this capability in action:

- Numerous Iran-leaning Shia Islamist groups and their affiliated media outlets have long pushed the narrative that the US and its allies created ISIS, and that US helicopters help resupply ISIS militants or evacuate ISIS leaders from the battlefield.

- Shia Islamist politicians from parties affiliated with militia groups roundly condemn US sanctions on Iran. The sanctions are described as oppressive and hypocritical. One common line of argument is a historical narrative linking US policy to Iran's 1979 revolution,[182] and some evoke Iraq's experience of US sanctions in the 1990s, commingling these examples of US intervention in a narrative of shared resistance.[183]

- Following the destruction of the Iranian consulate in Basra in September 2018, and several offices of Iraqi Shia Islamist parties/militias aligned with Iran, media outlets linked to both Tehran and its Iraqi allies have pushed the narrative that the US consulate helped foment the protests and the destruction of these facilities.[184]

the IRGC and Iraqi interlocutors is no longer a prerequisite to survival. There are other reasons that Iran values having a multitude of parallel relationships with a range of Iraqi militia groups, but it is no longer an operational necessity to the degree it was in the 2003–08 period.

Indeed, there is open-source information that Iran appears to engage directly with senior officials in its sphere of influence, such as Ameri, Muhandis and other top-tier militia leadership. Iran also engages directly with political parties (Kurdish and Shia Islamist) and militia groups (the Badr Organisation and other Shia militias), as well as PUK-aligned Peshmerga.

The blurred line between armed groups and political parties in Iraq means that Iranian political and military engagement often blend into each other. This may be one reason why Tehran opted for a long-time IRGC officer, Iraj Masjedi, who had served as an adviser to Qasem Soleimani, as its current ambassador to Iraq.[180] The line is blurred in large part because groups such as the AAH and the Badr Organisation are also political actors. The same is true in Iraq's Kurdistan Region, where the PUK and the Kurdistan Democratic Party (KDP) both control their own large Peshmerga forces, which are essentially party militias. In the case of the PUK, sources familiar with the party's relationship with Iran say there are a small number of PUK political officials that Iran sometimes uses to carry both political and security messages (though this is not to say that Iran exclusively engages the PUK through these interlocutors).[181] The same dynamic is probably true among Shia militia/political groups; Iran has preferred interlocutors, but is certainly willing to approach directly other officials of varying ranks, at its discretion.

Strategic assessment

The evolution of the Iraqi state from 2003 to the present day effectively guarantees significant Iranian influence in Iraq's political, economic and security affairs, barring a major change in the political and security environment. Iraq's importance to Tehran also helps to explain how Iran approaches its relationship to Iraqi militant groups differently from militias in other regional states. Iranian decision-takers pay close attention to Iraq, and move cautiously when it comes to Iraqi affairs. Indeed, Iranian policy seems designed to maintain relationships and keep open as many policy options as possible, rather than to force Iraq in a political direction that might lead to a decisive conflict that Iran's allies in Iraq might lose.

Nevertheless, through its local affiliates, Iran maintains the capacity to direct, commission and carry out violence in Iraq. In addition, through the expansion of militias that variously act as direct surrogates or over which Iran holds significant leverage through ideological affiliation, influence or practical support, Iran has deprived the Iraqi state of a monopoly on the use of force in the post-2003 era. This affords Tehran an unrivalled level of influence over Iraq's affairs.

Iran's support for Shia militant groups in Iraq has moved through many phases, and even now it must be seen as a developing phenomenon. From relationships seeded in the war with Ba'ath-era Iraq almost 40 years ago, Iran has developed a strong team of cadres, both Iranian and Iraqi, with extensive experience in both clandestine and battlefield operations. Much of Iran's military-asset base in Iraq was born of the 'resistance' to the US between 2003 and 2011, and the United States' relative tolerance of or refusal to

Table 4.1: PMU militia groups: relationship with Iran and assessment of strategic utility

Militia	Ideological affinity	Strategic convergence	Political expediency	Transactional value	Strategic value for Iran	Other 'patrons'	Assessment
Asaib Ahl al-Haq	●●	●●	●●●	●●	●●●	Yes	Strategic ally
Badr Organisation	●●●	●●●	●●●	●●●	●●●	Yes	Strategic and ideological ally
Harakat al-Nujaba	●●	●	●●	●●●	●●	Yes	Proxy
Kataib Hizbullah	●●●	●●●	●●●	●●●	●●●	Yes	State organ
Shabak and Yazidi militia	●	●	●	●●	●	Yes	n.k.

Source: IISS

●●● High ●● Medium ● Low

respond decisively to this resistance. Iran's assets in Iraq further adapted during the war against ISIS. This conflict provided a unique opportunity to assimilate hardline Iran-oriented militia assets into the Iraqi state and budget. The result is that the Iraqi state is essentially financing the degradation of its ability to hold a monopoly on force and enjoy the resultant political power, while giving disproportionate credit – and with it political heft – to the PMU and its component parts for victory against ISIS.

If the threat posed by ISIS continues to fade over the coming years to the point that it can no longer be used as a *raison d'être* for maintaining the PMU, the programme's militias will probably shift their rhetoric to justify their continued existence. In Lebanon, Hizbullah at one point ostensibly existed to drive the Israeli military out of the country; the group's relative power there has only grown in the nearly two decades since Israel's withdrawal. Potential rhetorical shifts that could be used by Iran-aligned PMU militias to justify their existence and budgetary allocations include:

- exaggerating the threat posed by continued pockets of insurgency;
- adopting a position that as long as Turkish and US forces continue to have a ground presence in Iraq – the former without legal justification – the continued presence of armed PMU militias is necessary;
- morphing the PMU into something of a national guard, mixing military readiness with an increase in the type of public-works activities already undertaken by the PMU in multiple locations across Iraq;
- defending Iran if it comes under attack;
- serving as an expeditionary or buffer force if the security environment in Syria deteriorates.

As the war with ISIS draws to a close, PMU groups show no sign of disbanding. The Iraqi state has considered various ways to tame these groups, either by building a national guard or integrating these militias into the country's armed forces. In July 2019, as tensions between the US and Iran threatened to destabilise Iraq, Prime Minister Abdul-Mahdi issued an order to bring all militias into the armed forces. In keeping with their previous stance, the militia commanders aligned with Iran gave lip service to the government announcement but carried on as usual, revealing the balance of power inside Iraq.

The PMU is looking for new missions that can enhance its factions' public visibility, political power and post-ISIS relevance. The transition is not yet an urgent matter, given that ISIS remains a threat and the fight against it continues to provide employment – and a justification – for PMU forces, especially in western Anbar, Diyala and the disputed territories. But already there are signs of a pivot: hundreds of PMU vehicles and personnel were sent to Basra and other southern provinces in spring 2019 to shore up dams and perform relief work in areas affected by winter flooding.[185] In a sign of the strategic value accorded to this effort by PMU leaders, Muhandis himself oversaw some of these works.[186] The PMU is also beginning to take on other public-works projects in southern Iraq.[187]

A higher-risk, higher-pay-off option for PMU capabilities would be to assume broad domestic intelligence and security roles. At least some PMU factions have extensive experience in surveillance, kidnapping and interrogation operations, and there are already some indications they have used these against domestic critics.[188] This path offers PMU factions the chance to serve as powerful gatekeepers in Iraqi politics, with a role parallel to that of the IRGC in policing domestic discourse. But the PMU is still far from achieving this kind of position, and moving too far too fast would mean risking a domestic backlash. It is not clear that various PMU factions could work together on these issues without falling into conflict with each other.

In terms of capacity-building, Iranian support for Iraqi Shia militias has been a major success. Since 2014, the militias have become politically and militarily normalised through their participation in the war against ISIS, which they have leveraged into increased political activity. Iranian-backed militias are larger, wealthier and more politically influential than ever before. They also have powerful military and intelligence capabilities, which can be used to check the influence of the US, Sunni powers and even domestic Iraqi critics on the political scene.

However, its support for Shia militias has not given Iran total domination in Iraq. The US–Iraq military relationship endures, with only a small US military footprint, and Iraq is complying, at least to a degree, with sanctions imposed on Iran by the Trump administration. Iraqi politics continues to be a balancing act: domestically, among Kurds, Shia and Sunnis, and internationally among Iran, the US and regional powers, especially Turkey.

Shia PMU militias have also helped to drive major demographic changes in Baghdad and elsewhere in Iraq through the displacement of Sunni Arab communities over the past 15 years, yet this often brutal campaign has generated new threats and resentments that have impeded the kind of security situation Iran desires in Iraq. Even as the influence of Shia militias has grown immensely over the past five years, Iraq's political structures and diplomatic position remain much as they were in 2012 or 2013, before the rise of ISIS and the creation of the PMU. And with each election cycle it is becoming harder for Tehran to corral the fracturing Shia body politic into the kind of government it wants.

The relative restraint shown by Iran's militias in the post-ISIS conflict environment – particularly in contrast to sectarian displacements in the 2005–08 period – may be a poor indicator of what lies ahead. Iran's paramilitary allies are planting deep roots in Iraq, building both military capacities and political networks. It seems unlikely that they will back down, withdraw or disarm willingly, and it is likely that they will try to use their growing power to win a greater say in government, putting them on a collision course with other political actors in Iraq, and with each other.

Indeed, the particular conduit that Iran has chosen to build its influence in Iraq creates high risks of destabilisation for the Iraqi political system. Unlike Lebanese Hizbullah, Iraqi Shia militias do not constitute a single political or military entity. Competition among them has so far been contained, apparently in large part by Iranian mediation. But it seems likely

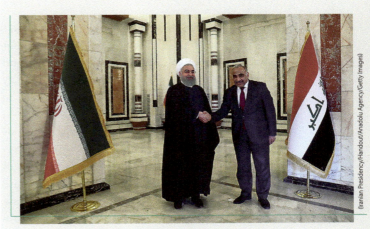

Iranian President Hassan Rouhani meets with Iraqi Prime Minister Adil Abdul-Mahdi, Baghdad, March 2019

that as these militias expand, it will become harder to contain them. This is especially so now that the threat of ISIS has receded, and the prospect of a greater role in government introduces more assets for militia leaders to dispute.

However, the fractured landscape of allies in Iraq also has upsides for Iran. When Iraq's domestic political winds shift, it is unlikely to harm all of Iran's allies at once. Instead, what hurts one ally may well boost another. In the case of the 2018 elections, Iraqi voters favoured individuals and parties perceived as not being part of the existing political establishment. The phenomenon was essentially a 'break even' proposition for Iran, given that it has both establishment (Badr Organisation, ISCI) and anti-establishment (AAH) allies.

Maintaining a stable of militias in Iraq rather than a single entity is Iran's choice at this time. But in some ways, this is a forced choice: Iraq's Shia militia leaders represent a spectrum of loyalty to Iran, and lack a clear vision for how to adapt Iran's Islamic Revolutionary ideology to Iraq's circumstances. Ideological alignment with Iran's revolutionary project is much stronger among ageing former exiles who command groups like the AAH and the Badr Organisation than it is among the majority of Iraqi Shia citizens, who in many cases spent the Iran–Iraq War in Iraq being targeted by Iranian military hardware. This factor also limits what Tehran can hope to achieve in Iraq. Broad acceptance of *Velayat-e Faqih* by a majority of Iraqi Shia is unlikely, even if militias espousing the concept increase their foothold in Iraq's political establishment.

Any attempt to force these competing groups into a single political movement would create resentful and underemployed losers, who would look for a new political home. Already, the Sadrist movement, which controls the largest coherent party in Iraq's parliament, has repositioned itself as a key counter-weight to pro-Iranian forces, including the AAH and the Badr Organisation, as seen in Sadr's July 2017 visit to Saudi Arabia and his December 2017 call to disband the militias.[189]

Tehran has previously manipulated rivalries between Sadrist and SCIRI-derived groups to diversify its investments and maximise the imbalance of relationships in its favour. Yet as Iraqi militias fuse their paramilitary and political activities, and draw continued support from the Iraqi state, their desire for domestic political influence and popular support may come into conflict with manifestations of active loyalty to Iran. This is evident in the exhortations of Sadr, whose rhetoric suggests he believes a majority of Iraqi Shia are more interested in Iraqi nationalism than they are in Iran's Axis of Resistance.

Although Iran has created a powerful group of militia allies in Iraq, they threaten to undermine Iraq's stability in unpredictable ways. Efforts by Tehran to use these militias to intervene forcefully in Iraqi domestic politics would risk further destabilising the situation, and any reconfiguration of the militias into a more stable pattern would be difficult and risky.

The anti-ISIS war may prove to be the high point for the success of Tehran's militia-based policy in Iraq. Militias alone cannot provide Iran with the broad influence it requires to prevent what Tehran would view as adverse political and security developments in its neighbour, such as strong Iraqi nationalism, the disbanding of the PMU or parliament pushing to defund the militias. At times, Tehran's closest allies seem unable to convert battlefield successes into political dominance: the Badr Organisation's post-ISIS management of Diyala governorate, for example, has largely been a failure. Iraqis have shown a high degree of resistance to and resentment of militarised Iranian influence, including popular protests in Iraq's south in summer 2018. The perceived brutality of militias in Sunni areas and the disputed territories has hindered stabilisation efforts and indirectly risked renewed threats, both of which run counter to Iranian interests. The continuation of Tehran's militarised policy has irritated Iraqis and could become counterproductive in the post-conflict environment.

The long-term prospects of Iran's militia-building project in Iraq are therefore still in doubt, despite the successes of the past few years. Just how destabilising these militias prove for Iraq and for the region depends on a number of factors, including whether or not Iranian policymakers recognise the risks and limitations inherent in their relationship with their militia allies; how the US responds to Iraqi militia groups, and whether US policies drive a self-fulfilling prophecy of increased Iranian influence; and how Iraq's population responds to the increased role of militia groups in political life.

Notes

1 'Iraq cleric issues call to arms against ISIL', Al-Jazeera, 14 June 2014, https://www.aljazeera.com/news/middleeast/2014/06/iraq-cleric-issues-call-arms-against-isil-2014613125518278210.html.

2 Iraq's 2018 budget law states that the PMU has 122,000 personnel and a budget of 1.683 trillion Iraqi dinars (US$1.4 billion); see chart E, p. 57, no. 4485, 2 April 2018, https://moj.gov.iq/upload/pdf/4485.pdf. In spring 2018 the Abbas Combat Division (a formation independent of Iran) had 44,000 fighters and the Sadrist Saraya al-Salam had 18,000, while the Badr Organisation had 24,000; see 'Qira'ah fi masa'i damj "al-hashd al-sha'abi" bi al-quwwat al-'iraqiyyah' [A reading of efforts to integrate the 'Popular Mobilisation Units' with the Iraqi forces], al-Sharq al-Awsat, 30 April 2018, https://aawsat.com/home/article/1253046. No official breakdown of fighters by faction has ever been released; even if it were, payroll numbers might be misleading due to the widespread presence of unpaid volunteers in some PMU formations and to chronic absenteeism (or outright payroll fraud) in others.

3 The US Treasury Department declared Kataib Hizbullah a terrorist group in July 2009 and placed Abu Mahdi Muhandis under sanctions for his role as the group's leader; see US Department of the Treasury, 'Treasury Designates Individual, Entity Posing Threat to Stability in Iraq', 2 July 2009, https://www.treasury.gov/press-center/press-releases/Pages/tg195.aspx.

4 'Li'annahum Rafadu Haymanat Iran, Abu Mahdi Muhandis harima Fasa'il fi al-Hashd al-Sha'abi min rawatibihim' [Because they denied Iran's domination, Abu Mahdi Muhandis deprived elements of the PMU of their salaries], Kalima, 3 February 2018, http://kalimaiq.com/contents/view/details?id=278.

5 'Declassified U.S. Tactical Intelligence Report of Qais al-Khazali', TIR 200243-062, 17 February 2008, pp. 159–61, American Enterprise Institute, https://www.aei.org/wp-content/uploads/2018/08/Enclosure-TAB-A-Documents-for-Release-49-66.pdf.

6 'Declassified U.S. Tactical Intelligence Report of Qais al-Khazali', TIR-28, 8 April 2007, p. 32, https://www.aei.org/

wp-content/uploads/2018/08/TIR-32.pdf.

7   Hamdi Malik, 'Shiite split heats up as Iraqi lawmakers fail to elect speaker', Al-Monitor, 5 September 2018, https://www.al-monitor.com/pulse/originals/2018/09/iraq-iran-election-parliament-shiite.html.

8   The idea that Iranian support is channelled through the federal government is often put forward by PMU leaders. See 'Hadi al-'Ameri – za'im al-Hashd al-Sha'abi – kamil al-muqabilah – istifta' al-aqlim wa al-kathir' [Hadi al-Ameri – a leader of the PMU – full interview – Referendum of the region], September 2017, 33:28–33:57, https://www.youtube.com/watch?v=VIDytvUkq5c.

9   'Madha Yaf'al al-Janaral al-Irani Qasim Sulaymani Fi al-Fallujah?' [What is Iranian general Qasem Soleimani doing in Fallujah?], al-Ghad Television, 29 May 2016, https://bit.ly/2Yehrzf.

10 'Kata'ib Hizbullah: al-Amn al-Qawmi al-Yuqas bi-l-Amtar wa-la Tu'fa Amrika min Mas'uliyat al-'I'itida' 'ala Mawaqa'ina' [Kataib Hizbullah: National security cannot be measured by a few metres, America will not escape responsibility for the attack on our positions], Kataib Hizbullah website, 25 June 2018, https://www.kataibhizbollah.com/news/2922; 'Nu'lin Fih Wuqufina ila Janib Nitham al-Jumhuriya al-Islamiya' [In which we announce that we stand side by side with the Islamic Republican regime], Kataib Hizbullah website, 23 June 2009, https://www.kataib-hizbollah.com/statment/1182.

11 Robert F. Worth, 'Kidnapped Royalty Become Pawns in Iran's Deadly Plot', New York Times, 14 March 2018, https://www.nytimes.com/2018/03/14/magazine/how-a-ransom-for-royal-falconers-reshaped-the-middle-east.html.

12 'Kata'ib Hizbullah: Nu'akkid Qararana al-Ladhi Itakhadhnah Mundh al-Bada' bi-'Adam Musharakatina 'aw 'ay min Kawadirina fi al-Intikhabat al-Qadima ka-Murashshahin' [Kataib Hizbullah: We affirm the decision we took from the beginning that neither we nor any of our cadres shall participate as candidates in the upcoming elections], Kataib Hizbullah website, 24 February 2018, https://kataibhizbollah.com/statment/2873.

13 'Laqa' khas ma'a Abu Ala' al-Wala'i amin 'am Kata'ib Sayyid al-Shuhada' [Exclusive interview with Kataib Sayyid al-Shuhada leader Abu Ala al-Walai], 6 July 2017, 5:15–5:54, https://www.youtube.com/watch?v=iNuVkz3ehYA.

14 Ibid., 9:20–9:30, 18:10–18:23.

15 Dexter Filkins, 'The Shadow Commander', New Yorker, 23 September 2013, https://www.newyorker.com/magazine/2013/09/30/the-shadow-commander.

16 'SCIRI leaders deeply concerned over al-Kut operation', WikiLeaks, 19 January 2007, https://wikileaks.org/plusd/cables/07BAGHDAD212_a.html.

17 Loveday Morris, 'Appointment of Iraq's new interior minister opens door to militia and Iranian influence', Washington Post, 18 October 2014, https://www.washingtonpost.com/world/appointment-of-iraqs-new-interior-minister-opens-door-to-militia-and-iranian-influence/2014/10/18/f6f2a347-d38c-4743-902a-254a169ca274_story.html?utm_term=.eaa391f2cb29.

18 Interviews with local Sunni PMU officials in Salahaddin governorate and with Peshmerga and local residents in Kirkuk.

19 'Frontline', 5 August 2017, 8:20–10:00, https://www.youtube.com/watch?v=XsxkPZC1ph4.

20 'Declassified U.S. Tactical Intelligence Report of Qais al-Khazali', TIR-7, 24 March 2007, p. 74, https://www.aei.org/wp-content/uploads/2018/08/TIR-7.pdf.

21 'Declassified U.S. Tactical Intelligence Report of Qais al-Khazali', TIR-200243-38, 20 October 2007, p. 96, https://www.aei.org/wp-content/uploads/2018/08/Enclosure-TAB-A-Documents-for-Release-33-48.pdf.

22 'Declassified U.S. Tactical Intelligence Report of Qais al-Khazali', TIR-200243-007, 11 June 2007, p. 18, https://www.aei.org/wp-content/uploads/2018/08/Enclosure-TAB-A-Documents-for-Release-1-16.pdf.

23 'Declassified U.S. Tactical Intelligence Report of Qais al-Khazali', TIR-200243-21, 18 July 2007, and 200243-22, 20 July 2007, pp. 54–57, https://www.aei.org/wp-content/uploads/2018/08/Enclosure-TAB-A-Documents-for-Release-18-32.pdf.

24 Ammar Karim, 'Baghdad Shootout Points to Growing Militia Threat', AFP, 21 October 2014, https://www.yahoo.com/news/baghdad-shootout-points-growing-militia-threat-115144527.html; 'Tajik al-Salifah ma'a al-amin al-'am li-'Asa'ib Ahl al-Haq al-shaykh Qays al-Khaz'ali' [Tajik al-Salifa with the leader of Asaib Ahl al-Haq, Qais al-Khazali], May 2017, 6:00–6:20, https://www.youtube.com/watch?v=tFMSQfpdQ4A.

25 Jonathan Spyer, 'Behind the lines: Who is Qais al-Khazali, and Why Should You Care?', Jerusalem Post, 15 December 2017, https://www.jpost.com/Arab-Israeli-Conflict/Behind-The-Lines-Who-is-Qais-al-Khazali-and-why-should-you-care-518131.

26 'Goftogu-ye Jam-e Jam Anlain Ba Pedar-e Shahid Morteza Hossein-Pur, Farmandeh-ye Haidariyun dar Suriyeh' [Jam-e Jam Online's Discussion with the Father of the Martyr Morteza Hosseinpour, Commander of the Haidariyoun in Syria], Jam-e Jam, 16 September 2017, http://jamejamonline.ir/online/2995242834952373792.

27 'Al-Sayyid 'Ali al-Yasiri fi mu'tamir Saraya al-Khorasani' [Sayyid Ali al-Yaseri in a Saraya al-Khorasani press conference], 5 April 2015, https://www.youtube.com/watch?v=DTTubkY2CJk.

28 Nour Samaha, 'Iraq's "Good Sunni"', Foreign Policy, 16 November 2016, https://foreignpolicy.com/2016/11/16/iraqs-good-sunni.

29 Several interviewees in Diyala governorate say that members of the Karawi tribe, displaced and unable to return home due to suspicions of their potential ties to ISIS, were able to use their AAH affiliation to reclaim prior status and property, 2018.

30 Personnel identifying themselves as the Ali al-Akbar Brigade (a Shrines Administration-sponsored PMU group) appear at a PMU training course in Karbala; see 'Popular Mobilisation Unit Karbala artillery branch concludes its fourth training course', Karbala Satellite Channel, 15 May 2018, 07:35, https://www.youtube.com/watch?v=KWi1uGetxM8.

31 'Al-Basrah: Munaththamat Badr Tuwazzi' al-'Iyad al—Naqdiya 'ala 'Adad min 'Awa'il Shuhada' fi al-Muhafatha' [Basra: Badr Organisation distributes holiday cash disbursements to a number of families of martyrs in the province], Badr Organisation, 17 June 2017, http://basra.badr.iq/?a=content.id&id=17505&lang=ar; 'Badr Tu'akkid Istimraraha Ma'a al-Firqa al-Kahmisa bi-Tathir Nahiyat al-Riyad bi-Kirkuk min Tanthim Da'ish' [Badr affirms it continues with the fifth division the cleansing of Riyadh sub-district in Kirkuk of Daesh], al-Sumaria News, 5 April 2015, https://www.alsumaria.tv/news/129987/iraq-news; interview with an Iraqi army officer in western Anbar, 2018.

32 PMU artillery-branch chief Abu Majid al-Basri describes a memorandum with the Iraqi Army on training, al-Ghadeer TV, March 2018, 51:28–52:30, https://www.youtube.com/watch?v=fYyOLZk2WxQ.

33 Specific individuals are said to have commanded both Badr Organisation forces and Federal Police units during the fight against ISIS. Dexter Filkins, 'The Dangers of the Iraqi Coalition Headed Towards Mosul', New Yorker, 19 October 2016, https://www.newyorker.com/news/news-desk/the-dangers-of-the-iraqi-coalition-headed-toward-mosul.

34 Interview with an ISF official who served in eastern Anbar, 2016, who said that a Federal Police unit controlled by 'Abu Dhargham' was primarily made up of Badr personnel, and that it was effectively a Badr unit.

35 Interview with a PUK Peshmerga officer based in Sulaimaniya governorate, 2018, who described the provision of light and medium weaponry to both KDP and PUK Peshmerga units in 2014 and early 2015. The source said Iran also provided artillery teams at least to PUK Peshmerga.

36 Ibid.

37 Interviews with KDP and PUK Peshmerga officers, 2018.

38 'Safqa Ab'adat al-Hashd 'An al-Anbar Muqabil Istikmal Tahrir Salah al-Din wa Khamsat Alaf Tikriti Yusharikun Fiha' [Deal to move Hashd away from Anbar in return for complete liberation of Salahaddin, with participation of 5,000 Tikritis], al-Mada, 13 October 2015, https://bit.ly/303gQ5l; Alah al-Din Governor Ahmad Abdullah al-Jibouri interview with al-Arabiya al-Hadath TV, 2 August 2018, 4:56–5:35, https://www.youtube.com/watch?v=jPBqLKu.

39 Interviews with multiple individuals affiliated with the PMU, 2018.

40 Ibid.

41 Interviews with Iraqi Security Forces and tribal PMU figures based in western Anbar, 2018.

42 An official in Qaim claimed that Kataib Hizbullah and other PMU militias had created a dedicated border point between Qaim and Akashat, 2018.

43 'Amaliyyat 'askariyyah li-tathir manatiq nahr al-Furat' [Military operations to clear out the areas around the Euphrates river], al-Mada, 16 July 2018, http://almadapaper.net/Details/211998; 'Al-I'ilam al-Amni: Istishhad Shaks wa-Isabat 16 bi-Tafjir al-Qaim' [Security spokesperson: one killed and sixteen wounded in al-Qaim bombing], al-Sumaria TV, 11 January 2019, https://www.alsumaria.tv/news/257565; multiple interviews with Anbar-based security officials, 2018–19.

44 Interviews with Iraqi Security Forces, tribal PMU and local government officials from or in Fallujah, Heet, Qaim and Ramadi districts, 2018.

45 Abbas Abd al-Karim, 'Tal'afar Madinat al-Turkman Ard al-Fitnah al-Muqbilah, Ma Lam Tatadarakaha al-Hukumah wa-Qiwa al-Iqlim' [Talafar, City of Turkmen and the next trouble spot: what the government and regional powers do not understand], al-Hayat, 26 January 2017, http://www.alhayat.com/article/805091; 'Absent government, fragile truce holds in Tuz Khurmatc', Iraq Oil Report, 8 November 2015.

46 'Jabhat al-Kurd al-fayliyyin: "adad mutatawwi'ina li-qital Da'ish tajawaza al-khamsah alaf mutatawwi"' [The Faili Kurdish Front: the number of our volunteers fighting against ISIS exceeded 5,000], al-Sumaria TV, 22 March 2015, https://www.alsumaria.tv/news/128459.

47 Interview with official familiar with the Shabak Brigade PMU group, 2018.

48 'Winning the Post-ISIS Battle for Iraq in Sinjar', International Crisis Group Report no. 183, 20 February 2018, p. 6, https://www.crisisgroup.org/middle-east-north-africa/gulf-and-arabian-peninsula/iraq/183-winning-post-isis-battle-iraq-sinjar.

49 In interviews, local Kurdish and Turkmen sources say that Badr Organisation officials – including Ameri – struggled to rein in groups like the AAH and Saraya Khorasani. Additionally, Badr Organisation and Kurdish political officials alike struggled to prevent their respective constituent groups from engaging in street violence.

50 Hamza Mustafa, 'Mas'ul 'Iraqi ya'zu istighlal <Da'ish> li-milaff Diyala ila al-siyasat al-khati'ah li-al-tayyarat al-siyasiyah' [Iraqi official attributes the exploitation of ISIS for the Diyala file to the erroneous policies of the political currents], al-Sharq al-Awsat, 14 July 2016, https://aawsat.com/home/article/689266; 'ISIS militants execute mukhtars,

militiamen in new video', Rudaw, 14 April 2019, http://www.rudaw.net/english/middleeast/iraq/140420191.

51 In interviews, local officials in multiple locations in Diyala said that the AAH and the Badr Organisation have clashed at times over localised control, 2016.

52 Interviews with Anbar residents, 2016.

53 Interview with Iraqi army officer based in Nineva, 2018.

54 'Muhandis min al-Basrah: narfud al-mathahir al-musallahah dakhil al-mudun' [Muhandis from Basra: we reject armed groups inside the cities], Muhandis Radio al-Mirbad, 24 January 2018, http://www.almirbad.com/news/view.aspx?cdate=24012018&id=ccb9d0e1-4ace-4d69-b8c6-980450a91f0f.

55 'Intishar Saraya al-Khorasani fi shawari' Baghdad li-hifth al-amn' [Deployment of Saraya Khorasani in the streets of Baghdad to preserve security], May 2016, 7:15–10:30, https://www.youtube.com/watch?v=hkA_QSjLiZ8.

56 The presence of these depots is known in part because of several accidents where munitions exploded, including in Baghdad and Karbala. See Rudaw Arabic TV, 6 August 2018, https://www.youtube.com/watch?v=3-miSFfv9n8; 'Baghdad mosque explosion kills 18 people', National, 7 June 2018, https://www.thenational.ae/world/mena/baghdad-mosque-explosion-kills-18-people-1.737712#2.

57 Basra residents constitute 29% of killed PMU fighters whose province of origin is known. See Ali Alfoneh, 'Forces Preparing for Post-Islamic State Iraq', Middle East Institute, 3 August 2017, https://www.mei.edu/publications/iran-backed-popular-mobilization-forces-preparing-post-islamic-state-iraq.

58 Interviews with provincial-level PMU officials, 2018.

59 Interviews with Iraqi Security Forces, tribal PMU and local administrators in Qaim and Rutba districts, 2018.

60 Ibid.

61 Ibid. Sources suggested most traffic occurs at night. Multiple sources suggested there is traffic across the border overseen by militias.

62 Interviews with Iraqi Security Forces officers, 2018.

63 'Iran expands regional empire ahead of Nuclear Deal', Reuters, 23 March 2015, https://www.reuters.com/article/us-mideast-iran-region-insight/iran-expands-regional-empire-ahead-of-nuclear-deal-idUSKBN0MJ1G520150323; Hannah Porter, 'September 5–11: Increased fighting before Eid, senators push ahead with joint resolution', Yemen Peace Project, 12 September 2016, https://www.yemenpeaceproject.org/blog-x/tag/joint+resolution.

64 Interview with Western government official.

65 Interview with former Western government official, 2018.

66 Aida Arosoaie, 'Hadi Al-Amiri's Grip on Iraq', Counter Terrorist Trends and Analyses, vol. 7, no. 10, November 2015, pp. 19–24, https://www.jstor.org/stable/pdf/26351397.pdf?refreqid=excelsior%3A5805157b7fedae8167004392223cc72c.

67 'Badr Organization of Reconstruction and Development', Mapping Militant Organizations, Stanford University, http://web.stanford.edu/group/mappingmilitants/cgi-bin/groups/view/435.

68 'Mostanad-e selfi ba Abu Mahdi (farmandeh-ye Hashd al-Sha'abi 'Eragh' [Biographical documentary of Abu Mahdi (leader of Iraq's PMU)], 2017, 11:13–11:55, https://www.youtube.com/watch?v=HOrEPnKdEZU.

69 Michael Knights, 'The Evolution of Iran's Special Groups in Iraq', CTC Sentinel, November 2010, https://www.washington-institute.org/uploads/Documents/opeds/4d06325a6031b.pdf.

70 'U.S. says arms link Iranians to Iraqi Shiites', New York Times, 12 February 2007, https://www.nytimes.com/2007/02/12/world/middleeast/12weapons.html.

71 'Against U.S. wishes, Iraq releases man accused of killing American soldiers', New York Times, 16 November 2012, https://www.nytimes.com/2012/11/17/world/middleeast/iraq-said-to-release-hezbollah-operative.html.

72 Matthew Levitt, Hezbollah: The Global Footprint of Lebanon's Party of God (Washington DC: Georgetown University Press, 2015), p. 300.

73 'Declassified U.S. Tactical Interrogation Report of Qais al-Khazali', TIR-16, 29 March 2007, https://www.aei.org/wp-content/uploads/2018/08/TIR-16.pdf.

74 'Declassified U.S. Tactical Interrogation Report of Qais al-Khazali', TIR-15, 28 March 2007, p. 121, https://www.aei.org/wp-content/uploads/2018/08/TIR-15.pdf.

75 Ibid.

76 'Declassified U.S. Tactical Interrogation Report of Qais al-Khazali', TIR 200243-008, 30 June 2007, pp. 21–23, https://www.aei.org/wp-content/uploads/2018/08/Enclosure-TAB-A-Documents-for-Release-1-16.pdf.

77 'Declassified U.S. Tactical Interrogation Report of Qais al-Khazali', TIR 200243-015, 1 July 2007, p. 41, https://www.aei.org/wp-content/uploads/2018/08/Enclosure-TAB-A-Documents-for-Release-1-16.pdf.

78 Interview with a PMU militia member, 2018.

79 Loveday Morris, 'Shiite militias in Iraq begin to remobilize', Washington Post, 9 February 2014, https://www.washingtonpost.com/world/middle_east/shiite-militias-in-iraq-begin-to-remobilize/2014/02/09/183816c6-8f59-11e3-878e-d76656564a01_story.html?utm_term=.52bdba577066.

80 'Laqa' khas ma'a al-qa'id al-hajj Abu Mahdi Muhandis – al-Hashd al-Sha'abi' [Exclusive interview with the PMU leader Abu Mahdi Muhandis], Muhandis, 12 June 2017, 2:10–4:42, https://www.youtube.com/watch?v=v-RhTjQEIDQ.

81 Interviews with multiple PMU fighters, 2018.

82 Interview with PMU fighter, 2018.

83 'Ma'rikat al-Saqlawiyyah: al-liwa' al-thalith Badr al-janah al-'askari wa al-shortah al-ittihadiyyah' [The Battle of Saqlawiyah: the third battalion of Badr's military wing

and the Federal Police], Al-Walaa TV, 1 June 2016, https://www.youtube.com/watch?v=c2NFQar-r-c; 'Abtal Keta'ib Sayyid al-Shuhada' fi madinat Al-Bukamal' [The heroes of Kataib Sayyid al-Shuhada in the city of Al-Bukamal], Al-Mawqif TV, December 2017, https://www.youtube.com/watch?v=P3ABf5xur3c.

84 Interview with PMU fighters, 2018.

85 Interviews with political official from PMU-linked party, 2018.

86 'Shahidu dawr katibat al-dubabat fi al-Hashd al-Sha'abi munthu bidayat al-fatwa ila tahqiq al-nasr' [Witness the role of the PMU's tank battalion in achieving victory since the beginning of the fatwa], 3 January 2018, 0:35–0:50 and 1:26–1:44, https://www.youtube.com/watch?v=EPHt7forhZ8.

87 'Basamat mudiriyyat al-midfa'iyyah al-tabi'ah li-al-Hashd al-Sha'abi li-sina'at al-nasr' [Traces of the PMU's artillery directorate in securing victory], 27 March 2018, 45:45 and 52:25–52:42, https://www.youtube.com/watch?v=fYyOLZk2WxQ.

88 Ibid., 54:50.

89 'Ikhtabarat maydaniyyah li-aslihat firqat al-'Abbas al-qital-iyyah wa quwwatiha' [Field testing of the Abbas Combat Division's weapons and forces], August 2017, https://www.youtube.com/watch?v=oTormoiHR00; 'Liwa' al-Tada-khkhul al-Sari' Yujri Isti'aradan 'Askariyan fi Samarra' al-Muqaddasah' [The brigade of swift intervention carries out a military review in the holy city of Samarra], Saraya al-Salam, May 2017, http://www.sarayasalam.net/2017/05/blog-post_81.html.

90 'Kalimat ra'is al-wuzara' Dr. Haydar al-'Abadi khilal istiqbalih jam'an min qadat al-Hashd al-Sha'abi' [Prime Minister Haidar al-Abadi's speech in a gathering of the PMU leadership], 25 March 2017, 37:38, 38:25, https://www.youtube.com/watch?v=7sk1e_W-u08.

91 'Iftitah Madrasat Muqatilat al-Duru' fi Hay'at al-Hashd al-Sha'abi' [Opening of an anti-armour fighting school among the PMU], al-Masalah, 18 July 2017, http://almasalah.com/ar/NewsDetails.aspx?NewsID=108834.

92 Ibid.

93 Interview with former Western intelligence official, 2018.

94 Interview with official from PMU-linked party serving in Iraqi police force, 2018.

95 Interviews with sources familiar with PMU operations in Diyala governorate, 2018.

96 Interview with former PMU militia member, 2018.

97 Interview with political official from PMU-linked party, 2018.

98 Interviews with multiple PMU members who went through training in the post-2014 period, 2018.

99 'Laqa' khas ma'a al-qa'id al-hajj Abu Mahdi Muhandis – al-Hashd al-Sha'abi' [Exclusive interview with the PMU leader Abu Mahdi Muhandis], June 2017, 47:15–48:15, http://www.youtube.com/watch?v=v-RhTjQEIDQ.

100 Members of multiple different PMU militias said in interviews that some members of their groups were selected for specialised training, implemented in Iran, 2018.

101 Levitt, Hezbollah: The Global Footprint of Lebanon's Party of God, pp. 299–300.

102 'Al-Tulab al-Turkman al-shi'ah yaltahiqun bi-ma'skarat al-Hashd al-Sha'abi al-Turkmani al-khasah li-al-tadrib 'ala al-silah' [Shia Turkmen Students join PMU army camps specifically for weapons training], June 2015, https://www.youtube.com/watch?v=j-etQ6YRVPk.

103 'Ra'is Majlis al-Wuzara' al-Qa'id al-'Amm li-l-Quwwat al-Musallahah al-Daktur Haydar al-'Abadi Yasdur Dhawabit Takyif 'Awda' Muqatili al-Hashd al-Sha'abi' [Prime Minister, Commander-in-Chief of the Armed Forces Dr Haider Al-Abadi issues regulations for adapting the Popular Mobilisation Units], Iraqi Prime Minister's Office, 8 March 2018, http://www.pmo.iq/press2018/8-3-201803.htm.

104 Interviews with officials based in southern Iraq, 2018.

105 Interviews with local officials based in Basra, 2018.

106 'Laqa' khas ma'a al-qa'id al-hajj Abu Mahdi Muhandis – al-Hashd al-Sha'abi', 46:30–46:52.

107 'Al-Khaz'ali yu'lin itlaq hamlatin li-izalat mathahir 'askarat al-Mujtama' wa-yu'akkid hasr al-silah bi-al-ajhizah al-amniyah' [Khazali announces the launch of a campaign to remove the society's militarised dimensions and confirms the inventorying of weapons with the security services], al-Sumaria TV, 13 December 2017, https://www.alsumaria.tv/news/224081.

108 Interview with PMU militia official, 2018; Abbas Combat Division chief Maytham al-Zaydi, al-Sumaria TV, July 2016, https://www.youtube.com/watch?v=A-ws7PIi5Ng.

109 Loveday Morris, 'Iraq's victory over militants in Sunni town underlines challenges government faces', Washington Post, 29 October 2014, https://www.washingtonpost.com/world/middle_east/iraqs-victory-over-militants-in-sunni-town-underlines-challenges-government-faces/2014/10/29/c53c4886-6f61-4567-904a-918060f6f2f5_story.html?utm_term=.ffdb8857682f.

110 Qassim Abdul-Zahra, 'Iran-backed militias accused of reign of fear in Iraqi Basra', Associated Press, 23 September 2018, https://www.apnews.com/7a043d89870c4c2bac69f25c5b399060.

111 Iraqi 2018 Federal Budget, 2 April 2018, https://moj.gov.iq/upload/pdf/4485.pdf; Ali Al-Mawlawi, 'Iraq's 2018 Federal Budget: Key features and trends', Al-Bayan Center, 17 March 2018, http://www.bayancenter.org/en/2018/03/1461.

112 According to Ministry of Finance data, Iraq spent US$6.5 billion on Ministry of Defence and Ministry of Interior forces in Q1 and Q2 2018.

113 For example, interviews conducted in 2018 suggest a Kataib Sayyid al-Shuhada official is a senior PMU official in east Mosul, while Badr Organisation-linked officials hold senior

114 PMU positions in a number of local sectors from Kirkuk to the Iranian border in northern Iraq.

114 Al-Mawlawi, 'Iraq's 2018 Federal Budget: Key features and trends'.

115 Sources in northern Salahaddin and Diyala say that this includes all Asaib Ahl al-Haq, Badr Organisation and Saraya al-Khorasani personnel recruited in the northern parts of those provinces in 2015 and 2016, with AAH and the Badr Organisation allegedly continuing in 2017.

116 Fanar Haddad, 'Understanding Iraq's Hashd al-Sha'bi', Century Foundation, 5 March 2018, https://tcf.org/content/report/understanding-iraqs-hashd-al-shabi/?agreed=1.

117 Interviews with tribal PMU officers based in Nineva, 2018–19.

118 Interview with militia fighter, 2018. Equipment levels reportedly improved as of 2016, when the PMU commission in Baghdad began distributing weapons. The distribution system was formalised, including paperwork.

119 The Ministry of Oil broadcasts the support provided by these groups. See, for example, 'Under the patronage of the Minister of Oil the Ministry of Oil honours 235 families of martyrs of the Popular Mobilisation Units in Muthanna province', 27 July 2017, https://oil.gov.iq/index.php?name=News&file=article&sid=1614; 'Under the patronage of the Minister of Oil the Ministry of Oil honours 338 families of martyrs of the Popular Mobilisation Units in Karbala', 27 May 2018, https://oil.gov.iq/index.php?name=News&file=article&sid=1965.

120 Interviews with officials in Nineva province.

121 'Muhkamah 'Iraqiyyah tawaqqafa amr al-'Abadi bi-iqalat al-Fayadh' [An Iraqi court blocks Abadi's decision to dismiss Fayadh], al-Hurra, 15 October 2018, https://www.alhurra.com/a/464474.html.

122 In interviews, multiple fighters from different PMU militias talked about receiving support, including rations, from 'donors', 2018.

123 For example, in interviews in 2016 and 2017, former PMU fighters suggested that civilian volunteers saying they were acting on guidance from Ayatollah Sistani could be found embedded with PMU units, providing catering at bases in Nineva and Mosul.

124 Interview with source familiar with the inner workings of Saraya al-Salam, 2018.

125 Order number 1229, issued to PMU regional commands by Abu Mahdi al-Muhandis, 18 August 2018.

126 'How the U.S. government should think about Iraq's Popular Mobilization forces', Washington Institute for Near East Policy, 9 May 2019, https://www.washingtoninstitute.org/fikraforum/view/how-the-u.s.-government-should-think-about-iraqs-popular-mobilization-force.

127 Multiple sources from Salahaddin governorate described the transportation of crude oil from a Hamrin Mountains area field from 2016, just after parts of the field were retaken from ISIS, 2016.

128 Sources in Salahaddin describe crude-oil tanker trucks from the Hamrin Mountains area selling their cargoes to local traders in disputed territories in northern Iraq, 2016.

129 Interviews with Iraqi Security Forces officials based in Nineva governorate during that time frame.

130 Interview with local source based in Salahaddin governorate, 2018.

131 Interview with Iraqi Security Forces official previously based south of Mosul, 2018.

132 Mark A. DeWeaver, 'Decentralized Rent Seeking in Iraq's Post-ISIS Economy: A Warning from the Concrete Block Industry', IRIS Iraq Report, 23 August 2017, p. 8, https://auis.edu.krd/iris/sites/default/files/IRIS%20Iraq%20Report_Decentralized%20Rent-Seeking%20post-ISIS%20Iraq_DeWeaver.pdf.

133 Nabih Bulos, 'Iraqi forces took Baiji from the Islamic State, but the former boom town may be doomed', *Los Angeles Times*, 11 June 2016, https://www.latimes.com/world/middleeast/la-fg-iraq-baiji-20160611-snap-story.html.

134 'Once fixable, Baiji refinery plundered beyond repair', *Iraq Oil Report*, 28 January 2016, https://www.iraqoilreport.com/news/fixable-baiji-refinery-plundered-beyond-repair-17812.

135 Order number 1392, issued to all PMU 'formations, commanders and departments' by Abu Mahdi al-Muhandis, 2 August 2018.

136 Interview with a former PMU administrative official, 2018.

137 'Declassified U.S. Tactical Interrogation Report of Qais al-Khazali', TIR-7, 24 March 2007, p. 75, https://www.aei.org/wp-content/uploads/2018/08/TIR-7.pdf.

138 For example, senior Badr Organisation official Qassim Araji is the minister of interior, which receives the largest spending allocation of any Iraqi ministry, and Badr Organisation commander Hadi al-Ameri previously served as minister of transportation, a post that entails control of Iraq's revenue-generating land, sea and air points of entry.

139 Interviews with Iraqi officials.

140 *Ibid*.

141 In interviews, officials say that when fighting broke out between Kurdish and Turkmen communities over checkpoints levying steep tariffs on Kurdish-manufactured products, Eghbali intervened to secure a truce, 2015–16.

142 Interviews with Kurdish officials.

143 Interviews with Tuz officials.

144 *Ibid*.

145 'Absent government, fragile truce holds in Tuz Khurmatu', *Iraq Oil Report*, 18 November 2015, https://www.iraqoilreport.com/news/absent-government-fragile-truce-holds-in-tuz-khurmatu-17090.

146 'IS targets Tuz again, exposing deep-rooted divisions', *Iraq Oil Report*, 20 June 2016, https://www.iraqoilreport.com/news/targets-tuz-exposing-deep-rooted-divisions-19198.

147 Interviews with Tuz officials.

148 Interviews with former PMU fighters, 2018.

149 *Ibid.*

150 'Watch the role of the tanks brigade of the PMU from the issuance of the fatwa to the realisation of the victory', 2018, 0:35, 1:00–1:50, 1:27–1:47, https://www.youtube.com/watch?v=EPHt7forhZ8.

151 Interview with local security official familiar with the incident, 2017.

152 'Declassified U.S. Tactical Interrogation Report of Qais al-Khazali', TIR-1, 21 March 2007, p. 19, https://www.aei.org/wp-content/uploads/2018/08/TIR-1.pdf; TIR-4, 23 March 2007, p. 63, https://www.aei.org/wp-content/uploads/2018/08/TIR-4.pdf; TIR-9, 25 March 2007, p. 85, https://www.aei.org/wp-content/uploads/2018/08/TIR-9.pdf.

153 'Declassified U.S. Tactical Interrogation Report of Qais al-Khazali', TIR.20043-015, 11 June 2007, p. 41, https://www.aei.org/wp-content/uploads/2018/08/Enclosure-TAB-A-Documents-for-Release-1-16.pdf.

154 'Declassified U.S. Tactical Interrogation Report of Qais al-Khazali', TIR-17, 29 March 2007, pp. 132–33, https://www.aei.org/wp-content/uploads/2018/08/TIR-17.pdf.

155 TIR Report no. 200243-008, 18 June 2007, p. 21, https://www.aei.org/wp-content/uploads/2018/08/Enclosure-TAB-A-Documents-for-Release-1-16.pdf.

156 'Declassified U.S. Tactical Interrogation Report of Qais al-Khazali', TIR-54, 18 April 2007, p. 351, https://www.aei.org/wp-content/uploads/2018/08/TIR-54.pdf.

157 'Declassified U.S. Tactical Interrogation Report of Qais al-Khazali', TIR-76, 4 May 2007, p. 213, https://www.aei.org/wp-content/uploads/2018/08/r_TIR-N1228A-67.pdf.

158 'Declassified U.S. Tactical Interrogation Report of Qais al-Khazali', TIR-46, 14 April 2007, p. 294, https://www.aei.org/wp-content/uploads/2018/08/TIR-46.pdf.

159 'Declassified U.S. Tactical Interrogation Report of Qais al-Khazali', TIR-31, 7 April 2007, p. 208, https://www.aei.org/wp-content/uploads/2018/08/TIR-31.pdf.

160 'Declassified U.S. Tactical Interrogation Report of Qais al-Khazali', TIR-49, 16 April 2007, p. 317, https://www.aei.org/wp-content/uploads/2018/08/r_TIR-N1228A-49.pdf.

161 'Declassified U.S. Tactical Interrogation Report of Qais al-Khazali', TIR-10(2), 26 March 2007, p. 98, https://www.aei.org/wp-content/uploads/2018/08/TIR-11.pdf.

162 'Declassified U.S. Tactical Interrogation Report of Qais al-Khazali', TIR-16, 29 March 2007, p. 127, https://www.aei.org/wp-content/uploads/2018/08/TIR-16.pdf.

163 *Ibid.*; 'Declassified U.S. Tactical Interrogation Report of Qais al-Khazali', TIR-10(2), 26 March 2007, p. 91, https://www.aei.org/wp-content/uploads/2018/08/TIR-11.pdf.

164 'Declassified U.S. Tactical Interrogation Report of Qais al-Khazali', TIR-47, 15 April 2007, p. 302, https://www.aei.org/wp-content/uploads/2018/08/r_TIR-N1228A-47.pdf.

165 'Declassified U.S. Tactical Interrogation Report of Qais al-Khazali', TIR-45, 14 April 2007, pp. 3–6, https://www.aei.org/wp-content/uploads/2018/08/TIR-45.pdf.

166 *Ibid.*; 'Declassified U.S. Tactical Interrogation Report of Qais al-Khazali', TIR-47, 15 April 2007, p. 300, https://www.aei.org/wp-content/uploads/2018/08/r_TIR-N1228A-47.pdf.

167 *Ibid.*

168 *Ibid.*

169 'Declassified U.S. Tactical Interrogation Report of Qais al-Khazali', TIR 200243-22, 20 July 2007, p. 56, https://www.aei.org/wp-content/uploads/2018/08/Enclosure-TAB-A-Documents-for-Release-18-32.pdf'; TIR 200243-023, 24 July 2007, p. 60.

170 'Declassified U.S. Tactical Interrogation Report of Qais al-Khazali', TIR-19, 30 March 2007, p. 143, https://www.aei.org/wp-content/uploads/2018/08/TIR-19.pdf.

171 'Declassified U.S. Tactical Interrogation Report of Qais al-Khazali', TIR 200243-016, 4 July 2007, p. 43, https://www.aei.org/wp-content/uploads/2018/08/Enclosure-TAB-A-Documents-for-Release-1-16.pdf.

172 'Declassified U.S. Tactical Interrogation Report of Qais al-Khazali', TIR 200243-023, p. 60.

173 'Declassified U.S. Tactical Interrogation Report of Qais al-Khazali', TIR-10(1), 26 March 2007, p. 91, https://www.aei.org/wp-content/uploads/2018/08/TIR-10.pdf.

174 *Ibid.*; 'Declassified U.S. Tactical Interrogation Report of Qais al-Khazali', TIR-47, p. 301, https://www.aei.org/wp-content/uploads/2018/08/r_TIR-N1228A-47.pdf.

175 TIR-10(1), 14 November 2007, p. 91, 'Declassified U.S. Tactical Interrogation Report of Qais al-Khazali', TIR 20043-0036, p. 92, https://www.aei.org/wp-content/uploads/2018/08/Enclosure-TAB-A-Documents-for-Release-33-48.pdf.

176 'Declassified U.S. Tactical Interrogation Report of Qais al-Khazali', TIR 200243-033, 20 October 2007, p. 87, https://www.aei.org/wp-content/uploads/2018/08/Enclosure-TAB-A-Documents-for-Release-33-48.pdf.

177 'Declassified U.S. Tactical Interrogation Report of Qais al-Khazali', TIR-31, 7 April 2007, p. 207, https://www.aei.org/wp-content/uploads/2018/08/TIR-31.pdf.

178 'Declassified U.S. Tactical Interrogation Report of Qais al-Khazali', TIR-43, 13 April 2007, p. 275, https://www.aei.org/wp-content/uploads/2018/08/TIR-43.pdf.

179 September 2018 indirect-fire attacks near the US embassy in Baghdad and the US consulate in Basra were most likely the work of Iran-aligned militia groups.

180 'Revolutionary Guard general takes over as new Iranian ambassador in Iraq', Reuters, 19 April 2017, https://af.reuters.com/article/worldNews/idAFKBN17L2EC.

181 Interview with PUK official, 2018.

182 Interview with several officials from parties within Iran-aligned PMU militias, 2018.

183 *Ibid.*

184 'Dawr al-qunsuliyyah al-Amrikiyyah fi al-Basrah fi tahrik al-shari' al-'Iraqi' [The US consulate in Basra's role in fomenting the Iraqi street protests], Mehr News, 13 September 2018, https://ar.mehrnews.com/news/1887618.

185 Interviews with officials in Basra, Dhi Qar and Maysan provinces, 2019.

186 *Ibid.*

187 *Ibid.*

188 Qassim Abdul-Zahra, 'Iran-backed militias accused of reign of fear in Iraqi Basra', Associated Press, 23 September 2018, https://www.apnews.com/7a043d89870c4c2bac69f25c5b399060. In May 2017, AAH's Qais al-Khazali denied that AAH had a policy of kidnapping domestic critics, but also confirmed that it had the capacity to do so and hinted that it may kidnap domestic opponents in certain exceptional cases, https://www.youtube.com/watch?v=tFMSQfpdQ4A.

189 'Al-nass al-kamil li-kilmah simahah hojjat al-islam wa al-muslimin al-qa'id al-sayyid Muqtada al-Sadr (a'azzahu Allah) bi-munasabat i'alan yawm al-nasr al-kabir wa allati alqaha bi-tarikh 11 Kanun al-Awwal 2017' [The Full text of His Eminence Hojjat ol-Eslam Sayyid Muqtada al-Sadr's Speech on the occasion of the declaring the Day of Great Victory, 11 December 2017], Muqtada al-Sadr website, 11 December 2017, http://jawabna.com/index.php/permalink/10325.html.

CHAPTER FIVE

YEMEN

- Iran's interests in Yemen are to threaten and bog down at a limited cost its rival Saudi Arabia but also to establish a forward presence in the strategic area of Bab al-Mandeb
- The Houthis have welcomed Iranian assistance and maintain a privileged relationship with Hizbullah
- Iran's contribution to the Houthis' battlefield performance has been limited, but its provision of advanced weaponry is indicative of more ambitious goals

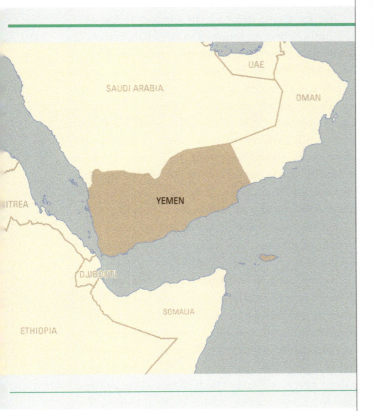

Iran's relationship with the Houthis (otherwise known as Ansarullah, or 'Helpers of God') has passed through three distinct phases – attraction, assistance and alliance – over the course of the past decade. Prior to that, there were three decades of sporadic visits and communications. In 1979, Badr al-Din al-Houthi, the founder of the movement, arrived in Iran in search of refuge. Several more visits followed, including by his son Hussein in 1994, during Yemen's civil war. Those visits and the relationships that grew out of them paved the way for the current relationship with Tehran.

Following the upheaval of the Arab Spring in 2011, Tehran began providing money, weapons, support and training to the group. After the Houthi takeover of the Yemeni capital Sanaa in 2014 and the subsequent intervention by Saudi Arabia, Iran started supplying heavy weapons and delivering significant economic support. It has become committed to the Houthis' survival and their ability to project power throughout the region – particularly into Saudi Arabia.

At the same time, the Houthis have a parallel relationship with Lebanese Hizbullah. The Houthi satellite channel, al-Masirah, is headquartered in Beirut; Houthi leaders increasingly travel to Lebanon, where reports suggest they have been gifted a

Houthis at a checkpoint in Saada, February 2010

number of residences; and there have been, and likely continue to be, Hizbullah trainers on the ground in Yemen. Hizbullah does not manage the relationship between Iran and the Houthis.

Tehran does not exercise command and control over the Houthis, but Iranian advice, aid and assistance buys influence. The Houthi goals of holding onto power in Yemen and projecting military power into the Red Sea are closely aligned with the broader Iranian goal of weakening Riyadh. Iran's increasing provision of military capabilities – primarily ballistic missiles and uninhabited aerial vehicle (UAV) technology – enables the Houthis to threaten Saudi Arabia, and Iranian economic aid sustains the organisation.

A history of the Houthi movement

In 1962, the Shia Zaydi imamate, which had largely held sway over much of northern Yemen for more than a millennium, was overthrown in a palace coup, which degenerated into a brutal eight-year civil war. The Yemen Arab Republic, in today's northern Yemen, emerged from this struggle.[1] The northern governorate of Saada was one of the last regions to submit to republican rule, in 1970. The last imamic family – the Hamid al-Dins – was sent into exile. Both Saada and Yemen's *sayyid*s – the descendants of the Prophet Muhammad[2] – suffered under republican rule.

Successive governments in Sanaa largely ignored Saada. Development money was funnelled to other regions; roads went unpaved; hospitals were left unbuilt and so too promised electrical grids. Zaydi *sayyid*s, who for centuries had been at the top of the country's social pyramid, were now discriminated against and often harassed by the state.

In the late 1970s and early 1980s, the threat to the *sayyids* became more acute as Saudi Arabia began to send money and Wahhabi missionaries across the border into Saada. Zaydi revivalists, particularly those who saw themselves as defenders of the faith, felt on the verge of cultural extinction.[3] Among the initial responses was the creation of a group called Al-Shabab al-Mumin, or the Believing Youth. This group, which was founded by Muhammad Izzan and Muhammad Badr al-Din al-Houthi,[4] would later form the nucleus of the Houthi movement.

Throughout the 1990s, then-president Ali Abdullah Saleh used Zaydi revivalists as a counterweight against other domestic rivals. For instance, in the wake of the 1994 civil war, in which Sunni Islamists had played a significant role, Saleh gave key positions, including minister of education, to traditionalist Zaydis. Saleh also provided money to Hussein Badr al-Din al-Houthi – a former member of parliament from the Islamist Zaydi Hizb al-Haqq party – through what was known locally as al-'itimad (support) – a way of bestowing presidential patronage on key figures.

But by 2000 Saleh had cut support to Hussein al-Houthi, who then returned to Yemen from Iran. In September, Hussein saw footage from Gaza of a boy being killed in the crossfire of a skirmish between Israeli and Palestinian forces. A Houthi reportedly exclaimed 'Death to America, Death to Israel, a Curse upon the Jews, Victory for Islam',[5] a slogan that would become the exhortation of the Houthi movement. Throughout 2002 and 2003, Hussein al-Houthi made speeches and gave sermons that increasingly, if implicitly, criticised Saleh's government. After the 9/11 attacks in the United States, the slogan was used to criticise US foreign policy and, from 2002, it served as a coded criticism of president Saleh's rule.

In June 2004, Saleh instructed the local governor in Saada to arrest Hussein, which sparked the first of what would become the six Saada wars of 2004–10. Hussein al-Houthi was killed – some reports claim he was summarily executed – in September 2004, ending the first war. Leadership of the Houthi movement passed first to his father Badr al-Din al-Houthi and then to his half-brother, Abdul Malik al-Houthi. The sixth war began in November 2009 and, for the first time, drew in the Saudi armed forces. The war ended inconclusively in early 2010, but the combination of growing Houthi military strength and direct Saudi involvement seems to have led to a deepening of ties between the Houthis and Tehran.

The gradual intensification of the relationship between Iran and the Houthis

The Houthis began as a local movement with local grievances. That did not, however, prevent Saleh from trying to link them to both Iran and Lebanese Hizbullah as soon as the fighting in Saada began in June 2004, essentially internationalising a domestic dispute. The government's allegations included that Hussein al-Houthi had declared himself imam and had raised the flag of Hizbullah.[6] Following the 9/11 attacks, Saleh had learned the benefits of repackaging local rivals as international threats. He did so with al-Qaeda, tying Yemen's domestic conflict into a broader war against terrorism, and was attempting to do the same with the Houthis.

Two years earlier, in January 2002, then US president George W. Bush had declared Iran part of an 'axis of evil', and Saleh knew that Saudi Arabia, his neighbour to the north, was particularly sensitive to Iranian actions in the Arabian Peninsula. However, despite Saleh's efforts, neither Saudi Arabia nor the US believed him when it came to claims of Iranian support for the Houthis.

In 2009, the US ambassador to Yemen wrote a cable to Washington saying that 'Iranian influence in Yemen has thus far been limited to informal religious ties between Yemeni and Iranian scholars and negligible Iranian investment in the energy and development sectors'.[7] In late 2009, the US embassy in Sanaa dispatched another cable, in which it quoted a member of Saudi Arabia's Special Office for Yemen Affairs saying: 'We know Saleh is lying about Iran.'[8]

Despite Saleh's likely exaggerated claims of Iranian influence on the Houthis, there was a history of contact and visits dating back to 1979.

Early ties: 1979–2009

In 1979, the same year as the Islamic Revolution in Iran, Badr al-Din al-Houthi wrote a small tract rebutting a fatwa from the Saudi cleric Abdul al-Aziz bin Baz 'prohibiting prayer behind a Zaydi imam'.[9] According to a biographical sketch, which the Houthis circulated in 2007 and 2008, Badr al-Din was targeted for assassination that same year.[10] Fearing that the assassins would return, he fled to Jordan before eventually making his way to Iran.[11]

In Iran, Badr al-Din reportedly remained true to his Zaydi heritage, rejecting attempts to convert him to Twelver Shi'ism.[12] Following his return to Yemen in the 1980s, Badr al-Din made additional trips to Iran, including in the early 1990s as Yemen appeared to be heading for a north–south civil war. Hussein al-Houthi, his eldest son from his first marriage, was at the time a member of parliament and also left the country to visit Iran. By the time the Saada wars began, the Houthis' relationship with Iran seemed to amount to several visits by Houthi leaders and some religious discussions. Indeed, even as late as 2008, when the Yemeni government claimed that the Houthis were an Iranian proxy group,[13] Sanaa continued to maintain cordial if modest relations

> **"IT WAS ONLY AFTER THE LAUNCH OF *OPERATION DECISIVE* STORM THAT IRAN SHIFTED FROM PROVIDING ASSISTANCE TO THE HOUTHIS TO FORMING SOMETHING CLOSER TO AN ALLIANCE WITH THEM"**

with Iran. In April 2008, Manouchehr Mottaki, Iran's then foreign minister, visited Yemen and Abu Bakr al-Qirbi, his Yemeni counterpart, travelled to Tehran the following month to discuss economic ties.[14] On 23 June, Iranian warships were allowed to refuel and resupply in Aden.[15]

Attraction: 2009–11

When the Saada wars commenced in 2004, Iran viewed the Houthi uprising as a Yemeni domestic affair. Its understanding of, and interest in, the Houthis changed in late 2009 when Saudi Arabia became directly involved in the conflict. However, while rhetorically supporting the Houthi movement, Iran remained primarily preoccupied with the intensification of its rivalry with Saudi Arabia at a time of tensions over Tehran's nuclear programme and regional role.

On 3 November 2009, amid the sixth war, a contingent of Houthi fighters crossed the Saudi border to take control of Mount al-Dukhan, which they said Yemeni soldiers were using to outflank them – violating Saudi sovereignty. In the process, the Houthi fighters came into contact with a Saudi border patrol, and in the ensuing battle they killed a Saudi soldier (another later died of his wounds) and took one captive.[16] Saudi Arabia's armed forces became increasingly involved in the fighting in the following weeks, often performing poorly. The Houthis uploaded videos of their barefoot fighters overrunning Saudi military camps or driving looted Saudi vehicles.

Figure 5.1: **Houthis: major events, 2004–2019**

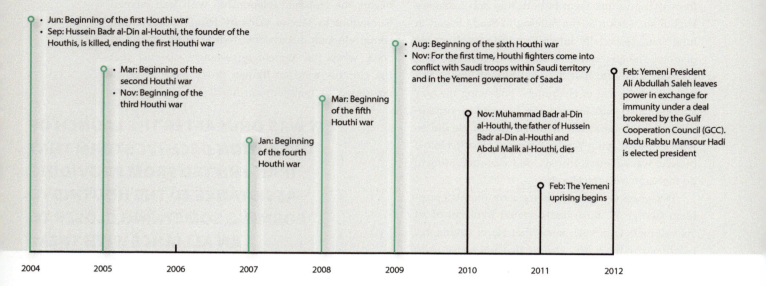

Assistance: 2011–14

Following the Arab Spring protests in 2011, Iran began providing military and financial assistance to the Houthis. Much of this came in the form of weapons sent into the country and cash distributed to Yemenis visiting Iran.

The protests changed calculations throughout the region. Saudi Arabia led a military intervention in Bahrain, while in Syria, Bashar al-Assad fought to hold onto power. Both developments were of concern to Tehran. US officials, who had previously dismissed allegations of Iranian assistance to the Houthis, began to make different assessments in 2011. Iran reached out to anti-Saleh activists, including the Houthis.[18]

In September 2011, and again in January 2012, Iran paid for a number of Yemeni activists to visit Iran.[19] The purpose of these visits, according to one of the attendees, was to offer the protesters financial help, training and encouragement.[20] In early 2012, the Yemeni government intercepted shipments of explosively formed penetrators (EFPs) that were transported to Aden on Egyptian- and Turkish-flagged ships.[21] US officials also claimed that smugglers backed by Iran's Islamic Revolutionary Guard Corps (IRGC) Quds Force were shipping small arms and rocket-propelled grenades to the Houthis to replace some of their older weapons.[22]

In January 2013, Yemeni authorities, supported by the US, seized a 130-foot Iranian dhow, *Jihan 1*, off the coast of Yemen.[23] The ship was carrying a significant quantity of arms, including *Katyusha* rockets, surface-to-air missiles, Iranian-made night-vision goggles, and RDX and C-4 explosives.[24] According to a Yemeni official, the weapons and ammunition were 'well packed in small containers, all of which were concealed inside several larger compartments filled with diesel fuel'.[25]

A United Nations monitoring team suggested that the ship may have been destined for Somalia.[26] However, the Houthis are known to use C-4 explosives to target the houses of their political opponents – a common tactic of local control – and other smuggling routes identified later suggested that weapons were sometimes unloaded in Somalia before being distributed onto smaller boats and sent to Yemen.

In 2014, two years after Saleh's resignation, political order in Yemen completely unravelled. The situation in Sanaa was particularly tense, as four different factions – former president Saleh, current president Abdu Rabbu Mansour Hadi, General Ali

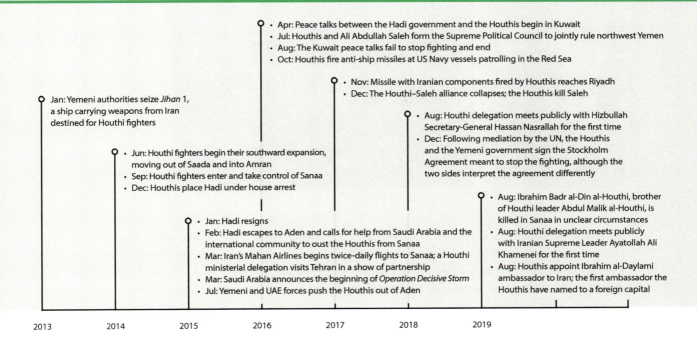

Mohsen al-Ahmar and the Ahmar tribal family – faced one another. The armed forces split, with units following the political preference of their commander. Military salaries were delivered to commanders, who then distributed them to their personnel; this did little to encourage loyalty to the central state. While these power centres were struggling for position in Sanaa, the Houthis consolidated their control over the governorate of Saada. According to an Iranian official, the Houthis also sent roughly 100 individuals to Iran to train at an IRGC base outside Qom.[27] Travelling to Iran would have also enabled the direct transfer of money, which could then be carried back to Yemen.

In July 2014, the Houthis moved out of Saada, overrunning a military base in the neighbouring governorate of Amran.[28] This was the beginning of a *coup d'état* that culminated on 21 September when the Houthis entered Sanaa. Saleh ordered troops loyal to him to stand down, and the Houthis entered the capital nearly unopposed. They quickly took control of Ahmar's military base, forcing him to take refuge in the Saudi embassy.[29] The Houthis also forced the resignation of Yemen's prime minister. Within hours they had effective control of the state. Within weeks, the Houthis had placed Hadi under house arrest, and he resigned his office. He later escaped to Aden where he rescinded his resignation and left for Saudi Arabia, from where he sent a letter asking for military support to overthrow the Houthi coup. A Saudi Arabia-led coalition responded by launching *Operation Decisive Storm* on 26 March 2015, which was intended to drive the Houthis out of Sanaa and restore Hadi to power.

From the Arab Spring until the Houthi takeover of Sanaa, Iran provided money, weapons, support and training. But this was an open-ended investment. It was only after the launch of *Operation Decisive Storm* that Iran shifted from providing assistance to the Houthis to forming something closer to an alliance with them.

Alliance: 2015–present

Following Saudi Arabia's intervention in Yemen, Iran changed its posture towards the Houthis, providing heavier weapons and more substantial economic support. In this current phase, Tehran is not only interested in resupplying the Houthis; it has become engaged in and committed to both their long-term survival and their ability to project power in the region.

On 14 April 2015, the UN Security Council imposed an arms embargo on Yemen.[30] In response, Iran significantly increased its support to the Houthis. As documented by the UN's Panel of Experts on Yemen, Iranian-manufactured ballistic missiles were cut into pieces, smuggled into Yemen and reassembled before being launched at Saudi Arabia.[31] The first known firing of an extended-range ballistic missile took place in May 2017, more than two years after Saudi Arabia entered the war. Possibly this attests to an increase in Iranian support over the period 2015–17. Yet it is also possible that Iran made the decision to provide extended-range

(l) Yemeni President Abdu Rabbu Mansour Hadi in Riyadh, Saudi Arabia, October 2015

(r) Yemeni soldiers loyal to the Houthis at a graduation ceremony for new cadets in Saada, April 2019

missiles to the Houthis in 2015 but that it took time to train the Houthis and set up a delivery pipeline. Iran has also provided UAV technology to the Houthis,[32] as well as the plans for a 'drone boat' (a waterborne remote-controlled explosive vessel).[33]

Size and structure

Iran provides financial support, military hardware and, most likely, some military advisers, but neither Iranian officers nor Iranian doctrine appear to be integrated into the Houthi command-and-control structure. Houthi military doctrine is derived mainly from the group's early years as a tribal militia in 2004–14. Latterly, it has absorbed doctrine from the Yemeni armed forces, partly because it has integrated conventional army units into its structure.

Estimates of the size of the Houthis vary widely, partly owing to the nature of the militia and tribal alliances in Yemen. In late 2014, when the Houthis entered Sanaa, they probably had about 20,000 fighters. That number has since grown significantly. Much of this development is a result of military units defecting and joining the Houthis following the group's takeover of Sanaa. Many of these units were loyal to Saleh, who had helped facilitate the Houthis' entry into the city. While several units wholly or mostly joined the Houthis, others, particularly in contested areas, splintered. This led to what the UN Panel of Experts on Yemen called 'shadow units'.[34] For instance, in Taizz, two units identified themselves as the 35th Armoured Brigade, one loyal to Hadi's government and one loyal to Saleh and the Houthis, until at least 2017. This reflects the trend in which both the government and the Houthis appoint governors and cabinet officials.

The Houthis have largely adhered to a two-tier approach when it comes to their fighters. The first is the tribal militia, which grew out of the six wars in Saada. These units do not wear uniforms and often rotate around the country to different battle fronts.[35] Their commanders are not given military ranks and are known by a *nom de guerre*. The second is made up of regular Yemeni Army units that have aligned themselves with the Houthis. As the UN Panel of Experts on Yemen noted, many of these units are headed by Zaydis of *sayyid* descent.[36] Other than trainers and advisers, there is no evidence of a large number of Iranian or Hizbullah forces fighting alongside the Houthis in Yemen.

Politically and militarily, the Houthis have maintained as much of the pre-existing bureaucratic structure as possible. They are a top-down organisation, with all key decisions made by Abdul Malik al-Houthi. On the political side, to the extent possible, they have attempted to maintain existing Yemeni government infrastructure and ministries. To facilitate this, they typically appoint a loyalist director and deputy to each office. On the military side, a similar process is followed, although a relatively small number of individuals surrounding Abdul Malik al-Houthi, including long-standing members of the Houthi network and those related to the family through marriage, continue to make key military decisions.[37] Militia commanders, the backbone of the movement, are given tactical flexibility within their areas of operation, and significant autonomy is granted to individual militia groups – which form the backbone of the Houthis' military wing. The regular military units that have joined the Houthis are either under the control of trusted Houthi commanders or have loyalist deputies in place.[38]

The Houthis have striven to develop specialist cadres, such as the Missile Brigades. In April 2013, Hadi named Major-General Muhammad Nasser Ahmed al-Atifi commander of the Missile Brigades. Atifi subsequently defected and joined the Houthis.

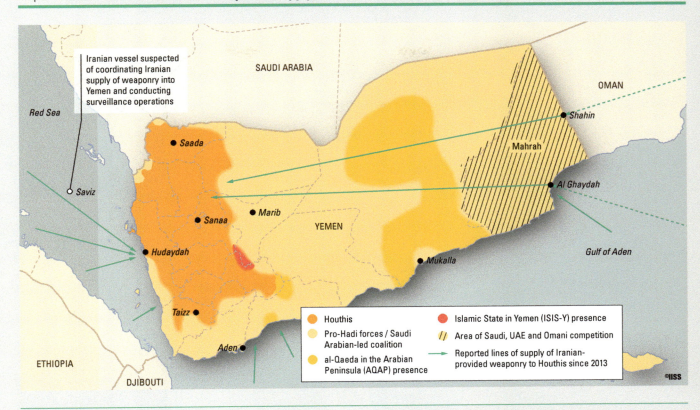

Map 5.1: **Yemen zones of control and suspected supply lines of the Houthis as of June 2019**

Source: IISS

In September 2016, Atifi was appointed defence minister in the Houthi–Saleh government.[39]

The Houthis have reportedly maintained their force strength in the face of ongoing aerial bombardments and fighting on the ground partly through the recruitment of child soldiers. Families, many of which are struggling economically because of the war, are paid premiums when their sons join Houthi militias.[40] On occasion, the Houthis also supplement their ranks by recruiting from local tribes. In late November and early December 2017, as the alliance between Saleh and the Houthis collapsed, Muhammad Ali al-Houthi,[41] a cousin and brother-in-law of Abdul Malik al-Houthi, and military commander Abdullah Yahya al-Hakim lobbied tribes around Sanaa to either join the Houthis or remain neutral in their fight with Saleh.[42] Sometimes called the 'collar tribes', the opportunism of seven tribes around Sanaa was instrumental in Saleh's defeat. After initially reclaiming many military installations from Houthi control, Saleh's forces were outnumbered as the tribes surrounding Sanaa allowed Houthi fighters to move in and block reinforcements from reaching Saleh. Although these tribal combatants do not always fight on behalf of the Houthis, they do represent a strategic reserve.

Finance

When the Houthis seized Sanaa in early 2015, they took control of the state's assets, revenues and patronage. In September 2016, worried that the Houthis were using the central bank to support their rule, Hadi ordered its closure. He opened an alternate bank in the temporary capital of Aden.[43]

Although the Houthis are opaque about their finances, the UN Panel of Experts on Yemen estimated that they may have as much as US$1.62 billion per year under their control (based on the 2011 national budget, the last year for which information is fully available).[44] In Sanaa, the largest single source of this money is the telecoms sector, which is estimated to pay the Houthis US$159 million per year,[45] followed closely by the customs and taxation dues paid by tobacco companies. A UAE official estimated in 2018 that the Houthis make roughly one-third of their annual income, or around US$30m a month, from taxing goods that enter the country through the port of Hudaydah.[46] However, Yemen is also suffering from a currency crisis in which the Yemeni riyal has lost much of its value since 2015 (in 2015, a dollar was worth 250 Yemeni rials; by October 2018, the rate had weakened to more than 700 rials per dollar).[47]

Figure 5.2: **Structure of the Houthi movement**

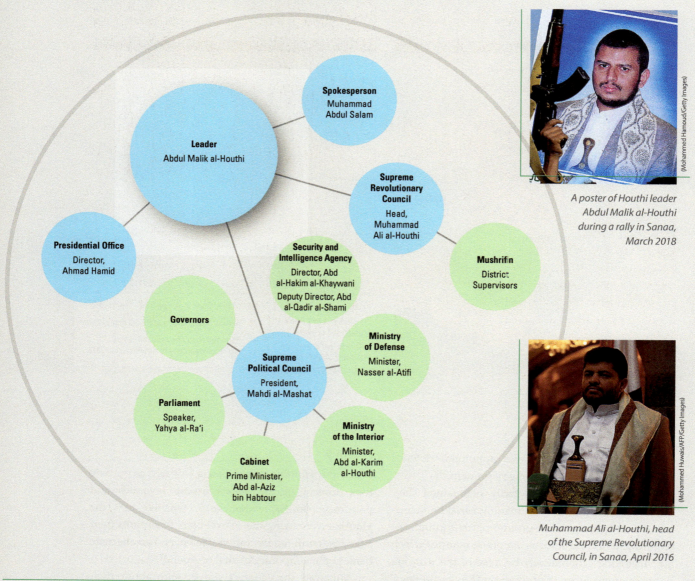

A poster of Houthi leader Abdul Malik al-Houthi during a rally in Sanaa, March 2018

Muhammad Ali al-Houthi, head of the Supreme Revolutionary Council, in Sanaa, April 2016

Source: IISS

Iranian financial aid moved from cash handouts and paid visits to Iran in 2011–14 to more sustained, organised and substantial support. For instance, in its 2018 midterm update, the UN Panel of Experts on Yemen said it was investigating reports that Iran was providing a monthly fuel donation valued at US$30m, something Tehran has denied.[48] Such a donation would allow the Houthis to generate revenue by selling the fuel on the black market amid the cash crisis, while also freeing up funds that would otherwise be spent on fuel to pay fighters' salaries or recruit new combatants.

In 2012, before the beginning of the current conflict, Khalil Harb, Hizbullah commander responsible for Yemen, was recorded telling a local group in Yemen that monthly funding of US$50,000 was ready for collection.[49] It is unclear from reports whether Harb was talking to a Houthi-linked group or another political party in Yemen. Shortly after Saudi Arabia entered the war in March 2015, it added Harb to its 'terrorist list' for a number of reasons, including channelling financial support to the Houthis. The US Department of the Treasury had previously sanctioned Harb for his role in transferring money to groups in Yemen. However, to what extent Hizbullah funding may have increased since the Saudi Arabian-led coalition entered the war is unknown.

(l) US Marine Corps and Saudi-led coalition personnel with suspected Iranian weapons seized from Houthi forces in Yemen

(r) A still from a video released by Houthis on 27 March 2018, purportedly showing Houthis launching a ballistic missile near Sanaa two days earlier

Equipment

The Houthis have three main sources of weapons: local stockpiles of light and medium arms; military-weapons depots seized when the Houthis took Sanaa and bases across the country; and smuggled Iranian weapons and military equipment.

Missiles and rockets

On 6 June 2015, the Houthis launched their first short-range ballistic missile, a *Scud*, against Saudi Arabia. They launched 59 more missiles and rockets against Saudi Arabia over the next 18 months, although none of them travelled very far into Saudi Arabia.[50] The vast majority of these were S-75 (SA-2 *Guideline*) surface-to-air missiles (SAMs) that had been converted into *Qaher* rockets, with a range of less than 300 kilometres.[51]

The Yemeni armed forces' ballistic-missile inventory seized by the Houthis when they took Sanaa was relatively small, consisting largely of shorter-range *Scud*-B missiles (300 km range) and North Korean-made *Hwasong*-6 missiles (a *Scud*-C copy with a range of 500 km).[52] Their S-75s, which were largely ineffective against modern Saudi coalition aircraft, were converted to augment their missile capabilities and reach.[53] It also meant receiving Iranian assistance to obtain longer-range systems.

On 19 May 2017, the Houthis launched an extended-range ballistic missile that landed in the Saudi province of Riyadh. The missile flew 965 km – well beyond the range of Houthi missiles to that date and well beyond that of the known missiles in Yemen's arsenal. Three subsequent missiles, fired on 22 July, 4 November and 19 December 2017, all flew at least 900 km, suggesting that the Houthis had access to new ballistic missiles.[54]

US missile experts and the UN Panel of Experts on Yemen both believe that these extended-range missiles, which the Houthis refer to as *Borkan*-2H, are part of Iran's *Qiam* family of missiles.[55] The UN Panel of Experts reported that fragments of these missiles – which were not known to exist in Yemen before the implementation of an arms embargo in April 2015 – indicate that they had been cut into pieces, most likely to be smuggled into Yemen, and then welded back together at clandestine sites.[56]

Maritime weapons

The Houthis are known to use sea mines. After examining three sea mines discovered in Mokha, on the Red Sea coast, in 2017, the UN Panel of Experts on Yemen concluded that they were similar to an Iranian-manufactured sea mine, which was first identified at an Iranian arms fair in October 2015.[57] The discovery was made after the Houthis took over Sanaa and after the UN imposed an arms embargo.

On 30 January 2017, a small boat struck a Saudi warship 30 km off the coast of Yemen, near Hudaydah.[58] In March 2017, experts inspected a similar vessel seized by the UAE.[59] Evidence examined by CAR, a research organisation, suggested that 'certain components were sourced from Iran or through Iranian channels'.[60] For instance, cables connecting the command and guidance elements of the device were reportedly from the Iranian Simia Cable Company, which exports commercial products and is used by the Iranian defence industry.[61] A Farsi-script keyboard was found on board. Although the experts did not have access to the vessel's computerised guidance system, a later examination of the system by UN and US officials showed Iranian military involvement.[62]

UAV technology

On 27 November 2016, forces loyal to Hadi's government stopped a Dubai-registered truck in Marib and uncovered parts for six complete UAVs and additional

Map 5.2: **Reported Houthi missile attacks against Saudi territory by province, 2015–19**

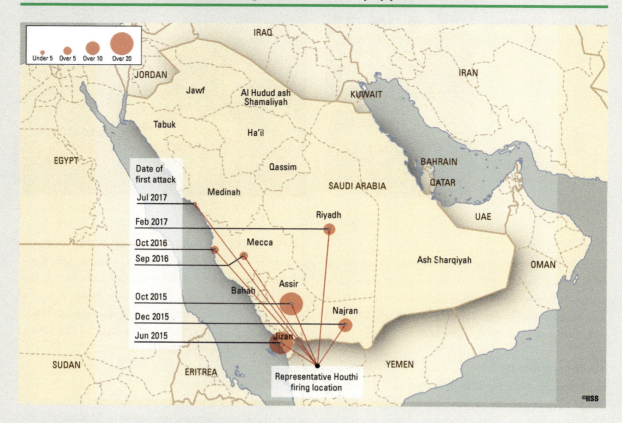

Table 5.1: **Inventory of Houthi-fired missiles since 2015**

Model	Type	Range	Origin	Examples of reported target
9K79 *Tochka* (SS-21 *Scarab*)	Rocket	<100 km	Yemen Armed Forces inventory	Across southwest Saudi Arabia; rival forces inside Yemeni territory
Scud-B/*Hwasong*-5	SRBM	300 km	Yemen Armed Forces inventory	Across southwest Saudi Arabia
Scud-C/*Hwasong*-6	SRBM	~500 km	Yemen Armed Forces inventory	Taif
Borkan-1 (likely *Scud*-B modification)	SRBM	<500 km	Yemen Armed Forces inventory – modified *Scud* with Iranian technical support	King Fahd Air Base (Taif); King Abdulaziz International Airport (Jeddah)
Qaher-1	SRBM	160 km	Yemen Armed Forces inventory – modified S-75 surface-to-air missile with Iranian technical support	Across southwest Saudi Arabia, including Jizan Regional Airport
Borkan-2H (*Qiam*-1)	SRBM	<900 km	Based on Iranian *Qiam*-1, likely shipped to and assembled in Yemen	King Khalid International Airport; Yanbu oil facility

SRBM: short-range ballistic missile
Source: IISS

components for as many as 24 more.[63] The UAV type known as the *Qasef*-1 is similar in design, dimensions and capability to the *Ababil*-2 family, particularly the *Ababil*-T, which is manufactured by Iran's Aircraft Manufacturing Industries.[64] This company is owned by the Iranian government and is part of the Defence Industries Organisation.[65] Additionally, the location of the seizure, at Milh checkpoint near Marib in a truck travelling east towards Sanaa, suggests that the UAVs were being smuggled either from Oman or the Yemeni governorate of Mahrah. This is similar to the suspected smuggling route used for transporting Iranian ballistic-missile parts to the Houthis.

Prior to this incident, on 16 November 2016, UAE forces had recovered a crashed UAV in Aden, and a UAV engine following an attack in Marib on 19 September the same year.[66] Several months later, in February 2017, the Houthis displayed four UAVs they

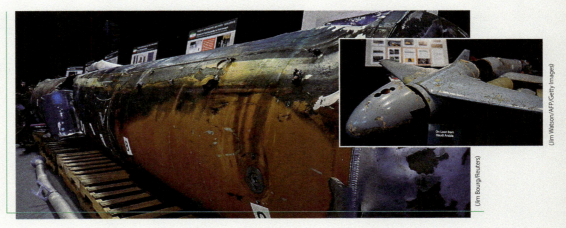

(l) Fragments from a ballistic missile, believed to have been made by Iran and fired into Saudi Arabia by the Houthis, presented at a press conference by Nikki Haley, then US ambassador to the UN, 14 December 2017

(r) A UAV displayed at the same press conference; like the missile, Haley said Iran had sent it to the Houthis in Yemen

claimed to have manufactured themselves.[67] One of the systems shown was identical to the *Qasef*-1 intercepted in Marib in November 2016.[68]

Two additional pieces of evidence strongly suggest that Iran is behind the transfer of UAV technology to Houthi forces. Firstly, the gyroscope seen in the captured *Qasef*-1 UAVs is identical to an Iranian-manufactured gyroscope recovered in Iraq.[69] Secondly, the serial numbers on the UAV components suggest that they were manufactured in the same location at roughly the same time.[70]

Mines and IEDs

Yemen signed the Mine Ban Treaty in 1997 and in April 2002 announced that it had destroyed its stockpile of anti-personnel mines, except for some 4,000, which it retained 'for training and research purposes'.[71] Despite those claims, in 2011 Republican Guard forces loyal to then-president Saleh laid thousands of mines in the Bani Jarmooz area near Sanaa.[72]

Since their takeover of Sanaa, the Houthis have used large numbers of anti-personnel and anti-vehicle mines, with one estimate suggesting that they have laid more than 500,000 since the beginning of 2015.[73] Some are from Saleh-era Yemeni military stockpiles that were not destroyed – they show a date of manufacture before Yemen's declaration in 2002 – while others are of Houthi manufacture.

There is no evidence to suggest that the Houthis are receiving imported mines from outside Yemen, but there is evidence to suggest that Iran supplies them with vital components for some of their own improvised explosive devices (IEDs). Passive infrared sensors and switches are particularly notable in this regard. In 2015, Bahraini forces seized several of these from an Iranian-backed militant cell, while their use in Yemen in 2016–18 has been documented.[74] The sensors seized in Bahrain and those used by the Houthis in Yemen are identical.[75] They have similar numbering and markings, strongly suggesting that they are from a common source, believed to be Iran.[76] These sensors and switches are also similar to the ones found on the *Jihan* 1 in 2013.[77]

Houthi usage of IEDs, which was rudimentary in 2015, has become increasingly sophisticated. IEDs are often camouflaged as rocks and many are radio-controlled. There are at least three possible explanations for the growing sophistication of IED construction and usage by the Houthis in Yemen, none of which are mutually exclusive. Firstly, the Houthis are gaining experience and expertise as the war continues. Secondly, it is possible that the Houthis are studying and adapting IED usage by al-Qaeda in the Arabian Peninsula (aka AQAP or Ansar al-Sharia) and the Islamic State in Yemen, also known as ISIS–Y. The third possibility is that trainers from a group such as Hizbullah may be assisting the Houthis.

Iran–Houthi communications

Iran communicates with the Houthis through a variety of means, both overt and covert. On the political front, Houthi officials such as Muhammad Abdul Salam, the group's spokesman, travel to Iran for consultations and discussions.[78] Iran also maintains an embassy in Sanaa, the only country to still do so, after Russia closed its embassy in December 2017 when Saleh was executed by the Houthis. However, Houthi leaders more frequently travel to Lebanon. These trips often involve consultations with Hizbullah. For instance, in August 2018, Abdul Salam and Abdul Malik al-Ajri, a member of the Houthis' political council, met Hizbullah Secretary-General Hassan Nasrallah.[79] Although it is widely believed that the Houthis have regular contact with Hizbullah, this was the first time a meeting between officials from the two sides had been publicised.

Map 5.3: **Reported Houthi uninhabited aerial systems attacks against rival forces and Saudi territory, 2015–19**

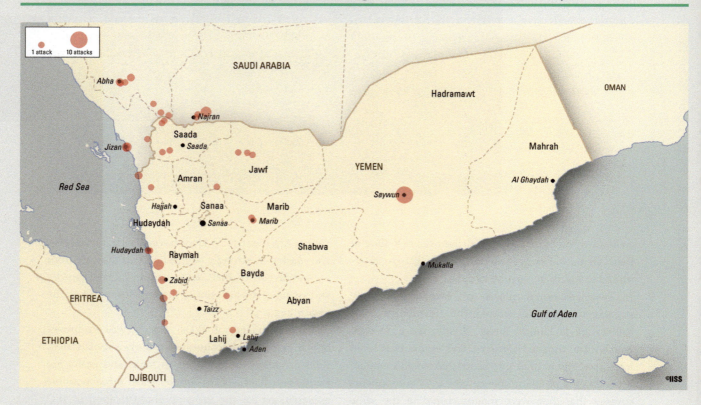

Table 5.2: **Inventory of known Houthi uninhabited aerial systems**

UAV System	Function*	Payload	Estimated operation radius	Origin
Qasef 1	ISR/Weapon	30 kg†	150 km	Reportedly a variant of the Iranian *Ababil*-T class of UAV
Qasef 2K	ISR/Weapon	30 kg†	100 km	Reportedly a variant of the Iranian *Ababil*-T class of UAV with indigenous engineering
Sammad 1	ISR	N/A	500 km†	Visually similar to one of Hizbullah's *Mirsad* UAVs
Sammad 2	ISR/Weapon	n.k.	100 km	An adaptation of the *Sammad* 1
Sammad 3	ISR/Weapon	n.k.	1,000 km (claimed)	An adaptation of the *Sammad* 1
Rased	ISR	N/A	30–40 km	Commercial (Skywalker X8)

*A number of these platforms carry a warhead payload, turning them into a form of improvised stand-off munition. † Reportedly. ISR – Intelligence, surveillance and reconnaissance
Source: IISS

Recent analysis suggests that there are differences between Hizbullah and IRGC military communications with the Houthis. IRGC advisers in Yemen in 2014–17 were reportedly confined to two locations: Sanaa and a 'missile construction site in Saada'.[80] US sources say that the number of Iranian advisers in Yemen is likely to be very small and that they are unlikely to be at missile-firing sites.[81] However, Hizbullah advisers have reportedly been 'allowed forward as far as command posts and the Red Sea coastal defense sites'.[82] Although relying heavily on Emirati and Saudi sources, this account matches the general pattern of Houthi–Hizbullah and Houthi–Iranian relations.

Smuggling routes

Owing to the UN Security Council arms embargo in place since April 2015, military aid to the Houthis is smuggled into the country. There are two main supply routes by which ballistic missiles and fuel can be smuggled into Houthi-controlled territory. The first runs from the east, originating either in Oman or in the eastern Yemeni governorate of Mahrah. Shipments are brought ashore and then smuggled across more than 1,000 km of government-controlled territory before reaching the Houthis. This is the route the UN Panel of Experts on Yemen has deemed 'most likely' in terms of ballistic-missile supply.[87] There is significant traffic and trade along

Houthi resupply

Throughout the Saada wars, Houthi fighters generally supplied themselves with weapons, ammunition and food, rather than relying on centralised supply.[83] This self-sufficiency reduced their need for some of the logistical and material support that the IRGC's Quds Force and Lebanese Hizbullah have supplied in other theatres. The practice of local scavenging by fighters in areas they knew well appears to have changed since the Houthis took control of Sanaa. Houthi fighters no longer operate solely in Saada or surrounding areas – they are now trans-ported to different fronts across the country.[84] For example, 12 Houthi prisoners who were released in September 2016 as part of a prisoner exchange were captured fighting in Marib but were from seven different districts, including Ibb, Mawhit, Raymah and Taizz.[85] This has changed the way the Houthis resupply. The Houthis are reported to oversupply militia posts with ammunition, water and food,[86] allowing fighters to remain in one place for extended periods and reducing exposure for both the fighters and those providing supplies.

this route, which crosses the front line from government-controlled territory into Houthi territory. Interceptions, such as the seizure of UAVs, have primarily been along this route.

The second, or western, route involves material coming into Houthi-controlled territory from the Red Sea coast, which appears to be the course the *Jihan 1* was taking in 2013 when it was intercepted. Along this route, ships depart Iran and head south to join the traffic of dhows delivering goods to Africa. Vessels halt in the Gulf of Aden or (less often) dock along the African coast or meet at sea before dispersing their goods to smaller wooden boats that then cross to Yemen, mingling with the local sea traffic. The use of such small boats provides the capability to land almost anywhere along the Yemeni coast.

Training and technical assistance

The Houthis gained much of their training and experience as a tribal militia group that has been fighting nearly continuously since 2004, along with specialised training FROM regular Yemeni military units affiliated with the movement. These military units that joined the Houthis had received professional training, although parts of the armed forces had been deliberately starved of attention and funding under Saleh as a way of preventing them from posing a threat.

Before their takeover of Sanaa in late 2014, the Houthis had access only to light and medium weapons and no access to the sea. By 2015 and 2016 they were a de facto government in control of large portions of Yemen and its military, along with multiple ports. One plausible reason for their relatively smooth transition from militia to governing body is the aid, advice and training provided by Iran and Hizbullah.

Hizbullah

Houthi leaders have been travelling to Lebanon for many years, often meeting in secret with Hizbullah officials. But evidence suggests that there was cooperation with and, perhaps, training provided by Hizbullah before the Houthi takeover of Sanaa in late 2014. As one analyst has noted: 'The parallels in the Hezbollah [sic] takeover of West Beirut in 2008 and the Houthi grab of power in 2014 … suggest some exchange on military strategy.'[88]

Throughout the current conflict, there have been frequent media reports of Hizbullah commanders being killed on the ground in Yemen. But many of these are published by pro-Saudi media outlets with no independent confirmation. It has been in the interest of both the Houthis and Hizbullah to downplay these claims.

On 16 August 2018, Khalid bin Salman, Saudi Arabia's then ambassador to the US, said on social media: 'Among the much ignored realities in Yemen is not only the direct assistance the Houthi militia receives from the Iranian regime, but also the existence of Hizbullah commanders on the ground.'[89] A few weeks later, on 2 September, it was reported that Tariq Haydrah, who was described as a Hizbullah commander, had been killed in a Saudi-led coalition airstrike.[90]

Although the Houthis had experience in infantry tactics and anti-tank guided-missile operations from the six Saada wars, evidence suggests that Hizbullah may have trained the Houthis in 'offensive mine operations and anti-shipping attacks',[91] areas in which the Houthis had less experience. It is also likely that the Houthis received training, assistance or at the very least advice from Hizbullah on the creation of 'small-scale military industries'[92] such as mine-production facilities. The Houthis have

Houthi members hold up portraits of Hizbullah Secretary-General Hassan Nasrallah and Houthi leader Abdul Malik al-Houthi in Sanaa, March 2016

relied heavily on mines since late 2014. Hizbullah has significant experience in building and securing similar underground facilities in an urban environment. It is possible that the Houthis had assistance from Saleh's military network, but given the years of mistrust and wars between the two sides, it is more likely that the Houthis looked to Hizbullah for guidance.

Iran

Iran has provided direct training and technical assistance to the Houthis, although probably on a smaller scale than that provided by Hizbullah.[93] In 2011–14, this likely took place either in Iran or Lebanon, or on a very small scale in Yemen. Notably, in late September 2014, days after the Houthis took control of Sanaa, at least three members of the IRGC were released from prison.[94]

Six months later, Iran's Mahan Air – which the US had sanctioned in 2011 for 'providing financial, material and technological support to the Islamic Revolutionary Guard Corps'[95] – operated a series of twice-daily flights from Tehran to Sanaa, beginning on 1 March 2015 and lasting a few weeks.[96] Saudi Arabia entered the war three weeks later and quickly worked to establish air superiority over Sanaa, bombing Sanaa International Airport in late April to prevent an Iranian aircraft from landing.[97]

Commentators noted that 14 flights per week to Yemen was a highly unusual number, particularly given the relatively few Yemenis living in Iran.[98] By contrast, Saudi Arabia, where more than 2m Yemenis live, did not have as many flights. It is unclear what was on the aircraft that landed in Sanaa, but it is likely that they carried military trainers and equipment. However, it is unlikely that these flights included the Iranian ballistic missiles the Houthis would later fire at Saudi Arabia.

Nevertheless, it is likely that at some point, either inside or outside Yemen, Iran provided at least minimal training to Houthi forces on the structure and operation of the *Qiam* missile. It seems unlikely that the Yemeni Missile Brigades under Atifi would have been able to reassemble and use the smuggled missile parts without some sort of training or instruction. The *Qiam* was a new type of missile that did not exist in Yemen's arsenal prior to the implementation of the arms embargo in April 2015. In May 2018, the US Department of the Treasury sanctioned five Iranian individuals for involvement in the transfer of ballistic-missile technology to the Houthis.[99] However, these sanctions centred on the transfer of technology and not on training.

Command, control and Iranian influence

Although neither Iran nor Hizbullah exercises direct command and control over the Houthis, there exists an alliance based on shared interests. These interests may change over time. The Houthis have a long history of accepting conditional outside aid and assistance, but executing their original plans regardless.

Perhaps the clearest example of this took place in September 2014. The Houthis advanced from Saada in June, where they had been in de facto control since 2012, overrunning a military base in Amran in early July 2014 before massing for a march on Sanaa. According to US diplomatic and security sources, Iran had advised them not to do this, although it is unclear whether Tehran opposed the timing or the takeover itself.[100] The Houthis, however, disregarded this advice and conducted a separate deal with Saleh to take Sanaa. A US National Security Council spokesperson said at the time: 'It remains our assessment that Iran does not exert command and control over the Houthis in Yemen.'[101]

In July 2018, the Houthis attacked two Saudi oil tankers as they were passing through the Red Sea.[102] An Iranian IRGC commander, Brigadier-General Naser Shabani, later took credit for the attacks, saying in the Iranian media: 'We told the Yemenis to strike two Saudi oil tankers, and they did.'[103] An IRGC spokesman later claimed that, despite evidence to the contrary, Shabani was not in the IRGC and that he had been misquoted; Iran, the spokesman said, gave no such order.[104] This situation is similar to the media pattern that played out in 2014 and 2015 over Iranian involvement in Syria.

The preponderance of evidence therefore supports the fact that even in the alliance phase, Iran does not exercise command and control over the Houthis, instead advising and suggesting. Regardless of Iran's intentions, the Houthis had their reasons for striking the Saudi oil tankers in July 2018. The Saudi-led coalition's military offensive to retake Hudaydah, the Houthis' main outlet to the sea, was gathering momentum and the Houthis had repeatedly threatened to target international shipping in the Red Sea.[105] Nevertheless, it is perhaps in Tehran's interests to overstate its role and influence with the Houthis. Iran wants to take part in peace negotiations in Yemen,[106] in order to maintain its influence along the Red Sea and against the Saudi southern border, something the US has strongly resisted. According to the Fars news agency, Iran has already named Hossein Jaberi-Ansari, a special assistant to Iran's foreign minister, as its negotiator in Yemen's international peace talks.[107]

Strategic assessment

The Houthis' domestic goal of holding power in Yemen and their regional goal of projecting military power into the Arabian Peninsula are closely aligned with the broader Iranian goal of weakening Riyadh. To that end, Iran has increasingly provided to the Houthis both the military capabilities to threaten Saudi Arabia and economic aid, in the form of fuel, to keep the group afloat. Although the Houthis and Tehran have effectively been part of an alliance since early 2015, Iran only began smuggling extended-range ballistic missiles to the Houthis in late 2016 or early 2017. Similarly, Iranian economic aid has increased significantly only since 2017. Iran is invested in both the Houthis' long-term political survival and their ability to project power throughout the Arabian Peninsula, particularly into Saudi Arabia.

Despite a public display of evidence by the US and the conclusion of the UN Panel of Experts on Yemen that Iran was in violation of a UN Security Council resolution, Tehran has suffered minimal consequences internationally. Russia vetoed a Security Council draft resolution condemning Iran in February 2018.[108] Following the veto, it appears that Iran has dramatically increased its economic support to the Houthis, providing much-needed aid during an economic blockade.

Houthi supporters in Sanaa, December 2018

In 2015 and 2016, the Houthis fired dozens of short-range ballistic missiles and rockets into Saudi Arabia. But given that these had maximum ranges of less than 300 km, they were of little strategic concern to Saudi Arabia. That changed in November 2017 when the Houthis demonstrated their capability of firing extended-range ballistic missiles that could reach Riyadh. Without so far causing significant damage or many casualties, these missiles altered Saudi perceptions and drew a harsh reaction from Riyadh. Following the 2017 strike, Saudi Arabia closed all air, land and sea ports in Yemen, effectively cutting the country off from aid and materiel.

Although the Houthis are not entirely reliant on Iranian military support to survive in Yemen, they do need such support to threaten inner Saudi Arabia and the UAE. They also need Iranian economic support in order to function as a government. Iran could easily cut off or reduce its support to the Houthis, depending on its strategic intentions, but it is more likely to increase. Iran's interests lie in continuing to back the Houthis. It preserves its strategic gains in Yemen and reinforces its narrative of solidarity and fidelity with regional partners. Instead of inserting itself in the tight organisational structure of the Houthi military, the Quds Force has prioritised the provision of weaponry and training on the use of missiles. It also left the role of mentor to Lebanese Hizbullah. Indeed, Hizbullah's deployment in Yemen surpasses that of

Table 5.3: Houthis (Ansarullah): relationship with Iran and assessment of strategic utility

Group	Ideological affinity	Strategic convergence	Political expediency	Transactional value	Strategic value for Iran	Other 'patrons'	Assessment
Houthis (Ansarullah)	●●	●●	●●	●●	●●	No	Strategic ally

Source: IISS   ●●● High   ●● Medium   ● Low

the Quds Force, probably because of cultural proximity and similar experiences, but also because of the Houthis' specific operational needs. This division of labour between Hizbullah and the Quds Force reflects Iran's desire to maintain some deniability but is also a way to keep the cost and exposure of its involvement in Yemen low and relations with the Houthis less entangled.

Unlike in Syria, where Iran has spent billions of dollars, its outlays in Yemen have been relatively modest. It has helped the Houthis where it can, giving them greater offensive capabilities, and provided them with enough economic support to remain viable, despite attempted blockades on the country. It is unlikely that the Houthis will become a full Iranian surrogate force in the near future. Instead, it is more likely that Iran will continue to increase military and economic aid to the Houthis, allowing the group to maintain a sense of independence, while preserving Tehran's deniability. Indeed, Iran does not need command and control over the Houthis: in terms of Saudi Arabia and the war in Yemen, their goals are, for the time being at least, largely the same.

Notes

1 During the 1960s, there was a separate civil war taking place in southern Yemen. North Yemen and South Yemen were two different states for much of the second half of the twentieth century, unifying only in 1990.

2 In order to qualify to be a Zaydi imam, it was necessary to meet 14 requirements, including descent from the Prophet Mohammad through Ali and Fatima.

3 Bernard Haykel, 'A Zaydi Revival?', Yemen Update, no. 36, 1995, http://www.aiys.org/no-36-1995/144-a-zaydi-revival.html.

4 Mohammad Badr al-Din al-Houthi is one of Badr al-Din al-Houthi's 14 sons and a brother and half-brother respectively of Hussein al-Houthi, the first leader of the movement, and Abdul Malik al-Houthi, the current leader of the movement.

5 Abdullah Lux, 'Yemen's Last Zaydi Imam', Contemporary Arab Affairs, vol. 2, no. 3, pp. 369–434; Marieke Brandt, Tribes and Politics in Yemen: A History of the Houthi Conflict (Oxford: Oxford University Press, 2017), pp. 132–33.

6 Iris Glosemeyer, 'Local Conflict, Global Spin', Middle East Report, no. 232, Autumn 2004, https://www.merip.org/mer/mer232/local-conflict-global-spin.

7 'Iran in Yemen: Tehran's Shadow Looms Large, but Footprint is Small', cable from ambassador Stephen Seche, US Embassy Sanaa Yemen, 12 September 2009, WikiLeaks, Cable 09SANAA1662_a, https://wikileaks.org/plusd/cables/09SANAA1662_a.html.

8 'Yemeni Tribal Leader: For Saleh, Saudi Involvement in Sa'ada Comes not a Moment too Soon', cable from Angie Bryan, US Embassy Sanaa Yemen, 28 December 2009, WikiLeaks, Cable 09SANAA2279_a, https://wikileaks.org/plusd/cables/09SANAA2279_a.html.

9 Haykel, 'A Zaydi Revival?'

10 The author of this chapter has seen this document.

11 Ibid.

12 Zaydi Islam is often referred to as 'Fiver' Shi'ism and is doctrinally distinct from the 'Twelver' Shi'ism that is practised in Iran, Iraq and Lebanon.

13 'Iran in Yemen: Tehran's Shadow Looms Large, but Footprint is Small', cable from ambassador Stephen Seche, US Embassy Sanaa Yemen, 12 September 2009.

14 'Al-Houthi Rebellion: No End in Sight', Cable from Ambassador Stephen Seche, US Embassy Sanaa Yemen, 14 July 2008, WikiLeaks, Cable 08SANAA1165_a, https://wikileaks.org/plusd/cables/08SANAA1165_a.html.

15 Ibid.

16 Robert F. Worth, 'Yemen Rebels Routed, Saudi Arabia Says', New York Times, 9 November 2018, https://www.nytimes.com/2009/11/10/world/middleeast/10yemen.html.

17 Michael Knights, 'The Houthi War Machine: From Guerilla War to State Capture', CTC Sentinel, vol. 11, no. 8, September 2019, https://ctc.usma.edu/houthi-war-machine-guerrilla-war-state-capture.

18 Eric Schmitt and Robert F. Worth, 'With arms for Yemen rebels, Iran seeks wider Mideast role', New York Times, 15 March 2012, https://www.nytimes.com/2012/03/15/world/middleeast/aiding-yemen-rebels-iran-seeks-wider-mideast-role.html.

19 Ibid.

20 Ibid.

21 *Ibid.*

22 *Ibid.*

23 Thom Shanker and Robert F. Worth, 'Yemen Seizes Sailboat Filled with Weapons, US Points to Iran', *New York Times*, 28 January 2013, https://www.nytimes.com/2013/01/29/world/middleeast/29military.html.

24 Yara Bayoumy and Mohammed Ghobari, 'Iranian Support Seen Crucial for Yemen's Houthis', Reuters, 15 December 2014, https://www.reuters.com/article/us-yemen-houthis-iran-insight/iranian-support-seen-crucial-for-yemens-houthis-idUSKBN0JT17A20141215; Monitoring Group on Somalia and Eritrea, 'Report of the Monitoring Group on Somalia and Eritrea pursuant to Security Council resolution 2060 (2012): Somalia', 12 July 2013, Annex 6.1.F, pp. 313–14, http://www.un.org/ga/search/view_doc.asp?symbol=S/2013/413.

25 Monitoring Group on Somalia and Eritrea, 'Report of the Monitoring Group on Somalia and Eritrea pursuant to Security Council resolution 2060 (2012): Somalia', p. 292.

26 UN Monitoring Teams, unlike UN Panels of Experts, do not have an investigative mandate and are dependent upon material provided to them by member states.

27 Bayoumy and Ghobari, 'Iranian Support Seen Crucial for Yemen's Houthis'.

28 United Nations Office for the Coordination of Humanitarian Affairs, 'Situation Report No. 5: Yemen: Amran conflict', 9 July 2014, https://reliefweb.int/sites/reliefweb.int/files/resources/2014_07_10%20Sit.rep%20Amran%20i.pdf.

29 Mohammed Khalid Alyahya (@7yhy), Twitter, 22 May 2018, https://twitter.com/7yhy/status/998911079764946949?lang=en.

30 UN Security Council, 'Resolution 2216 (2015)', 14 April 2015, sections 14–17, p. 6, https://www.un.org/ga/search/view_doc.asp?symbol=S/RES/2216%20%282015%29.

31 UN Panel of Experts on Yemen, 'Final Report of the Panel of Experts on Yemen 2018', 26 January 2018, http://www.un.org/en/ga/search/view_doc.asp?symbol=S/2018/594.

32 'Iranian Technology Transfers to Yemen', Conflict Armament Research, March 2017, http://www.conflictarm.com/perspectives/iranian-technology-transfers-to-yemen.

33 'Anatomy of a Drone Boat', Conflict Armament Research, December 2017, http://www.conflictarm.com/perspectives/anatomy-of-a-drone-boat.

34 UN Panel of Experts on Yemen, 'Final Report of the Panel of Experts on Yemen 2017', 31 January 2017, pp. 17–18, http://www.un.org/en/ga/search/view_doc.asp?symbol=S/2018/193.

35 *Ibid.*, pp. 20–21.

36 *Ibid.*, pp. 20–21.

37 UN Panel of Experts on Yemen, 'Final Report of the Panel of Experts on Yemen 2018', p. 20.

38 UN Panel of Experts on Yemen, 'Final Report of the Panel of Experts on Yemen 2017', p. 21.

39 *Ibid.*, p. 20.

40 Interviews with Yemenis living in Houthi-controlled territories, December 2018 and March 2019.

41 Muhammad Ali al-Houthi is the head of the Supreme Revolutionary Committee (SRC), which was formed in February 2015 and served as the Houthis' governing body until July 2016, when it was replaced by the Supreme Political Council. The SRC, however, was not disbanded.

42 UN Panel of Experts on Yemen, 'Final Report of the Panel of Experts on Yemen 2018', p. 11.

43 UN Panel of Experts on Yemen, 'Final Report of the Panel of Experts on Yemen 2017', p. 10.

44 UN Panel of Experts on Yemen, 'Final Report of the Panel of Experts on Yemen 2018', p. 37.

45 *Ibid.*, p. 38.

46 Mohammed Ghobari and Mohamed Mokashef, 'Civilians Flee Bombardment as Arab States Pound Yemeni Port', Reuters, 14 June 2018, https://www.reuters.com/article/us-yemen-security/civilians-flee-bombardment-as-arab-states-pound-yemen-port-idUSKBN1JA0N2; Jeremy M. Sharp, 'Yemen: Civil War and Regional Intervention', Congressional Research Service, 21 March 2019, p. 2, https://fas.org/sgp/crs/mideast/R43960.pdf.

47 Stephen Kalin, 'UN Envoy says top priority in Yemen is fixing the economy', Reuters, 4 October 2018, https://af.reuters.com/article/worldNews/idAFKCN1ME1ZK.

48 'UN Panel Finds Further Evidence of Iran link to Yemen Missiles', Agence France-Press, 31 July 2018, https://www.thenational.ae/world/mena/un-panel-finds-further-evidence-of-iran-link-to-yemen-missiles-1.755610; 'Yemen: Chronology of Events', Security Council Report, 6 December 2018, https://www.securitycouncilreport.org/chronology/yemen.php. It should be noted that the Panel of Experts' midterm updates are confidential to the UN Security Council. However, these reports are traditionally leaked to news outlets.

49 US Department of the Treasury, 'Treasury Sanctions Hezbullah Leadership', 22 August 2013, https://www.treasury.gov/press-center/press-releases/Pages/jl2147.aspx.

50 UN Panel of Experts on Yemen, 'Final Report of the Panel of Experts on Yemen 2017', pp. 149–50.

51 *Ibid.*, pp. 143–50.

52 *Ibid.*, p. 143.

53 *Ibid.*, p. 143.

54 *Ibid.*, p. 27.

55 *Ibid.*, p. 28.

56 *Ibid.*, p. 29.

57 *Ibid.*, p. 34.

58 'Anatomy of a Drone Boat', Conflict Armament Research, p. 1.

59 *Ibid.*

60 *Ibid.*

61 *Ibid.*, p. 4.

[62] Interviews with US intelligence source, March 2018.

[63] UN Panel of Experts on Yemen, 'Final Report of the Panel of Experts on Yemen 2018', p. 32; 'Iranian Technology Transfers to Yemen', Conflict Armament Research.

[64] UN Panel of Experts on Yemen, 'Final Report of the Panel of Experts on Yemen 2018', p. 32.

[65] Ibid., p. 32, note 128.

[66] Ibid., p. 32.

[67] 'Iranian Technology Transfers to Yemen', Conflict Armament Research, pp. 1–2.

[68] Ibid.

[69] UN Panel of Experts on Yemen, 'Final Report of the Panel of Experts on Yemen 2018', p. 156.

[70] 'Iranian Technology Transfers to Yemen', Conflict Armament Research.

[71] UN Panel of Experts on Yemen, 'Final Report of the Panel of Experts on Yemen 2017', p. 159.

[72] 'Landmine Ban: Yemen Admits Using Mines', Human Rights Watch, 1 December 2013, https://www.hrw.org/news/2013/12/01/landmine-ban-yemen-admits-using-mines.

[73] Elana DeLozier, 'The Problem of Landmine Proliferation in Yemen', Washington Institute for Near East Policy, Policy Watch 2987, 3 July 2018, https://www.washingtoninstitute.org/policy-analysis/view/the-problem-of-landmine-proliferation-in-yemen.

[74] 'Radio-controlled, Passive Infrared-Initiated IEDs', Conflict Armament Research, March 2018, http://www.conflictarm.com/perspectives/radio-controlled-improvised-explosive-devices-rcied/.

[75] Ibid., p. 2.

[76] 'Radio-controlled, Passive Infrared-Initiated IEDs', Conflict Armament Research; 'Mines and IEDs employed by Houthi Forces on Yemen's West Coast', Conflict Armament Research, September 2018, http://www.conflictarm.com/dispatches/mines-and-ieds-employed-by-houthi-forces-on-yemens-west-coast.

[77] 'Radio-controlled, Passive Infrared-Initiated IEDs', Conflict Armament Research, p. 10.

[78] 'Iranian, Yemeni Officials Discuss Ways to Speed Up Peace Process', Fars News Agency, 1 October 2018, http://en.farsnews.com/13970709001047.

[79] Mohammed Abdul Salam (@abdusalamsalah), Twitter, 18 August 2018, https://twitter.com/abdusalamsalah/status/1030886841069826048; Mohammed Abdul Salam (@abdusalamsalah), Twitter, https://twitter.com/abdusalamsalah; Abdul Malik Al Ajri (@alejri77), Twitter, https://twitter.com/alejri77.

[80] Knights, 'The Houthi War Machine: From Guerilla War to State Capture', p. 21.

[81] Interviews with US officials, 2018.

[82] Knights, 'The Houthi War Machine: From Guerilla War to State Capture', p. 21.

[83] Barak A. Salmoni, Bryce Loidolt and Madeleine Wells, 'Regime and Periphery in Northern Yemen: The Huthi Phenomenon', RAND Corporation, 2010, p. 196, https://www.rand.org/content/dam/rand/pubs/monographs/2010/RAND_MG962.pdf.

[84] UN Panel of Experts on Yemen, 'Final Report of the Panel of Experts on Yemen 2017', p. 101.

[85] Ibid.

[86] Knights, 'The Houthi War Machine: From Guerilla War to State Capture', p. 19.

[87] UN Panel of Experts on Yemen, 'Final Report of the Panel of Experts on Yemen 2018', pp. 127–28.

[88] Mareike Transfeld, 'Iran's Small Hand in Yemen', Sada Middle East Analysis, Carnegie Endowment for International Peace, 14 February 2017, http://carnegieendowment.org/sada/67988.

[89] Khalid bin Salman (@kbsalsaud), Twitter, 16 August 2018, https://twitter.com/kbsalsaud/status/103015836971216890?s=12.

[90] 'A Lebanese Hezbollah leader was killed in a raid by the alliance in Saada', Al Arabiya, 2 September 2018, https://www.alarabiya.net/ar/arab-and-world/yemen/2018/09/02/%D8%A7%D-9%84%D8%AA%D8%AD%D8%A7%D9%84%D9-%81-%D9%8A%D9%82%D8%AA%D9%84-%D9%82%D9%8A%D3%A7%D8%AF%D9%8A-%D8%A8%D8%AD%D8%B2%D8%A8-%D8%-A7%D9%84%D9%84%D9%87-%D8%A7%D9%84%D9%84%D8%A8%D9%86%D8%A7%D9%86%D9%8A-%D9%85%D8%B9-%D9%82%D9%8A%D8%A7%D8%A7%D8%AA-%D8%AD%D9%88%D8%AB%D9%8A%D8%A9.html.

[91] Knights, 'The Houthi War Machine: From Guerilla War to State Capture', p. 21.

[92] Ibid.

[93] Ibid.

[94] Mohammed Ghobari, 'Yemen Frees Members of Iran's Revolutionary Guards – sources', Reuters, 25 September 2014, https://www.reuters.com/article/uk-yemen-iran/yemen-frees-members-of-iran-revolutionary-guards-sources-idUKKCN0HK1K320140925.

[95] US Department of the Treasury, 'Treasury Designates Iranian Commercial Airline Linked to Iran's Support for Terrorism', 12 October 2011, https://www.treasury.gov/press-center/press-releases/Pages/tg1322.aspx.

[96] 'Arrival of the first direct flight from Iran to Yemen', Al-Jazeera, 1 March 2015, http://www.aljazeera.net/news/arabic/2015/3/1/%D9%88%D8%B5%D9%88%D9%84-%D8%A3%D9%88%D9%84-%D8%B1%D8%AD%D9%84%D8%A9-%D8%AC%D9%88%D9%8A%D8%A9-%D9%85%D8%A8%D8%A7%D8%B4%D8%B1%D8%A9-%D9%85%D9%86-

%D8%A5%D9%8A%D8%B1%D8%A7%D9%86-
%D8%A5%D9%84%D9%89-
%D8%A7%D9%84%D9%8A%D9%85%D9%86; Farea al-Muslimi, 'Iran's Role in Yemen Exaggerated, but Destructive', Century Foundation, 19 May 2017, https://tcf.org/content/report/irans-role-yemen-exaggerated-destructive.

97 'Aid Flights to Yemen Blocked after Saudi Arabian Jets Bomb Airport Runway', Reuters, 28 April 2015, https://www.theguardian.com/world/2015/apr/28/aid-flights-to-yemen-blocked-after-saudi-arabia-bombs-airport-runway.

98 Farea al-Muslimi, 'Iran's Role in Yemen Exaggerated, but Destructive'.

99 US Department of the Treasury, 'Treasury Targets Iranian Individuals Providing Ballistic Missile Support to Yemen's Huthis', 22 May 2018, https://home.treasury.gov/news/press-releases/sm0392.

100 Ali Watkins, Ryan Grim and Akbar Shahid Ahmed, 'Iran Warned Houthis Against Yemen Takeover', *Huffington Post*, 20 April 2015, https://www.huffingtonpost.com/2015/04/20/iran-houthis-yemen_n_7101456.html; Elisabeth Kendall, 'Iran's Fingerprints in Yemen: Real or Imagined?', Atlantic Council Issue Brief, October 2017, p. 3, http://www.atlanticcouncil.org/images/Irans_Fingerprints_in_Yemen_web_1019.pdf.

101 Watkins, Grim and Ahmed, 'Iran Warned Houthis Against Yemen Takeover'.

102 Rania El Gamal, 'Saudi Arabia halts oil exports in Red Sea lane after Houthi attacks', Reuters, 25 July 2018, https://www.reuters.com/article/us-yemen-security/saudi-arabia-halts-oil-exports-in-red-sea-lane-after-houthi-attacks-idUSKBN1KF0XN.

103 Amir Toumaj, 'Did IRGC commander say Houthis were ordered to strike tankers?', *Long War Journal*, 9 August 2018, https://www.longwarjournal.org/archives/2018/08/did-irgc-commander-say-houthis-were-ordered-to-strike-tankers.php.

104 Hossein Bastani, 'Naghl-e ghowl-e janjali-ye khabargo-zari-ye Fars az yek sartip-e sepah' [Fars News Agency's controversial quote of one IRGC brigadier-general], BBC Persian, 7 August 2018, http://www.bbc.com/persian/iran-features-45106676.

105 Aziz El Yaakoubi, 'Yemen's Houthis threaten to block Red Sea shipping lane', Reuters, 9 January 2018, https://uk.reuters.com/article/uk-yemen-security/yemens-houthis-threaten-to-block-red-sea-shipping-lane-idUKKBN1EY2AX.

106 Interviews with United Nations source, January 2018.

107 'Iranian, Yemeni Officials Discuss Ways to Speed up Peace Process', Fars News Agency.

108 Rick Gladstone, 'Russia Vetoes U.N. Resolution to Pressure Iran Over Yemen Missiles', *New York Times*, 26 February 2018, https://www.nytimes.com/2018/02/26/world/middleeast/iran-yemen-security-council.html.

CHAPTER SIX

BAHRAIN, SAUDI ARABIA AND KUWAIT

- Iran's support for militant groups in Bahrain, Saudi Arabia and Kuwait is primarily meant to irritate and pressure their governments, and impose a political cost for their partnership with the United States
- Tehran's nurturing of partners in these Gulf states has been both ideological and opportunistic, but the return on this investment has been limited given local circumstances, the relative strength of their states and Iran's own risk appetite
- Iran's networks in these Gulf states pose a manageable security threat rather than an existential challenge

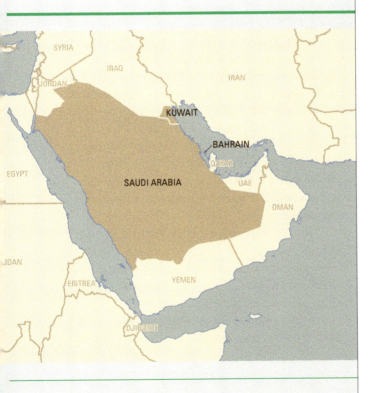

Since the Islamic Revolution in 1979, Iran has mounted ideological, strategic and security challenges against Bahrain, Saudi Arabia and Kuwait, the three countries hosting the largest Twelver Shia communities on the Arabian Peninsula. After rising tensions in the 1980s, relations between Iran and these Gulf states reached a detente in the late 1990s, but worsened considerably with the war in Iraq in 2003 and more so since the regional uprisings of 2011.

Forty years after the revolution, Iran's quest for influence faces more obstacles in Bahrain, Saudi Arabia and Kuwait than elsewhere in the Middle East. The factors that have enabled the growth of pro-Iranian militancy across the states of the northern Middle East or Yemen – civil war, foreign occupation, weak and poor governments, welcoming Shia communities, ease of logistical supply and low risk of blowback – are either absent or considerably less pronounced in Bahrain, Saudi Arabia and Kuwait. Consequently, Iran's attempts to cultivate and direct local partners in these countries have failed to deliver results comparable to Iran's achievements elsewhere.

Geopolitically, the Arabian Peninsula states' conventional superiority and privileged security relationships with Western countries, as well as global aversion to instability in the energy-rich Gulf

Iraqi soldiers in front of a mural of Ayatollah Ruhollah Khomeini near the border with Iran, September 1980

region, have also constrained Iran's power projection. Iranian policy towards these three Gulf states is in large part a corollary to the paramount need to stand up to the military presence of the United States in the region, whose expulsion from the region would allow Iranian hegemony.

Iran perceives most Gulf states as rivals for regional influence, pawns in the hands of Western powers and enablers of their aggression, monarchical oppressors of their own people and facilitators of anti-Shia extremism. The rivalry with Saudi Arabia is particularly salient: the two countries vie for the religious and political leadership in the region. From Tehran's perspective, Iran's efforts to secure regional dominance would be greatly facilitated by the expulsion of US and other Western forces from the region, since Iran's attributes of power exceed those of its immediate Gulf neighbours by most metrics: population; size and experience of the military; industrial output; and non-oil economy. In contrast, Saudi Arabia, the United Arab Emirates and other Gulf states considerably outspend Iran on defence and have access to better technology. They are also financially wealthier and better integrated in the global economy, and maintain a broader network of geo-economic and diplomatic ties.

In the meantime, Iran's priority is to make it politically costly and controversial for the key Gulf states that are actively opposed to Iran (Bahrain, Saudi Arabia, the UAE and Kuwait) to host US bases and allow US military operations.[1] Given the extreme difficulty of replicating the conditions that have enabled pro-Iranian militancy in other parts of the Middle East, Iran has been opportunistic in these Gulf states, exploiting social rifts in the respective societies to expose and widen domestic vulnerabilities and provoke and divide leaderships. To this end, Tehran has focused on developing covert capabilities of nuisance and punishment, opting for a combination of rhetorical provocation, ideological mobilisation and covert and limited support for local groups, rather than building groups with mass and overt appeal.

Assessing the nature, extent and potency of Iran's networks of influence in Bahrain, Saudi Arabia and Kuwait is more challenging than elsewhere. The inherently covert nature of the networks and the difficulty of conducting primary research contrast with the increasingly overt and open relations Iran maintains with groups in Iraq, Lebanon, Syria and even Yemen. While Gulf governments routinely complain about Iranian-backed activities in their countries, their security services and their Western counterparts are loath to reveal the extent of their knowledge. Iran itself has a political interest in amplifying its reach or understating it, depending on regional conditions.

1979: revolution, sectarianism and geopolitics

Before the Islamic Revolution in 1979, Iranian support for Shia political movements in the Gulf was limited to calls for reform, social change and religious tolerance. This changed with the coming to power of Ayatollah Ruhollah Khomeini, who pursued a more activist regional policy as a natural extension of the revolution.[2] Khomeini's claim – to be working towards the empowerment of all Muslims in the Arab Gulf states – was ostensibly non-sectarian, with Khomeini asserting in 1980 that '[w]e should set aside the thought that we do not export our revolution, because Islam does not regard various Islamic countries differently'.[3] The Islamic Revolution energised Islamist movements, both Sunni and Shia, across the Middle East. In its early years, Muslim Brotherhood movements in Egypt and Syria but also Palestinian nationalist groups (such as Fatah) hoped for Iranian material and political support.

Iran's pan-Islamist appeal was, however, underwritten by a pro-Shia agenda and the destabilising posture of exporting the revolution. The Iranian Shia clerical establishment openly challenged the Saudi monarchical and clerical establishment. In Iran's view, the empowerment of all Muslims was incompatible with the status quo in the Gulf monarchies, with Khomeini declaring that '[w]hen people have self-confidence and high morale, they will begin to demand their rights and oppose the authorities' policy and conduct. Indeed, it is this which the

A US Air Force sergeant in front of the damaged Khobar Towers, Saudi Arabia, June 2001

corrupt monarchies fear most.'[4] Iran's appeal to non-Shia groups was also blunted by Khomeini's claims to absolute leadership as the ultimate *marja al-taqlid* under *Velayat-e Faqih*. Iran primarily appealed to disaffected Shia communities in the Gulf states, seeking to manipulate and amplify the pre-existing social and political grievances and to present Iran's own revolutionary progress as a model of liberation. A violent uprising known as the 'Intifada of the Eastern Province' in Saudi Arabia between 1979 and 1980 was the culmination of a multi-decade movement to protest Shia social and economic exclusion that found inspiration and support in Iran's revolution.[5] Iran's early outreach to large Shia communities in Bahrain, Saudi Arabia and Kuwait at a time of geopolitical tensions in the early 1980s had mixed results, but it would validate post facto a long-lasting perception in Arab capitals that Tehran was intent on nurturing a fifth column.

Iran's geopolitical interests also complicated its revolutionary vision of a unified, pan-Islamic region and further highlighted its pro-Shia agenda. In Syria, Iran sided with the Alawite regime of Hafez al-Assad – its ally against Saddam Hussein in Iraq and its facilitator in Lebanon – against the Syrian Muslim Brotherhood uprising that ended in 1982. During the 1980–88 Iran–Iraq War, Khomeini and his revolutionary followers portrayed the fight as a continuation of Shia revolt and martyrdom against tyranny, opposing Saddam Hussein's repression of Iraq's Shia community and its clergy and Hussein's pretence to be the defender of the Sunni Arab world.

Starting in 1980, the Gulf states' support for Hussein's regime against Iran raised tensions between the latter and the Gulf states. This added a strategic and security imperative to Iranian activities in the Gulf states beyond the export of the revolution as mandated by Khomeini. The financial and political support extended by the Gulf states to Hussein's Iraq was a direct threat to Iran's national security, while these states' reliance on Western security provision since the issuance of the Carter Doctrine in 1980 blunted Iran's regional ambitions and rendered it vulnerable to military attacks.[6] In response, Iran's activities in the Gulf states were aimed not only at the Gulf states, but also regional and international partners of the Gulf. For example, attacks against Western embassies in Kuwait in the 1980s mounted by Shia militants with connections to Iran were motivated by Western and Kuwaiti support for Iraq.

Iran and Shia activism in the Gulf: 1979–2011

From 1979 until 2011, Iran attempted a friendly takeover of the Iraqi-origin Shia networks in the Gulf. It did so by providing refuge in Iran and assistance to sympathetic senior Iraqi and associated Gulf clerics and operatives, and by co-opting part or the entirety of their organisations in Bahrain, Kuwait and Saudi Arabia. The most sophisticated and ambitious attacks conducted in the Gulf states after the 1979 Sunni extremist takeover of the Grand Mosque in Mecca and up to al-Qaeda's 2003–07 terror campaign were Iranian-ordered or inspired.

Iran's outreach in Bahrain, Saudi Arabia and Kuwait was facilitated by the growing politicisation of Shias in the 1970s and 1980s, as was the case in Lebanon and Iraq. Iran's clerical class, which propounded a revolutionary ideology of transnational theocracy, competed with other Shia clerical and political players for the leadership of the newly politicised Shia communities. Iran came to this competition with strong arguments: the success of its revolution carried prestige and inspiration, while the

Hadi al-Mudarrisi delivers a speech to supporters in Baghdad, July 2003

Origins of Shia activism

Gulf Shia Islamist activism can be traced back to Ayatollah Muhammad Baqir al-Sadr's al-Da'wa al-Islamiyya (the Islamic Call), which he formed in the late 1950s in Najaf, Iraq, and Ayatollah Muhammad al-Shirazi's Message Movement, which originated in Karbala, which was renamed the Islamic Action Organization after the Iranian revolution. The organisations were similar in their ideology and objectives. Opposing the secular and nationalist ideologies promoted by post-colonial Arab regimes, they sought the re-Islamisation of Shia politics and revolutionary toppling of the Iraqi government to establish an Islamic state in which Shia clerics would have a supervisory rather than a directing, hands-on role. The organisations were also rivals, and their rivalry resonated in the Gulf where the movements grew under the influence of both exiled Iraqi and local activists and militants.

The Shirazist movement

Muhammad al-Shirazi fled Iraq in the early 1970s, relocating to Lebanon, Kuwait and later Iran, where he became a powerful clerical figure. One of his Kuwait-based Iraqi followers, Muhammad Taqi al-Mudarrisi, recruited and trained a number of Saudi activists, including Hassan al-Saffar, who became the leader of the Shirazist revolutionary organisation in Saudi Arabia in 1975. After the Islamic Revolution, this group renamed itself the Organization for the Islamic Revolution in the Arabian Peninsula (OIRAP). (One of its most notable members was Sheikh Nimr al-Nimr, who would go on to play a major role in the Eastern Province's unrest in Saudi Arabia in 2011.) Muhammad Taqi al-Mudarrisi's brother, Hadi al-Mudarrisi, established himself in Bahrain, where he created the Islamic Front for the Liberation of Bahrain (IFLB) in 1976.

The Shirazists never created a revolutionary organisation in Kuwait, where the Shia community was seen as co-opted by and integrated within the state, but focused instead on Saudi Arabia and Bahrain. In 1979, inspired by Iran's revolution, OIRAP initiated an opportunistic rapprochement with Iran, and in November played a key role in prompting violent riots in Qatif in Saudi Arabia's Eastern Province. In later years, OIRAP deepened its relationship with Iran.

The IFLB also initiated a rapprochement with Iran. In 1980, Muhammad Mudarrisi, now based in Iran after being deported from Bahrain alongside other clerics, announced the IFLB's allegiance to Khomeini:

financial and organisational resources it could deploy dwarfed those of competing Shia leaderships.

Over time, however, personal and theological rivalries, as well as tensions between Iran's ideological goals and its security and strategic priorities, affected the nature of their relationship and Iranian levels of support. Iran failed to recruit large numbers of adherents or dominate a group, let alone set the politics of Shia communities in Bahrain, Saudi Arabia and Kuwait. Iran's efforts to directly appeal to the Shia professional and middle class, divided between loyalty to the state and adherence to the Shirazist- or Da'wa-aligned political movements, remained ineffective. However serious, the attempts against the Gulf monarchies did not attract sizeable and sustained Shia approval. Regardless of their level of disaffection toward their respective governments, many Shia Gulf citizens did not abide by *Velayat-e Faqih*.

Despite its relatively limited influence, however, Iran remained a source of concern to the Gulf states throughout the period. Even the moderate foreign policy of Hashemi Rafsanjani's and Mohammad Khatami's presidencies from 1989 to 2005 did not mollify Bahrain, which kept a watchful eye on the remnants of the Iran-aligned opposition and applied political and security measures to weaken it. Indeed, the Khobar Towers attack in Saudi Arabia in 1996 (in which 20 were killed and 498 wounded) illustrated that Iran continually maintained a capability to inflict harm, made possible in part by Lebanese Hizbullah. When political expediency required Iran to reduce or recalibrate its activities, as happened in the 1990s, it did so.

'Imam Khomeini is the leader and axis around which our oppressed peoples should rally if they truly seek freedom, since Imam Khomeini is the summit of jihad and faith and the symbol of challenge and endurance. He is the hope of all the oppressed in the world.'[7] In 1981, the IFLB organised a coup attempt against the monarchy in Bahrain that received Iranian encouragement and guidance.[8] The ensuing crackdown considerably weakened the Shirazist movement, but its legacy was felt in the violent unrest in the 1990s. Small numbers of IFLB militants, trained by the Islamic Revolutionary Guard Corps (IRGC), would also join the Iranian war effort against Iraq.

The Shirazists subsequently distanced themselves from the Iranian state. Shirazi's concept of rule by *shurat al-fuqaha* (a council of the religious scholars) clashed with Iran's *Velayat-e Faqih*, and Shirazi was gradually marginalised by Khomeini and his successors and starved of resources. Personal rivalry between Shirazi and Khomeini also contributed to this marginalisation, which became even more pronounced with Khamenei, whose religious credentials as Supreme Leader were disputed by many Iraqi and Lebanese ayatollahs.

The Shirazists also objected to the post-Khomeini regional polices of Iran. Rafsanjani, who served as president from 1989 to 1997, sought to end Iran's international and regional isolation and to reconcile with its Gulf neighbours. The detente with Saudi Arabia proceeded gradually, and included the resumption of diplomatic relations, while Iran-backed public manifestations of anti-Saudi sentiment decreased substantially. The Shirazists bitterly complained that Iran, while committing rhetorically to transnational revolution, actually behaved opportunistically, ceasing to support revolution in Iraq, Bahrain and Saudi Arabia in order to further its international agenda.

These setbacks prompted a rethinking and splits within the Shirazist movement. In 1991, Saudi Shirazists renamed their organisation the Reform Movement, reflecting the conclusion that revolution in Saudi Arabia would fail and that their ideology had to be tailored to fit the Saudi context. The Reform Movement concluded an agreement with the Saudi government in 1993, under which the movement's leaders were allowed to return to Saudi Arabia and Saffar effectively became the figurehead of the Saudi Shia.

Not all of the membership supported the Shirazists' rapprochement with the Saudi government. Radical Saudi anti-Shirazist students based in Qom also established in the kingdom a militant group called Hizbullah al-Hijaz (also known as Saudi Hizbullah), which at Iran's behest conducted the 1996 Khobar Towers bombing against a US facility in Saudi Arabia's Eastern Province. The attack was motivated by Iran's long-standing opposition to the US military presence in the region and came after the US passed the Iran and Libya Sanctions Act and began imposing sanctions on its oil sector and a trade and investment embargo. According to the US investigation of the attack, Hizbullah al-Hijaz was supported by Lebanese Hizbullah operatives.[9] This multi-actor coordination reflected Iran's persistent cultivation of local networks across countries, even at a time of ostensible detente with its regional adversary, Saudi

> ## "THE WEAKENING POWER AND COHESION OF THE SHIRAZIST MOVEMENT WAS BEST REFLECTED BY THE DECISION OF SAFFAR TO CHOOSE AS HIS MARJA' GRAND AYATOLLAH ALI AL-SISTANI"

Arabia. The bombing marked the apex of Hizbullah al-Hijaz, whose decline followed after a sustained Saudi counter-terrorism campaign.[10]

The Shirazist movement also fell into decline. Upon the death of Muhammad al-Shirazi in 2001, his brother Sadiq became the *marja* (spiritual reference) of the Shirazists and chose to live in Qom, Iran. However, he became decreasingly influential, in large part because of Iranian-imposed constraints. The weakening power and cohesion of the Shirazist movement was best reflected by the decision of Saffar to choose as his *marja* Grand Ayatollah Ali al-Sistani, a critic of direct clerical involvement in political affairs based in Najaf, Iraq, instead of Sadiq.

The Da'wa movement

Da'wa also pursued the goal of exporting the revolution and dominated the Shia political space in Kuwait and Bahrain from the 1970s, although it failed to make significant inroads in Saudi Arabia. In Kuwait, Iraqi clerics officiating in mosques and working as teachers spread the revolutionary ideology, and were joined by Iraqi exiles who expanded the party's constituency. From the mid-1970s to the late 2000s, Da'wa dominated Shia political representation in the Kuwaiti parliament, where it has operated as the Islamic National Alliance (INA) since 1998 and was the largest organised Shia political grouping in parliament. In recognition of the Kuwaiti context, where the

Ayatollah Isa Qasim gives a speech at a mosque near Manama, May 2013

Shia community has fewer grievances and is politically better integrated, the INA's political behaviour has been pragmatic: while it lauded *Velayat-e Faqih* as a perfect system of government, Da'wa in Kuwait maintained that the system could work only in Iran.

In parallel with its political involvement, Da'wa also resorted to violence. In 1983, it carried out several terrorist attacks in Kuwait against Western embassies and critical infrastructure; it later hijacked planes and targeted prominent Kuwaiti figures, including the Emir.[11] Tellingly, the 1983 attacks were conducted in conjunction with Lebanese Hizbullah, itself deeply influenced by Da'wa theology, and obtained support from Iran. The aim of these attacks, in the context of the Iran–Iraq War, was primarily to dissuade the Kuwaiti government from supporting the Iraqi war effort. Seventeen militants were arrested over the attacks against the embassies, three of whom were Lebanese and several others Iraqi. (Few Kuwaitis were apparently involved in Da'wa's violent activities, and none were senior operatives: this suggests either a calibrated division of labour or simply unwillingness among Kuwaitis to engage in such activities.) One of the Lebanese militants, Mustafa Badreddine, escaped from prison in 1990 and became one of Hizbullah's most senior commanders until his death in 2016. Badreddine was also the cousin and brother-in-law of Imad Mughniyah, Hizbullah's security chief. When Mughniyah was assassinated in Damascus in 2008, prominent members of the INA publicly mourned his death. This caused widespread outrage in Kuwait, which the government used to neuter the INA's oppositionist stance and revamp the Shia political landscape. The INA folded, coalescing with other Shia groups to secure its political survival.

Also convicted in absentia for the 1983 attacks was Jamal Jaafar Mohammad al-Ibrahimi, also known as Abu Mahdi al-Muhandis.[12] An Iraqi holding Iranian citizenship, Muhandis was a former Da'wa member who later became the head of the Badr Brigade, an Iraqi Shia militia that fought alongside Iran during the 1980–88 war. He returned to Iraq in 2003 with the Badr Brigade, founded Kataib Hizbullah in 2006 and oversaw the Special Groups, an Iranian-controlled array of militias that fought US forces in Iraq. He has been the deputy commander of Iraq's Popular Mobilisation Units (PMU, or *al-Hashd al-Shaabi*) since 2014.

Da'wa also spread to Bahrain through students returning from Iraq in the late 1960s, the most noteworthy of which was Isa Qasim, who had studied under Muhammad al-Sadr and spent several years in Qom in the 1990s under Khomeinist and Da'wa teachers. In Bahrain, Da'wa fiercely competed with the Shirazists to present itself as the pre-eminent supporter of the revolution. Like Da'wa in Kuwait, it was deeply embedded in the local Shia community, but the group's evolution in Bahrain was more complex, with the group splitting into two camps, one aiming to achieve political reform and the other resolutely revolutionary. Following the 1981 Shirazist IFLB attempted coup, the space for activism was reduced. Da'wa's political affiliate, the Islamic Enlightenment Society, was closed in 1984 and many of its members agreed to cease political activity.

Bahrain experienced several acts of terrorism and frequent disturbances between 1994 and 1999. It was at this time that Ali Salman, a young graduate of the Qom seminary in Iran, came to prominence. After a year in prison and several in exile, Salman returned to Bahrain in 2001 when Emir Hamad bin Isa Al Khalifa instituted participative reforms. Operating under the tutelage of Qasim, Salman led al-Wifaq, a broad-based Islamist political society. After boycotting the 2002 elections, he decided to participate in the 2006 elections after a heated internal debate within al-Wifaq. A dissenting minority chose to boycott the elections and formed a separate radical movement, al-Haqq Movement for Liberties and Democracy. Splits within the Bahraini Shia political scene continued, culminating in 2011 during the large-scale revolts when al-Wifaq declared that its goal was the establishment of a genuine constitutional monarchy and that it rejected violence, while more radical groups called for a republic and endorsed violence. Inside al-Wifaq too, there were divisions between Qasim, who is a follower of *Velayat-e Faqih*, and Salman and other clerics, who did not embrace this Khomeinist principle.

Figure 6.1: **Gulf states: major events, 1976–2018**

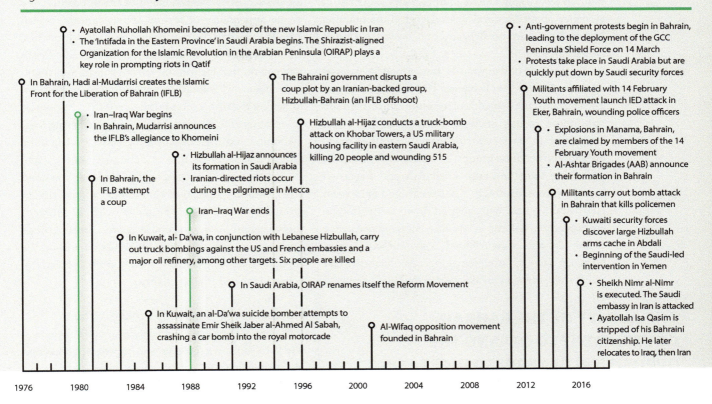

The tribulations of the Shirazist and Da'wa movements and their offspring from the late 1970s to 2011 illustrate how Iran attempted to co-opt, at times successfully, dissident and violent actors in Saudi Arabia, Bahrain and Kuwait. Despite the general paucity of social, economic and political reforms in the Gulf states, neither Iran nor its closest radical partners managed to establish mass followings or build a sustained insurgency, given adverse local conditions and tensions between Iran's priorities and their own.

Iranian outreach since 2011

The 2003 US invasion of Iraq and the subsequent civil war opened space for Iran's regional influence. The empowerment of the Iraqi Shia community and the emergence of powerful Iran-aligned political and military groups had a transformative impact on Shia communities in the Arab world. This was amplified by Hizbullah's military performance during its 2006 war with Israel, which raised concern among the Gulf states and generated prestige and momentum for the group and its main patron, Iran.

The 2011 uprisings that shook the Arab world provided Iran with more opportunities to challenge its rivals. Iranian Supreme Leader Ali Khamenei heralded the Arab revolutions as part of the Islamic Awakening long predicted by the ideology of the Islamic Revolution.[13] Discounting the Syrian uprising as a product of Western and Israeli machinations, he saw the fall of then Egyptian president Hosni Mubarak and other Western-aligned autocrats as an opportunity to overturn the Western-backed order.

Bahrain

In February 2011, large protests, inspired by uprisings elsewhere in the region, rocked Bahrain. The movement was initially peaceful and focused on long-standing demands for political reforms. As it grew in size, however, calls became bolder and more sectarian, with Shia-dominated political parties in the lead. The al-Wifaq party, which was engaged in talks with the government, competed for the crowd's support with more radical groups who were calling for outright revolution and a republican system. There were a number of incidents on the outskirts of Manama and near the Pearl Roundabout. The security forces attempted to restore civil order but did so initially with the application of disproportionate force.

Iran was particularly gratified with the dissent in Bahrain. Iranian officials had periodically disparaged the small kingdom-island, questioning its independence and referring to it in 2009 as Iran's 'fourteenth province'.[14] Such rhetorical provocations against

Bahrain were a convenient if indirect way to stir Saudi anxieties about Iran and were useful in maintaining low-cost pressure on Bahrain, that hosts the United States' 5th Fleet.

In the wake of the protests, Iranian media (such as Al-Alam TV but also Lebanese Hizbullah's Al-Manar TV) amplified the demands of the more radical Bahraini opposition groups such as al-Haqq and al-Wafa, amounting to incitement. Bahraini authorities made allegations that these groups, as well as al-Wifaq, were consulting with Lebanese Hizbullah and hardened their position accordingly. The background of Hossein Amir Abdollahian, who stepped down as the Iranian ambassador to Bahrain in late 2010 but remained active in Bahraini affairs, contributed to government perceptions of Iranian troublemaking: Abdollahian had previously served as an assistant to the IRGC-affiliated

> ## "THE ABILITY OF THE BAHRAINI GOVERNMENT TO DEFANG THE OPPOSITION GENERATED INCREASING FRAGMENTATION AND FRUSTRATION AMONG ACTIVISTS"

Iranian ambassador in Iraq until 2007 and was accused of having radicalised the opposition in Bahrain. Appointed in early 2011 as deputy foreign minister with oversight over the Arab world, Abdollahian would quickly become the most vociferous critic of the Gulf monarchies and a main interlocutor of Lebanese, Iraqi and Syrian militias with Iran.

Once the restoration of civil order exceeded the abilities of the Bahraini security forces and the wider region became concerned, the Gulf Cooperation Council (GCC) deployed the Peninsula Shield Force in March 2011. In response, the speaker of the Iranian parliament Ali Larijani warned that 'the treason of the Saudi regime and its massacres against the Muslim people of Bahrain will never be forgotten', while Khamenei declared that 'the victory of the people of Bahrain was inevitable'. However, in a report released in November 2011, the independent international commission appointed by King Hamad was not able to establish whether Iran had been involved in assisting or orchestrating the 2011 protests, and the government of Bahrain did not provide any public evidence of a significant Iranian role.[15]

The humiliation and weakening of al-Wifaq, following its failed attempts to control the opposition and to negotiate with the government, together with

the subsequent dismantlement of the opposition, led to the appearance of several activist groups, which adopted varying degrees of violence. One of the first and most notable was the nebulous 14 February Youth movement, that focused on street protests and small-scale violence.[16] The ability of the Bahraini government to defang the opposition through coercive responses, co-optation and incentives resulted in increasing fragmentation and frustration among activists. The more radical members of the 14 February Youth began joining forces with members of al-Haqq, al-Wafa and other radical political organisations and insurgent groups such as al-Ashtar Brigades (AAB), al-Mukhtar Brigades and al-Muqawama Brigades. These groups operated in small cells from Shia villages around the capital Manama, with the main centres of activity being Sanabis, Budaiya and Sitra.

Increased Iranian support to Bahrain militants

In the rise of these activist groups, Iran saw an opportunity to fuel unrest in Bahrain and impose a political and reputational cost to its Gulf rivals. After being largely uninvolved in the 2000s, Iran resumed its provision of assistance to those willing to engage in militant activity starting in late 2011. In 2013, Iran began facilitating the movement of higher-quality explosive material into Bahrain through Iraqi intermediaries[17] and also training small numbers of Bahrainis in improvised explosive device (IED) construction and employment, as well as rudimentary small-arms tactics and communications security. IED training occurred primarily at IRGC camps in Iran and by Kataib Hizbullah in Iraq.[18] As of 2019, the number of individuals trained in IED operations is estimated to be between 50 and 100.[19] At the operational level, Iran provided material support, funding and training for (IED) operations both directly and also through Kataib Hizbullah and Lebanese Hizbullah.[20] The resort to Iraqis is explained by the cultural and political affinities between Iraqi and Bahraini militants and Iran's desire to maintain deniability. Iran encouraged the activists and protesters but wanted to avoid being seen as the orchestrator of the revolt.[21]

Bahraini militants living in exile in Iran and Iraq, such as Murtadha Alawi and Ahmad Yusuf, leaders of the AAB, were the conduit between the IRGC, Iraqi and Lebanese militias, and the new militant groups.[22] At the tactical level, much was left to the Bahraini armed groups, although targeting guidance – including what not to attack, notably the US navy base – was also given, highlighting Iran's unwillingness to risk an escalation with Saudi Arabia or the US. Notably, the AAB and other groups refrained from

Proscribing Bahraini militant groups

The United Kingdom proscribed the AAB in December 2017, with the US designating the group a Foreign Terrorist Organization in July 2018.[23] The US designation specifically highlighted the AAB's ties and loyalty to Iran, which the AAB reaffirmed publicly in 2018. In addition to the AAB, at least six other groups have claimed responsibility for attacks in Bahrain from 2012 to 2017. The numerous names create the impression of a larger campaign and could be used to confuse the Bahraini security services.

Some of these groups are indeed unique and separate, the product of personal and regional rivalries, but they are largely connected by past experience and membership has been fluid. Several of these groups even report to the same Bahraini leaders based in Iran. These leaders appear to have little political following and serve essentially as intermediaries for militants operating inside Bahrain. They were eclipsed in 2019, when Ayatollah Isa Qasim moved to Iran after being stripped of his Bahraini citizenship in 2016.[24]

targeting civilians, insisting that their targets were Bahrain's security services and symbols of the state. ATMs and other public infrastructure were occasionally attacked between 2012 and 2017, but care was taken to avoid civilian casualties. Attacks against the police were often presented as being in response to police action against demonstrations and protests.

A clear indication of increased foreign support to violent groups in Bahrain was the growing sophistication of technology used in attacks against security forces. In the months following the February 2011 protests, tactics included throwing paint at Ministry of Interior vehicles, causing traffic jams by putting chains or oil on roads, and setting fire to tyres on major roads. Incidents of Molotov-cocktail attacks on the police increased in subsequent months, along with occasional use of simple improvised devices.[25] By late 2011, groups affiliated with the 14 February Youth movement began experimenting with simple IEDs. The attack on a police foot patrol in Eker on 10 April 2012 wounded seven police officers (three seriously) – the first casualties from an IED since the start of the protests in February 2011.[26] With Iranian assistance, the quality of the IEDs improved: they became more reliable, had greater explosive power and could be remotely detonated. An IED in March 2014 killed three police officers, one of whom was an Emirati deployed to serve in Bahrain. Three men convicted for these murders were executed in January 2017.[27]

Weaponry and explosives similar in design to those delivered and used by Iran-supported groups in Iraq also began appearing in 2013.[28] In December 2013, a boat was boarded near Bahraini coastal waters carrying 38 C4 explosives, 31 Claymore antipersonnel mines and 12 explosively formed penetrator (EFP) charges.[29] In June 2015, the police found an industrial press that had been modified to make EFP liners along with sensors to activate EFP devices. In July 2015, a boat was seized with C4 explosives, detonators and AK-47s.[30] In September 2015, another large cache of weapons was found in the village of Nuwaidrat, ten kilometres south of Manama, that included C4, TNT and EFP components.[31] In December 2016, men who fled security forces were tracked to a bomb-making workshop. Two men connected to the address had recently travelled to Iran.[32]

Despite the influx of explosive materials, violent incidents involving sophisticated charges were limited. Early on, Iran seems to have restricted the use of high explosives (RDX and C4), perhaps because it did not want to escalate the situation while it was engaged in other battlefields in the region as well as in nuclear diplomacy. Tehran has shown a preference for being able to direct an increase in terrorist activity when necessary, while ensuring that a stockpile of materiel would be available should it be needed.

This ramping-up of Iranian assistance came in concert with more inflammatory Iranian rhetoric over Bahraini affairs and in parallel with a steep deterioration in relations between Iran on the one hand and Saudi Arabia and Bahrain on the other over the execution of Saudi dissident Nimr in January 2016 and attacks by mobs linked to hardline factions on their embassies in Tehran. Tensions rose further in June 2016 when Bahrain revoked Qasim's citizenship, with Qasem Soleimani, commander of the IRGC's Quds Force, stating

> They certainly know that trespassing the sanctuary of Ayatollah Sheikh Isa Qasem is a red line whose crossing will set fire to Bahrain and the entire region and leave people with no other option but armed resistance. The Al-Khalifa will pay the price of such an action whose endpoint will be nothing but annihilation of this tyrannical regime.[33]

Table 6.1: Al-Ashtar Brigades: relationship with Iran and assessment of strategic utility

Group	Ideological affinity	Strategic convergence	Political expediency	Transactional value	Strategic value for Iran	Other 'patrons'	Assessment
Al-Ashtar Brigades	●●	●●	●●	●●	●●	No	Strategic ally

Source: IISS ●●● High ●● Medium ● Low

Starting in 2017, there was an increase in the sophistication and ambition of the attacks. An attack on Jau prison in January freed several Shia militants linked to bombings in previous years; several of the escaped men attempted to board boats toward Iran.[34] In March, the police announced that they had disrupted several sophisticated plots, including surveillance of the US Navy Support Facility, for possible intimidation in the context of rising regional tensions and more confrontational US policy as well as potential future attacks.[35] When police raided Isa Qasim's house in May, ostensibly to arrest individuals hiding there, five civilians were killed in the operation.[36] Rioters also threw hand grenades at the police, who responded with lethal force.[37] In November, an attack temporarily disabled Bahrain's main oil pipeline.[38]

It remains unclear if the escalation between 2016 and 2017 was primarily driven by Iran's need to appear to be responding to Qasim's isolation and legal travails, by the pressure on militant groups inside Bahrain to protect their spiritual leader or by Iranian security interests in a context of regional escalation, or a combination of all three.

Iranian support: limitations and challenges

Despite this evidence of increased support, Iran has faced logistical challenges in supplying the militants. Bahrain is an island whose coastal waters are relatively easy to monitor and whose only land entry is the causeway from Saudi Arabia. Unlike Iran's provision of materiel to groups in Iraq, Syria, Lebanon and Yemen, smuggling weapons into Bahrain must be done primarily by sea and is much harder. There is no black market for weapons or explosives, as is the case in Iraq, Syria, Yemen or Lebanon.

Bahrain's small size and population also makes it difficult to prepare and conduct complex terrorist attacks while levels of recruitment have remained low, hindering the growth of militant groups. Throughout 2017 and 2018, policing operations seemed to have disrupted many of the armed groups. In 2019, a Western government report assessed that intelligence-led police operations had broken up several cells manufacturing IEDs and that the level of insurgent violence was contained, although militant groups continued to attract recruits.[39] Importantly, however, the same analysis determined that the groups were unlikely to attract greater numbers and would be unable to pose a serious challenge to security. The AAB, which is considered the largest militant group, can only muster a few dozen core militants. Recruitment tends to be localised and village-based, and militant activities lack any countrywide character. A senior member of the Bahrain government observed in 2016 that perhaps only about 5% of Bahraini Shia, who represent between 55% and 65% of the 700,000-strong Bahraini Muslim population, adhere to the Khomeinist principle of *Velayat-e Faqih*.[40] This has worked to the advantage of the Bahraini security forces, who are well equipped and better trained than the militants, and who have been able to monitor, isolate, contain and dismantle militant cells through a mix of intelligence, the containment of Shia communities and coercion of violent groups.

Divisions among Shia political forces have also contributed to the demoralisation of the community and weakening support on the ground for activism, with al-Wifaq (which was banned in 2016, with Salman sentenced to life in prison in 2018) and the more radical groups all failing to achieve notable and lasting results. From the perspective of many Shia citizens, the wisdom of relying on Iran is questionable: Iran is often seen as an opportunistic, cunning actor that could manipulate or taint Bahraini Shia interests as it suits its interests. Iran's own internal travails and repression of the 2009 popular uprising have eroded its credibility and the portrayal of the Islamic Revolution's achievements. As a result, many politicised Shia citizens have retreated from politics, disappointed by the performance of al-Wifaq but also unwilling to take on the cost of active confrontation. Better Bahraini policing, combined with targeted social and economic projects, have at present mollified the politically ambivalent and those who prefer reform over revolution. As a Western assessment concluded, this was the stage in a counter-terrorist campaign where effective social, economic and political programmes could further undermine the armed groups' cause.[41]

The Bahrain government maintains that the IRGC supports the armed groups, a finding corroborated by US government analysts.[42] Without Iranian assistance, Bahraini militants would be forced to resort to propane-tank IEDs and other crude and more symbolic weapons. That said, Bahraini armed groups' training and capability falls short of that of a militia, and there is no evidence that Bahraini armed groups are either integrated into Iranian command structures or afforded the same levels of respect and support as Iraqi militias or Lebanese Hizbullah. There has never been any assertion that IRGC members have deployed clandestinely in Bahrain (or any other GCC state) to support local partners. Contrary to Iraq, Syria and Yemen, where the IRGC works 'by, with and through' indigenous Shia groups, the IRGC can only work 'through' militant groups in Bahrain. The relationship is rendered more complex by the differing risk appetite of Iran and the militant groups: Iran's geopolitical considerations may dictate or prevent the targeting of Western military bases in Bahrain, which may contradict the militant groups' domestic agendas. Additionally, while the militant groups' association with Iran creates a perception of strength, it also undermines the goals of the broader Shia opposition by tarnishing it as a mere tool of the Iranian government.

Inevitably, because IRGC expertise cannot be directly applied in Bahrain, and given the geographical, demographic and policing constraints, the prospects for indigenous militants to pose an existential threat to the Bahraini government are significantly reduced. Iran itself seemingly lacks confidence in the Bahraini militants' ability to carry out actions and deliver results.[43] It has no expectation that they can threaten the government's hold on power, putting a ceiling to how much effort and how many resources it will pour into the venture. Iran's main objective is to goad the Bahraini government into taking violent actions that would keep the island unsettled, tarnish the government's public image among various constituencies, including Western governments, and make it politically costly for the US to maintain a military presence there. Indeed, criticism of the US presence in Bahrain gained momentum after 2011, with prominent US senators, activists and former officials calling for the closing of the US base.[44] However, the US Department of Defense and many senior officials have rejected this idea, arguing that it would weaken US alliances and defence posture while delivering a symbolic victory for Iran.[45]

Saudi Arabia

Bahrain has clearly been the main focus of Iranian activities in the GCC states since 2011. In neighbouring Saudi Arabia, Shia unrest, episodic since the 1930s but mostly contained since the early 1990s, flared up again, but did not attract the same level of Iranian interest.

The unrest centred on the town of Qatif in the Shia-dominated Eastern Province which sits across from Bahrain. Qatif has always been a hotbed of anti-monarchy activity and social unrest. The 1979 uprising was put down brutally, but its memory remained a tool of political mobilisation for radical Shia movements.[46] In 2011 and 2012, as unrest grew, the standing of Nimr al-Nimr increased, although his appeal remained limited: he was described in 2008 as 'a second-tier political player in the Eastern Province'

> **"THE BAHRAIN GOVERNMENT MAINTAINS THAT THE IRGC SUPPORTS THE ARMED GROUPS, A FINDING CORROBORATED BY US GOVERNMENT ANALYSTS"**

in WikiLeaks cables. Nimr, a radical Shirazist who had studied in Iran and Syria for 15 years and rejected the accommodation reached by Hassan al-Saffar with the Saudi government, was particularly critical of the Al Saud, Al Khalifa and al-Assad rulers, saying 'we don't accept Al Saud as rulers. We don't accept them and want to remove them.'[47] Nimr was arrested in 2012 and sentenced to death in 2014, accused of terrorism but also of 'seeking "foreign meddling"'.[48] Protests in Qatif continued throughout the following years, but at lower intensity.[49]

There is no public evidence of any direct material Iranian support for Nimr before his arrest, but Nimr had been opportunistically supportive of Iran and suggested that he would welcome Iranian support under certain conditions.[50] Once jailed, Iran's media and officials raised Nimr's case regularly in an effort to tarnish Saudi Arabia's reputation and warned against harming him. The more Iran's media elevated his profile, the more he was seen in Saudi Arabia and elsewhere as an Iranian agent. After he was executed in 2016, Khamenei warned that Saudi Arabia would face 'divine revenge', while Iranian mobs, directed by hardliners, stormed Saudi diplomatic facilities in Iran.[51] Iran clearly saw a benefit in highlighting at low cost Nimr's resistance and fate to irritate Saudi Arabia without necessarily caring for him as a person.

Iranian protesters outside the Saudi embassy in Tehran after Nimr al-Nimr is executed in Saudi Arabia, January 2016

There was further unrest in 2017 in western Qatif when Saudi security forces cordoned off the town of Awamiya – a prominent centre of Shia dissent and the hometown of Nimr – in order to raze the old town and rebuild it. The Saudi government maintained that the old town harboured criminals and weapons caches and needed to be cleared to make the area safe. The intense fighting in Awamiya ended, unsurprisingly, with a government victory. It received limited attention in Arab, international and Iran-aligned media. Tellingly, there was no mass uprising among Saudi Shia in solidarity with Awamiya, underlying both the factional nature of Saudi Shiism and the deep-seated aversion to confrontation with the state among many. The judgement of Western intelligence analysts following Awamiya was that the calibrated, low-profile Saudi security response had deprived Iran of the opportunity to act strongly in its self-declared role as the protector of the Shia.[52]

Iran is generally more inclined to disregard Shia unrest if it leads to an unwanted escalation with a superior power, preferring to use its networks for more serious contingencies linked to Iranian national security. Even if it chose to get involved, geographic and local constraints, and superior Saudi policing developed during the fight against al-Qaeda from 2003, would complicate Iranian support for large-scale dissent. Even Nimr recognised in the WikiLeaks cable that 'foreign powers – including Iran … act out of self-interest, not out of piety or religious commonality'.[53]

Excluding an all-out war, the threat to the Saudi state from dissent in the Eastern Province remains limited. Iran can upset Saudi Arabia far more effectively in other theatres of operation, such as Yemen, than it can inside the country, and has primarily sought to irritate Saudi Arabia whenever it can at low risk.

Kuwait

Even if Iran does not perceive Kuwait as an enemy on a par with Saudi Arabia and Bahrain, it has still maintained a minimal infrastructure to conduct activities there on a need-basis. The presence of US forces in Kuwait remains a powerful rationale for Iran's preservation of local armed partners in case of an escalation. In 2015, Kuwaiti security forces discovered a Hizbullah cache that contained 2,000 pounds of ammonium nitrate, over 300 pounds of explosives, 68 weapons and 204 grenades. While the cache was old, the militant cell was assessed to have been operational.[54] In 2017, several members of the cell (Kuwaiti nationals in touch with Hizbullah handlers) were captured. The Kuwaiti government accused Iran of overseeing the cell and in response expelled Iranian diplomats and partially shut down the Iranian embassy.

For Kuwait, the memory of the 1980s attacks, the continued presence of Hizbullah operatives, the power of Iran-backed militias in neighbouring countries and the return to prominence of Abu Mahdi al-Muhandis as deputy commander of Iraq's PMU all contribute to a climate of concern, albeit one that is counterbalanced by the greater loyalty of the Shia community to the state than in Bahrain or Saudi Arabia.

Strategic assessment

The Islamic Revolution was inspirational for the Iraqi-shaped Shia networks that were already established in the Gulf, but Iran failed to completely dominate or control the Shirazist and Da'wa movements.[55] The Islamic Republic did attempt to export the revolution to the Gulf through these existing networks but after Khomeini's death sought a regional detente, appearing to accept that exporting the revolution was

Map 6.1: **US, UK and France: selected military facilities, presence and transit routes in the Gulf region**

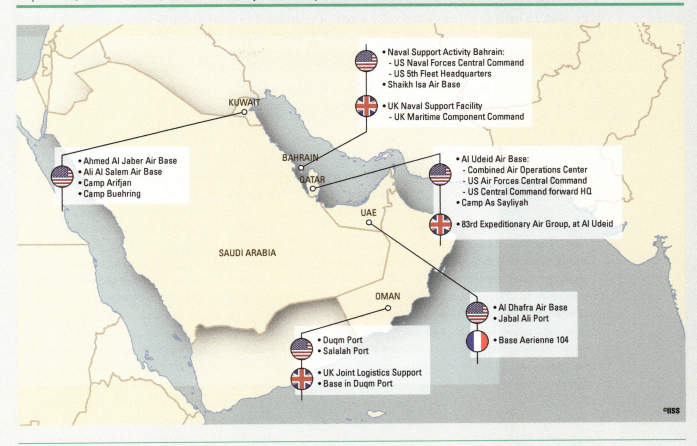

Source: IISS

a long-term goal. This in turn tempered the demands of many Shia Islamist groups in the Gulf, suggesting that local groups scrutinised Iranian policy changes to adapt accordingly to local realities.

Other groups, however, rejected accommodation with Gulf governments and remained committed to revolution through violent means. The ascent of Shia movements in Iraq since 2003, the Lebanese Hizbullah 'victory' of 2006 and Iran's more assertive foreign policies under the presidency of Mahmoud Ahmadinejad between 2005 and 2013 gave succour to Shia movements in Saudi Arabia and Bahrain, but it was the regional uprisings of 2011 that galvanised Shia militancy in these countries. Post-2011, Iran and the groups it supports in the Gulf have been highly opportunistic, exploiting pre-existing social and political rifts that were exacerbated by the 2011 uprisings.

However, neither Iran nor the groups it supports have scored significant and tangible results. In none of the three countries covered in this chapter have they been able to sway public opinion, eliminate powerful rivals or capture territory and resources, let alone alter the domestic balance of power. Iran has no realistic chance through its partners of penetrating, let alone capturing, parts or the totality of a Gulf state. In contrast to Syria, Iraq, Lebanon or Yemen, none of the Gulf countries is in conflict and the Shia communities' grievances alone do not create enough space for decisive foreign interference. The primarily local nature of the Shia complaints has denied Iran a foothold in Gulf societies. States in the Gulf are considerably stronger and wealthier than their counterparts in the Levant and are able effectively to deploy instruments of co-optation and coercion to foster obeisance among their populations.

Iran very likely never expected to profit greatly from its efforts in the GCC states. It remains content to nurture, at low cost, the threat of irritation and violence, viewing unrest as a way of signalling to the Gulf monarchies that it considers them to be non-representative and anachronistic. Iran has particularly sought to emphasise Saudi and Bahraini brutality and alleged support for Sunni Islamist movements across the region to harden internal divides.

In penetrating Shia communities in Bahrain, Saudi Arabia and Kuwait, Iran has also had to strike a balance between its self-declared role as the protector of the Shia, its security priorities and the dangers of unwanted escalation. Tehran understands that its local partners cannot mount a takeover of their respective countries but hopes that in the long term they will achieve greater influence within the Shia communities and eventually over government decision-making, either institutionally or through active dissent. In addition to maintaining the ability to irritate its Gulf neighbours at low cost, Iran also aims at developing a capability to threaten the Western military presence in case of a conflict or impose a domestic cost on Gulf states for their support for increased, US-led pressure on Iran.

Notes

[1] As of early 2019, all GCC states except Saudi Arabia host US bases. This includes Oman and Qatar, two countries that are distrustful of Iranian policy but have chosen to accommodate rather than oppose their large neighbour, in part to maintain a regional balance with Saudi Arabia and out of aversion to conflict. As a result, Iran has been considerably less strident in its criticism of both countries and their hosting of US military bases, focusing on the other four Gulf states.

[2] Ali Ansari and Kasra Arabi, 'Ideology and Iran's Revolution: How 1979 Changed the World', Tony Blair Institute for Global Change, 11 February 2019, https://institute.global/insight/co-existence/ideology-and-irans-revolution-how-1979-changed-world.

[3] *Ibid.*

[4] William B. Quandt, *Saudi Arabia in the 1980s: Foreign Policy, Security, and Oil* (Washington DC: Brookings Institution Press, 1981), pp. 39–40.

[5] Joshua Teitelbaum, 'The Shiites of Saudi Arabia', *Current Trends in Islamist Ideology,* vol. 10, 2010, The Hudson Institute, p. 75, https://www.hudson.org/content/researchattachments/attachment/1288/teitelbaum.pdf.

[6] In his final State of the Union Address on 23 January 1980, President Jimmy Carter said: 'Let our position be absolutely clear: An attempt by any outside force to gain control of the Persian Gulf region will be regarded as an assault on the vital interests of the United States of America, and such an assault will be repelled by any means necessary, including military force.' Jimmy Carter, 'State of the Union Address 1980', Jimmy Carter Library, https://www.jimmycarterlibrary.gov/assets/documents/speeches/su80jec.phtml.

[7] Hasan Tariq Alhasan, 'The Role of Iran in the Failed Coup of 1981: The IFLB in Bahrain', *Middle East Journal*, vol. 65, no. 4, Autumn 2011, pp. 603–17.

[8] *Ibid.*

[9] Bruce Riedel, 'Captured: Mastermind behind the 1996 Khobar Towers attack', Brookings Institute, Markaz, Middle East Politics and Policy, 26 August 2015, https://www.brookings.edu/blog/markaz/2015/08/26/captured-mastermind-behind-the-1996-khobar-towers-attack.

[10] Toby Matthiesen, 'Hizbullah al-Hijaz: A History of the Most Radical Saudi Shia Opposition Group', *Middle East Journal*, vol. 64, no. 2, Spring 2010, pp. 179–97.

[11] Abdul-Reda Assiri, *Kuwait's Foreign Policy: City-State in World Politics* (Boulder, CO: Westview Press, 1990), pp. 100–01.

[12] James Glanz and Mark Santora, 'Iraqi Lawmaker Was Convicted in 1983 Bombings in Kuwait That Killed 5', *New York Times*, 7 February 2007, https://www.nytimes.com/2007/02/07/world/middleeast/07bomber.html.

[13] Payam Mohseni, 'The Islamic Awakening: Iran's Grand Narrative of the Arab Uprisings', *Middle East Brief*, no. 71, April 2013, https://www.brandeis.edu/crown/publications/meb/MEB71.pdf.

[14] 'Bahrain as Iran's Fourteenth Province', 17 February 2009, released by WikiLeaks as Cable 09MANAMA91_a, https://wikileaks.org/plusd/cables/09MANAMA91_a.html.

[15] 'The evidence presented to the Commission by the GoB on the involvement by the Islamic Republic of Iran in the internal affairs of Bahrain does not establish a discernable link between specific incidents that occurred in Bahrain during February and March 2011 and the Islamic Republic of Iran. Given that most of the claims made by the GoB related to allegations of intelligence operations undertaken by Iranian operatives, sources of which, by their nature, are not publicly available, the Commission has not been able to investigate or independently verify these allegations of Iranian involvement in the events of February and March 2011.' Bahrain Independent Commission of Inquiry, 'Report of the Bahrain Independent Commission of Inquiry', 10 December 2011, p. 387, http://www.bici.org.bh/BICIreportEN.pdf.

[16] Toby C. Jones and Ala'A. Shehabi, 'Bahrain's revolutionaries', *Foreign Policy,* 2 January 2012, https://foreignpolicy.com/2012/01/02/bahrains-revolutionaries.

[17] 'Wazir kharijiyat al-bahrain: al-mutafajirat al-lati arsalatha Teheran takfi li-izalat al-manama' [Bahraini foreign minister: the explosives sent by Iran are sufficient to destroy Manama], As-Shark al-Awsat, 10 December 2015, https://aawsat.com/home/article/449246/وزير-خارجية-البحرين-المتفجرات-التي-أرسلتها-طهران-تكفي-لإزالة-المنامة.

[18] Interviews with former Western intelligence officials, April and July 2019.

[19] *Ibid.*

[20] Interview with Western intelligence official, April 2019.

[21] Farishta Saeed, 'Bahrain puts groups on terrorism list

after bomb kills three police', Reuters, 4 March 2014, https://www.reuters.com/article/us-bahrain-unrest/bahrain-puts-groups-on-terrorism-list-after-bomb-kills-three-police-idUSBREA231FC20140304.

22 Michael Knights and Matthew Levitt, 'The Evolution of Shi`a Insurgency in Bahrain', Washington Institute, policy analysis, January 2018, https://www.washingtoninstitute.org/policy-analysis/view/the-evolution-of-shia-insurgency-in-bahrain.

23 UK Home Office, 'Proscribed terrorist organisations', 12 April 2019, https://assets.publishing.service.gov.uk/government/uploads/system/uploads/attachment_data/file/795457/Proscription_website.pdf; US Department of State, 'State Department Terrorist Designation of al-Ashtar Brigades (AAB)', 10 July 2018, https://www.state.gov/state-department-terrorist-designation-of-al-ashtar-brigades-aab.

24 'Bahrain's Shiite Leader Announces Move To Iran After Losing Citizenship', Radio Farda, 3 February 2019, https://en.radiofarda.com/a/bahrain-shiite-leader-qassim-moves-to-mashhad-iran/29748500.html.

25 'Bahrain struggles to police the protests', BBC News, 1 February 2012, https://www.bbc.co.uk/news/world-middle-east-17076387.

26 'Bahrain police injured in bomb attack', BBC News, 10 April 2012, https://www.bbc.co.uk/news/world-middle-east-17663642.

27 'Bahrain executes three Shia men over 2014 police killing', BBC News, 15 January 2017, https://www.bbc.com/news/world-middle-east-38627679.

28 Matthew Levitt and Michael Knights, 'Iranian-Backed Terrorism in Bahrain: Finding a Sustainable Solution', Washington Institute, policy watch, no. 2750, 11 January 2017, https://www.washingtoninstitute.org/policy-analysis/view/iranian-backed-terrorism-in-bahrain-finding-a-sustainable-solution.

29 Habib Toumi, 'Bahrain foils weapon smuggling attempt', Gulf News, 30 December 2013, https://gulfnews.com/world/gulf/bahrain/bahrain-foils-weapon-smuggling-attempt-1.1272184.

30 Michael Knights, 'Iranian EFPs in the Gulf: An Emerging Strategic Risk', Washington Institute, policy watch no. 2568, 23 February 2016, https://www.washingtoninstitute.org/policy-analysis/view/iranian-efps-in-the-gulf-an-emerging-strategic-risk.

31 Habib Toumi, 'Large explosives cache, bomb-making facility discovered in Bahrain', Gulf News, 1 October 2015, https://gulfnews.com/world/gulf/bahrain/large-explosives-cache-bomb-making-facility-discovered-in-bahrain-1.1593042.

32 Levitt and Knights, 'Iranian-Backed Terrorism in Bahrain: Finding a Sustainable Solution'.

33 'IRGC Warns Manama to Meet Bahraini People's Demands, Condemns Stripping Sheikh Qassim's Citizenship', Fars News Agency, 21 June 2016, https://en.farsnews.com/newstext.aspx?nn=13950401001458.

34 Levitt and Knights, 'Iranian-Backed Terrorism in Bahrain: Finding a Sustainable Solution'.

35 Souad Mekhennet and Joby Warrick, 'U.S. increasingly sees Iran's hand in the arming of Bahraini militants', Washington Post, 1 April 2017, https://www.washingtonpost.com/world/national-security/us-increasingly-sees-irans-hand-in-the-arming-of-bahraini-militants/2017/04/01/be5e61fc-1329-11e7-833c-503e1f6394c9_story.html.

36 'Bahrain unrest: Death toll from raid on cleric's home rises to five', BBC News, 24 May 2017, https://www.bbc.com/news/world-middle-east-40026813.

37 British government source, 2017.

38 Reem Shamseddine,'Bahrain calls pipeline blast "terrorism" linked to Iran', Reuters, 11 November 2017, https://www.reuters.com/article/us-bahrain-pipeline/bahrain-calls-pipeline-blast-terrorism-linked-to-iran-idUSKBN1DB0NW.

39 Interviews with former Western intelligence sources, April and July 2019.

40 Discussion with senior Bahraini official, 2016.

41 Interviews with former Western intelligence sources, April and July 2019.

42 Interview with a Bahrain government official, 2019; interview with US government analyst, 2019.

43 Former US intelligence official, July 2019.

44 Dennis C. Blair, 'False trade-off on Bahrain', The Hill, 12 February 2013, https://thehill.com/blogs/congress-blog/foreign-policy/282337-false-trade-off-on-bahrain.

45 Emile Hokayem, 'U.S. Has Few Options to Curb Crackdown in Bahrain', Atlantic, 19 October 2011, https://www.theatlantic.com/international/archive/2011/10/us-has-few-options-to-curb-crackdown-in-bahrain/246942.

46 Toby Craig Jones, 'Rebellion on the Saudi Periphery: Modernity, Marginalization, and the Shia Uprising of 1979', International Journal of Middle East Studies, vol. 38, no. 2, May 2006, pp. 213–33, https://www.jstor.org/stable/3879971?read-now=1&seq=7#page_scan_tab_contents.

47 'آية الله الشيخ نمرالنمردرع الجزيره يتفضل 6/4/2012' [video], YouTube, published 17 April 2012, https://youtu.be/l9C3DMGSXIU; 'ماذا قال الشيخ نمر النمر عن سوريا وبشار الأسد؟' [video], YouTube, published 8 July 2012, https://youtu.be/iJyEETz2Mlo.

48 'Sheikh Nimr al-Nimr: Saudi Arabia executes top Shia cleric', BBC News, 2 January 2016, https://www.bbc.co.uk/news/world-middle-east-35213244.

49 Frederic Wehrey, 'Eastern promises', Carnegie Endowment for International Peace, 12 February 2013, http://carnegieendowment.org/sada/?fa=50920.

50 'Meeting with controversial Shi'a Sheikh Nimr al-Nimr', 23 August 2008, released by WikiLeaks as Cable 08RIYADH1283_a, https://wikileaks.org/plusd/cables/08RIYADH1283_a.html.

51 'Iran: Saudis face "divine revenge" for executing al-Nimr',

BBC News, 3 January 2016, https://www.bbc.com/news/world-middle-east-35216694.

52 British government source, 2017.

53 'Meeting with controversial Shi'a Sheikh Nimr al-Nimr', 23 August 2008, released by WikiLeaks as Cable 08RIYADH1283_a.

54 Interview with a Kuwaiti security official, December 2017; 'Kuwait says arrests 12 convicted in 2015 Iran spy case', Reuters, 12 August 2017, https://www.reuters.com/article/us-kuwait-iran-lebanon/kuwait-says-arrests-12-convicted-in-2015-iran-spy-case-idUSKBN1AS07F.

55 Laurence Louër, 'The Limits of Iranian Influence Among Gulf Shi`a', CTC Sentinel, vol. 2, no. 5, May 2009, https://ctc.usma.edu/the-limits-of-iranian-influence-among-gulf-shia.

CONCLUSION

'The Iran of today does not have the geographical constraints of the past. Today Iran is also the PMU of Iraq, Lebanon's Hizbullah, Ansarullah in Yemen, Syria's National Front, Palestinian Islamic Jihad and Hamas. All of these have come to represent Iran and therefore Iran is no longer just us. The sayyid of the resistance declared that the region's resistance has one leader and that leader is the Supreme Leader of the Islamic Revolution of Iran.'[1]

Ayatollah Ahmad Alam ol-Hoda, Supreme Leader's Representative in Khorasan Razavi Province, 2019

Iran's networks of influence have become its way of war. It rests on a developed doctrine, and a sophisticated capability within the Islamic Revolutionary Guard Corps (IRGC) Quds Force, for conducting remote warfare through third parties in foreign jurisdictions. This has high strategic value for Iran. It enables Iran to raise costs for its adversaries at low cost to itself. It is flexible, low risk and sustainable but allows Iran to maintain a remote, defensive cordon and to project military and cultural influence deep into target countries. It has deep roots in the ideology and war-fighting experiences of the Iranian regime. But its development has been accelerated, its effectiveness enhanced and its resilience deepened by extensive deployments in varying configuration across theatres of conflict in the Middle East, in particular Syria and Iraq.

Three developments in Iran's networks of influence have been particularly significant. Firstly, Hizbullah's autonomous capability for conducting asymmetric and conventional campaigns outside Lebanon has matured, making it an expeditionary force in its own right. Secondly, Iran has developed a 'whole-of-theatre' approach, making use of different territories and domains to respond to adversaries, and deploying personnel and expertise across national boundaries. Thirdly, Hizbullah and other groups serve as an international reserve of combat-hardened manpower loyal to the IRGC Quds Force, as well as penetrating and subordinating state structures and authorities in Lebanon, Syria and Iraq.

The network has weaknesses and risks. It is extended; partners cannot always be controlled; and Arab communities are resistant to Iranian hegemony. Hizbullah remains the model of a group that has been accepted in its host state and has changed the nature of the polity. However, this will be difficult for Iran to emulate elsewhere and if it fails to do so, this will pose a strategic long-term risk to the capability. Regional security forces and external actors will also seek to degrade Iran's networks, as they apprehend more clearly the nature and scale of the threat.

That said, the capability gives Iran a greater fitness than its adversaries to fight in complex and remote battlespaces. It will fight through third parties, both Shia and non-Shia, for ideological and logistical reasons; they are Iran's most natural and easily deployed response to external threat. This doctrine is unlikely to change until the regime itself does and it will continue to draw strength from successful deployments, the coalition of state and non-state allies within which it is now placed, and broader, non-sectarian opposition to the United States in the Middle East.

Neither international nor domestic pressure is currently sufficient to force the regime to retrench.

Iran will continue to see its network capability as the most efficient and effective way of confronting and harming its principal regional adversaries, Israel and Saudi Arabia, and of signalling intent to the US. It is too woven into the ideology of the regime and of too high a practical value for it to be readily abandoned.

Power projection through partners: a strategic capability

From the war which followed the Iranian Revolution and its experience in foreign theatres in which it has since intervened, the regime has developed a way of war which blends both ideology and pragmatism, self-reliance and the use of third parties, conservatism and innovation. The doctrine has as its defining and avowed purpose the defence of the Islamic Revolution and by extension Shia communities, and specifically Shia shrines, outside Iran. But what was originally a defensive doctrine has evolved into a powerful expeditionary capability.

Internationally isolated, Iran has formed strategic relationships with non-state actors. Iran remained connected to and active in the Muslim world – particularly the Middle East, where the Shia communities and distribution of shrines provided a natural network – despite a repressive security regime which imposed long-term restrictions on inward visits and travel abroad. Its military and defence doctrine transformed this connectivity into an asset. It became a vector for projecting Iranian force (through terrorism or subversion), a source of intelligence and influence, and a means of finding allies who shared broad objectives and were prepared to play by Iran's rules.

The design and implementation of Iran's third-party doctrine were shaped by survival imperatives for the regime: to minimise Iranian casualties or attacks on its territory, while being able to inflict harm on its regional adversaries in a deniable manner. Iran and its partners have used strikingly overt means (such as deployments in battle formations in Syria and Iraq beneath recognisable flags) and covert means, including cyber attacks on Saudi Arabia and terrorism within Gulf states. But the principles governing the deployment of all capabilities have been the same: most notably to avoid escalation and reprisal which would threaten the survival of the regime. Although this doctrine has become far from defensive in its implementation, the capability which Iran has developed to fight through third parties has become its weapon of choice.

In the decades which followed the revolution, Iran developed the theology and military doctrine of asymmetry. Whilst at home the state security and defence machinery enjoyed and used its superior force to control and intimidate, overseas Iran projected a narrative appealing emotively to Shia minorities. It sought partnerships with groups who were ideologically aligned through common Shia beliefs, or whose cause aligned with the regime's strategic objectives. The critical, early adoption of the Palestinian cause was an attempt both to establish a broader non-sectarian base of support for the regime in Arab states and to put direct pressure on its long-standing adversaries, the US and Israel.

In Lebanon, and to a lesser extent the Gulf, Iran intervened ostensibly to protect a Shia minority from a strong Sunni or Christian state. Further afield, Iran has supported resistance movements who were by definition fighting against superior forces. Resistance became a cardinal principle in Iranian activism. The act of resistance was dignified with a theological context and extended, in an early example of Iranian strategic

196   CONCLUSION

ecumenism, beyond the Shia community to embrace Sunni (Palestinian) and even secular organisations (such as the Irish Republican Army). Resistance reinforced the doctrine of asymmetry. It became almost axiomatic for the regime that the dispossessed, the disenfranchised or the secessionist was a natural affiliate, whatever the political cause. Yet from its inception, the Quds Force saw the fostering and mobilisation of Shia groups as its primary purpose and strategic base. This was intimately tied to the perception of the Islamic Revolution as the historic opportunity to reverse the tradition of Shia subservience and marginalisation in the Arab world.

Revolutionary Iran failed to form any meaningful relationships with states. It deliberately did not appropriate the military apparatus and doctrine of the deposed regime, partly because US hostility made it impossible to maintain the largely Western-supplied inventory and partly because the army (Artesh) was distrusted and had been decimated by purges. Conventional military doctrine did not suit the revolution's early need to create its own defining structures and doctrines. Iran had not, for example, until the civil war in Syria, experienced war fighting as a member of a coalition, nor had it participated in a strategic relationship or developed interdependent weapons or intelligence systems. It remained isolated and insular as a military power with the exception of accessing missiles and warheads from North Korea, another pariah state, an exception which emphasised Iran's isolation.

Iran thus appropriated and redirected elements of the Shia community abroad. That community has always been complex and fractured, and many Shia Muslims had rejected Iran's hegemony or had already reached a satisfactory modus vivendi with non-Shia rulers (as in Kuwait). Lines of loyalty ran along theological rather than national axes. Shia communities were loyal primarily to their spiritual sources of emulation (*marja al-taqlid*), which could be in Iraq or Lebanon rather than in Iran. Over time, Iran learned not to try to impose Iranian *Marja'iyya* on Shia communities but to work with the multiple loyalties this traditional feature of Shia society created. In Iraq and the Gulf states, this is still an effective brake on the extent of Iranian influence and control of Shia communities.

The Iranian regime's instrumentalisation of Shia in other states has been along lines of strategic and ideological convergence which do not map automatically onto lines of loyalty to ayatollahs. In Iraq, communities loyal to Ayatollah Sistani and Sadrist ayatollahs did not automatically succumb to Iranian influence; in some instances, they opposed it. The regime has blended elements of ideological affinity, strategic convergence, political expediency and transactional value in all of its relationships with groups beyond its borders. This has resulted in an unusually wide range of relationships and a pragmatic approach to the development of relationships from ephemeral, task-based engagement (as in Syria and Iraq) to long-term strategic ambitions (as with Lebanese Hizbullah).

Iran has neither succeeded in exporting its revolution to the wider Shia and Muslim community as the early revolution pledged, nor established absolute hegemony which would allow it to command and control their resources. But it has succeeded in appropriating Shia iconography, and in mobilising those willing, or vulnerable, to organise and redefine what it means to be Shia. It has achieved the influence and authority to mobilise Shia opinion and in some cases personnel behind its agenda. This confederation of actors is not sustained by any treaty or constitution. Instead, Tehran relies on appeals to shared enemies and cultural affinities, supplemented by material assistance.

The creation of the Popular Mobilisation Units (PMU, or *al-Hashd al-Shaabi*) in Iraq is only the most recent example of Iran using the concept and practice of mobilisation as a means of achieving a military objective. In its early days, the Islamic Revolution depended for its legitimacy upon the breadth of popular support not only in Iran but among the wider Shia community. Mass mobilisation met the immediate military manpower needs generated by high-casualty warfare against Iraq, but it also tied the Iranian populace to the revolution. It replaced expertise lost by the purging of the Shah's officer class and made up for lack of skills and weapons systems through troop numbers. Although Iran's strategy is now geared to avoid mass-casualty warfare, conscription has remained for other social and ideological reasons. The utility of the concept of mobilisation to Iran overseas was evidenced in the intimate role the Quds Force played in raising the PMU. As an irregular and mass movement, fighting against an existential threat (the Islamic State, otherwise known as ISIS or ISIL) across the sectarian divide, the PMU was the Quds Force's ideal partner. But as those defining features changed, the partner became less ideal. As a regular, non-mass movement, formally if not in practice integrated into the Iraqi government and seeking a role in politics, it poses significant challenges for the Quds Force. The integration of the PMU, as the Iraqi government has long intended, could pose a dilemma to Iran: whether to buttress the government or reinforce its client. Tehran's attachment to irregular, mass mobilisation complicates this question.

Similarly, the first strategy of the Quds Force in Syria was to raise a force through mass mobilisation similar to the Basij. Although this failed, it was an indication of the value and usefulness of the concept. Its successor, the Syrian Local Defence Forces, still relied on mobilisation but is located inside rather than outside the Syrian state structures. It was also indicative of the Quds Force's operational pragmatism; having tried and failed to foster an independent, effective partner, it settled for one that was less independent, but nevertheless effective.

In locations far from the Middle East battlefields, Tehran succeeded in recruiting Shia elements (in Afghanistan and Pakistan) willing to fight in Syria and Iraq. Iranian recruitment techniques met local discontent and sectarian concerns. Shia iconography – in particular the motivating reverence felt for shrines – has provided a major strand in the recruitment narrative and offered recruits a clear cause and objective. Many of those recruited beyond Syria and Iraq were deployed to defend Shia shrines in Syria. As with Sunni jihadis recruited into ISIS, it also offered a chance to escape local circumstances where Shia may be subject to persecution, and provided a sense of purpose and adventure to (often unemployed) young Shia men. Their susceptibility to recruitment and Iran's determination to exploit them will persist where Shia are marginalised or perceive themselves to be. In countries where that is not the case (like Kuwait), Iran can make fewer inroads.

Transnational Shia networks have over time represented both a survival mechanism and a strategic tool for political and economic ends. For Iran, they were viewed as a potential defensive cordon, pushing the first line of defence beyond Iranian territory. They subsequently became a source of manpower, influence and intelligence.

But the Shia community beyond Iran is more than a diaspora bound by an ethnic or sectarian identity. The existence of the Islamic Republic of Iran has radically redefined Shia identity. This is a source of regret for many more moderate and liberal Shia, but Iran has exploited its position as the most populous, aggressive and homogenous Shia state to inspire Shia from other countries. Wherever possible, Iran recruits foreign nationals voluntarily rather than through coercion – although it has exploited Afghan refugees. It has done so by playing on local grievances, sectarian fears and the spiritual authority of the Supreme Leader. Hizbullah has, in parallel, played a major role in fostering Arab insurgent groups – in particular the Houthis. Neither Iran nor Hizbullah has so far shown ambition to establish secessionist or autonomous Shia enclaves in other jurisdictions. However, the footholds they have established in countries at war (Yemen and Syria) leave them well placed to do so, whether formally (via peace agreements) or de facto.

Hizbullah's expeditionary capability: the revolution's arm in the Arab world

Iran's most emphatic strategic achievement beyond its own frontiers has been the establishment of a sympathetic politico-military entity in Lebanon now larger and more powerful than its host: Hizbullah. Conditions at the time of its inception favoured Iran: the central government was weak and so too the rule of law; there was a defined and established Shia community; and in Hafez al-Assad's Syria, there was a strong local patron. Iran was additionally served by the proximity of Israel, which provided a focus of hostility, an impetus to militarisation and an embodiment of the unfavourable asymmetry of power which defines resistance. Yet despite the success of Hizbullah, it has not been replicable elsewhere because the local conditions and circumstances are less propitious, and Iran has not invested sufficient resources to overcome those hurdles. Instead, in each theatre Iran has adapted its working methods and strategic ambition. Iran's and Hizbullah's presence in other countries has been, and will remain, highly adaptive. The demonstrated ambition is to achieve a level of influence similar to that in Lebanon, but thus far without attempting to build Hizbullah-like entities. Whether it might seek to do so is a question of strategic significance.

In Iraq and Syria, Tehran has so far worked pragmatically with and through governments, but that does not preclude the possibility that it might seek to build a power base beyond the state if the government of either country is further weakened or tilts against Iran. In Yemen, Iran and Hizbullah have so far been unwilling to build beyond their current discreet presence. This has enabled them to maintain deniability (however implausible that may be given the evidence). However, this does not rule out Iran and Hizbullah maintaining a relationship with the Houthis such that they retain, through them, a permanent presence in northern Yemen. Iran will not surrender lightly the strategic advantage over Saudi Arabia conferred by the Houthis' ability to target Saudi Arabia directly with ballistic missiles. Similarly, the partnership gives them reach into the Bab al-Mandeb Strait and a base from which to operate into Saudi Arabia, either through paramilitary personnel or uninhabited aerial vehicles (UAVs), while maintaining plausible deniability. But neither the Houthis nor the Shia of Saudi Arabia's Eastern Province or elsewhere in the Gulf have the same potential for coalescence into a powerful political entity as did Hizbullah in Lebanon in the 1980s. Neither do they have religious leaders of sufficient stature or the proximity to Israel which would make them as attractive and secure an investment as Hizbullah.

Over the course of the Syrian conflict, Hizbullah, already a partner of Iran enjoying a special status, matured from a powerful but local militia into a fighting force capable of deploying beyond its borders. Hizbullah showed itself, along with the Iranians, capable of conducting kinetic operations within a complex coalition comprising systems and capabilities as diverse as those of the Russian Armed Forces and local militias. Hizbullah's expeditionary land capability is a new force in the region. If the conditions for deployment are right, it is a force with a ready advantage over conventional, including joint, forces in that it has recent experience of combat, a regional network of supporters and enablers, and a proven capability to fight in complex theatres.

Hizbullah has greater traction in the Arab world, and can deploy more easily, because of its Arab ethnicity and reputation as a successful fighting force that confronts Israel. It has the potential to be more widely and effectively deployed in the Islamic world than Iranian forces. This suits the Iranian objective of limiting the profile of its own intervention, which risks reaction from the international community and Arab populations resistant to Iranian influence. More cynically, Iran is also prepared for Hizbullah and other partners to suffer higher casualty rates – as in Syria – than the Iranian regime would risk with its own troops.

Hizbullah has become the most effective Shia fighting force and organiser of fighting Shia in the Arab world. Its leadership role is likely to become more pronounced as Iran faces limitations on its own ability to project force and the character of conflict continues to be that in which Hizbullah is expert: predominantly asymmetric and urban but with conventional phases and partners. Moreover, for potential future conflicts in which Iran or Hizbullah

may seek to intervene, Hizbullah compares favourably with sovereign armed forces of Arab states for its competence and conduct in the field. Its reputation is a material asset. In the absence of a credible process to resolve the future of the Palestinians and with the wider demographic problem in the Arab world, the possibility exists that Hizbullah will broaden its franchise to include Sunna. Gulf states already regard Hizbullah as a hostile and menacing entity. They will be further unnerved if Hizbullah, on the back of its performance in Syria, makes inroads into the Sunni community. It has shown itself pragmatic in this regard, entering into political alliances with Lebanese Christians and working with Hamas in Gaza.

The question is whether Hizbullah now seeks to extend the principle of mobilisation beyond sectarian limits. Both current Hizbullah Secretary-General Hassan Nasrallah and consecutive Iranian leadership figures have been careful to use inclusive language that appeals to all Muslims, not just to Shia. The most vitriolic parts of Nasrallah's invectives against Israel straddle the sectarian divide. So too does the rhetoric of Iranian Supreme Leader Ali Khamenei on defiance of the US. While fear of Iran is widespread in the Gulf states and part of the Levant, it falls off markedly further west in the Arab world. Elsewhere in the Levant and North Africa, Iran hardly features as a threat compared to Israel or the US. Thus the battle lines in the 'sectarian' conflict are not clearly drawn between Iran and the Shia satellites on the one side and Saudi Arabia, the US and the Sunna on the other. Lines of loyalty across the Arab world may well be as complex as they have proved in the Levant, both in politics and on the battlefield. In those circumstances an actor with a defined identity, established reputation and a ready capability is at a distinctive advantage.

In the course of its expeditionary warfare in Iraq, Syria and Yemen, Hizbullah has displayed its ability to mobilise foreign non-Lebanese forces into military action. This has become a source of pride – in 2017, Nasrallah boasted of the Muslim forces which would come to Hizbullah's aid if attacked by Israel – and one which Hizbullah has growing confidence it can deliver following experiences in Syria and Iraq. Moreover, it also has the power to leverage through the Arabic language and its status as the front-line resistance to Israel a wider diaspora than the Iranians. Hizbullah has, in short, both cause and capability to rally support beyond its borders. It has become the Islamic Revolution's arm in the Arab world.

As an ideological twin, and a wholly indigenised, competent fighting force, Hizbullah is a model partner for Iran. Iran has preferred to rely on Hizbullah, rather than deploy it as a Trojan horse through which to pursue territorial annexation: it has avoided directly seizing power in foreign countries. This has been consistent with the regime's status as an idiosyncratic outsider to the international system. There are also traces in this non-territorial strategy of the traditional Shia disavowal of secular states and borders which conveniently leaves the regime free to redefine over whom, under *Velayat-e Faqih*, it has a right to exercise power, require loyalty and offer patronage. It has been careful not to define this but in times of heightened tension is quick to speak on behalf of the wider community in terms that imply a feudal due. But although taking sovereign territory has not so far been its objective, Iran has worked consistently to secure lines of communication and 'ink spots' of direct influence (mostly around shrines) beyond its borders. Most notably, it has secured through Syria a land corridor from the Iraqi border to Lebanon which it is protecting through local forces. Similarly, it has invested in the protection of shrines in Syria, and to an extent in Iraq, as enclaves of Iranian state power.

Despite an overarching doctrine, the overall objective of the Iranian way of war is less clearly defined. Iran has proved pragmatic and opportunistic in the application of its capabilities, modulating commitments to the point where it has appeared ready to settle for an inconclusive result. Denying a state-level adversary victory counts as success. Nor is there a single, desired, political end-state or security structure detailed in a treaty. Hizbullah is a product of local circumstances as much as Iranian strategic design. What Iran seeks in Yemen remains to be seen. In Iraq it has achieved a high degree of state penetration, but there is no entity which resembles Hizbullah.

Iran's enemies – and Saudi Arabia in particular – see on Tehran's part a clear intent to encircle. There is some truth in this: Iran is intent on preserving leverage through sub-state groups over its principal regional adversaries, Saudi Arabia and Israel. The missile attacks on Saudi soil launched by the Houthis have given Iran the ability to respond to pressure by menacing Saudi Arabia from the south. To deliver and maintain a ring of uniformly and wholly pro-Iranian states is beyond Tehran's diplomatic and military capacity. What it can achieve is a string of entities of varied shape and strength loosely harnessed to its strategic priorities.

The entities through which Iran can most effectively advance its objectives are in the Middle East. But Iran is well placed to exploit Shia communities in a second defensive circle at greater remove. Beyond the Arab world, Iran's most natural leverage is in the large Shia populations of Pakistan and Afghanistan. So far, Iran has used these as sources of manpower for conflicts in other theatres rather than as bridgeheads for militant activity within those countries. But authorities in both countries are concerned about Iran's ties to political groups and the capabilities Iran has gained through the cadres of Shia it has trained and deployed to fight in Syria. In Pakistan, Iran has links to separatist Baluch and Sindhi groups, including the twice-banned Tahrik-e-Jafaria Pakistan (TJP). In the case of TJP, the absolute fealty pledged by its Pakistani leadership to Khamenei is striking. The emergence of pro-Iranian Shia fighters and political groups has heightened tensions and raised the possibility of clashes with Sunni groups whose origins go back to the violently anti-Shia groups. But any aspirations on the part of the Quds Force or indigenous groups to establish a Shia, sub-state entity would meet with fierce resistance from the Pakistani military and local anti-Shia groups. Iran and its local partners have not pushed for this but have generally calibrated their activities and manifestos so as to avoid provoking a damaging reaction. What they have misjudged, and may continue to do so in the fervid sectarian atmosphere of Pakistani politics, is their affiliate's use of violence and terrorism. That may be a failing locally or centrally in Tehran. But that may not matter for Iran, which will be implicated regardless: TJP has claimed that it takes its guidance from Tehran.

In Afghanistan, Iran continues primarily to exercise its influence through its cultural affinity with the Hazara, but the political relationship is complicated by Iran's sponsorship of elements of the Taliban – in itself a powerful example of Iran extending its influence beyond its natural sphere. However, Iran's potential local partner in Afghanistan is the refugee community from which the Quds Force raised a large contingent (estimates range up to 15,000 men) to fight in Syria as the Liwa Fatemiyoun. This hard core of ideologically affiliated fighters can be deployed either in defence of Shia and Hazara interests (one-third of the Fatemiyoun were Hazara), or in other theatres.

Afghan authorities face the ongoing challenge of preventing the further marginalisation of the Hazara which will only enhance Iranian influence. The potential force at Iran's disposal inside Afghanistan is not enough to establish a grouping resembling Hizbullah but it is enough to mount asymmetric attacks. It is noteworthy that Iran has developed a strong cultural presence in northern and western Afghanistan but has not attempted to create a militarised, politically independent entity. Both Afghanistan and Pakistan have traditionally been lower priorities for Iran than the eastern Arab world, which is reflected in the allocation of effort (for example, in visits of senior Quds Force personnel). But in both countries strategies adapted to local sectarian politics are likely to generate for Iran opportunities to deepen its influence.

Iran potentially has, therefore, some presence in various countries across South Asia which it can use for either political or militia activity. The potential for unpredictable instability creates a Shia 'ring of fire' which is a strategic asset for Iran. While widely variable in the degree of direction it takes from Tehran, it would, if required, offer some degree of support if Iran faced an existential threat.

A capability held and deployed at risk

The IRGC- and Hizbullah-backed militias in Iraq dramatically expanded their partner network in the country to defeat ISIS but, rhetoric aside, there was no serious attempt to convert this into a militarily significant escalation against Israel. The deployments of personnel and missiles in Syria and the subsequent strikes on the Golan Heights led to a demonstration of Israeli firepower sufficient to deter Iran from any escalation. Instead, Tehran sought to capitalise on its deployments and missile launches to confirm its status as the state which heads the resistance. But Hizbullah, which mans the military front line with Israel, may not share the same calculation.

Tehran is wary of the risk that any of its partners would hazard a conflict in which Iran loses face, suffers an attack on its territory or sustains mass casualties. A major concern for the Quds Force, which manages relations with Iran's partners, is to ensure that the partners respect those red lines. This has not always been easy, because some partners lack Iran's finely tuned sense of how to calibrate attacks to avoid a harsh response. The Houthis, for instance, attacked targets in Saudi Arabia on their own initiative and reportedly against Iranian wishes. Hizbullah famously triggered a war with Israel in 2006 which Iran did not want as it feared fatal damage, or indeed the annihilation, of its most valuable partner. Hizbullah's value to Iran and the remarkable intimacy of their relationship were illustrated by Soleimani himself. In a 2019 interview, he revealed that he was present and active in the Hizbullah command room throughout the war alongside Hassan Nasrallah and Imad Mughniyah, his top military commander.[2]

The risk for Iran of local partners moving unbidden beyond its red lines will persist. This is an inherent part of relationships between a distant patron and groups fighting in a local, intense conflict. Local agendas will dominate in times of tension, as they did in Lebanon and Yemen. Conversely, there will be times when a partner refuses to act with sufficient vigour for Iran's liking. For instance, they may be disinclined to mount an operation for which they will suffer the retaliation, as is sometimes the case with Hizbullah. The prospect may increase in situations where external pressure on Iran mounts, changing the power relationship between Iran and its proxies in favour of the latter.

Iran has ways of managing partners inclined to do too much or too little. Its presence in-country gives Iran channels of real-time influence on decision-making and an understanding of when the risks of divergence are greatest. Quds Force and Hizbullah advisers remain in Yemen and Iraq and are close to the command structure of the groups and militias they support. Ultimately, partners know that without Iranian support and patronage they would be greatly diminished.

Iranian influence versus national identities

Iran's extension of its influence has not gone wholly unchecked by local Shia communities. In Iraq, Iranian influence has chafed against nationalism as witnessed in the attacks on the Iranian consulate in Basra in September 2018 by a Shia population once considered comfortable in its pro-Iranian orientation. Muqtada al-Sadr's career has typified the tension between Iraqi Shia nationalism and Iranian influence, and his exploitation of it. Early in his career he was backed by Iran but later he stood against it and its proxy, Hadi al-Ameri. This is the latest iteration of the historic rivalry between Iraq and Iran for authority over the Shia of Iraq. The leaders of Shia factions themselves are struggling to find a formula which reconciles Iranian ideological influence and a measure of dependency on the one hand, and Iraqi nationalism on the other: an 'Iraqi Khomeinism'. In the long term, a failure to indigenise Iranian ideology in Iraq could cost Tehran its influence.

Iran has not sought to force the template of Hizbullah on its other regional partners. But there is one significant sense in which Hizbullah is the model: it is an indigenous and self-governing entity, albeit one that relies on Iran for financial support and its strategic parameters. For Iran, this is close to ideal. There is a high degree of ideological alignment, Hizbullah has compatible military capabilities and it has a dominant position in its host state, making it a model of political acceptance. This is most manifest in Hizbullah's appropriation of the national voice: protestations of Lebanese patriotism and identity are a recurring meme in Nasrallah's rhetoric. Mainly this concerns resistance to Israel, but more recently Nasrallah sought to speak for the nation in rebutting Saudi efforts to replace Lebanon's prime minister in 2017. Hizbullah's allies won more seats in the subsequent parliamentary elections.

Affirming a nationalist identity is a challenge in itself for Shia, as they must define themselves as separate from Iran and in a manner that does not exclude the Sunni community. Some pro-Iranian groups in Iraq have avoided being drawn into conflicts with local Sunni populations. Yet by exploiting sectarian identity, Iran has reinforced it and made more complicated the search for an inclusive political formula. Iran cannot render its partners able to exercise power beyond the confines of the sectarian entity. Whilst it can teach and equip them to resist, it will not train them how to rule a multi-confessional country.

Similarly, Iran's practice of supporting multiple armed groups in one country is effective when there is a clear, uniting enemy such as ISIS in Iraq. The policy is harder to sustain where there is no enemy or several. In such cases, Iran must work hard to manage rivalries and it risks having disgruntled partners or occasionally losing a client. In Iraq, for instance, Agha Eghbali played a successful mediating role in disputes between factions in Tuz. More of this mediation may be required in complex theatres such as Syria and Iraq. It is clear from the course of domestic politics in Iraq that in any post-conflict settlement in Syria, Iran will be an active power broker both in defence of its own interests and as a mediator between the proliferation of actors it has sponsored.

There is also a tension between the partner's local agenda and ideology, and that of Iran. The Houthis are committed to resisting Saudi influence over their territory and political fate; they are not invested in Iran's regional agenda or the fate of the Iranian Revolution. This limits the potential of the relationship beyond Yemen. Nevertheless, the Houthis are valuable for Iran as they fight Saudi forces in Yemen and attack targets within Saudi Arabia. This is a transactional partnership with strategic value.

The revolutionary fervour which translated the concept of clerical authority, *Velayat-e Faqih*, into the institutions of government in Iran is no longer sufficiently strong to enable its export. For Iran's partners operating in states where Arab influences and agendas are dominant and Western influences often strong, *Velayat-e Faqih* is manifestly not a viable form of government nor a desirable end-state. It does not have a compelling record of delivery. It will disenfranchise and alienate too large a sector of the population. Although the concept was conceived by Iraqi theologians, its practical manifestation is still too peculiarly Iranian to be accepted elsewhere. The only exception would be territories with cohesive and belligerent Shia monocultures. In Lebanon, Hizbullah has entered into power-sharing arrangements with groups who could never accept *Velayat-e Faqih*. So while it has considerable utility within Iran, its usefulness as a mobilising and organising principle beyond its borders is limited.

Iran's expansion of its influence outside sympathetic jurisdictions has been opposed. The work of local security services against pro-Iranian and pro-Hizbullah operational cells over the past decade has also created a hostile environment for the Quds Force. Similarly, political and social developments – and in some cases a long-standing distrust of Iranian influence – have stymied Iran. In Bahrain, the tempo of violence and rhetoric has reduced after 2018. Since then, Bahrain has implemented reforms to improve the situation of lower-income groups and give young offenders community service rather than prison terms. These and other measures may have diminished the strength of the motivating narrative of exclusion, on which the Quds Force relies. Possibly too, Iran has responded by directing fewer resources towards Bahrain. However, Iran may perceive that Bahrain is a useful location as it seeks to respond to the US policy of 'maximum pressure'. It is one of a few locations where the IRGC can act through indigenous partners, and where there are US targets in-country.

In seeking entry to countries of strategic interest, Iran will continue to be reliant on excluded minorities or parties at war who have an immediate need for material support. It will not be able to appropriate groupings more widely or penetrate more deeply into Arab polities. While the tide of conflict is in its favour, its ideological appeal is limited. This restricts the strategic value of the relationships.

The future: consolidate, expand or rehabilitate?

Iran is most likely to continue to deploy its capability at near-current levels, unless either it is pushed back by concerted international activity – including critically from the countries in which it is most active – or domestic pressures cause it to retrench. Neither of these seem likely.

It is similarly unlikely that Iran will surrender or curtail its network to achieve international rehabilitation. The regime leverages its difference to attract minorities and the disenfranchised beyond its borders. As an outsider, it arrogates to itself the power to license and proscribe behaviour. It can sanction and legitimise otherwise unlawful activity, such as terrorism, which other states seeking the benefits of inclusion in the international order cannot. Its charisma in the eyes of its partners derives from its survival as an outlaw and alternative. While rehabilitation and inclusion in the international order would have economic benefits, it would require constraints to be placed on its remote warfare capability and the mission of the Quds Force. If this were not explicitly a condition for rehabilitation, it would certainly be incompatible with it. Put simply, Iran and the Quds Force cannot be both revolutionary and part of the international order. This must have been an element of the dispute between Foreign Minister Mohammad Javad Zarif and Quds Force Commander Qasem Soleimani over the possibility of international rehabilitation through the Joint Comprehensive Plan of Action (JCPOA).

The status which Iran enjoys by virtue of being an anti-establishment power is a strong disincentive to detente, certainly among the military and clerical leadership. This has added significance in a time of weakening cohesion within the international community and of rising anti-establishment activity in Eurasia and Latin America. In a multipolar order, there is increasing space for Iran to forge partnerships with movements and parties challenging the international system. At the state level, Iran has developed a workable relationship with Russia and Turkey, both challenger states, despite the differences between the three. It maintains relationships with Nicolás Maduro in Venezuela and Kim Jong-un in North Korea. Below the state level, Iran has so far restricted its network to groups in its near abroad. But that may change: there is, for example, a growing pro-Iran Shia community in Nigeria. With a successful formula for calibrated intervention which is adaptive to local circumstances, Iran is well placed to venture further afield either as asymmetric retaliation for hostile acts or to bolster its credentials as an alternative patron and power centre. The cost of doing so is modest. The benefits, manifest in widening Iran's defensive cordon and broadening its options to respond to threats or aggression, would represent a good return on investment.

Indeed, the dividends Iran has reaped from proxy warfare have so far outweighed the risks and costs. Iran has not been punished or contained by the international community for the development and projection of this capability as it has for the development of its nuclear capability. Former US secretary of defense James Mattis reportedly commented that the IRGC commander 'has every reason to believe that Iran is the rising power in the region … We've never dealt him a body blow.' Iran has met resistance and retribution when it has deployed its capability offensively outside established tolerances (most notably from Israel), but that has not arrested its further development.

Even if other states had been more effective in checking and deterring Iran, there are internal imperatives that promote overseas projection. Hardliners are committed to the strategy and it is integral to Iran's claims for regional hegemony. Past successes and current narratives sustain the approach. Moreover, it is affordable, politically and financially. With the exception of Hizbullah, Iran is not committed to large-scale payments to its partners in the region. It has accepted responsibility for the welfare of recruits from Afghanistan and Pakistan whom it has trained and deployed, and in the case of those killed, for their relatives. As economic sanctions reduce revenues for the government and the IRGC, it is possible that Iran will reduce funding for some partners. Yet that does not necessarily mean that relationships will deteriorate or that security threats will diminish. The degree of fealty which groups have sworn to Iran and the person of the Supreme Leader is reminiscent of the Bay'a sworn to Osama bin Laden by Sunni jihadis. It suggests that the motive for such groups in working with Iran is not primarily financial. Some groups will adapt their operations if financial support decreases. It is conceivable that the network could become in some ways more cohesive under financial pressure, which will amplify the patron's narrative of persecution.

In short, Iran will be able to take a 'whole-of-theatre' approach in the face of mounting external pressure, using capabilities and partners in specific theatres to respond to threats against the homeland. It will also seek to retain escalation dominance, demonstrate capabilities and give substance to its threats. It will strive to keep this within Western tolerances to avoid a damaging response it cannot manage. It probably feels it can now judge those tolerances with confidence. Its attacks on Gulf shipping and Saudi oil infrastructure in 2019 vindicated such confidence. However, Iran has not succumbed to hubris by moving beyond the red lines it set out of self-preservation.

In practice, we are likely to see Iran pursue several goals. Firstly, it will seek to maintain influence in Syria, Iraq and Yemen as conflicts in those states wind down. It is probable that Tehran will seek to insert proxy leaders into positions of political and security authority in order to protect Iran's interests and deflect approaches from regional or Western powers. This will be contested by Gulf and Western states.

Secondly, Iran is likely to work to ensure political and economic stability in those territories in which it has gained influence. Doing so will cement its partners' security and Iran's local reputation. It will also benefit the IRGC-connected businesses operating in these countries and allow Tehran to recoup some of its expenditure during the conflicts. In Iraq, Tehran has already sought to consolidate its commercial influence through agreements on oil, trade and healthcare projects. Iran also exports gas and electricity to Iraq, which provides hard currency and economic influence. In Syria, Tehran has signed agreements to operate as a mobile-telephone service provider, as well as to restore a portion of the Syrian power grid. It hopes also to build an oil refinery, expand phosphate production and possibly construct a new port.

Thirdly, Tehran might seek to exploit its new territorial reach with a possible deployment of new militia partners to other theatres. Although hundreds of Israeli airstrikes have prevented Iran from building a force on Israel's border with Syria or expanding its missile transfers to Hizbullah, these strikes do not yet seem to be sufficient to deter Quds Force ambitions in Syria. The governments of Afghanistan and Pakistan may be considering how they would respond to the Quds Force using the Fatemiyoun and Zainabiyoun, respectively, in their countries.

Finally, Tehran will probably maintain a close relationship with Russia, which is a powerful diplomatic and military partner. This is despite Tehran's frustration at the growth of the Moscow–Riyadh relationship or their competition for influence inside Syria. Iran's military budget is small compared with those of its neighbours, yet it needs to upgrade its air-

defence and combat and transport aircraft. Russia is its supplier of choice.

External events could encourage Iran to cease expanding its network, and perhaps even to scale it back. An improvement in local conditions for Shia communities in states of interest for Iran, for instance through political reforms, would weaken local demand for Iranian support and alter Tehran's calculations. Also, if Iran were to overreach and be repelled by the government of a friendly power, this would be a damaging blow to the prestige of the Quds Force and to Iran's reputation as a revolutionary, non-colonial power. That said, it would take more than the persistent attempts by the government of Iraq to bring the PMU under its formal control to prompt a strategic rethink in Tehran. A third potential trigger would be an economic downturn in Iran sufficient to persuade the Supreme Leader of the need to sacrifice some limited external reach in return for economic or political support – although the scope for such exchange is limited in the context of existing US sanctions. Finally, personnel changes in Tehran, either in the IRGC or the Supreme Leader himself, could test the relationships with partners.

Iran's strategy will continue to focus on its two principal regional adversaries, Israel and Saudi Arabia. It will seek to injure them while avoiding a climactic confrontation. Its best means of doing so is through the continued development of its network of partners. Israel's consistently firm approach to dealing with aggression by Iran and Hizbullah has taught Tehran to be cautious about escalation. Hizbullah, however, may take a different view and if it were to attack Israel at a moment when a hawkish US administration were looking for a *casus belli*, the result could be catastrophic for Iran, Hizbullah and their relationship.

Saudi Arabia and Iran are locked in an ideological and sectarian struggle, largely eschewing direct confrontation in favour of indirect efforts to injure and weaken each other. Since its foundation, the involvement of the Quds Force in Saudi Arabia has been intermittent, ranging between intelligence collection through to (most recently) drone attacks on Saudi infrastructure. Iran has struggled to co-opt a sufficiently large body of the Saudi Shia population to its revolutionary cause, who orientate spiritually to Iraqi *Marja'iyya* and who are not, in the main, supporters of *Velayat-e Faqih*. Serious unrest among Shia in Saudi Arabia would undoubtedly offer an attractive opportunity for the Quds Force to intervene. However, that is not likely in the short term. A more plausible scenario is the escalation of tensions between the two countries, with Iran gradually encroaching on Saudi security through stand-off, asymmetric attacks. The Quds Force has recently shown its capability and appetite for this through drone and sabotage attacks on shipping in the Gulf of Oman. It could expand such attacks without the need to develop a sympathetic local militia or political grouping. All it would need is an ability to collect intelligence and, in some cases, to gain physical access to targets. It is likely that the Quds Force has already developed these capabilities.

Attacks originating within Saudi Arabia are also possible. The Saudi authorities appeared to suggest that Iran was directing a network of Saudis, whose members were executed in April 2019. If the Quds Force cannot recruit in Saudi Arabia, it could draw upon an international reservoir of fighters to deploy there. There is a precedent for IRGC terrorism inside Saudi Arabia: the 1996 attack on the Khobar Towers took place at a time when Iran had a far less developed network of regional influence than it has now.

Gulf Cooperation Council (GCC) countries and Saudi Arabia in particular will be most affected by Iranian escalation, especially in the Gulf waters. The rhetoric and diplomatic messaging from both sides seems to preclude any kind of immediate rapprochement. However, the GCC states have diplomatic and economic options for containing Iranian influence in their own countries and in Iraq, Afghanistan and Pakistan. Confrontation plays to Iran's strengths, in particular those of the Quds Force, whereas containment frustrates it.

GCC countries also have influence with Russia, which has expanded Iran's operating space and served as its patron on the international stage. However, Iranian and Russian interests are not congruent and Russia stands to be damaged by the expansion of Iranian influence through militant proxies.

Containing the influence which Iran has generated through its partnerships will be a defining challenge for the Middle East and for the international community. Whilst Iran may eventually enter into negotiations over the extent of its influence, so far its reaction to mounting pressure has been to defend and hold fast to its partnerships, narrative of resistance and focus on asymmetry. The Supreme Leader could reverse this strategic choice. However, Iran's unique approach to projecting influence flows from, and reinforces, the defining concepts and narrative of the Iranian revolution. Renouncing it entails not only a loss of influence, but of identity. It is hard to envisage any change under the current regime. While it may still hold, as US President Donald Trump commented in a tweet in July 2019, that Iran has 'never won a war but never lost a negotiation' that could now be reversed.[3] Iran has lost faith in negotiations following the collapse of the JCPOA but, as demonstrated in both Syria and Iraq, it found a way to win in war.

Notes

[1] 'Bekhahid beh Iran tajavoz konid, Esra'il nesf ruzeh khak shodeh ast' [Go ahead and invade Iran, Israel would be destroyed in half a day], Iran Online, 20 September 2019, http://www.ion.ir/news/502091/%D8%B3%DB%8C%D8%AF-%D8%A7%D8%AD%D9%85%D8%AF-%D8%B9%D9%84%D9%85%D8%A7%D9%84%D9%87%D8%AF%DB%8C.

[2] 'Soleimani Reveals Role in 2006 Israel-Hizbullah War', Naharnet, 3 October 2019, http://www.naharnet.com/stories/en/265124-soleimani-reveals-role-in-2006-israel-hizbullah-war#new-comment.

[3] Donald Trump (@realDonaldTrump), Twitter, 29 July 2019, https://twitter.com/realdonaldtrump/status/1155941248705761280.

APPENDIX

KEY INDIVIDUALS

IRAN

Major-General Abdolrahim Mousavi	Chief commander of the Artesh (2017–)
Abdul Reza Shahlai (aka. Hajji Yousef)	Middleman for IRGC Quds Force's supplying of materiel to Iraqi militias in the 2000s and sanctioned by the US in 2011 for his role in the failed plot to assassinate the Saudi ambassador to the US
Ahmad Madani	IRGC commander identified as Sayyid Javid, coordinator of IRGC activities in northern Syria
Major-General Ahmad Motevasselian	IRGC commander who disappeared in Lebanon in 1982 after the Israeli invasion
Brigadier-General Ahmad Vahidi	First commander of the IRGC Quds Force (1988–98)
Ali Akbar Mohtashami-Pour	Adviser of Khomeini with strong links to Hizbullah's founders; Ambassador to Syria (1982–86); Minister of Interior (1985–89)
Ali Akbar Velayati	Senior foreign-policy adviser to the Supreme Leader; Minister of Foreign Affairs (1981–97)
Grand Ayatollah Ali al-Sistani	The most influential Iraqi-based Shia cleric and *marja al-taqlid*
Ali Larijani	Speaker of Parliament (2008–); formerly chief nuclear negotiator of Iran and secretary of Supreme National Security Council
Ali Omid Mehr	Former Iranian diplomat in Pakistan and subsequent defector
Brigadier-General Ali Reza Asgari	Retired IRGC general who disappeared in Turkey in 2007
Major-General Gholam Ali Rashid	Commander of the IRGC Khatam al-Anbia Central Headquarters
Hojjat ol-Eslam Ghorban Gholampour	Iranian official arrested in Herat reportedly for recruiting Afghan Shia to fight in Syria for Iran
Major-General Hadi Kajbaf	IRGC commander killed in southern Syria in 2015
Ayatollah Hashemi Rafsanjani	President of the Islamic Republic of Iran (1989–97); Chairman of Expediency Council (1989–2017)
Major-General Hassan Firouzabadi	Senior military adviser to the Supreme Leader; Chief commander of the Armed Forces (1989–2016)
Hojjat ol-Eslam Hassan Rouhani	President of the Islamic Republic of Iran (2013–)
Major-General Hassan Shateri (aka Hesam Khushnevis)	IRGC commander killed in Syria in 2013, allegedly by Israeli agents
Hossein Amir Abdollahian	Special adviser to the Speaker of Parliament (2016–); Deputy minister of foreign affairs (2011–16); Ambassador to Bahrain (2007–10)
Brigadier-General Hossein Dehghan	Senior military adviser to the Supreme Leader; former IRGC officer who served in Lebanon in the 1980s
Major-General Hossein Hamadani	Former IRGC commander and lead proponent of creating a 'Syrian Basij', killed near Aleppo in October 2015

207

Hossein Jaberi-Ansari	Senior adviser to the minister of foreign affairs
Ayatollah Hossein Montazeri	Shia cleric who was deputy Supreme Leader (1985–89) before becoming a critic of the Islamic Republic of Iran's governance
Major-General Hossein Salami	Chief commander of the IRGC (2019–)
Hossein Taeb	Shia cleric and chief of the IRGC's intelligence unit
Hossein Yekta	IRGC media figure and former commander of the Khatam al-Osya Headquarters
Brigadier-General Iraj Masjedi	Iranian ambassador to Iraq and former IRGC commander
Mahmoud Ahmadinejad	President of the Islamic Republic of Iran (2005–13)
Manouchehr Mottaki	Minister of foreign affairs (2005–10)
Mansour Arbabsiar	Iranian national convicted for participating in a plot to assassinate the Saudi Arabian ambassador to the US in 2011
Hojjat ol-Eslam Mehdi Taeb	Influential Shia cleric and head of the Ammar Strategic Advisory Base; brother of Hossein Taeb
Brigadier-General Mohammad Ali Falaki	Retired IRGC general who commanded Iranian-led forces in Syria, including Fatemiyoun fighters
Major-General Mohammad Ali Jafari	Chief commander of the IRGC (2007–19)
Mohammad Ali Shahidi Mahallati	Director of Foundation of Martyrs and Veterans Affairs (2013–)
Brigadier-General Mohammad Allahdadi	Quds Force officer killed in southern Syria near the Golan Heights in 2015 alongside Jihad Mughniyah
Major-General Mohammad Bagheri	Chief commander of the Armed Forces (2016–)
Brigadier-General Mohammad Esmail Kousari	Former IRGC commander and go-between with Hizbullah's Hassan Nasrallah
Mohammad Hajji Ali Eghbalpour	IRGC representative in Tuz Khurmatu, Iraq, known locally as Agha Eghbali
Mohammad Javad Zarif	Minister of Foreign Affairs (2013–)
Mohammad Khatami	President of the Islamic Republic of Iran (1997–2005)
Mohammad Reza Hakim Javadi	IRGC officer during the Iran–Iraq War
Brigadier-General Mohammad Zahedi	Senior IRGC commander who oversees security relations and coordination over Syria; former commander of the IRGC Ground Forces
Mohsen Chizari	IRGC commander captured in Iraq by the US armed forces in 2007
Brigadier-General Mohsen Rafighdoust	Former IRGC commander and minister of the Revolutionary Guards (1982–89)
Major-General Mohsen Rezai	Chief commander of the IRGC (1981–97)
Morteza Hosseinpour	Commander of the Haidariyoun killed in Syria
Mostafa Chamran	First minister of defence of the Islamic Republic of Iran (1979–80); killed in 1981 during the Iran–Iraq War
Mostafa Sadrzadeh	IRGC commander killed in Syria while leading the Fatemiyoun
Musa al-Sadr	Lebanese-Iranian Shia cleric who trained in Iran and created the Amal Movement and militia in Lebanon
Hojjat ol-Eslam Musa Fakhr Rouhani	Former Iranian ambassador to Lebanon in the 1980s
Second rank Brigadier-General Naser Shaabani	IRGC commander known for admitting to Iran's role in Houthi attacks on Saudi oil tankers in 2018
Major-General Qasem Soleimani	Commander of the IRGC Quds Force (1998–)
Brigadier-General Reza Khavari	Senior IRGC commander of the Fatemiyoun, killed near Hama in Syria in 2015
Ayatollah Ruhollah Khomeini	Supreme Leader of the Islamic Republic of Iran (1979–89)
Sadegh Ganji	Iranian consul general assassinated in Lahore in 1991
Sayyid Abbas Mousavi	Supposed commander of the Zainabiyoun
Ayatollah Vahid Khorasani	One of the most senior *marja al-taqlid*s based in Qom, Iran
Major-General Yahya Rahim-Safavi	Special military adviser to the Supreme Leader; former chief commander of the IRGC (1997–2007)
Zohair Mojahed	Cultural and media representative of the Fatemiyoun

LEBANON

Abbas al-Musawi	Shia cleric, co-founder of Hizbullah and its second secretary-general (1984–92) until being killed in 1992 by an Israeli airstrike
Ali Fayyad	Hizbullah commander in the Radwan Unit, Hizbullah's special forces, killed in action in Aleppo in 2016
Ali Musa Daqduq	Senior Hizbullah commander believed to be commanding a unit in southern Syria near the Golan Heights
Ali Shabib Mahmoud	Hizbullah commander responsible for creating the special forces in Damascus's Sayyida Zainab district in 2013, killed later that year
Anis al-Naqqash	Lebanese political activist with connections to Imad Mughniyah; was arrested in Paris in 1980 for a failed assassination attempt on a former Iranian prime minister
Fawzi Ayyoub	Hizbullah commander who was on the FBI's most wanted list until he was killed in action in Deraa in 2013
Haitham Tabatabai	Senior Hizbullah commander believed to be the head of the Radwan Unit, Hizbullah's special forces, in Syria and Yemen
Hamza Ibrahim Haidar	Hizbullah commander involved in establishing Quwat al-Ridha in Syria, killed while fighting in Homs in 2013
Hassan al-Hajj	Hizbullah commander killed in action in Idlib in 2015
Hassan al-Laqqis	Senior Hizbullah officer who was believed to be a member of Hizbullah's Jihad Council and was head of R&D, logistics and procurement until his assassination in 2013
Hassan Najib Madlaj	Hizbullah official who fought in Quwat al-Ridha's artillery and missile force, killed while fighting in the Homs desert in 2016
Hassan Nasrallah	Secretary-General of Hizbullah (1992–)
Ibrahim al-Amin	Editor of Al-Akhbar, a pro-Hizbullah Lebanese media outlet
Imad Mughniyah	Senior Hizbullah security commander and the organisation's second most powerful man until his death in 2008 in an Israeli-orchestrated operation
Jihad Mughniyah	Hizbullah commander and son of Imad Mughniyah; killed in Quneitra in January 2015 by an Israeli strike alongside a top IRGC official
Khalil Harb	Senior Hizbullah commander known to have provided training and financial support to Houthi fighters in Yemen
Michel Aoun	President of Lebanon (2016–) and founder of the Free Patriotic Movement, the largest Christian political party in the Lebanese parliament
Grand Ayatollah Muhammad Hussein Fadlallah	Senior Shia cleric whose opposition to the Iranian clerical leadership caused a rift between him and the Hizbullah leaders
Muhammad Issa	Senior Hizbullah commander who was responsible for military operations in Syria and Iraq, killed in Quneitra by an Israeli attack in 2015
Muhammad Kawtharani	Senior Hizbullah commander in the group's Political Council who has been a key representative in Iraq promoting Hizbullah's interests
Muhammad Yazbek	Shia cleric and head of Hizbullah's Shura Council, with strong ties to Iran
Mustafa al-Yakoubi	Hizbullah commander who supported Iran's efforts to build reliable Iraqi political partners in the post-2003 landscape
Mustafa Badreddine	Senior Hizbullah commander and cousin and brother-in-law of Imad Mughniyah who spent seven years in prison in Kuwait for his part in the 1983 Kuwait bombings and was killed in Syria in 2016
Mustafa Dirani	Senior Hizbullah military operative who was abducted by Israel in southern Lebanon in 1994 and exchanged in a prisoner swap in 2004
Naser Akhdar	Hizbullah official who is alleged to be responsible for liasing with the Houthis
Rafiq al-Hariri	Prime minister of Lebanon (1992–98; 2000–04) who was assassinated in 2005, allegedly by Hizbullah operatives
Ragheb Harb	Shia cleric and member of Amal Movement whose supporters went on to found Hizbullah and seen as a key figure in the Shia Lebanese resistance movement in the 1980s

Talal Hamiyah	Head of Hizbullah's External Service Organisation, the body responsible for planning its attacks abroad
Tareq Haidarah	Hizbullah commander reported to have been killed in a Saudi airstrike in Yemen in 2018
Wissam Sharafeddine	Experienced Hizbullah commander killed in action in eastern Ghouta in 2013
Yasser al-Musawi	Son of former Hizbullah secretary-general, Abbas al-Musawi, who has acted as a go-between with the commander of Liwa al-Baqir
Yousef Hashim	Hizbullah commander who oversees the group's operations and protects its interests in Iraq

PALESTINIAN TERRITORIES

Hisham Salem	Leader of Gaza-based Harakat al-Sabireen and former Palestinian Islamic Jihad commander
Ismail Haniyah	Head of Hamas's politburo (2017–) and former disputed prime minister (2006–14)
Khaled Mashal	Head of Hamas's politburo (1996–2017)
Mahmoud Zahar	Politician and member of Hamas's politburo who was exiled by Israel to Lebanon in 1992; later appointed foreign minister (2006–07)
Musa Abu Marzouq	Senior official in Hamas's politburo and an influential member since the group's establishment
Osama Hamdan	Representative of Hamas in Lebanon and member of its politburo
Saleh al-Arouri	Deputy political leader of Hamas and founder of the Ezzeddine al-Qassam Brigades
Yahya Sinwar	Hamas' spolitical leader in the Gaza Strip (2017–) and former commander of the group's military wing

SYRIA

Ali al-Hamo	Commander of the Local Defence Forces (LDF) in Hama governorate
Ali Reza Tavassoli (Abu Hamed)	Afghan; co-founder and commander of the Fatemiyoun who was killed in fighting in southern Syria in 2015
Ali Younis	Commander of the LDF in Homs governorate
Aziz Asbar	Leading rocket scientist with close links to the Syrian and Iranian governments who was assassinated in a car bombing in 2018
Bashar al-Assad	President of Syria (2000–)
Basil Ali Abdullah	Commader of the Saraya Fursan al-Basil, an Aleppo LDF unit
Fadi Dahdouh	Founder of Fawj al-Sayyida Zainab
Hafez al-Assad	President of Syria (1971–2000)
Haitham Abd al-Rasul al-Nayef	First commander of the LDF; died in 2018
Hisham Ikhtiyar	Key military official, head of intelligence and national security adviser until his death in 2012
Hussein Ajeeb Jazzah	Co-founder of Liwa Abu al-Fadl al-Abbas
Hussein Tawfiq al-Assad	Commander of Liwa Usud al-Hussein
Mahir Qawarma	Commander of the LDF in the town of Mahrada and a Ba'ath Party MP
Mahmoud al-Jubouri	Senior cleric who provides spiritual leadership for the Shia militia Liwa al-Baqir and is director of the Imam Mahdi Centre in Sayyida Zainab
Muhammad Nasif Kheirbek	Long-standing Assad family ally with decades of managing the Syrian–Iranian military alliance; deputy vice-president for security affairs from 2006 until his death in 2015
Muhammad Suleiman	Special presidential adviser for arms procurement and strategic weapons assassinated in 2008, with close links to Hizbullah and Iranian officials
Rami Makhlouf	Cousin of Bashar al-Assad and head of the charity al-Bustan Association

Rami Yousef	Commander of Ghaliboun militia and allegedly participated in the 2006 war in Lebanon
Reza Bakhshi	Afghan; deputy commander of the Fatemiyoun who was killed in Deraa in 2015
Sayyid Mohammad Hassan Hosseini (Sayyid Hakim)	Afghan; senior commander of the Fatemiyoun who was killed in a battle near Palmyra in 2016
Yousef al-Hassan	Commander of the LDF who succeeded Haitham Abd al-Rasul al-Nayef

IRAQ

Abdul Aziz al-Hakim	Shia cleric and former leader of the Supreme Council for Islamic Revolution in Iraq who died in 2009
Abu Ala al-Walai	Commander of Kataib Sayyid al-Shuhada
Abu Bakr al-Baghdadi	Leader of ISIS
Abu Dhar	Middleman in Iran's weapons-smuggling operations into Iraq during the 2000s who operated from Abu Dhar
Abu Mahdi al-Muhandis (Jamal Jaafar Mohammad al-Ibrahimi)	Deputy commander and effective leader of the Popular Mobilisation Units (PMU) with strong links to Qasem Soleimani
Abu Majid al-Basri	Commander of a Badr Organisation artillery directorate
Abu Mustafa al-Shaibani	Alleged founder and commander of Kataib Sayyid al-Shuhada with strong historical ties to the Quds Force
Abu Sajjad al-Gharawi	Weapons smuggler who supplied arms to various militias with close links to Iran during the 2000s
Abu Thanun al-Khaledi	Commander of a PMU tank force in 2014 chosen by Abu Mahdi al-Muhandis
Adil Abdul-Mahdi	Prime Minister of Iraq (2018–); former vice-president of Iraq (2005–11)
Ahmad Kayarah	Founder of Liwa Abu al-Fadl al-Abbas who lived in Syria prior to the outbreak of the civil war
Ali al-Yasiri	Commander of Saraya al-Khorasani
Ammar al-Hakim	Shia cleric and president of the Islamic Supreme Council of Iraq
Faleh al-Fayadh	Nominal leader of the PMU (2014–18)
Hadi al-Ameri	Commander of the Badr Organisation
Hadi al-Mudarrisi	Shia cleric and nephew of Muhammad al-Shirazi who was a leading Iraqi opposition figure to Saddam Hussein living in Bahrain in exile
Haider al-Abadi	President of Iraq (2014–18)
Hanin al-Qadu	Nineveh MP and supposed leader of the Shabak Brigade's recruitment campaign
Karim Hattab	Deputy minister of oil and former head of the ministry's PMU Support Committee
Maitham al-Zaidi	Commander of the Abbas Combat Division
Mishan al-Jabouri	Sunni politician and leading figure of the Jabouri tribe
Muhammad al-Shirazi	Shia cleric, *marja al-taqlid* and founder of the Message Movement who fled Iraq in the 1970s
Muhammad al-Tabatabai	Shia cleric and leading figure in Asaib Ahl al-Haq with history of close contact with Iranian officials
Muhammad Baqir al-Sadr	Shia cleric and political activist and leading member of the Da'wa Party executed in 1980, father-in-law of Muqtada al-Sadr
Muhammad Sadiq al-Sadr	Shia cleric and *marja al-taqlid* who was assassinated in 1999 and father of Muqtada al-Sadr
Muhammad Taqi al-Mudarrisi	Shia cleric, *marja al-taqlid*, nephew of Muhammad al-Shirazi and former leader of the Islamic Action Organisation
Muqtada al-Sadr	Shia cleric, leader of the Sadrist Movement and a leading Iraqi nationalist politician
Nouri al-Maliki	President of Iraq (2006–14) and leader of the Islamic Da'wa Party

Qais al-Khazali	Shia cleric, founder and leader of Asaib Ahl al-Haq
Qasim al-Araji	Minister of interior (2017–18); arrested by US forces in 2007 for weapons smuggling
Grand Ayatollah Sadiq al-Shirazi	Shia cleric and *marja al-taqlid* based in Qom whose followers disagree with the current relationship between Iran's political and religious establishment
Sheikh Akram al-Kaabi	Co-founder and leader of Harakat al-Nujaba
Yazan al-Jabouri	Commander of Liwa Salahaddin, a Sunni militia supported by the US and Iran against ISIS

YEMEN

Abdu Rabbu Mansour Hadi	Disputed president (2012–) supported by the Saudi-led coalition
Abdul Malik al-Ajri	Member of the Houthi's political council who has met with Hassan Nasrallah in Lebanon
Abdul Malik al-Houthi	Leader of the Houthi Ansarullah movement (2004–)
Abdullah Yahya al-Hakim	Senior Houthi military commander who has been sanctioned by the United Nations
Abu Bakr al-Qirbi	Diplomat and former minister of foreign affairs (2001–14)
Ali Abdullah Saleh	President of Yemen (1990–2012) and occasional ally of the Houthis until he was assassinated in 2017
Ali Mohsen al-Ahmar	Vice-president (2016–) of Abdu Rabbu Mansour Hadi and senior commander in the Yemeni army
Hassan al-Mulusi	Former Yemeni special-forces soldier who defected to the Houthis
Hussein Badr al-Din al-Houthi	Founder and the first leader of the Houthi movement and former member of parliament of the Zaydi Hizb al-Haqq party in the 1990s; killed in 2004
Muhammad Abdul Salam	Spokesman of the Houthi movement who is known to have travelled to Lebanon and Iran to meet with officials
Muhammad Ali al-Houthi	Cousin and brother-in-law of Abdul Malik al-Houthi and head of the Houthis' Supreme Revolutionary Committee
Muhammad Badr al-Din al-Houthi	Zaydi cleric and revivalist who was temporary leader of the Houthi movement in 2004 after the death of his son, Hussein Badr al-Din al-Houthi
Muhammad Izzan	Co-founder of Al-Shabab al-Mumin, a Zaydi revivalist group that was the precursor to the Houthi movement
Muhammad Nasser Ahmed al-Atifi	Former minister of defence of the Yemeni government (2006–14) who later defected to the Houthis to become their minister of defence
Yousef al-Madani	Senior Houthi military commander and brother-in-law of Abdul Malik al-Houthi

BAHRAIN

Ahmad Hassan Yusuf	Senior member of the Al-Ashtar Brigades residing in exile in Iran
Ali Salman	Shia cleric and leader of al-Wifaq (2006–)
Hamad bin Isa Al Khalifa	King of Bahrain (2002–); formerly Emir of Bahrain (1999–2002)
Ayatollah Isa Qasem	Bahrain's foremost Shia cleric and spiritual leader of al-Wifaq
Murtadha Alawi	Senior member of the Al-Ashtar Brigades residing in exile in Iran

IRAN-BACKED MILITIAS

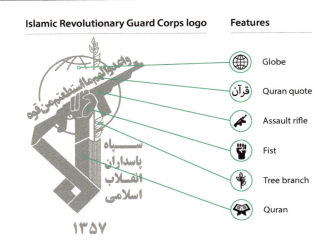

Islamic Revolutionary Guard Corps logo

Features
- Globe
- Quran quote
- Assault rifle
- Fist
- Tree branch
- Quran

Name	Alternative name	Date of formation	Territory of formation	Main areas of current operation	Current leader	US-designated terrorist status	Iconography
Proto-Lebanese Hizbullah	Islamic Resistance in Lebanon	1982–85	Lebanon	Lebanon Kuwait	Various	n/a	n/a
Palestinian Islamic Jihad	Islamic Jihad Movement in Palestine	1982	Palestinian Territories	Israel Lebanon Palestinian Territories Syria	Ziyad al-Nakhaleh	Aug 1997	
Badr Organisation	(formerly Badr Corps), Badr Brigade	c.1983	Iran	Iraq Syria	Hadi al-Ameri	n/a	
Lebanese Hizbullah	Islamic Resistance in Lebanon	1985	Lebanon	Lebanon Iraq Syria Yemen	Hassan Nasrallah	1995	
Kataib al-Shahid Ezzeddine al-Qassam (Hamas)	Ezzeddine al-Qassam Brigades, Al-Qassam Brigades	1991	Palestinian Territories	Palestinian Territories	Mohammed Deif	Aug 1997	

Name	Also known as	Formed	Origin	Operates in	Leader	Designated	Symbols
Saraya al-Muqawama al-Lubnaniyah (Hizbullah affliate)	Lebanese Resistance Brigades	1997	Lebanon	Lebanon Syria	Various	n/a	
Asaib Ahl al-Haq	League of People of Righteousness	2004	Iraq	Iraq Syria	Qais al-Khazali	n/a	
Ansarullah	Ansarullah, Ansar Allah, Houthi Movement	2004	Yemen	Yemen	Abd al-Malik al-Houthi	n/a	
Kataib Hizbullah	Hizbullah Battalions	2007	Iraq	Iraq Syria	Abu Mahdi al-Muhandis	Jul 2009	
Liwa Abu al-Fadl al-Abbas	Abu al-Fadl al-Abbas Brigade	2012	Syria	Iraq Syria	Abu Ajib	n/a	
Liwa al-Sayyida Ruqayya	Sayyida Ruqayya Brigade, The Jaafari Force	2012	Syria	Syria	n.k.	n/a	
313 Force	313 Brigade, Liwa al-Rasul al-Adham	c.2012	Syria	Syria	Al-Hajj Abu al-Abbas	n/a	–
Quwat al-Wad al-Sadiq	Forces of the True Promise	c.2012	Syria	Syria	n.k.	n/a	
Liwa al-Fatemiyoun (Afghans)	Fatemiyoun Division	2013	Iran	Iran Syria	n.k.	n/a	
Harakat al-Nujaba	Harakat Hizbullah al-Nujaba, Movement of the Noble Ones	2013	Iraq	Iraq Syria	Akram al-Kaabi	n/a	
Kataib Sayyid al-Shuhada	–	2013	Iraq	Iraq Syria	Abu Ala al-Walai	n/a	
Liwa Zhulfiqar	Zhulfiqar Brigade, Liwa Dhu al-Fiqar	2013	Syria	Iraq Syria	Haidar al-Juburi (Abu Shahad al-Juburi)	n/a	
Quwat al-Ridha	Ridha Forces, Liwa al-Imam al-Ridha, Imam Ridha Brigade	2013	Syria	Syria	n.k.	n/a	
Saraya al-Khorasani	Khorasani Brigades	2013	Syria	Iraq Syria	Ali al-Yasiri	n/a	
Liwa Zainabiyoun (Pakistanis)	People of Zainab Brigade	c.2013	Iran	Syria	n.k.	n/a	

Name	Translation	Year formed	Country formed	Active in	Leader	Disbanded	Icons
Kataib Imam Ali	Imam Ali Battalions	2014	Iraq	Iraq, Syria	Shabal al-Zaidi	n/a	
Kataib Jund al-Imam	Imam's Soliders' Battalions	2014	Iraq	Iraq	Abu Jaafar Ahmad al-Asadi	n/a	
Liwa Ali al-Akbar	Ali al-Akbar Brigade	2014	Iraq	Iraq	Ali al-Hamdani	n/a	
Quwat Abu al-Fadl al-Abbas	Abu al-Fadl al-Abbas Forces	2014	Iraq	Iraq, Syria	Aws al-Khafaji	n/a	
Saraya Ashura	Saraya Ansar al-Ashura, Ashura Brigades	2014	Iraq	Iraq	Kazim al-Jabri	n/a	
Harakat al-Sabireen	Sabireen Movement, Al-Sabireen, Movement of Those Who Endure	2014	Palestinian Territories	Palestinian Territories	Hisham Salem	Jan 2018	
Liwa al-Baqir	Baqir Brigade	2014	Syria	Syria	Khalid Ali al-Hassan	n/a	
Ghaliboun	Al-Ghaliboun: Saraya al-Muqawama al-Islamiyah fi Suriya, The Victors: the Companies of the Islamic Resistance in Syria	2015	Syria	Syria	Rami Yousef (aka Abu al-Meqdad)	n/a	
Liwa Usud al-Hussein	The Lions of Hussein Brigade	c.2015	Syria	Syria	Hussein Tawfiq al-Assad	n/a	
Saraya al-Arin	Brigades of the Den	c.2015	Syria	Syria	Yisar Talal al-Assad	n/a	
Faylaq al-Mudafieen an Halab	The Legion of the Defenders of Aleppo	2016	Syria	Syria	Al-Hajj Mohsen	n/a	–
Fawj al-Sayyida Zainab	The Regiment of Sayyida Zainab	c.2016	Syria	Syria	Al-Hajj Mahdi	n/a	–
Liwa Ashbal al-Hussein	The Cubs of Hussein Brigade	2017	Syria	Syria	Al-Hajj Abu al-Ayham	n/a	
Saraya Fursan al-Basil	Knights of al-Basil Brigade	2017	Syria	Syria	Basil Ali Abdullah	n/a	n/a
Quwat Shahid al-Sadr	Martyr Sadr Forces	n.k.	Iraq	Iraq	n.k.	n/a	
Liwa al-Abbas	Abbas's Brigade (formerly Liwa al-Rasul al-Akram/The Most Noble Messenger Brigade)	n.k.	Syria	Syria	n.k.	n/a	

ORDER ORGANISING THE SYRIAN LOCAL DEFENCE FORCES

ISSUED BY THE SYRIAN ARMED FORCES COMMAND (APRIL 2017)

Syrian Arab Republic
General Command for the Army and Armed Forces
Organisation & Admin Branch
Organisation and Arming Division
No. 1455

Date: / /1438 AH
Corresponding to 4 April 2017 CE

Memorandum

(l) front

(r) back

Dear Lieutenant-General [/field marshal]: the general commander for the army and armed forces, President of the Republic [Bashar al-Assad]:

- Implementing the decision of the brigadier-general, the deputy general commander, deputy head of the council of ministers, minister of defence, on the memorandum of the leadership of the popular army – operations and training division – no. 45 on date 19 January 2017 guaranteeing the formation of a committee headed by the organisation and administration branch in order to organise the forces working with the Iranian side within the organisation and propriety of the local defence units in the provinces and put forward suggestions to your excellence.

- The committee specified by admin order no. 562/67 date 11 February 2017 held a number of meetings and studied and discussed the situation from different angles, including organisation, leadership, combat and material guarantee, rights of the martyrs, wounded and disappeared, sorting out the affairs of those commissioned who have avoided obligatory and reserve service and deserters, and the civilians working with the Iranian side. And it culminated in the following suggestions:

1. Organising the Syrian personnel (military and civilian) who are fighting with the Iranian side within the local defence units in the provinces according to the following table.

No.	Province	Those who have avoided obligatory service	Those who have avoided reserve service	Desertion	Civilians	Affairs sorted out	Provincial total	Notes
1	Damascus	4,106	4,824	600	9,485	601	19,616	
2	Deraa	421	359	658	857		2295	
3	Tartous	321			679	100	1,100	
4	Homs	980	1,124	1,127	4,314	1,506	9,051	
5	Hama	2,144	2,654	2,549	3,915	864	12,126	
6	Aleppo	3,925	5,687	1,213	10,241	4,864	25,930	
7	Idlib	1,123	211	279	2,929	3,487	8,029	
8	Latakia	790	302	477	3,165	700	5,434	
9	Raqqa	213	235	148	220		817	

10	Deir ez-Zor	461	870		645		1,976	
11	Hasakah	388	465	952	554		2359	
Grand total		14,873	16,721	8,003	37,004	12,122	88,723	

2. Sorting out the affairs of the military personnel (deserters) and those commissioned who have avoided obligatory and reserve service, and transferring them, appointing them, and modifying the party of their summoning to the local defence units in the provinces and including those personnel who have sorted out their affairs and are working with the Iranian side within the local defence units according to the following table:

No.	Description	No.	Notes
1	Those who avoided compulsory service	14,873	
2	Deserted the army	8,003	
3	Avoided reserve service	16,731	
4	Personnel who have sorted out their affairs	12,122	
Total		51,729	

3. Organising recruitment contracts for the interest of the armed forces – the people's army, for a period of two years for the civilians working with the Iranian side for whosoever desires, regardless of the conditions of recruitment implemented in the armed forces (permanent matter no. 1 and its modifications/recruitment) and renewing it by agreement of the two sides according to the following table:

No.	Description	No.	Notes
1	Civilians working with the Iranian side	37,004	

4. Commissioning an administration of the affairs of the officers by sorting out of the affairs of session 69 of active officers and those who are working with the Iranian side currently in Aleppo province, their number being 1,650.

5. The leadership of the local defence units in the provinces that work with the Iranian side remain affiliated with the Iranian side while coordinating with the general command for the army and armed forces until the end of the crisis in the Syrian Arab Republic, or issuing of a new decision.

6. Combat and material guarantee in all its types for Syrian military personnel and civilians working with the Iranian side on the shoulder of the Iranian side after organizing them into the local defence units in the provinces in coordination with the relevant parties.

7. Guaranteeing the material rights for the martyrs, wounded, and disappeared who have been working with the Iranian side since the beginning of the events, placed on the shoulder of the Iranian side. As for the rest of the determined rights for the martyrs, wounded and disappeared according to the systems and laws as follows:
a) Military personnel and those commissioned who have avoided obligatory service after sorting out of their affairs in principle.
b) Civilians in the framework of the comprehensive solution.

8. Issuing organisation instructions guaranteeing implementation instructions for military personnel and civilians working with the Iranian side after organising them into the local defence units in the provinces.

Attached is a table of the combat equipment handed to the Iranian side from the popular army and that which is present with it.

Please review and decide.

Brigadier-General Adnan Mahraz Abdo
Head of the organisation and administration branch.

. Opinion of the major-general, head of the general chief of staff for the army and armed forces.

I agree to the suggestions: 5 April 2017

. Opinion of the major-general, deputy general commander, deputy head of the council of ministers, minister of defence.

I agree to the suggestions: 5 April 2017.

. Decision of the lieutenant general [/field marshal], general commander for the army and armed forces.

Agreed – 11 April 2017.

218 APPENDIX

INDEX

A

al-Abadi, Haider 123, 125, 133, 141
Abdollahian, Hossein Amir 186
Abdullah, Basil Ali 94
Abdul-Mahdi, Adil 141, 148, 149
Aden (Yemen) 26, 161, 162, 163, 165, 168
Afghanistan 10, 15, 17, 18, 19, 23, 29, 32, 33, 67, 92, 93, 101, 103–106, 108, 110, 112, 114, 198, 200–205
Agha Eghbali 144, 145, 155, 202
Ahmadinejad, Mahmoud 24, 40, 55, 191
al-Ahmar, Ali Mohsen 162
Ahvaz (Iran) 12, 135
al-Ajri, Abdul Malik 169
Aknaf Beit al-Maqdis Brigade (Syria) 73
Alawi, Murtadha 186
Al-Bukamal (Syria) 70, 91, 101, 105, 109, 110, 111, 113
al-Bustan Association (Syria) 97
al-Da'wa al-Islamiyya (Iraq) 182
Aleppo (Syria) 23, 24, 51, 55, 69, 70, 76, 86, 90, 91, 94, 96, 104, 105, 106, 108, 111
Allahdadi, Mohammad 23, 68, 99, 100
Al Massira television channel 71
al-Qaeda 18, 74, 161, 181, 190
al-Qaeda in the Arabian Peninsula 169
Al-Shabab al-Mumin (Yemen) 160
al-Ameri, Hadi 21, 124, 125, 126, 131, 134, 136, 138, 139, 147
Amerli (Iraq) 131, 144, 145
al-Amine, Ibrahim 42
Amran (Yemen) 163, 172
Anbar (Iraq) 125, 128, 129, 131, 133, 148
Ansar al-Sharia 169
Aoun, Michel 51
Arabian Sea 26
Arab Movement Party (Lebanon) 62
Arab Spring 13, 21, 24, 159, 162, 163
al-Araji, Qasim 124
Argentina 18, 48, 75
al-Arouri, Saleh 73, 74
Arsal (Syria) 108
Asaib Ahl al-Haq (Iraq) 21, 22, 69, 70, 91, 123–129, 131, 133, 134, 136, 138, 140, 142–150
Asapov, Valery 109
Asbar, Aziz 60
al-Assad, Bashar 21–24, 33, 40, 50, 51, 53, 54, 55, 56, 59, 70, 73, 78, 85–97, 99, 100–103, 105, 106, 109, 112, 113, 114, 162
al-Assad, Hafez 43, 44, 86, 198
al-Assad, Hussein Tawfiq 97
al-Assad, Maher 86, 92
al-Atifi, Muhammad Nasser Ahmed 164, 165, 172

Awamiya (Saudi Arabia) 190
Axis of Resistance 18, 32, 40, 46, 72, 86, 101, 102, 123, 125, 150
Ayash, Yahya 72
Ayyoub, Fawzi 111

B

Baalbek (Lebanon) 95, 102
Bab al-Mandeb Strait 26, 33, 71, 159, 199
Badiya (Syria) 108
Badreddine, Mustafa 42, 50, 55, 68, 75, 76, 87, 111, 184
Badr Organisation (Iraq) 19, 21, 22
Baghdad (Iraq) 11, 129, 131, 132, 133, 139, 144
Bagheri, Mohammad 24
Bahrain 10, 12, 14, 18, 29, 42, 75, 133, 162, 169, 179–191, 202
　14 February Youth movement 185, 186, 187
　al-Ashtar Brigades 185–188
　al-Haqq 184, 186
　al-Mukhtar Brigades 186
　al-Muqawama Brigades 186
　al-Wafa 186
　Al-Wifaq 184–188
Balkans 18
Balochistan (Pakistan) 104
Bani Jarmooz (Yemen) 169
al-Baqir, Mohammad 96
Basra (Iraq) 122, 124, 132, 134, 138, 139, 146, 147, 148, 201
Basri, Abu Majid 136
Battle of Badr 97
bin Baz, Abdul al-Aziz 161
Beheshti, Mohammad 42
Beirut (Lebanon) 18, 42, 43, 46, 50, 51, 58, 64, 70, 72, 73, 75, 87, 100, 101, 102, 108, 111, 159, 171
　Hariri International Airport 57
Bekaa Valley (Lebanon) 23, 42, 43, 62, 65, 98, 102
Ben Ali, Zine al-Abidine 21
Brazil 67
Budaiya (Manama) 186
Al-Bukamal (Syria) 70, 91, 101, 105, 109, 110, 111, 113
Buenos Aires (Argentina) 18
　AMIA bombing 1994 18
Bulgaria 49, 75
Bush, George W. 161

C

Camp David Accords 86
Canada 27, 64
Carter, Jimmy 181
Chabahar (Iran) 12
Chamran, Mostafa 41, 42
China 32, 56, 61, 64
Chizari, Mohsen 134
Cloudstrike (US) 27
Crown Prince Abdullah 44
Czech Republic 67

D

Dahduh, Fadi 94
Dahieh (Lebanon) 102
Damascus (Syria) 22, 50, 64, 68, 70, 72, 73, 74, 86, 87, 90, 91, 94, 95, 97, 98, 100, 101, 102, 105, 106, 108, 111, 112, 184
Daqduq, Ali Musa 68, 69, 133, 134
Da'wa movement 182–185, 190
al-Daylami, Ibrahim 163
Dehghan, Hossein 43
Deir ez-Zor (Syria) 70, 86, 90, 91, 92, 105, 108, 109, 110, 113
Deraa (Syria) 23, 51, 90, 99, 100, 102, 105
Dhar, Abu 146
Dhi Qar (Iraq) 132
DigiNotar virus 27
Diyala (Iraq) 127, 130, 131, 136, 148, 150
Doha Agreement 46, 55
Druze Arab Tawhid Party (Lebanon) 62
Dubai (UAE) 167

E

Eastern Province (Saudi Arabia) 181, 182, 183, 185, 189, 190, 199
Eghbalpour, Mohammad Hajji Ali 144
Egypt 21, 56, 72, 73, 76, 180, 185
Eker (Bahrain) 185, 187
Erbil (Iraq) 131
Euphrates River 101, 109, 110
Eurodif (France) 75
European Union 66
　Integrated Border Management programme 66
Ezzeddine al-Qassam Brigades (PT) 72, 73, 74

F

Falaki, Ali 104
Fallujah (Iraq) 129, 133, 135
Fars news agency 173
Fatah (PT) 180
al-Fayadh, Faleh 122, 141
Fayyad, Ali 55, 111
Firouzabadi, Hassan 24
France 45, 52, 54, 55, 75, 185
Fuah (Syria) 108

G

Gaza 19, 71, 72, 74, 102, 160, 199
Geneva (Switzerland) 22, 33
Gerdab.ir hacker group 27
al-Ghabban, Mohammad 124
Gharawi, Abu Sajjad 146
Ghazieh (Lebanon) 102
Ghouta (Syria) 86, 105, 111
Gilgit-Baltistan (Pakistan) 104
Golan Heights 44, 45, 68, 70, 99, 100, 201
Gulf Cooperation Council 162, 185, 186, 189, 191, 205
　Peninsula Shield Force 185, 186
Gulf of Aden 171
Gulf of Oman 205
Gulf War 132

H

Hadi, Abdu Rabbu Mansour 162–165, 167
Haidar, Hamza Ibrahim 95, 111
al-Hajj Asghar 94
al-Hajj Hamza 96
al-Hajj Khalid 96
al-Hajj Mahdi 94
al-Hajj Mohsen 94
al-Hakim, Abdullah Yahya 165
al-Hakim, Ammar 125
Hamadani, Hossein 22, 23, 78, 87, 89, 93
Hama (Syria) 23, 94
Hamas 9, 32, 56, 71–74, 195, 199
Hamdan, Osama 73
Hamid al-Dins 160
Hamiyah, Talal 75
al-Hamo, Ali 94
Haniyah, Ismail 73
Harakat al-Sabireen (PT) 74
Harakat Ansar al-Awfiyah (Iraq) 101
Harakat Hizbullah al-Nujaba (Syria) 70, 91
Harb, Khalil 70, 166
Harb, Ragheb 42
al-Hariri, Rafiq 46, 50, 55
Hariri, Saad 47
Hashim, Yousef 68
Hassakeh (Syria) 51
al-Hassan, Khalid Ali 90
al-Hassan, Yousef 94
Haydrah, Tariq 171
Hermel (Lebanon) 102
Hizbullah al-Hijaz (Saudi Arabia) 183, 185
Hizbullah-Bahrain 185

Hizbullah (Lebanon)
  Al-Manar TV 186
  Badr Unit 111
  External Security Organisation 48, 68, 72, 74, 75
  Imam al-Mahdi Scouts 62, 90, 99
  Islamic Resistance 43, 48, 68
  Jihad al-Binaa 45, 53, 64, 90, 99
  Jihad council 48, 66, 68
  Missile Accuracy Project 60
  Nasr Unit 111
  Open Letter 41, 43, 54
  Radwan Unit 111
  Shura council 48
  Unit 1800 68
  Unit 3800 68
Homs (Syria) 23, 51, 55, 90, 91, 94, 95, 98, 108, 111
al-Houthi, Abdul Malik 71, 160, 162–166, 172
al-Houthi, Hussein 159–162
al-Houthi, Ibrahim Badr al-Din 163
al-Houthi, Muhammad Ali 165
al-Houthi, Muhammad Badr al-Din 159–162
Hudaydah (Yemen) 26, 165, 167, 173
Hussein, Saddam 19, 42, 44, 75, 85, 91, 97, 125, 134, 181

I

al-Ibrahimi, Jamal Jaafar Mohammad 21, 132, 184
Idlib (Syria) 23, 90, 94, 111
Ikhtiyar, Hisham 86
International Monetary Fund 32
Iran
  65th Airborne Special Forces Brigade 24
  Aircraft Manufacturing Industries 168
  Al-Alam TV 186
  Al-Thaqlin Charity Center 99
  Artesh 15, 16, 24, 28, 92, 197
  Astan Quds Razavi Foundation 99
  Complete Regulations of the Islamic Republic of Iran
      Armed Forces 15
  Defence Industries Organisation 168
  Green Movement 87
  Hamadan air base 24
  Hikma 134
  Imam Hossein University 25
  Imam Khomeini Relief Foundation 99
  Iranian Cyber Army 27
  Iranian Reconstruction Authority 99
  Irano Hind Shipping Company 99
  Iran Powerplant Repair Company 99
  Islamic Azad University 99
  Islamic Culture and Relations Organization 99
  Islamic Revolution 7, 12, 17, 19, 27, 41, 42, 98, 103, 104,
      124, 132, 134, 161, 179, 180, 182, 185, 188, 190, 195,
      196, 197, 199, 202
  Islamic Revolutionary Guard Corps 9, 13, 15–18, 20,
      22, 23–29, 40, 42, 43, 48, 50, 54, 55, 56, 59, 60, 64,
      66–70, 72, 74, 75, 78, 87–95, 97, 99, 100, 101, 103, 104,
      108–113, 123, 125, 126, 134, 135, 137, 138, 143–148,
      162, 163, 170–173, 183, 186, 187, 189, 201–205
    Cyber Defence Command 27
    Ground Force 22
    Mohammad Rasulullah Corps of Greater Tehran 22
    Quds Force 9, 13, 16–23, 28, 32, 48, 50, 68, 85, 87, 104,
        105, 109, 112, 121, 123, 124, 125, 145, 146, 162, 171,
        173, 174, 187, 195–198, 200–205
  Joint Chiefs of Staff Cyber Command 27
  Khatam al-Anbiya Construction Headquarters 24, 99
  Mahan Airlines 163, 172
  MAPNA Group 99
  Mazarat Ahl al-Bayt Authority 99
  Ministry of Construction Jihad 45
  Ministry of Defence 18
  Ministry of Intelligence and Security 146
  Mobile Telecommunication Company of Iran 99

Shah 41, 75, 197
Supreme Council for Cyber Space 27
Supreme Council for the Islamic Revolution in Iraq 132,
    133, 134, 150
Supreme National Security Council 87
Tehran Construction Engineering Organization 99
Iran–Iraq War 11, 15–18, 23, 24, 42, 43, 44, 75, 105, 124, 132,
    134, 146, 149, 181, 184, 185
Iraq 8, 9, 11–24, 26, 28, 29, 32, 33, 41–44, 46, 55, 56, 67–71,
    75, 78, 85, 86, 88, 91, 93, 95, 101, 103, 105, 106, 108–113,
    121–150, 169, 179, 180–191, 195–202, 204, 205
  51st Brigade 126
  Abbas Combat Division 129, 141, 142
  Army 127, 131, 137, 145, 152
  Ba'ath Party 89, 97, 125, 126, 132, 134, 137, 145, 147
  Badr Organisation 69, 124, 125, 127–136, 139, 140, 142,
      143, 144–150, 184
  Beladi TV 124
  Camp Speicher 136
  Dawa Party 144
  Fatah coalition 125
  Federal Police 124, 127, 128, 131, 140
  Green Movement 22, 27
  Hadi al-Ameri 201
  Hamrin Mountains 142
  Harakat al-Nujaba 126, 129, 133, 146, 148
  Imam Ali Brigades 144
  Iran-backed Special Groups 125, 132, 134, 135, 143, 145,
      146, 184
  Iraqi Security Forces 109, 128, 129, 133, 142
  Islamic Supreme Council of Iraq 125, 134, 149
  Jaish al-Mahdi 126, 134, 135
  Jund al-Imam 126, 135
  Kataib Hizbullah 22, 69, 70, 91, 122, 123, 124, 129, 133, 135,
      144, 145, 146, 148, 184, 186
  Kataib Imam Ali 129, 131, 142
  Kataib Sayyid al-Shuhada 124, 131
  Kurdistan Democratic Party 147
  Liwa Salahaddin militia 126
  Mahdi Army 135
  Ministry of Defence 139
  Ministry of Interior 124, 127, 139
  Ministry of Oil 140
  Nasr Alliance 125
  National Wisdom Movement 125
  Popular Mobilisation Units 21, 26, 69, 109, 111, 121–146,
      148, 149, 150, 184, 190, 195, 197, 204
  Qayara oilfield 142
  Sairun Alliance 125
  Saraya al-Khorasani 126, 131, 132, 133, 135, 140
  Saraya al-Salam militia 141
  Saraya Ashura militia 125
  Shabak Brigade 130
  Shahid al-Sadr 144
  Supreme Council for the Islamic Revolution in Iraq 19
Iraq war 14, 46
Irish Republican Army (UK) 197
Islamic Action Organization (Iraq) 182
Islamic Front for the Liberation of Bahrain 182, 183, 184, 185
Islamic Resistance in Syria 95
Islamic State 21, 23, 24, 63, 69, 74, 88, 91, 92, 101, 102, 105–109,
    111, 112, 113, 122, 123, 124, 126, 128–133, 135, 136, 137,
    139, 140, 142, 143, 144, 145, 147–150, 197, 198, 201, 202
Islamic State in Yemen 169
Israel 8, 13, 21, 22, 24, 27, 28, 32, 33, 40–61, 63, 65–68, 70–78,
    85, 86, 88, 93, 96, 99–102, 111, 112, 113, 125, 148, 160, 185,
    196, 198–204
  Air Force 56, 86, 99, 100
  Defense Forces 47, 53, 54, 56, 60, 61, 63
  Operation House of Cards 100
Issa, Muhammad 111
Italy 54
Izzan, Muhammad 160

J

Jaberi-Ansari, Hossein 173
al-Jabouri, Mishan 126, 127
al-Jabouri, Yazan 126
Jafari, Mohammad Ali 17, 18, 22, 26, 59, 72
Jamal Jaafar Mohammad al-Ibrahimi. *See* al-Muhandis, Abu Mahdi
Javad, Sayyid 94, 95
Jazza, Hussein Ajeeb 91
Jeddah (Saudi Arabia) 28
Jerusalem 51, 71
al-Jibouri, Ahmad Abdullah 128
Jisr al-Shughour (Syria) 106
Joint Comprehensive Plan of Action 27, 32, 203, 205
Jordan 18, 21, 56, 100, 161
al-Jubouri, Mahmoud 90

K

al-Kaabi, Akram 70, 126, 146
Kajbaf, Hadi 23
al-Karbalai, Abdul al-Mahdi 133
Karbala (Iraq) 102, 127, 129, 141
Kataib Imam Ali militia (Syria) 110
Kataib Sayyid al-Shuhada (Iraq) 21, 95, 101, 124
Kawtharani, Muhammad 68
Kayara, Ahmad 91
Kefraya (Lebanon) 108
Kerman (Iran) 18
Khaledi, Abu Thanun 136
Khamenei, Ali 15, 17, 27, 43, 50, 55, 76, 77, 87, 88, 93, 95, 96, 102, 103, 104, 106, 126, 134, 145, 146, 183, 185, 186, 189, 199, 200
Khatami, Mohammad 44, 50, 182
Khavari, Reza 23
al-Khazali, Qais 21, 69, 70, 123, 125, 133, 134, 138, 143, 145, 146
Kheirbek, Muhammad Nasif 86
Khobar (Saudi Arabia) 18, 44, 75
Khomeini, Ruhollah 16, 18, 41–44, 74, 180–183, 185, 190
Khushnevis, Hesam 22
Khuzestan (Iran) 102
Kim Jong-un 203
King Hamad (Bahrain) 186
King Salman al Saud (Saudi Arabia) 28
Kirkuk (Iraq) 130, 144, 145
Kiswah (Syria) 100
Kousari, Mohammad Esmail 88
Kurdistan 18, 19, 21, 32, 63, 122, 124, 128, 130, 131, 132, 140, 142, 144, 145, 147, 149
   Kurdistan Regional Government 128, 130, 131
   Patriotic Union of Kurdistan 128, 144, 145, 147
   Peshmerga 21, 128, 144, 145, 147
Kuwait 10, 14, 18, 54, 75, 123, 132, 179–185, 190, 191, 197, 198
   Islamic National Alliance 183, 184

L

bin Laden, Osama 203
al-Laqqis, Hassan 50, 66
Larijani, Ali 186
Las Vegas (US) 27
Latakia (Syria) 65, 94, 96, 97, 100
Lebanon
   Amal Movement 41, 42, 43, 47, 54, 63
   Armed Forces 45, 56, 57, 66
   Baabda Declaration 51
   Ceasefire Understanding 52, 54, 59
   Civil War 41
   Dawa Party 43
   General Security Directorate 66
   Masnaa border crossing 65
   Nasr Brigade 56
   Resistance Brigades 62
   Supreme Islamic Shia Council 42
   Taif Agreement 44
Libya 41, 54
Litani River 56, 64, 111

M

Maaloula (Syria) 108
Madani, Ahmad 94
Madlaj, Hassan Najib 95
Maduro, Nicolás 203
Mahmoud, Ali Shabib 95
Mahrada (Syria) 96, 97
Mahrah (Yemen) 168, 170
Makhlouf, Rami 97
al-Maliki, Nouri 19, 133, 135
Manama (Bahrain) 184–187
Manbij (Syria) 94
Marib (Yemen) 167, 168, 169, 171
Marzouq, Musa Abu 73, 74
Mashal, Khaled 73
Mashhad (Iran) 104
Masjedi, Iraj 147
Masyaf (Syria) 60
Mattis, James 203
Mayadin (Syria) 109, 110
Maysan (Iraq) 135
Mecca (Saudi Arabia) 181, 185
Mediterranean Sea 111, 112
al-Meqdad, Abu 96
Message Movement 182
Midi (Yemen) 162
Mikati, Najib 47
Mine Ban Treaty 169
al-Moghassil, Ahmed 75
Mohtashami-Pur, Ali Akbar 42, 43
Mojahed, Zohair 105
Mokha (Yemen) 167
Montazeri, Hossein 41, 42
Morocco 67
Morsi, Muhammad 73, 76
Mostafa, Abu 95
Mosul (Iraq) 23, 131, 133, 135, 136, 138, 142
Motevasselian, Ahmad 43, 89
Mottaki, Manouchehr 161
Mousavi, Abdolrahim 24
Mousavi, Ahmad 102
Mubarak, Hosni 21, 185
al-Mudarrisi, Hadi 182, 185
al-Mudarrisi, Muhammad 182
Mughniyah, Imad 42, 49, 50, 55, 68, 72, 75, 99, 100, 112, 184, 201
Mughniyah, Jihad 68, 99
al-Muhandis, Abu Mahdi 21, 69, 122, 123, 126, 127, 129, 132, 133, 134, 136–143, 146, 147, 148, 184, 190
al-Musawi, Abbas 42, 48, 54, 75
Muslim Brotherhood 71, 73, 76, 86, 180, 181

N

Nabi Chit (Lebanon) 65
Najaf (Iraq) 41, 102, 122, 127, 135, 141, 182, 183
Nasrallah, Hadi 68
Nasrallah, Hassan 28, 40, 42, 44, 50, 51, 53–56, 66, 67, 68, 70, 71, 72, 75–78, 87, 88, 99, 102, 106, 163, 169, 199, 201, 202
Nasrallah, Jawad 68
NATO 109
al-Nayef, Haitham Abd al-Rasul 94
Netanyahu, Benjamin 99
Nigeria 67, 203
al-Nimr, Nimr 182, 185, 187, 189, 190
9/11 160, 161
Nineva (Iraq) 130, 137, 140
North Korea 53, 167, 197, 203
Nubl (Syria) 91, 108, 110

O

Obama, Barack 24
Oman 26, 168, 170
Organization for the Islamic Revolution in the Arabian Peninsula 182, 183, 185

P

Pakistan 10, 23, 29, 67, 92, 93, 103–106, 112, 114, 198, 200, 201, 203, 204, 205
Palestinian Islamic Jihad (PT) 32, 74
Palestinian Liberation Organisation 42, 54
Palestinian Territories 18, 21, 29, 32, 41, 42, 43, 51, 53, 54, 68, 70–74, 102, 160, 180, 195, 196, 197, 199
  Palestinian Authority 71
Palmyra (Syria) 23, 70, 105, 108, 109, 110, 113
Parachinar (Pakistan) 104
Paraguay 67
Persian Gulf 16, 33
Petraeus, David 19
Putin, Vladimir 24, 93, 99, 100

Q

al-Qaedu, Hanin 130
Qaim (Iraq) 109, 110, 128, 129
Qalamoun (Lebanon) 51, 108
Qardaha (Syria) 97
Qasim, Isa 184, 185, 187, 188
Qasir, Muhammad 66, 68
Qatar 46, 72, 73, 88, 102
Qatif (Saudi Arabia) 182, 185, 189, 190
al-Qirbi, Abu Bakr 161
Qom (Iran) 41, 104, 163, 183, 184
Quneitra (Syria) 99, 111
Qusayr (Syria) 23, 55, 57, 58, 108
Quwat Abu al-Fadl al-Abbas (Syria) 91
Quwat al-Wad al-Sadiq (Syria) 97

R

Rafighdoust, Mohsen 43
Rafsanjani, Hashemi 44, 182, 183
Rahim-Safavi, Yahya 40
Ramadi (Iraq) 129, 131
Raqqa (Syria) 90, 106
Rashid, Gholam Ali 24
Red Sea 12, 13, 26, 28, 33, 160, 162, 163, 167, 170, 171, 173
Reform Movement (Saudi Arabia) 183, 185
Rezai, Mohsen 89
al-Ridha, Ali 95
Riyadh (Saudi Arabia) 28, 167
Rouhani, Hassan 32
Rouhani, Musa Fakhr 42
Russia 8, 20, 24, 26, 27, 32, 57, 60, 61, 62, 76, 78, 85, 86, 90, 91, 92, 93, 96, 99, 100, 109–114, 136, 169, 173, 199, 203, 204, 205
Rutba (Iraq) 129
Ruways, Abu Turab 95

S

Saada (Yemen) 160–164, 170, 171, 172
al-Sadr, Muhammad Baqir 182
al-Sadr, Muhammad Sadiq 141
al-Sadr, Muqtada 19, 21, 122, 125, 134, 135, 141, 145, 150, 201
al-Sadr, Musa 41, 43, 54, 69
Sadrzadeh, Mostafa 104
al-Saffar, Hassan 182, 189
Salahaddin (Iraq) 126, 127, 128, 130, 142, 144, 145
Salam, Tammam 47
Salami, Hossein 60
Salam, Muhammad Abdul 169
Saleh, Ali Abdullah 160–165, 169, 171, 172
Salem, Hisham 74
Salman, Ali 184, 188
bin Salman, Khalid 171

Salman, Sayyid 94
Sanaa (Yemen) 12, 26, 159, 160–173
Sanabis (Manama) 186
Saraya al-Arin (Syria) 96, 97, 110
Saudi Arabia 10, 12–14, 18, 26–28, 44, 55, 70, 71, 73, 74, 75, 88, 102, 127, 150, 159–164, 166–174, 179–183, 185–191, 196, 199, 200, 201, 202, 204, 205
  Khobar Towers attack 182, 183, 185, 205
  Mount al-Dukhan 161
  Operation Decisive Storm 161, 163
  Special Office for Yemen Affairs 161
Sayyida Zainab (Syria) 90, 94, 95, 97, 105, 106
Second World War 24
Shabani, Naser 173
Shahlai, Abdul Reza 145
al-Shaibani, Abu Mustafa 21, 146
Shallah, Ramadan 74
Shamoon virus 27
Sharafeddine, Wissam 111
Shateri, Hassan 22, 64, 87
Shikaki, Fathi 74
al-Shirazi, Muhammad 182, 183
al-Shirazi, Sadiq 183
Simia Cable Company (Iran) 167
Sinai Peninsula 72
Siniora, Fouad 47
Sinwar, Yahya 73, 74
al-Sistani, Ali 21, 122, 127, 133, 144, 146, 183, 197
Sitra (Manama) 186
Six-Day War 56
Small Media (UK) 27
Soleimani, Qasem 18–24, 32, 33, 50, 68, 75, 76, 87, 89, 90, 92, 93, 105, 109–112, 123, 124, 126, 145–147, 187, 201, 203
Somalia 162
South Lebanon Army (Lebanon) 45
Soviet Union 15, 24, 103
Strait of Hormuz 26, 33
Stuxnet 27
Sudan 17, 18
Sukhna (Syria) 108, 110
Suleiman, Muhammad 86
Suqaylabiya (Syria) 97
Suwayda (Syria) 51, 92, 99
Syria
  101 Battalion 96
  313 Force 94, 95, 96, 110
  Army 89, 94, 100, 109, 110
    4th Division 86, 92, 100, 110
    5th Corps 109, 110
    Special Force 94, 95, 96
  Basij militia 22, 89, 93, 113, 198
  Desert Hawks 92, 113
  Fawj al-Imam al-Hujja 96
  Fawj al-Nayrab 96
  Fawj al-Sayyida Zainab 94, 96
  Fawj Raad al-Mahdi 96
  Fawj Sheikh al-Jabal 96
  Faylaq al-Mudafieen an Halab 94, 96
  Ghaliboun militia 96, 97
  Golan Liberation Brigade 70
  Imam Mahdi Center 90
  Liwa Abu al-Fadl al-Abbas 91, 108
  Liwa Ahrar 96
  Liwa al-Abbas 95
  Liwa al-Baqir 90, 91, 95, 96, 97, 114
  Liwa al-Doushka 96
  Liwa al-Rasul al-Akram 95
  Liwa al-Safira 96
  Liwa al-Sayyida Ruqayya 95, 96
  Liwa al-Shahid Zain al-Abideen 96
  Liwa Ashbal al-Hussein 95, 96
  Liwa Fatemiyoun 23, 92, 101, 103, 104, 105, 110, 114, 200
    Amar Battalion 104

Liwa Suqur al-Sahara militia 92
Liwa Usud al-Hussein 96, 97
Liwa Zainabiyoun 9, 200, 204
Liwa Zhulfiqar (Syria) 91
Local Defence Forces 93–97, 108, 110, 113, 114, 198
Majmuat al-Ghadab 96
National Defence Forces 9, 22, 23, 26, 88, 89, 91, 92, 93, 95, 108, 113
National Ideological Resistance 96
National Resistance Brigades in Syria 97
National Security Bureau 87
Operation Fajr 108, 109, 110
Quwat al-Ridha militia 95, 96
Quwwat al-Nimr militia 92
Republican Guard 86, 92
Saraya al-Muqawama 96
Saraya al-Raad 96
Saraya Fursan al-Basil 94
Scientific Studies and Research Center 60
Shaer gas fields 109
Social National Party 62, 90
Syrian Democratic Forces 94
Tiger Force militia 92, 110, 113
V Corps 100
Syrian Hizbullah 88, 93, 95, 97

T

Tabatabai, Haitham 70
al-Tabatabai, Muhammad 146
Taeb, Mehdi 22, 102
Tahrik-e-Jafaria Pakistan 200
Taizz (Yemen) 164, 171
Tal Afar (Iraq) 131, 137
Taliban (Afghanistan) 12, 18, 23, 32, 103, 106, 200
Tanf (Syria) 90, 95, 113
Tartus (Syria) 65
Tavassoli, Ali Reza 23, 104, 105
Tehran (Iran) 42, 74, 104, 134, 161, 172, 187
Tikrit (Iraq) 123, 133, 144, 146
Trump, Donald 149, 205
Tufayli, Subhi 42
Tunisia 21
Turkey 57, 72, 73, 87, 88, 90, 127, 148, 149, 162, 203
Tuz Khurmatu (Iraq) 131, 142, 144, 202

U

United Arab Emirates 12, 26, 28, 73, 88, 163, 165, 167, 168, 173, 180, 187
United Kingdom 20, 27, 54, 66, 133, 187
United Nations 32, 45, 46, 53, 56, 66, 162–167, 169, 170, 173
  Interim Force in Lebanon 53, 54, 56, 57
  Panel of Experts on Yemen 163–167, 170, 173
  Security Council 13, 24, 32, 163, 170, 172, 173
    Resolution 425 53
    Resolution 1559 45, 46
    Resolution 1701 55, 56, 66

United States 7, 11, 13, 15, 18–22, 24, 26–28, 32, 33, 40, 41, 44–47, 49, 52–55, 58, 62, 64, 66–69, 71, 74–78, 85, 86, 88, 90, 91, 93, 94, 95, 100, 101, 102, 109, 110, 113, 114, 121–125, 127, 128, 131–137, 143–150, 160–163, 166, 167, 169–173, 179–181, 183–192, 196, 197, 199, 202–205
  5th Fleet 186
  Army 21
  Department of Defense 189
  Iran and Libya Sanctions Act 183
  Navy 27
  Navy Support Facility 188
  Operation Desert Storm 15
  Operation Inherent Resolve 109
  Treasury 66, 166, 172

V

Vahidi, Ahmad 17, 18
Velayati, Ali Akbar 87, 90, 91, 93
Venezuela 203

W

al-Walai, Abu Ala 124
West Bank 72
WikiLeaks 189, 190

Y

Yabroud (Syria) 108
al-Yakoubi, Mustafa 68
Yassin, Ahmed 71
Yazbek, Muhammad 42
Yazidi 130, 131
Yemen 8, 9, 12, 13, 14, 26, 28, 29, 32, 33, 55, 67, 68, 70, 133, 159, 160–174, 179, 180, 185, 188–191, 195, 198, 199–202, 204
  35th Armoured Brigade 164
  Army 164
  Hizb al-Haqq Party 160
  Missile Brigades 164, 172
  Republican Guard 169
  Shia Zaydi 160, 161
  Stockholm Agreement 163
Yom Kippur War 56
Yousef, Hajji 145, 146
Yousef, Rami 96
Yunis, Ali 94
Yusuf, Ahmad 186

Z

Zabadani (Syria) 51, 65, 108
Zahedan (Iran) 104
Zahedi, Mohammad 50
Zahraa (Syria) 108, 110
Zainabiyoun (Syria) 92, 103, 104, 105, 114
Zarif, Mohammad Javad 22, 32, 33, 203
Zia-ul-Haq 103